Teaching
World
Literature

Modern Language Association of America
Options for Teaching

For a complete listing of titles,
see the last pages of this book.

Teaching World Literature

Edited by
David Damrosch

The Modern Language Association of America
New York   2009

MLA and the MODERN LANGUAGE ASSOCIATION are trademarks owned
by the Modern Language Association of America. For information about
obtaining permission to reprint material from MLA book publications, send
your request by mail (see address below), e-mail (permissions@mla.org), or fax
(646 458-0030).

Library of Congress Cataloging-in-Publication Data

Teaching world literature / edited by David Damrosch.
        p. cm. — (Options for teaching series)
    Includes bibliographical references and index.
    ISBN 978-1-60329-033-3 (hardcover : alk. paper) — ISBN 978-1-60329-034-0
(pbk. : alk. paper)
    1. Literature—Study and teaching.   I. Damrosch, David.
    PN59.T46 2009
    807'.1—dc22   2008054600

Options for Teaching 23
ISSN 1079-2562

Cover illustration of the paperback edition: woodcut by Heinrich Bünting,
1581. The title reads, "Die ganze Welt in einem Kleberblat" ("The Whole
World in a Cloverleaf"). At the center is Jerusalem.

Published by The Modern Language Association of America
26 Broadway, New York, New York 10004-1789
www.mla.org

Contents

Part III: Teaching Strategies

Part V: Resources

Valerie Henitiuk

David Damrosch

Introduction:
All the World in the Time

This is an exciting, and unsettling, time to be teaching world literature. The geographic reach of the field has expanded enormously in recent years, and courses that formerly concentrated exclusively on the Western tradition now often spend at least as much time on a range of non-Western literatures. At the same time, the boundaries of "the West" have been shifting significantly, with new attention paid to minor literatures within and beyond the borders of the few major powers long favored in world literature courses. As recently as 1990, most North American courses still embodied the perspective criticized in 1960 by Indiana University's Werner Friederich, who regretted that "world literature" rarely encompassed much of the world:

> Apart from the fact that such a presumptuous term makes for shallowness and partisanship which should not be tolerated in a good university, it is simply bad public relations to use this term and to offend more than half of humanity. . . . Sometimes, in flippant moments, I think we should call our programs NATO Literatures—yet even that would be extravagant, for we do not usually deal with more than one fourth of the 15 NATO-Nations. (15)

Today, Western literature courses that would formerly have begun with Homer now often start with *The Epic of Gilgamesh*, and writers from several Eastern European countries can be found on syllabi that would once have included Russia and Germany but no points in between. Courses of fully global scope are becoming common.

Many teachers are trying to include much more of the world than ever before, yet as they do so, they come up against some serious difficulties. First is the problem of time. The length of the school year hasn't expanded along with our growing global vision, and so the task of selection becomes more and more vexed. Not only has the school year not expanded in tandem with this growth, but many teachers report that students are coming to campus less prepared to read long assignments, which puts teachers under pressure to do more with fewer pages all told. Teachers' own preparation, moreover, is increasingly challenged by the demands of world literature courses, as an ever-widening range of languages, cultures, and subcultures comes into view.

Even within the boundaries of Europe, *Don Quixote* now shares the stage with Arabic and Hebrew writing from al-Andalus, while Welsh laments, Norse sagas, and the poems of the Polish Nobel Prize winner Wisława Szymborska further expand the linguistic boundaries of courses that once viewed Europe exclusively in terms of the Romance languages, English, German, and perhaps Russian. The challenges are even greater for the increasing number of courses that move well beyond Europe, including works originally written in Akkadian, Chinese, Japanese, Kikuyu, Korean, Nahuatl, Quechua, Swahili, Vietnamese, Zulu, and many other languages. Translation becomes a newly complex issue, and problems of social context and cultural translation are now heightened in courses that no longer focus exclusively on an evolving conversation among writers working within a common Western tradition.

Far from paralyzing the field, however, these challenges have stimulated a great deal of creative pedagogical work over the past decade and a half.[1] This book is designed to showcase a range of solutions that have been worked out at different kinds of institutions around the United States, from community colleges to research universities. The book would undoubtedly have been much shorter if it had been put together twenty years ago; many different approaches are being tried today, and it is important to give as full a sense as possible of the varieties of literary experience now being presented in world literature courses throughout the country. The essays included here show that solutions are usually highly institution-specific, crucially shaped by departmental and college structures, student backgrounds and interests, and faculty training and availability. As the canon has been expanding, models for presenting world literature have been multiplying.

At the same time, certain patterns and sets of options have begun to emerge in recent years and can now be described. No single program has developed a template that can be mechanically applied elsewhere, yet collectively the three dozen essays in this volume offer a wealth of creative ideas, together with illuminating discussions of the problems and solutions that emerged when these ideas were put into practice. The discussions should be useful for people engaged in thinking freshly about how to teach world literature in many different settings and circumstances.

Teaching world literature poses intellectual as well as institutional challenges. Whatever their approach, people who teach this subject must develop a working sense of what they mean by the term. What literature? Whose world? How has *literature* been understood in its myriad manifestations over time and across space? Pedagogically, just how much time can and should be spent in class on issues of definition, literary history, and cultural context?

In his valuable book *The Idea of World Literature*, John Pizer argues that world literature courses should include direct discussion of the history of the term *Weltliteratur*, placing Goethe's coinage in the context of German Romanticism and its subsequent heritage. Even if a teacher decides to assign exclusively primary texts and not include critical or theoretical readings, it is necessary to come to some personal terms with the concept and its implications for curriculum and pedagogy, simply in order to be able to design a coherent syllabus and an effective opening lecture.

From Goethe's time onward, definitions of world literature have oscillated among three basic paradigms: as classics, as masterpieces, and as windows on the world.[2] These alternative conceptions are implied in such titles as, respectively, *The Harvard Classics* (1910 [Eliot]), *The Norton Anthology of World Masterpieces* (1956 [Mack et al.]), and *The HarperCollins World Reader* (1994 [Caws and Prendergast]). The dates of these collections correspond to a gradual shift of emphasis, but the three conceptions are not mutually exclusive, and ideas of the classic and the masterpiece continue to figure in many courses and collections today. All three paradigms still need to be taken into account.

As Frank Kermode has argued in *The Classic*, classics are foundational works for their culture, most often of imperial or aristocratic origin, often ancient and certainly influential over time. As enshrined academically in departments of classics, the term was used to refer to Greek and Latin literature *tout court*. In principle, the study of classics could encompass virtually any author active in those ancient cultures, whether major authors such as Sophocles and Vergil or figures of far less exalted literary status, such as the Roman playwright Livius Andronicus. As the *Encyclopaedia Britannica* admitted in 1910, "to judge from the insignificant remains of his writings, and from the opinions of Cicero and Horace," Livius Andronicus "can have had no pretension either to original genius or to artistic accomplishment." Yet the *Britannica* devoted a respectful article to his work as a translator and a pioneer of Greek techniques on the Roman stage. "His real claim to distinction," the article declares, "was that he was the first great schoolmaster of the Roman people" ("Livius Andronicus"). Though classical culture retains a definite prestige today, minor Roman writers can no longer be assured of the attention they received in 1910; the current online edition of the *Britannica* regrets to inform a searcher that it can find no references at all (much less a freestanding article) for Livius Andronicus in its myriad electronic pages.

Whereas collections such as the Loeb Classical Library never hesitated to make room for minor as well as major authors, aesthetic criteria come to the fore in conceptions of world literature as the corpus of the world's masterpieces. For a practicing author such as Goethe, an emphasis on world masterpieces had the considerable advantage that his best works could take their place in this pantheon during his lifetime rather than only long after his death. In contrast to the vertical orientation of the classical tradition, extending upward in time from the deep past, the category of masterpiece works just as well on a contemporary, horizontal plane. The world masterpiece can be recognized almost as soon as it is published to glowing reviews and begins to circulate in translation. Far from needing to live in a cultural capital such as imperial Rome, the writer of a masterpiece can come from a small country (such as the duchy of Saxe-Weimar in a not yet unified Germany) and quite modest origins, as Cervantes and Shakespeare did: Johann Wolfgang Goethe himself was granted the aspirational "von" by his duke only at age thirty-three.

The emphasis on masterpieces has advantages for the teacher as well as for the writer, since it is a highly selective category. A teacher is thus free to take up only a few works in a course, with no need to set the major authors in a frame of the much larger body of less transcendent writing around them. Where *The Harvard Classics* ran to fifty volumes, the *Norton Anthology of World Masterpieces* could content itself with two, conveniently arranged for use in a two-semester survey course. The masterpiece thus offers a kind of inverse economy of scale: the greater the works, the fewer of them you need to teach. A culturally grounded course in Dante might logically entail assigning dozens of associated writers, from the theologians Thomas Aquinas and Bernard of Clairvaux to the poets Brunetto Latini and Bertran de Born—all of whom appear as characters in the *Commedia*—but a masterworks course can leap directly from peak experience to peak experience: from the *Aeneid* to the *Commedia* and on to *Paradise Lost* and *Faust*.

Such a course can emphasize the gradual unfolding of a classical tradition, but the presentation of world masterpieces can equally take the form of a multipolar "great conversation" among works grouped in an ideal simultaneity. This conversation can be held among works that are linked by genre or theme, with little reference to historical influence or national context. The conversation may be inscribed in the texts themselves, in references to predecessors or to contemporary rivals, but it can also be constructed at will by the instructor, as when a course pairs the *Iliad* and the *Mahabharata*, with no need to show any genetic connection from one to the other.

Since the mid-1990s, the classical and masterpiece approaches have increasingly been supplemented by an emphasis on a view of world literature as a set of windows on the world. Reacting to the tendency of earlier models to focus largely or even exclusively on works by a few privileged (usually white and male) authors from a handful of Western countries, many teachers have broadened their focus to include intriguing conjunctions of compelling works of many origins. These works may be included regardless of whether they can be described as masterpieces—or at least as what Western readers might readily recognize as masterpieces. Thus the *HarperCollins World Reader* includes substantial sections on African and Amerindian oral works, which aren't even literature at all in the etymological sense of "written in letters." In her preface to the collection, the general editor, Mary Ann Caws, emphasizes that the anthology has been created from "a global perspective" and with the selections and arrangement "determined by their own cultural context rather than by Western or Eurocentric preconceptions" (lxxii, lxxiii). Not only do these writers represent different cultural circumstances and artistic norms; they also need not be dominant figures even in their home culture. The collection showcases "marginal as well as mainstream voices in literature, particularly the inclusion of women's voices" (lxxiii).

Distinct in theory, the three definitions of world literature are often combined in practice. Goethe, indeed, held all three views simultaneously, cherishing the Greek and Latin classics he read in the original, promoting the modern masterpieces he and his friend Friedrich Schiller were composing, and enjoying Chinese novels and Serbian folk poetry as windows on very different worlds of culture and aesthetic expression. World literature surveys have long combined all three approaches, as in Columbia University's venerable great-books course Literature Humanities, which has a classics-based fall semester giving a window onto Greco-Roman literary culture, followed by a spring semester of European masterworks. Conversely, courses using the new global anthologies may include works far beyond the purview of traditional Western-based courses, but they still typically give most of their time to works long recognized as masterpieces in their culture of origin. *The Tale of Genji* can't be read in the same way as *Don Quixote*, but it is equally a masterwork, and Murasaki Shikibu and Miguel de Cervantes offer windows on their respective worlds of Heian Japan and early modern Spain.

A blending of perspectives of this kind is nothing new, and it can already be seen in a multivolume collection published over a century ago under the title *The World's Great Classics* (Hawthorne et al.). The title shows the collection's debt to the classicist ideal, while the use of the term "great" shows that the collection will be made up of a subset of classics: great books or masterpieces. Interestingly, the series first appeared in 1900 under the title *The World's Greatest Literature*; the following year the publisher decided to up the ante from "Literature" to "Classics," but at the same time toned "Greatest" down to "Great." This second choice reflects the editors' ambition to move beyond the ranks of what their readers would have recognized as the greatest names in world literature. The sixty-one-volume series came to include volumes on East Asia, the ancient Near East, "Moorish literature," and even Armenian literature. A 450-page volume is devoted to Turkish literature—"Comprising," as its subtitle says, "Fables, Belles-Lettres and Sacred Traditions, Translated into English for the First Time." The volume's editor, Epiphanius Wilson, included anonymous folktales together with upper-class poetry and bourgeois drama, offering his readers a mimetic view of literature as directly reflecting national character and culture. One Turkish playwright's works, for example, "reflect domestic, forensic, and official life at Constantinople during the last century as truly as those of Molière reflect the speech and manners of Parisian society as they existed in the reign of *le grand monarque*" (iv).

Writing for the all too aptly named Colonial Press, Epiphanius Wilson wasn't finally prepared to set Turkish culture on a par with European civilization. "The weaknesses of the Turkish character," he announces at the outset, are "reflected in fables which contain but little wisdom, [displaying] the apathy which puts up with everything" and "the want of enterprise and energy which is characteristic of the Turk" (vii). Yet against his own prejudices, Wilson asserts that the fables "bear a reality about them which is lacking in the artificial productions of Gay and Lessing" (vii), and he makes unequivocal claims for Ottoman poetry: "In imagination and passion these Ottoman poems will hold their own in any company" (iv).

Though we can hope to go beyond Wilson in achieving a cosmopolitan equality of regard for the world's cultures, the reality principle is useful only up to a point. Artifice and realism mingle in the works of Fuzuli, Nedîm, and Orhan Pamuk as much as in the productions of John Gay and Lessing, and in any case humankind cannot bear all that much reality, at least not within a short fourteen weeks. Taken to a logical extreme, the view of literary works as windows into distant times and places would lead to extensive culture-specific study: truly to see Dante in his world, we should have at least two semesters devoted to him and his immediate contemporaries, ideally surrounded with a penumbra of courses on Roman and Florentine history, art, religion, and literature. Often used as a way of opening out world literature courses beyond the boundaries of Western Europe, the windows-on-the-world approach can equally underwrite a close focus on a single period or country.

In the past, the study of world literature often found itself in tension with the study of national literatures. Many specialists based in one or another national literature department were suspicious of world literature courses as culturally superficial and linguistically hobbled by their reliance on translation. Such courses were allowed, if at all, only as introductory surveys, preparatory to the serious work that would be done once students committed to mastering a language and studying a national culture in depth. Comparatists, in turn, could speak dismissively of "the nationalistic heresy," as Albert Guérard put it in a lead article of the

Yearbook of Comparative and General Literature in 1958, looking forward to a coming integration of literary studies across national borders. The only real question for comparatists, Guérard claimed, was "How and When Shall We Commit Suicide?" "Not yet," he replied: "we are needed so long as the nationalistic heresy has not been extirpated" (5).

Happily, the persistence of national literature departments during the past half century has allowed comparatists to cling a while longer to life. Comparatists must admit that even the most influential works of world literature usually achieve their first life in a national tradition that deserves attention together with the work's circulation abroad. Yet national literature specialists should also allow that most of their favorite authors were deeply influenced by a wide range of foreign works, sometimes read in the original but often read in translation. Equally, the serious decline in language study in many American high schools means that teachers of works written in languages other than English and Spanish can no longer rely on a substantial cohort of students coming to college already with a basic competence in the language. National language departments are commonly offering literature courses in translation, both so as to serve a nonspecialist population and also in the expectation of inspiring some students to begin language study once they've become excited by the literature in translation. Nor is the use of translation confined today to introductory courses: a seminar on the medieval European lyric may include works in Irish, Welsh, Arabic, Hebrew, Icelandic, and Occitan in addition to Old and Middle English, Latin, French, Italian, Spanish, and Middle High German, while a full survey of postmodern fiction should ideally include works in Arabic, Bengali, English, French, Italian, Japanese, Polish, Russian, Spanish, and Turkish, among other languages. Upper-level classes and published scholarship alike increasingly need to engage at least some material in translation rather than leave it out of account altogether.

Few teachers of world literature today have any wish to ignore the complex issues raised by translation, much less to confine students within the imperial boundaries of English. Introductory survey courses are increasingly devoting direct attention to the problematics of translation, and many who teach these courses hope that an initial exposure to unfamiliar languages and cultures will inspire students to learn new languages and seek to encounter more of the world in greater depth. Problems of language and culture are highlighted when a course takes a fully global perspective, but these challenges have really existed in world literature courses as long as those courses have been offered. A 1930 course that included Isaiah, Homer, Sophocles, Vergil, Ovid, Dante, Shakespeare, Cervantes, Molière, Goethe, and Dostoevsky already far exceeded anyone's ability to convey the many periods and cultures involved in any depth. Good teachers have always found ways to focus on illuminating moments or conjunctions that can open up distinctive social, historical, and aesthetic contexts for the works treated. The often broader scope of today's courses sharpens this issue in what can be a salutary way, prompting us to face openly matters of language and context that may have been elided under the pressure of time or the anxieties of limited academic training.

World literature surveys can never hope to cover the world. We do better if we seek to *un*cover a variety of compelling works from distinctive traditions, through creative combinations and juxtapositions guided by whatever specific themes and issues we wish to raise in a particular course. We can't do everything in a single semester or year, and it's impossible to give equal time to every language, country, or century. So world literature courses need to be exploratory rather than exhaustive, creating a teachable progression of issues and works rather than striving after some impossible proportional representation or near-native cultural literacy in each region involved. Particularly in introductory undergraduate survey courses, it can be an exhilarating experience for students and teachers alike to get an overview of the extraordinary wealth of the world's literatures, before going into greater depth in later courses on specific areas, periods, genres, and themes. By the same token, an in-depth study of a national tradition can lead far beyond the nation's boundaries, as we follow a writer's multinational literary heritage or look to see how comparable techniques and concerns have been developed by more distant authors. The study of world literature is increasingly seen not in competition but in symbiosis with the study of national and regional traditions.

Achieving an overview of world literature has always been a challenge. Erich Auerbach famously began his great book *Mimesis* with a melancholy epigraph, "Had we but world enough and time. . . ." Magisterial though *Mimesis* was, Auerbach dealt solely with Western literature, and indeed confined himself largely to Italy and France, home to fifteen of his twenty chapters. *The Representation of Reality in Latin, Italian, and French Literature* would have been a more accurate if less dramatic subtitle for his book. The challenges of world and of time have greatly increased since Auerbach chose his epigraph from Andrew Marvell, and yet, as the essays in this volume demonstrate, colleagues around the country are finding creative ways to present a rapidly changing field in an unstable world. The ready agreement of the contributors to write these essays and the pedagogic passion and scholarly creativity displayed in their contributions testify to the timeliness and the interest of the topic.

It is a pleasure for me also to acknowledge the strong support of Sonia Kane and Joseph Gibaldi at the Modern Language Association for the idea of this volume. Kane gave wise guidance throughout the process of review, itself a model of collaborative work. The volume has benefited from thoughtful advice from the MLA's Publications Committee and the press's readers, as well as the input of the board and membership of the American Comparative Literature Association, several of whose members are also contributors. These collegial interactions make this a wonderful time to be seeking new ways to fit all the world into the time.

Notes

1. Two valuable essay collections in the mid-1990s discussing new approaches to world literature are Lawall's *Reading World Literature* and Carroll's *No Small World*.

2. I discuss these definitions further, and Goethe's relation to them, in *What Is World Literature?* (1–36).

Works Cited

Auerbach, Erich. *Mimesis: The Representation of Reality in Western Literature.* Trans. Willard R. Trask. Introd. Edward W. Said. Princeton: Princeton UP, 2003. Print.

Carroll, Michael Thomas, ed. *No Small World: Visions and Revisions of World Literature.* Urbana: NCTE, 1996. Print.

Caws, Mary Ann. Preface. Caws and Prendergast lxxii–lxxviii.

Caws, Mary Ann, and Christopher Prendergast, eds. *The HarperCollins World Reader.* Single-vol. ed. Boston: Addison, 1994. Print.

Damrosch, David. *What Is World Literature?* Princeton: Princeton UP, 2003. Print.

Eliot, Charles W., ed. *The Harvard Classics.* 50 vols. New York: Collier, 1910. Print.

Friederich, Werner, "On the Integrity of Our Planning." *The Teaching of World Literature.* Ed. Haskell Block. Chapel Hill: U of North Carolina P, 1960. 9–22. Print.

Guérard, Albert. "Comparative Literature?" *Yearbook of Comparative and General Literature* 7 (1958): 1–6. Print.

Hawthorne, W., et al., eds. *The World's Great Classics.* 61 vols. London: Colonial, 1901. Print.

Kermode, Frank. *The Classic.* London: Faber, 1975. Print.

Lawall, Sarah, ed. *Reading World Literature: Theory, History, Practice.* Austin: U of Texas P, 1994. Print.

"Livius Andronicus." *Encyclopaedia Britannica.* 11th ed. London: Britannica, 1910. Print.

Mack, Maynard, et al., eds. *The Norton Anthology of World Masterpieces.* 2 vols. New York: Norton, 1956. Print. Expanded ed. as *The Norton Anthology of World Literature.* Ed. Sarah Lawall et al. 6 vols. 2nd ed. 2002.

Pizer, John. *The Idea of World Literature: History and Pedagogical Practice.* Baton Rouge: Louisiana State UP, 2006. Print.

Wilson, Epiphanius, ed. and trans. *Turkish Literature: Comprising Fables, Belles-Lettres and Sacred Traditions, Translated into English for the First Time.* London: Colonial, 1901. Print. World's Great Classics.

Part I

Issues and Definitions

Introduction

Our volume begins with six essays dealing with broad definitional questions that underlie any particular construction of world literature programs and courses. Broadly speaking, the first three essays explore some leading conceptions of "the world," while the next three discuss the treatment of "literature" as it circulates from other times and places into the contemporary American classroom.

Sarah Lawall offers an illuminating history of constructions of world literature, in terms first of Western literature and then in terms of oppositions or interrelations between "the West and the rest." Her history is illustrated through the changing shape of the Norton anthology of world literature in its various manifestations over the half century of its existence. Vilashini Cooppan then looks at the ethics of reading world literature in the context of historical imbalances between imperial powers and their colonies or former colonies. She focuses her discussion on the change that the events of September 11, 2001, wrought in the teaching of Arabic literature in her world literature classes. *The Thousand and One Nights* began to read differently as the Baghdad of Haroun al-Rashid suddenly became overlaid with a place of current military and cultural conflict. Next, Emily Apter, writing on literary world-systems, surveys attempts by

Franco Moretti, Pascale Casanova, and others to set the creation and reception of world literature in a global framework, in a way that is sensitive to the dynamics of relations between metropolitan centers and peripheral zones, a dynamics now often in view in world literature courses.

Zhang Longxi finds commonalities across literary and cultural boundaries, offering examples of themes and strategies in both Asian and Mediterranean works, including some striking similarities in theories of signification and uses of metaphor in Buddhist sutras and Saint Augustine. Looking at religious, philosophical, and fictional works, Zhang argues that cross-cultural study benefits from a broad emphasis on the literary rather than an exclusive focus on narrower conceptions of literature. At once complementary to Zhang's essay and contrasting with it, Anuradha Dingwaney Needham's contribution stresses the importance of a nuanced approach to cultural difference. Particularly intriguing manifestations of difference can be found in cross-cultural texts, both those that embody themes of migration and cultural transfer and those that come to be taught in North America from a distant culture of origin. Instead of homogenizing such works as expressions of a common globality, courses should foster a cross-cultural literacy that is attuned to the difference that is produced when Third World works are read in a North American setting.

A critical arena in which difference is mediated is translation. Concluding this section, Lawrence Venuti discusses the need to raise translation openly as an issue in the classroom, engaging students collaboratively in teasing out translators' strategies for mediating or minimizing the difference of the texts they are bringing into English. In Venuti's account, translation is never a simple transfer of information but a dynamic process of interpretive recontextualization.

Collectively, these six essays can aid teachers in thinking through the systematic or antisystematic ways their courses present the life of literature in the world and in the classroom.

Sarah Lawall

The West and the Rest: Frames for World Literature

The catchphrase "the West and the rest" pokes mild fun at such simpli-fied opposites: what West and what rest? Is the rest everything perceived to be non-Western (culturally or geographically), according to the per-ceiver's principles? Geography alone does not provide an answer, even if one narrows the range of choice. Boundaries shift, and geographic iden-tity is hard to establish,[1] most obviously for hybrid literatures stemming from a "transnational, cross-lingual process of pollination" (Rushdie 69) and for the modern literature of migrant consciousness. If "West" refers to something more than geography (for example, a strain of great ideas or industrialized society or imperialist principles), then the excluded "rest" becomes even more problematic. The way we frame the terms of the West-rest opposition, or try to evade them, becomes a large part of what we teach—part of the "hidden curriculum" in our classrooms (Finke). The case of world literature is interesting because each of these issues di-rectly engages contemporary beliefs not just about what is right and true, or aesthetically or culturally valuable, but also about the authoritative or correct way of viewing the world. In this essay, I consider this framing and also some of the factors involved in the evolution of the *Norton An-thology of World Literature* from an anthology of the literature of Western tradition to paired editions representing literary traditions around the globe.

It is only to be expected that "the West" and "Western tradition" are immediate reference points for American education, given the long-standing educational and cultural ties with a Europe that has considered itself politically Western since the division of the Roman Empire in 395 CE.[2] In the world literature curriculum, the and-or opposition has been most visible as paired semesters—one on Western literature, one on non-Western literature—designed to introduce American students to their Western heritage and to the larger world of which they are a part. Often, the teacher explains the non-Western works (the list varies) by relating them to previously established Western models and then to universal themes. Thus, as Hazel Alberson wrote in 1959 about innovative courses at the University of Wisconsin:

> Shakuntala and Sita took their places beside Helen and Dido, Deirdre and Nicolette as superb feminine characters, understandable, universally human, while at the same time they revealed the differing role of women in their specific cultures. (50)

Not surprisingly, other countries have other definitions of the rest and different ideas of the traditional center and its periphery. Like early map projections with "Here Be Dragons" marking unknown realms or the Hindu geography in which India is both "Central" and the "Land of Virtues" (Jones 29), representations of the world tend to be anchored at home. This is not to say they are monolithic: scholars and travelers provide diversified images of foreign parts, and ideological groups—Edward Said's "communities of interpretation"—compete to define the meaning of those images. In objecting to current stereotypes of the Orient, Said notes the different versions of Islam given by "the media's Islam, the Western scholar's Islam, the Western reporter's Islam, and the Muslim's Islam" (41). Of the various perspectives alive at different times, some are lost in history, others recur or are rediscovered, and a few take on the appearance of cultural consensus. Canons of world literature are one such example of cultural consensus—of dominant practice—and, along with other canons in recent decades, they have been scrutinized in historical and comparative context as never before. In 1966, the French comparatist Étiemble examined various canons of world literature and found that a Japanese list included works from Western Europe but not from India or the Arab world and that an Egyptian list of two thousand masterpieces

constituting the "common patrimony of humanity" omitted Latin literature as well as any mention of India, China, or Japan. Some countries—
China and Japan, most famously—looked outside and found the West
barbarian when compared with their own civilized selves. The American
contrast of West and rest enters world literature in an unusually systematic manner, however, reflecting the nineteenth-century belief in fact-
based or objective cultural comparisons to be derived from science and
social theory.

Here, Darwinian theories of evolution sustain an overarching view of
human history (inspired by Herder) that describes different cultural communities' making their way, with more or less speed and success, through
successive stages of cultural evolution. Conspicuous throughout the period of colonialism is the notion of the contemporary West as the civilized
pinnacle of this evolution and of other communities as less advanced
peers—even if neither Charles Darwin nor J. G. Herder authorized such
invidious comparisons.[3] A corollary assumption holds that Western literature and languages embody the best of Western culture and are therefore
superior models for the rest of the world. Thomas Macaulay's famous
"Minute on Indian Education" (1835) remarks not only that English literature is more valuable "than all the literature which three hundred
years ago was extant in all the languages of the world together" but also
that learning Western European languages (and thus gaining access to
Western knowledge) has "civilized" the once barbarous state of Russia
(723, 724). The combination of these three beliefs—in scientific authority, in the successive stages of cultural evolution, and in the superiority of
Western civilization—became a standard cluster repeated in various contexts from academic essays to encyclopedia articles and early anthologies
of world literature. It contributes to a canonical image of the West that
functions as a cultural reference point and, in that capacity, is often opposed to a rest found both inside and outside the tradition.

These beliefs are visible in the entry on civilization in the eleventh
edition of the *Encyclopaedia Britannica* (1910), a consensus of current
knowledge that outlines the "successive stages of human progress" from
"bestiality to civilization": from the ethnological categories of "Savagery"
and "Barbarism" (H. Williams 403b) up to the invention of writing, after
which man has "graduated out of barbarism" and become "a civilized
being" (405a). Dispassionate in style (specific civilizations are "a localized
phase of society bearing the same relation to civilization as a whole that a
wave bears to the ocean" [405a]) and eager to avoid the appearance of

bias (preliterate societies nonetheless demonstrate "certain stages of civilization" [403a]), the essay uses a neutral and authoritative tone in describing the development of human society toward its contemporary apogee in the "Upper Period of Civilization"(406b)—a period that turns out to be cosmopolitan, colonial, and European (esp. English).

Like the scholarly works cited in its list of authorities, the *Encyclopaedia Britannica* essay treats civilization, Western civilization, and European civilization as interchangeable, thus diminishing, if only by implication, the achievements of the non-Western, non-European remainder. Its emphasis on literacy as the milestone of civilization suggests that other modes of expression, whether those of oral tradition or performance-oriented mixed media, are less advanced. Other civilizations are referred to—briefly—as existing in the remote past or the equally remote and mysterious East: neither receives much analysis, for their importance consists only in their contributions to the contemporary Western model. Thus inventions that "were destined to change the entire aspect of European civilization . . . appear to have been brought into Europe by the Moors, whether or not they originated in the remote East" (405b), and the ancient civilizations of Egypt, Babylonia, Assyria, Greece, and Rome created "only minor and transitory ripples in the great ocean of civilization" (405a). Small wonder that this picture of the West as the culmination (or high tide) of civilization leads to a perspective that Rosemary Haskell describes as a "Progress Trap," in which modern non-Western countries are defined as "developing" regions and analyzed primarily in a subsidiary relation (25).[4]

There is more. The next stage of civilization, according to the 1910 *Encyclopaedia Britannica* entry, will extend Western frames of thought "to the utmost habitable confines of the globe," creating a "single family" that is governed by an "absolute standard of ethics" and includes "the remotest member of the human race" (H. Williams 409b). At this point, the West has effectively obscured the rest as a viable other. Locally, the same situation holds: the achievements of Western civilization are to be preserved through the practice of eugenics so that "the survival and procreation of the unfit" (an internal rest) will "cease to be a menace to the progress of civilization" (408b).[5]

These rigid prescriptions seem little related to the teaching of world literature today, or indeed to the canonical works themselves, which have a habit of escaping narrow definitions. Yet the overall picture presented by the essay has been remarkably influential, its assumptions persisting either

relatively unchanged or as problematic issues and fruitful subjects for debate. Many early anthologies—whether intended for the classroom or the
general public—saw themselves as illustrating the rise of civilization to its
current apogee in Western culture and transmitting the moral lessons of
that rise. The educator Charles W. Eliot's *Harvard Classics* (1910) claims
to demonstrate humanity's "intermittent and irregular progress from barbarism to civilization" in works that convey "the permanent, elemental
sentiments and passions of mankind, and of the gradually developed ethical means of purifying those sentiments and controlling those passions"
(3, 9). Selections in Stith Thompson's popular textbook, *Our Heritage of
World Literature* (1938), illustrate the "age-old striving of the human
spirit" (6). This idealist assumption frees us from problematic definitions
of West and rest, but only because the rest has been erased. Such timeless
frameworks are suggested by Robert Hutchins and Mortimer Adler for
their *Great Books of the Western World* (1952): omitting notes and introductions, they offer instead an alphabetical list of great ideas and encourage readers to consider what "great men" had to say about the "greatest
issues" and "what is being said about these issues today" (Hutchins xxv,
xxvi; for further discussion of Hutchins and Adler's collection, see Lawall, "Canons"). Unfortunately, neither the rise of civilization nor attri-
butions of greatness are very useful markers in trying to understand the
variety of texts around the world or the relations among them.

Such is some of the baggage associated with "the West" as it has anchored Western world literature in the undergraduate curriculum. Sym-
bolically, "the West" is a shared reference point whose function is to create
a sense of community—a long-standing priority of public education. In
1981, a Carnegie report on the aims of general education surveyed public
documents from 1918 to 1981,[6] finding repeated mention of the need "to
provide a global or 'world' perspective" and "to educate people to a 'common' heritage rather than their individual differences" (Boyer and Levine
55–56).[7] The editors conclude that all three revivals of general education
(1918–30, 1943–55, and 1971–81) "moved in the direction of community, and away from fragmentation," with an emphasis on "shared values,
shared heritage, shared responsibilities, shared governance, and a shared
world vision" (58). Later in the century, numerous books and national reports drew on the image of Western tradition to combat what was seen as
cultural fragmentation and a loss of common values.[8]

Although the Western heritage was widely represented as an agreed-on
wisdom that must be rediscovered by the modern era, this interpretation

did not go unchallenged. From the 1970s on, expanded reference works increased knowledge of diverse linguistic and ethnic traditions in America and around the world. Revisionary criticism documented overlooked narratives of gender, race, class, and ethnicity that shed new light on canonical versions of cultural evolution.[9] Different conclusions can be drawn from this newly complex image: for some, it demonstrates the need to teach a more inclusive image of Western society and of the West as part of global culture; for others, its confusing variety threatens to dissolve social bonds and shows the need for an anchoring tradition. Alternative course patterns reflect this debate: the traditional Western world literature survey expands to include works by women and minorities, and world literature courses generally become more open to other traditions, with attendant problems of selection and balance.[10]

Many of these tensions appear in the work of Philo Buck, a professor of comparative literature at the University of Wisconsin, whose course World Literature in Translation was the first to include non-Western works in the traditional syllabus. Raised in India, Buck emphasized Indian literature in the non-Western section of his course (Alberson 50) and was forced to consider the implications of choice in a truly world syllabus. He explains his procedures in the various prefaces to his influential *Anthology of World Literature* (1934). English or American writers are excluded because they are already anthologized and have been studied in high school and college ([1934] vi)—a businesslike solution that in practice isolates English and American literature from the rest of the world's expression. Buck prefers non-Western sources that can be shown to have a strong relation with European tradition: difference as such is not a value. "All national literatures have been excluded whose vital influence upon the European tradition has been negligible or very recent": thus "the Chinese and Japanese classics were finally discarded, and Oriental literature limited to a few classics of India, Persia, Arabia, and Palestine" (v). As a result, the survey is not so much global literature as an extension of European literature in translation with a selected opening onto non-Western traditions. Despite these limitations, it is noticeable that the rise "from barbarism to civilization" is no longer a central theme for this anthology, which proposes instead to give a broader picture of cultural expression.

Buck's choices are governed by his desire to discover an author's "philosophy of life, and its significance to life today" (v), an impulse that leads Buck to change selections in succeeding editions in a way that radically revises his definition of modern Western literature. Although he concludes the first edition of the *Anthology of World Literature* by describing a "new age of realistic experiment" that extends the "great tradition" in science and art—exemplified by the stylistic experiments, ambiguities, and currents of consciousness in James Joyce, Luigi Pirandello, and Marcel Proust (1005b, 1003a, 1003b)—he finds such a panorama of ambiguities unacceptable during World War II, when the country is already permeated by a "fatal sense of insecurity" ([1951] v), and replaces it, in the second and later editions, with a more positive section addressing his concerns (beginning with the second edition of 1940, the conclusion is subtitled "Some Problems Today"). The unsettling Pirandello disappears (as does a section on literary criticism), and the socially engaged perspectives of Mikhail Sholokhov and Thomas Mann emerge as examples of literature's humanistic power to assert "the moral world of man's conscience" ([1951] 1101). Dismayed by the fragmentation of modern society and society's rejection of the past, Buck retreats from his previous description of modern Western literature and anchors the anthology to a reassuring tradition: "[I]t is well that in at least one college course, open to all, there be a reassessment of the ideas that have made human civilization. . . . The result ought to be a pattern . . . the symphony of Western culture" ([1951] v–vi). The global perspective recedes once more into the background as the emphasis on civilization returns, showing how easy it is to revise a view of cultural tradition (West or rest) with a few changes in the table of contents.

World literature courses multiplied in the expansion of higher education after World War II, but there were few guidelines for a course that was neither specifically humanities nor great-books, and there was little professional preparation for a course in literature that drew on different linguistic and cultural traditions. Foreign-language departments preferred to teach a single national tradition, few comparatists were available, and most courses were taught in the English department by faculty members trained in English literature and translations of Western classics. The number of modern English-language works included in the courses grew, leading Calvin Brown to complain in 1953 of "debased standards in world literature courses," which would only "confirm the student's linguistic, geographical, and chronological provincialism" (13).

In 1959, a unique Conference on the Teaching of World Literature brought together a group of world literature teachers to discuss principles and standards. The conference organizer declared at the outset that "world literature is so large a subject that it cannot be studied systematically" (Block, "Objectives" 3)—that is, studied as a whole—and that discussions concentrate almost entirely on the Western model. Only one participant argues for "non-Western literatures in the world literature program" (Alberson 51); two other speakers note the paradox of world literature restricted to the Western tradition but then move on to other topics.[11] It is a pragmatic focus, reflecting the fact that almost all participants teach Western literature as a mandated part of the curriculum. For some, Western literature, being transnational, is already world literature, and literary expression in the rest of the world is best studied in separate semesters. Four manageable units could thus be made of Asian literature: "four distinct centers . . . the Mahometan World, especially the Arabs, though one might extend this to Iran and perhaps even farther east; India, China, and Japan" (Friederich 13). Part of this deferral in rooted in scholarly conscience—the fear of linguistic and cultural ignorance—but part stems from a belief in mapped-out blocs of cultural tradition, alternative sites whose separate history remains to be explored before comparisons are made with the West.[12] The resulting object of study promises a panorama of global literature organized by sequences rather than world literature's initial, and ambitious, project of inclusion.

The rest recedes as part of the world literature equation at midcentury, because of widespread emphasis on the Western heritage as part of general education and possibly also because of developments in literary criticism that replace generalizations about civilization with the close reading of texts. In some anthologies, the rest retains a sample presence that is heavily domesticated: witness Dagobert Runes's *Treasury of World Literature* (1956), which includes Asian texts but excludes, as too different, those that show "a decidedly Oriental mannerism" (vii).

A new kind of anthology, however, makes a break with the project of global inclusion. In 1956, the first edition of Norton's *World Masterpieces: Literature of Western Culture* presents itself as

> an anthology of Western literature. . . . The literatures of the Far East have been omitted, on the ground that the principal aim of a course in world literature is to bring American students into living contact with their own Western tradition, and that this aim cannot be adequately realized in a single course if they must also be introduced to a very different tradition, one requiring extended treatment to be correctly understood. (Mack et al., *World Masterpieces* 1: ix)

Conceived as a teaching anthology, with extensive notes and critical introductions, it seeks to go beyond the "usual generalizations about periods and philosophies" and to use the analysis of imaginative literature as a key to understanding a cultural epoch in "its unformulated aspirations and intuitions as well as its conscious theorems and ideals" (x, ix).

World Masterpieces was enormously successful and widely imitated. Its image of Western literary tradition was exported around the world, taught not only for the works it contained but also as an example of Western literary-critical perspective.[13] This work-centered perspective generates period introductions that insert the discussion of literary texts inside a framework of intellectual history. It prints complete works or large coherent sections of long works, rejects the broad coverage afforded by numerous excerpts ("no snippets"), and seeks to acquire a more "effective understanding" by analyzing individual works in depth (x). The role of translation is examined in a "Note on Translation," printed at the end of each volume, that demonstrates how different eras put their own stamp on translations of the same text (e.g., on translations of Homer). The organization of material replaces previous century divisions with cluster titles derived from intellectual or aesthetic history: "The Ancient World," "The Middle Ages," "The Renaissance," "Neoclassicism," "Romanticism," "Realism and Naturalism," and "Symbolism and the Modern School." Cultural evolution disappears as a theme, replaced by an affirmation of universal human nature and human dignity. History is given a contributing but not dominant role, and the previously all-important biographies of individual authors are relegated to fine-print columns at the end of each section introduction. It was a lucid and persuasive model that worked well in the classroom and suggested various contexts for discussion.

By 2005, the Norton anthologies of world literature had gone through eight editions.[14] The original Western focus was preserved through the sixth edition in 1992, shifting in 1995 to include a parallel global track with the expanded sixth edition. The Western focus was maintained in the seventh and eighth editions, in 1999 and 2005, and the global focus continued in the six-volume *Norton Anthology of World Literature* (2002). A brief overview of this evolution brings out significant issues of organization and coverage, which became even more crucial as the editors grappled with the projected balance of a global format.[15] In this perspective, the first edition acts as a reference point for later changes and even for broader differences among anthologies: it reflects the literary-theoretical decision to work with complete texts or substantially autonomous sections (and thus represents the dominant mode of literary criticism at the time); it chooses to focus on the Western tradition, though it does not ignore the existence of other traditions; it is based in the traditional Western canon of the mid–twentieth century (before the challenges of the 1960s); and it is firmly positioned as a pedagogical instrument.

The anthology's preference for complete works leads to a shorter list of readings, which focuses attention on principles of selection (it is easier to see what is left out). The first edition of *World Masterpieces: Literature of Western Culture* is based on the prevailing Western canon, which it diversifies along linguistic or national lines, with an unusually wide range of "English, Irish, American, Russian, German, Scandinavian, French, Italian, Spanish, Portuguese, Latin, Hebrew, and Greek" works (Mack et al., *World Masterpieces* 1: ix). It famously contains no women writers or writers of color, situating them by implication at the margins of Western literary tradition—an invisible, internal rest. This list has been transformed over the decades, offering a more complex representation of Western culture in its diverse writers (e.g., Sappho, Sor Juana, Frederick Douglass, Virginia Woolf, and Derek Walcott), its topics (including social issues of gender and class, the impact of colonialism), and in new types of writing. The anthology's primary focus remains the close reading of texts, but the contextual supports for that reading have been greatly strengthened. Maps, time lines, and reproductions of contemporary art are currently coordinated with clusters of historical and philosophical writings—from Hesiod to Salman Rushdie—that reinforce cultural contexts by showing how influential thinkers view the central issues of their time.

Though focused for curricular reasons on Western literature, the editors of the first *World Masterpieces* were conscious of being situated inside a larger framework, to which they regularly alluded and which ultimately became the global edition of 1995. Just as the first edition apologized for not including the literature of the Far East, the second edition listed a companion volume, *Masterpieces of the Orient*, edited by G. L. Anderson (1961), which it specifically recommended in the preface to the fourth edition (Mack, Introduction [1979]). *Gilgamesh* was introduced as a forerunner in the sixth edition (Mack, Introduction [1992]). As early as the fifth edition of 1985, this list of Western masterpieces included three works by non-Western authors (R. K. Narayan, Yukio Mishima, and Wole

Soyinka), which were carefully described as "windows opening on experiences and ways of life which are not part of the cultural tradition students brought up on the American continent usually know best" (Mack, Introduction [1985] xxi). They were replaced in the sixth edition with the Egyptian Naguib Mahfouz and the Nigerian Chinua Achebe. The notion of a window on the world (recalling Keats's magic casements) is not unique; it echoes world literature's curricular mission to educate citizens in their own tradition while situating them in a broader framework. How to execute this mission is another matter: the stories by Narayan and Mishima serve as sharp cultural contrasts, while the works by Soyinka, Mahfouz, and Achebe act as a bridge by openly comparing Western and non-Western values.

The sixth edition became the basis for a new global anthology that would retain the Western selections as a core and add a series of major non-Western works with canonical status in their own cultures. The task of preparing this anthology, both as the expanded sixth edition (1995) and as the later—enlarged and revised—*Norton Anthology of World Literature* (2002), raised many questions and highlights the way that Western frameworks shape our understanding of texts from other parts of the world. It is not merely a matter of identifying canonical works for India, China, Japan, Africa, and the Near East (although there are passionate disputes there too, especially as we approach the modern period) but also a matter of how they are presented to an audience used to Western thematic and temporal groupings. Western section titles like "Renaissance," "Enlightenment" (previously "Neoclassicism") and even "Romanticism," which usefully initiate discussion of shared themes and cultural context, do not have counterparts in other areas of the world; "classical" periods flourish at different times and with different connotations in India, China, and Western Europe. Consequently, the scholars in charge of various sections chose titles that expressed conventional groupings in that cultural tradition, such as "Vernacular Literature in China," "India's Heroic Age," or "The Rise of Popular Arts in Premodern Japan," and let those groupings determine chronology.

Because the resulting variety of titles and chronologies could be confusing in the classroom, a dual organization was devised to maintain cultural autonomy on the one hand and to offer a relatively neutral inclusivity on the other: an inner sequence of sweeps that follow each tradition's definition of its own artistic continuities and an overall structure of six consecutive blocks of time, from approximately 2500 BCE to the present. Accordingly, the second volume of the *Norton Anthology of World Literature* runs from 100 to 1500 and contains seven distinct sweeps from Western Europe, India, China, the Near East, and Japan that fall within the larger chronological pattern but have their own temporal identity. The final, twentieth-century section abandons the organization by sweeps in the name of a new global consciousness that experiences reality in terms of worldwide interrelations and has not yet responded to cognitive mapping.

Finally, literature in translation constitutes a special challenge for a world literature anthology charged with conveying other linguistic and cultural traditions. The first step is to locate accurate, readable translations of the work in question, but unfortunately there are not many of those in the public domain. If a work is poorly translated, it conveys little of its original character: it represents the other without letting it speak. If a work is not translated, if the person holding translation rights refuses to allow it to be translated, or if the publisher does not grant rights for reprinting (all of which happen more often than one would like), that part of the rest will not be represented at all. Nor can one predict the way a translation will be received. A version that conscientiously tries to reproduce original linguistic effects may outrage its audience if (for example) an existing Southern dialect is chosen to represent the speech of a country bumpkin in Greek comedy. In the happy event that several good translations are available, the editor looks for a readable version that also preserves cultural difference. For the Malian epic *Son-Jara* (also *Sundiata*), the Norton section editor chose a verse translation that preserved the rhythmic chant, the responses, and the interpolated songs of African oral performance, without which, he affirmed, it became a Westernized narrative. In another sweep, the editor coordinated two translations to represent different aspects of the *Mahabharata*, feeling that the Indian epic's scope and flow emerged from a fluid prose translation but that the dramatic and poetic qualities of the crucial dice-game episode were best represented by emulating the original poetry. The old saying that world literature is literature that can be translated (i.e., literature that does not depend on form) is disavowed in instances like these, where the artistic setting is visibly part of cultural identity.

The catchphrase "the West and the rest" does more than poke gentle fun at simplified opposites. Its ironic echo reminds us that the two are inextricable: one cannot be defined without open or implicit reference to the other. Perhaps it is for this reason that national reports on general education recommend a global or world perspective in addition to grounding in the Western tradition (see "Appendix A: Historical Purposes of General Education" in Boyer and Levine 53–58). In practical terms, it is unlikely that any global perspective can be truly decentered, providing equal representation and a neutral framework. Even if there is a balance of texts selected from different traditions, basic supporting structures establish patterns of expectation that relate to a local audience: maps (projections imply different centers), chronologies (calendars differ), appended time lines (differing in type, number, and origin of entries), and the necessary sequences of syllabus organization (the significant first example of a theme, genre, or any anchor point). Western tradition, moreover, is not a fixed reference point; growing over time, it incorporates new elements and recognizes new relations—unless it is frozen as a cultural icon, an available pawn in canon wars or the epitome of humanity's rise "from barbarism to civilization."

It may be best to see "West" and "rest" as templates, models executed differently at different times. Classroom dynamics will create the final variation, as both Western and global approaches come to terms with the myriad perspectives of a diverse student population. In the meantime, current anthologists build on these templates—on conventional images of West vis-à-vis rest—in ways that loosen up rigid definitions and shed light on interrelations. Some anthologists emphasize textual analysis; others, broad and diverse representation. Together, they devise frameworks that encourage teachers to maximize comparison and contrast and point the way to richer readings of two erstwhile cultural icons—the monolithic West and its shapeless counterpart, the rest—while supplying more precise yet flexible strategies for the teaching of world literature.

Notes

1. "There is an Arab literature in Morocco, which is 1500 miles west of Athens, and there is a Western literature in Vladivostok, almost a thousand miles east of Peking" (Anderson x).

2. For further discussion from two different perspectives, see Roberts; Gillespie.

3. "If we take the idea of European culture for our standard, we shall, indeed, only find it applicable to Europe. If, however, we establish arbitrary distinctions between cultures and modes of enlightenment, we are liable to lose ourselves in cloud-cuckoo-land . . ." (Herder 284).

4. "It is difficult for Americans and Europeans to teach recent 'third-world' texts without implying that these are 'developing' literatures—embryonic versions of first-world works which will improve in time. Such an attitude is especially enticing because much post–World War II Indian, African and West Indian literature is, after all, about colonialism and its aftermath" (Haskell 25).

5. "There are millions of men in Europe and America to-day whose whole mental equipment—despite the fact that they have been taught to read and write—is far more closely akin to the average of the Upper Period of Barbarism than to the highest standards of their own time" (409a).

6. ". . . committee reports, accounts of institutional reforms, descriptions of new programs, philosophical statements, commentaries on general education, news accounts historical treatises, analyses of the curriculum position papers, and empirical studies" (Boyer and Levine 53–54).

7. Similar debates over American identity, whether pluralistic or a new unified whole, emerge in relation to the "Americanization movement" of the early twentieth century (see Cremin 112–13).

8. The National Endowment for the Humanities report *To Reclaim a Legacy* (1984) recommends the study of great books (Bennett). *Challenges to the Humanities* begins with the question, "Is there no common heritage that belongs to us all?" (Finn, Ravitch, and Roberts 8). The *Dictionary of Cultural Literacy* (Hirsch, Kett, and Trefil) undertakes to provide a common (English) vocabulary for modern American society, or "what every American needs to know" (see subtitle of Hirsch).

9. Early examples are Kampf and Lauter; *Cassell's Encyclopedia*; Fetterley; Fitzgerald; and DiPietro and Ifkovic.

10. Aldridge discusses similar problems in relation to Asian literature.

11. Samuel Golden alludes to the lack of global cross-currents in the course at his institution and asks, "Would it be impertinent to suggest that world literature does not exist, that what we have been teaching is only an approximation of it?" (100). Weldon M. Williams, contrasting two pedagogic methods, mentions that the course is "addressed to the Western tradition and is not 'World' Literature" and the "most notable and serious omission . . . is the literature of the East" (75, 76). Further discussion of this conference and of the teaching of world literature in the United States can be found in Lawall, "Reading" 7–12, 20–32.

12. A more interactive version of this blocking appears in Fredric Jameson's idea of cognitive mapping, notably in his essay "Third World Literature in the Era of Multinational Capitalism" (1986), as criticized by Aijaz Ahmad for its reliance on monolithic images of First and Third Worlds.

13. The political impact of such exportation of cultural capital has been discussed separately in, for example, Viswanathan; Guillory.

14. I joined the anthology as twentieth-century editor in 1977 and was soon working on other aspects of it with General Editor Maynard Mack; I became general editor with the seventh edition (1999).

15. A more detailed discussion of changes in various editions is available in Lawall, "Anthologizing."

Works Cited

Ahmad, Aijaz. "Jameson's Rhetoric of Otherness and the 'National Allegory.'" *Social Text: Theory/Culture/Ideology* 17 (1987): 3–25. Rpt. in *In Theory: Classes, Nations, Literatures*. By Ahmad. London: Verso, 1992. 95–122. Print.

Alberson, Hazel S. "Non-Western Literatures in the World Literature Program." Block, *Teaching* 45–52.

Aldridge, A. Owen. *The Reemergence of World Literature: A Study of Asia and the West*. Newark: U of Delaware P, 1986. Print.

Anderson, George L., ed. *Masterpieces of the Orient*. New York: Norton, 1961. Print.

Bennett, William. *To Reclaim a Legacy: A Report on the Humanities in Higher Education*. Washington: Natl. Endowment for the Humanities, 1984. Print.

Block, Haskell M., "The Objectives of the Conference." Block, *Teaching* 1–7.

———, ed. *The Teaching of World Literature: Proceedings of the Conference on the Teaching of World Literature at the University of Wisconsin, April 24–25, 1959*. Chapel Hill: U of North Carolina P, 1960. Print. U of North Carolina Studies in Compar. Lit. 28.

Boyer, Ernest L., and Arthur Levine. *A Quest for Common Learning: The Aims of General Education*. Washington: Carnegie Foundation for the Advancement of Teaching, [1981]. Print.

Brown, Calvin S. "Debased Standards in World Literature Courses." *Yearbook of Comparative and General Literature* 2 (1953): 10–14. Print.

Buck, Philo M., ed. *An Anthology of World Literature*. 1934. 3rd ed. New York: Macmillan, 1951. Print.

Cassell's Encyclopedia of World Literature. Rev. ed. London: Cassell, 1973. Print.

Cremin, Lawrence Arthur. *Popular Education and Its Discontents*. New York: Harper, 1990. Print.

Di Leo, Jeffrey R., ed. *On Anthologies: Politics and Pedagogy*. Lincoln: U of Nebraska P, 2004. Print.

DiPietro, Robert J., and Edward Ifkovic, eds. *Ethnic Perspectives in American Literature*. New York: MLA, 1983. Print.

Eliot, Charles W. *The Harvard Classics*. Vol. 50. New York: Collier, 1910. Print.

Étiemble, [René]. "Faut-il réviser la notion de *Weltliteratur*?" *Proceedings of the International Comparative Literature Association* (1966): 5–16. Print.

Fetterley, Judith. *The Resisting Reader: A Feminist Approach to American Fiction*. Bloomington: Indiana UP, 1978. Print.

Finke, Lauri. "The Hidden Curriculum." Di Leo 395–404.

Finn, Chester E., Jr., Diane Ravitch, and P. Holley Roberts, eds. *Challenges to the Humanities*. New York: Holmes, 1985. Print.

Fitzgerald, Frances. *America Revised: History Schoolbooks in the Twentieth Century*. Boston: Little, 1979. Print.

Friederich, Werner. "On the Integrity of Our Planning." Block, *Teaching* 9–22.

Gillespie, Michael Allen. "Liberal Education and the Idea of the West." *America, the West, and Liberal Education*. Ed. Ralph C. Hancock. Lanham: Rowman, 1999. 7–25. Print.

Golden, Samuel. "The Teaching of World Literture at Wayne State University." Block, *Teaching* 97–100.

Guillory, John. *Cultural Capital: The Problem of Literary Canon Formation.* Chicago: U of Chicago P, 1993. Print.

Haskell, Rosemary. "From Third World to First: Minimizing Bias in the Teaching of Third World Literature." *Studies in the Humanities* 18.1 (1991): 25–34. Print.

Herder, J. G. "Ideas for a Philosophy of History." *J. G. Herder on Social and Political Culture.* Trans., ed., and introd. F. M. Barnard. Cambridge: Cambridge UP, 1969. 253–326. Print.

Hirsch, E. D., Jr. *Cultural Literacy: What Every American Needs to Know.* New York: Houghton, 1987. Print.

Hirsch, E. D., Jr., Joseph F. Kett, and James Trefil. *Dictionary of Cultural Literacy.* Boston: Houghton, 1988. Print.

Hutchins, Robert M. "Preface: The History and Purpose of This Set." Hutchins and Adler 1: xi–xxvii.

Hutchins, Robert M., and Mortimer Adler, eds. *Great Books of the Western World.* 3 vols. Chicago: Encyclopaedia Britannica, 1952. Print.

Jameson, Fredric. "Third-World Literature in the Era of Multinational Capitalism." *Social Text* 15 (1986): 65–88. Rpt. in *The Jameson Reader.* Ed. Michael Hardt and Kathi Weeks. Oxford: Blackwell, 2000. 315–39. Print.

Jones, William. "The Third Anniversary Discourse, on the Hindus, Delivered 2nd of February, 1786." *The Works of Sir William Jones, with the Life of the Author by Lord Teignmouth.* Vol. 3. London: Stockdale; Walker, 1807. 24–46. Print.

Kampf, Louis, and Paul Lauter, eds. *The Politics of Literature: Dissenting Essays on the Teaching of English.* New York: Random, 1972. Print.

Lawall, Sarah N. "Anthologizing 'World Literature.'" Di Leo 47–89.

———. "Canons, Contexts, and Pedagogy: The Place of World Literature." *Comparatist* 24 (2000): 39–56. Print.

———. "Reading World Literature." *Reading World Literature: Theory, History, Practice.* Ed. Lawall. Austin: U of Texas P, 1994. 1–64. Print.

Lawall, Sarah N., et al., eds. *The Norton Anthology of Western Literature.* 8th ed. 2 vols. New York: Norton, 2005. Print.

———, eds. *The Norton Anthology of World Literature.* 2nd ed. 6 vols. New York: Norton, 2002. Print.

———, eds. *The Norton Anthology of World Masterpieces: The Western Tradition.* 7th ed. 2 vols. New York: Norton, 1999. Print.

Macaulay, Thomas Babington. "Minute on Indian Education (February 2, 1835)." *Macaulay Prose and Poetry.* Comp. G. M. Young. Cambridge: Harvard UP, 1952. 719–30. Print.

Mack, Maynard M. Introduction. *The Norton Anthology of World Masterpieces: Literature of Western Culture.* 4th ed. Ed. Mack et al. 2 vols. New York: Norton, 1979. xiii–xv. Print.

———. Introduction. *The Norton Anthology of World Masterpieces.* 5th ed. Ed. Mack et al. Vol. 1. New York: Norton, 1985. xiii–xvi. Print.

———. Introduction. *The Norton Anthology of World Masterpieces.* 6th ed. Vol. 1. New York: Norton, 1992. xv–xix. Print.

Mack, Maynard M., et al., eds. *The Norton Anthology of World Masterpieces.* Expanded ed. 2 vols. New York: Norton, 1995. Print.

———, eds. *World Masterpieces: Literature of Western Culture.* 1st ed. 2 vols. New York: Norton, 1956. Print.

Roberts, J. M. "The Birth of the West." *The Triumph of the West.* Boston: Little, 1985. 55–77. Print.

Runes, Dagobert D. *Treasury of World Literature.* New York: Greenwood, 1969. Print.

Rushdie, Salman. "'Commonwealth Literature' Does Not Exist." *Imaginary Homelands: Essays and Criticism, 1981–1991.* London: Granta, 1992. 61–70. Print.

Said, Edward. "Communities of Interpretation." *Covering Islam: How the Media and the Experts Determine How We See the Rest of the World.* Rev. ed. New York: Random, 1997. 33–64. Print.

Thompson, Stith. Preface. *Our Heritage of World Literature.* Comp. Thompson. New York: Dryden, 1938. 5–6. Print.

Viswanathan, Gauri. *Masks of Conquest: Literary Study and British Rule in India.* New York: Columbia UP, 1990. Print.

Williams, Henry Smith. "Civilization." *Encyclopaedia Britannica: A Dictionary of Arts, Sciences, Literature and General Information.* Vol. 6. Cambridge: Cambridge UP, 1910. 403–10. Print.

Williams, Weldon M. "Intensive and Extensive Approaches in the Teaching of World Literature." Block, *Teaching* 73–81.

Vilashini Cooppan

The Ethics of World Literature: Reading Others, Reading Otherwise

In spring 2004, I taught a course entitled World Literatures at Yale University. It was the fourth time I had taught it since developing it in a flush of millennial optimism, when it seemed to me and some of my colleagues that world literature might revitalize, reorient, and transform a comparative literature long mired in an autogeography of Europeanisms. This course was a little different, however. Our initial reading of the ancient Akkadian *Epic of Gilgamesh*, worldly grounding in an epic tradition that went on to encompass, in whole or part, Homer's *Odyssey*, Derek Walcott's *Omeros*, the Sanskrit *Mahabharata*, and the fourteenth-century West African *Epic of Sunjata*, took place only days after the looting of the library in Baghdad, a library that had once housed cuneiform tablets like those on which *Gilgamesh* had been written some four thousand years ago. Later that spring, our focus shifted from world epics to world novels, and we turned for a week to *Alf Layla wa-Layla* ("The Tales of a Thousand and One Nights"), a magical hinge among the tenth-century Japanese *Tale of Genji*; Honoré de Balzac's *Le Père Goriot*, with its talismanic nineteenth-century Paris of love and money; the Chinese novelist Dai Sijie's recent fable of cultural translation in the Cultural Revolution, *Balzac and the Little Chinese Seamstress*; and finally, Salman Rushdie's

Midnight's Children, a postcolonial alchemist's mix of East and West, epic and novel. As we read a week's worth of the *Nights* and discussed their famously nested structure and palimpsestic history of recensions, migrations, translations, and rewritings, we tried to give some shape to what Franco Moretti in *Modern Epic* has called "world texts" (5). *World* here was an adjective denoting large-scale processes or systems of global literary movement—a trajectory of travel, borrowing, and transculturation through which texts like the *Nights* were initially made and through which they continued to surface. In spring 2004, as my students were quick to notice, the *world* in *world literature* was also uneasily allied to the national-imperial ground unfolding before them.

How different this Baghdad and Mosul are, said one student, describing the geography of Caliph Haroun al-Rashid's wanderings in the *Nights*, from the cities we know. Or, I might add, don't know. For by that time, Mosul had become a cave, Baghdad a toppled statue: metaphors whose reductionist verities and one-to-one equivalences bore little resemblance to what Jorge Luis Borges described as the "infinite" energies of the *Nights* (50), a text in the shape of a moving target, a narrative organism of almost cellular capacity, regenerating itself endlessly and everywhere. If the deadly couplet of United States imperial nationalism and Iraqi insurgency had reduced a place and its inhabitants to a narrow set of recognizable markers (us and them), would a return to the prenational, cosmopolitan geographies of the *Nights* recode a place we knew only in the Manichaean modalities of war? A Mosul we can embrace, a Baghdad we can marvel at.

This recoding, I confess, was my hope *and* my fear. My students in this moment, as in so many, were on the verge of a romantic attraction to otherness and a well-intentioned desire to turn admiration for other cultures, literatures, and aesthetic practices into a shorthand "understanding" of the other, what I would see as the Scylla and Charybdis of that self-styled epic project, world literature. From the heterogeneous mix of Muslim, Jewish, Christian, and Zoroastrian cultures, and Arabic, Persian, Hebrew, Turkish, Syriac, and Byzantine Greek languages that constituted the cosmopolitan medieval world chronicled in the *Nights*, to the distinct imprints placed on the text by its successive translators, the *Nights* has always seemed to pose, only to refuse, the question of what, exactly, is "Arabian" about it.

Antoine Galland's early-eighteenth-century translation of a fourteenth-century Arabic manuscript sent to Galland from Syria was liberally filled out with additional stories, stories gleaned from other written and oral sources, such as the iconic tales of Sindbad the sailor and Aladdin and the magic lamp. Galland translated both the original manuscript (a heterogeneric mix of fable and folklore, parable and poetry, ribald jokes and courtly disquisitions) and its ghostly companions into the uniform style of the French fairy tale. Subsequent nineteenth-century versions by European scholars, colonial civil servants, and imperial adventurers continued in this vein, omitting here, adding there, and transforming the collection by turns into an ethnographic source text on Arab language and custom (Edward William Lane), a nursery entertainment (Jonathan Scott's English version of Galland), a philologic exercise (Joseph von Hammer-Purgstall and Gustav Weil in German, John Payne in English, Joseph Charles Mardrus in French), and a set piece of orientalist sexual fantasy replete with Victorian racial stereotypes and anthropological nuggets (Richard Burton) (for discussions of these versions, see Irwin 9–41; Haddawy). Each translation reflected the compass of the cultural knowledge it sought. In spring 2004, this looking-glass function of the *Nights* had a peculiar force and a particular urgency. Then, and since, the elusive Arabianness of the *Nights*, with the work's fragmentary, heterogeneous, and historically differentiated notion of cultural identity, seemed precisely what we needed to embrace, an alternative to that will to knowledge that regularly enlists other literatures to the twin task of representing them and refracting us.

Gayatri Chakravorty Spivak recently identified

> the arrogance of the radical European humanist conscience, which will consolidate it*self* by imagining the other, or, as Sartre puts it, "redo in himself the other's project," through the collection of information. . . . Much of our literary critical globalism cannot even qualify to the conscientiousness of this arrogance. (*Critique* 7; for a similar argument, see Spivak, *Death* 72, 108)

Literary globalism in the mode of imperialism becomes a suspect ethics of (dis)engagement in which other literatures and cultures are recognized, even valorized, in order that their existence in some temporal anteriority or spatial exteriority may rehabilitate; shore up; and, to use a popular term, globalize the privileged narratives of the West. Such "technologies of recognition," writes Shu-mei Shih, reinscribe a familiar divide, "produc[ing] 'the West' as the agent of recognition and 'the rest' as the object of recognition, in representation" (17). We have parsed the meter of this old rhyme many times, as Dipesh Chakrabarty reminds us: "first in Europe, and then elsewhere" (7). This is the law of nations, of democracy, of rights-based discourse, all modeled as gifts bestowed by the West on territories variously seen as undeserving, unready, inhospitable, or selectively unwilling to be brought along on modernity's time line. Even when the West's others resist its organizing narratives, they remain defined by them, visible only insofar as they mirror or mask the self-image of the West.

Must the project of world literature, in what Spivak calls the arrogance of its ambition, mime the imperial certitudes of the West's recognition of itself through its others? The mere domestication of other literatures, languages, cultures, geographies, and histories does indeed turn world literature into imperial knowledge. But I prefer to imagine my students' surprise at discovering another Mosul and Baghdad than the one flashing forth in fire and smoke on CNN as the mark of a moment of incommensurable knowledge. Who are "they" and what is "their culture"? These unspoken questions of the classroom that read one Baghdad in the shadow of another were in the end unanswered by the *Nights*.

If I have lingered on the resolutely contemporary context of the United States war on Iraq, it is not to present this moment as simultaneous test case and limit point for the project of understanding the other but rather to suggest how some version of this impasse structures the project of world literature generally. To undertake the teaching of world literature without a detour to this dead end is to fail our students by allowing them to imagine that they are receiving something they cannot entirely have—namely, knowledge of the other. Students read world literature to know something of the world. It is my job to help to complicate that ambition quite as much as to enable it, through a reading of literature that is as temporally deep, historically informed, textually sensitive, and culturally nontotalizing as I, with my many limitations, can make it. In the supplementary logic of world literature, it is not to singularities of cultural reference, certainties of cultural meaning, and origins of literary culture that we must turn but rather to other rubrics of space and time: the gaps of translation; the nonlinear networks of transmission; and the spectral logics of hauntings, trace discourses, and residues. I have elsewhere sketched these patterns of space and time and considered the possibility they offer to the teacher and theorist of world literature (Cooppan, "Ghosts," "Hauntologies," and "World Literature"). Here I wish to concentrate on the specific ethical obligations of world literature.

Ethics, Derek Attridge reminds us, is in part a reading practice that

> involves working against the mind's tendency to assimilate the other
> to the same, attending to that which can barely be heard, registering
> what is unique about the shaping of language, thought, and feeling in
> a particular work. (25)

In a foreword to the English translation of Michel de Certeau's *Heterologies* (itself an important exploration of the practice of reading others through reading otherwise), Wlad Godzich observes, "Western thought has always thematized the other as a threat to be reduced, as a potential same-to-be, a yet-not-same" (xiii). We can well imagine a world literature version of this plot, in which other literatures are handily turned into a "potential same-to-be," the tenth-century Japanese *monogatari* prose narrative into the novel *avant-la-lettre*, *The Tale of Genji* into *La Princesse de Clèves*, Naguib Mahfouz into the Egyptian Marcel Proust, Rushdie into the Indian Gabriel García Márquez, and so on and so forth. There is a limit to comparability, as any comparatist knows. And it is at that limit point that the ethics of reading must take its stand. This is an ethics of reading whose goal cannot be conversion of otherness to sameness, an ethics of reading that must instead choose to stay blocked from that final assimilative moment, at home in the very moment of nonrecognition.

What is needed in the field of world literature is a practice of reading that seeks difference as much as sameness, a practice that preserves the distinct historical formation and trajectory, the sometimes forbidding opacity and alienness of, say, the Urdu *ghazal* or the Southern African praise poem even as it simultaneously urges students to ask questions and perform readings that lead them toward some kind of claim, no doubt many claims—if we are lucky, even competing claims—about the capacities of the lyric per se. This is not world literature reduced to the novel, nor is it world literature so thoroughly localized so as to refute any and all possibilities of someday thinking globally. And it is certainly not a world literature that leaps, Superman-style, over wide geographies and long histories to find a reassuring sameness to every story in its book. To look for the universal presence of the journey theme or the identity theme in the texts of world literature is no better than to turn Mahfouz into Proust. The *world* in *world literature* does not denote an object of knowledge, variously familiar or foreign, ours or theirs. World literature is not an ontology but an epistemology, not a known but a knowing. The ethics of reading turns on the moment in which we fail to recognize the familiar and claim that failure as a modality of knowledge. One culture's Baghdad is not another's.

The observation of this fact stages both an ethical obligation to imagine the other as the other and a historical obligation to locate the other in space-times not our own. To parse the logic of my student's surprise at finding another Baghdad in the city of Haroun al-Rashid is to uncover a telling clash between two historical narratives. In the first, an updating of the familiar trajectory from empire to decolonization, Iraq plays colony to a newly muscularized United States imperialism at the same time that it also begs to be understood as a new nation, created by us in some semblance of our image. The second historical narrative owes less to the nation-state in either its hegemonic or emergent form. Here it is not Iraq that signifies so much as Baghdad, one seat of a vital, cosmopolitan intellectual and literary culture that stretched far to the West between the seventh and thirteenth centuries. To recover this meaning of Baghdad is perhaps one modest task of world literature. The nonnational dimensions of literary Baghdad offer an alternative to the nonnational spaces of the global cell or network. They argue for us to continue to decouple *Arab* from *terrorist* in the present quite as much as to recast *Arabian* in the past as a complex sign whose reference was never just *Arab* and *Islamic*.

In my most optimistic moments I imagine a world literature that trains its readers in the revisualization of both literary histories and ethical-political futures. On the one hand, it is the task of our transnational, diasporic, global times to rethink the national paradigm. On the other hand, it is imperative to understand the continued relevance of the nation-state form to the still unfinished project of decolonization. Without some account of the nation and its work, the new world literature will have little to say about the new world order. But without some grasp of categories of political and cultural imagining beyond the nation—I do not say "after," for the nation is not, to my mind, dead—we will be unable to do more than read the record of the last three hundred years in the West and its colonies, unable to conceive of a practice of literary representation that does much more than allegorize the nation or simulate the processes, variously economic, cultural, political, psychic, of nation building. Even as we interrogate and retain the nation in some literary-critical *Aufhebung*, we have also to open ourselves to the regressive temporality of "once upon a time." This fairy-tale formulation serves as a critical open sesame, inviting the reading back of a different presence onto a space gridded by a long history of nationalist ambitions and nationalist long-ings, of which the United States war is only the latest installment. Once upon a time, Baghdad was different.

In "once upon a time"—"that paradigmatic phrase of all narrative or storytelling"—Homi K. Bhabha finds "literature's rule of fiction":

> Suddenly past and the present intersect and interact; histories and cultures cross; and the plot of literary narrative locates us in the region of allusion and articulation; we are in the world of the "as if." . . . The "as if" of literary language, its instructive fictionality, now reveals the ground for its ethical claims. Against the hard face of facts and the burden of experience, the fictional "as if" opens up the counterfactual ethical narrative of the "what if": "What if I, the son of slaves, daughter of the diaspora, exile of the Enlightenment—what if I read be-tween the lines of these great traditions, write against the grain of classics and canons, and in turning tropes to my own advantage, I es-tablish my right to narrate?" (197)

Bhabha's voicing of the right to narrate, with its attendant notion of the enunciative claim that any act of narration (understood quite simply as communication) makes for recognition and response, is a thinking of literature precisely as ethics, the ethics of relationality. This is the ethical imperative nested into the very structure of the *Nights* with its famed frames marking the endless circulation of story from teller to listener.

Walter Mignolo calls for the "decolonizing" of literary history. This means questioning the hegemony of Western schemas, from the "ma-cronarratives" of civilization and capitalism, with their sequential prog-ress through the stages of history; to such privileged languages as Greek, Latin, English, French, and German; to the notion of alphabetic written languages as the only languages that count; to quite recently invented Western categories of genre, whose ahistorical, transcultural imposition on other literatures is merely assimilation masquerading as comparativ-ism. Finally, Mignolo claims, this line of inquiry will cease to assume the existence of something called literature and instead seek through com-parison "to illuminate the processes by which certain aural and visual practices came to be conceived as literature" (170).

Here is a truly epic task: to provide a sense of such epochal shifts as nationalism, capitalism, colonialism, diaspora, globalization; to give a version of the view from places that lived those shifts that is very different from the view at the centers of the West; to take on more than simply the slice of the modern that coincides with the nation form and its global afterlife—indeed, to incorporate actively the literary cultures of earlier polities, linguistic and religious imperiums, and cosmopolitan trade routes; and, finally, to interrogate and contest the process of power by which literature is named, defined, canonized, and taught. Not to mention the charge to access as much of this material as possible in the original language, no matter if it be one of the European languages in which so many United States academics were trained or Arabic, Chinese, Norwegian, Tibetan, Hungarian, or Korean (I name a small selection of the languages my students and colleagues work in).

How are we to resist the temptation to let world literature go the way of a true mission impossible and self-destruct in the very grandeur of its ambition? No course can deliver all that we presently ask World Literature to do. But every course offered under that rubric can, I believe, undertake to transmit a reading method that regularly imagines, sometimes models, and occasionally invents some alternative to the conventional plots of literary history. World literature asks us to change not only the object but also the line of literary history, eschewing the narratives of literary-cultural progress for those of ghostly repetition and uncanny haunting, preferring the network of surprising transnational and transtemporal connections to the cartographic divisions of a world literature composed of the known and unknown, the named quantities and what Joseph Conrad's Marlow calls "the blank spaces." *The Tales of a Thousand and One Nights*, with its complex history of composition and transmission; its many translations, recensions, and imaginative rewritings; and its hybrid blending of the poetic and didactic traditions, of oral and written culture, resists the logic of straight lines and the logic of imperial filling in.

To take the *Nights*, as I have done here, as an occasion for the practice of that reading method known as world literature, perhaps even as a defense of it, is to claim the ethical as one task of literary criticism in the worldly mode. I do not read the *Nights* in Arabic, but I, and my students, read it nonetheless. I consult Galland's eighteenth-century version, Burton's Victorian version, and Husain Haddawy's recent version (now the authoritative choice for English readers), as well as Borges's wide-ranging homage, Tzvetan Todorov's narratological dissection, Rushdie's postmodern Indian riff, and a host of critical commentaries by scholars versed in Arabic. I rely on the generous expertise of a medieval Arabist colleague, Beatrice Gruendler, to guide me through the text with an eye to all that those various readers could not capture or communicate.

Perhaps most important, I tell my students that when they enter the fictional space of the *Nights* particularly and world literature generally, they should go for the moments that don't make sense, not the ones that do. Start, I say, with the place that refuses your understanding. Enter that other set of representational conventions, imaginative geographies, literary histories, and cultural ideals, and learn the view from there. Know what you don't know. Fully cognizant of the limitations of any reading methodology ever to allow us unmediated and total access to other cultures, times, and languages, all of which we may agree remain at least partially forever lost in translation of one sort or another, we may nonetheless hope to enter on the reading of others, otherwise.

Works Cited

Attridge, Derek. "Innovation, Literature, Ethics: Relating to the Other." *PMLA* 114.1 (1999): 20–31. Print.

Bhabha, Homi K. "Afterword: A Personal Response." Hutcheon and Valdés 194–204.

Borges, Jorge Luis. "The Thousand and One Nights." *Seven Nights.* Trans. Eliot Weinberger. New York: New Directions, 1984. 42–57. Print.

Chakrabarty, Dipesh. *Provincializing Europe.* Princeton: Princeton UP, 2000. Print.

Conrad, Joseph. *Heart of Darkness.* Electronic Text Center, U of Virginia Lib., 1993. Web. 15 Jan. 2008.

Cooppan, Vilashini. "Ghosts in the Disciplinary Machine: The Uncanny Life of World Literature." *Comparative Literature Studies* 41.1 (2004): 10–46. Print.

———. "Hauntologies of Form: Race, Writing, and the Literary World-System." *Gramma: Journal of Theory and Criticism* 13 (2005): 71–86. Print.

———. "World Literature and Global Theory: Comparative Literature for the New Millennium." *Symploke* 9.1–2 (2001): 15–43. Print.

Godzich, Wlad. Foreword. *Heterologies: Discourse on the Other.* By Michel de Certeau. Trans. Brian Massumi. Minneapolis: U of Minnesota P, 1986. vii–xxi. Print. Theory and History of Literature 17.

Haddawy, Husain. Introduction. *The Arabian Nights.* Trans. Haddawy. New York: Norton, 1990. ix–xxxi. Print.

Hutcheon, Linda, and Mario J. Valdés, eds. *Rethinking Literary History: A Dialogue on Theory.* New York: Oxford UP, 2002. Print.

Irwin, Robert. *The Arabian Nights: A Companion.* London: Penguin, 1994. Print.

Mignolo, Walter D. "Rethinking the Colonial Model." Hutcheon and Valdés 155–93.

Moretti, Franco. *Modern Epic: The World-System from Goethe to García Márquez.* Trans. Quintin Hoare. New York: Verso, 1996. Print.

Shih, Shu-Mei. "Global Literature and the Technologies of Recognition." *PMLA* 119.1 (2004): 16–30. Print.

Spivak, Gayatri Chakravorty. *A Critique of Postcolonial Reason: Toward a History of the Vanishing Present*. Cambridge: Harvard UP, 1999. Print.

———. *Death of a Discipline*. New York: Columbia UP, 2003. Print.

Todorov, Tzvetan. *The Fantastic: A Structural Approach to a Literary Genre*. Trans. Richard Howard. Ithaca: Cornell UP, 1975. Print.

Emily Apter

Literary World-Systems

In his editorial preface to *The Novel*, an ambitious study of the world history of the genre involving many contributors, Franco Moretti uses the term "ecosystem" to describe the work's global lexicon of narrative critical concepts. *The Novel*'s "Critical Apparatus," he writes, refers to a "wider ecosystem, focusing, for instance, on how the semantic field of 'narrative' took shape around keywords such as *midrash, monogatari, xiaoshuo, qissa*—and, why not, *romance*" (1: x). His adoption of the term *ecosystem* from the natural and environmental sciences as his methodological fulcrum for the book indirectly raises a key question: What is the status of *system*, eco- or otherwise, in literary history and theory today?

Constituted at a moment of reaction against deconstruction (with its heuristic of close reading and attention to poetic figuralism), Moretti's school stands for macrocomparative approaches to literary history. As a tendency in comparative literature, the intellectual purchase of these approaches is strong. They deliver linguistic and cultural breadth, historicize autonomous texts, illuminate waves of influence and circulation, juxtapose canonical and noncanonical literary works as objects of analysis, and rely on a transnational economy that takes critical stock of symbolic capital and institutional market forces. They marshal book history, reader reception, narratology, aesethetics, philology, and genetics for a genre analysis that is at once materialist and ideologically progressive. Ultimately, however, Moretti's survey of world literature, even if eclectic in methodology, is hardly neutral. It defaults to terms like *ecosystem* to describe its project, thus signaling an avowed if not fully articulated relation to systems theory in the sciences and world-systems theory in the social sciences.

That world-systems theory has gained traction in literary studies over the last twenty years is due in large measure to the influence of Fredric Jameson, Perry Anderson, Andre Gunder Frank, and Moretti, all of whom have drawn on the work of Immanuel Wallerstein. A sociologist by training, Wallerstein was himself indebted to a host of thinkers, including historians, economists, and systems theorists.[1] Specifying that the hyphen in "world-system" was "intended to underscore that we are talking not about systems, economies, empires *of the* (whole) world, but about systems, economies, empires *that are* a world," he analyzed interstate markets in early capitalism as a causal condition (rather than symptom) of world making (*World-Systems Analysis* 16–17). In *The Modern World-System* (1977) and its sequels, he demonstrated how war, transportation networks, technological know-how, capital accumulation, the size of bureaucracies, and the organization of empire enabled cities in early modern Europe to gain ascendancy as core centers of power, around which peripheral nations orbited. In later studies—*Antisystemic Movements* (1989) and *Geopolitics and Geoculture* (1991)—he updated the core, periphery, and semiperiphery coordinates of early modern world-systems for a global age that witnessed the rise of antiglobalization or antisystem social movements: green parties, feminism, minority and human rights groups, anti-NGO (nongovernmental organization) activists. The one-world model of market-driven world-systems was revised to reflect the impact of nationally unbordered oppositional networks and political countercultures.

Applications of Wallerstein's world-systems theory extended well beyond his historical and cultural purview to premodern, non-European world-systems. Janet Abu-Lughod traced trade loops through world cities such as Baghdad and Cairo and language hubs such as Arabic, Greek, Latin, Chinese. Frank and Barry K. Gills proposed a five-hundred-year world-system, with special pertinence to transcivilizational markets based in Eurasia and Africa (xi). And in Georgi M. Derluguian's portrait of a late-twentieth-century Chechen nationalist one finds an example of world-systems extended to post-Soviet neoimperialism.

Whether ascribed to history, sociology, or literature, the paradigm of the world-system bore little resemblance to systems theory proper, which flourished in the social sciences from the 1940s to the 1960s, often as a result of self-conscious discussions of cross-disciplinary paradigms.[2] The social theorist Talcott Parsons published *The Social System* in 1951, and the biologist Ludwig von Bertalanffy, often considered the movement's intellectual anchor, published his *General Systems Theory* in 1968.[3] Starting in the early 1970s, Gregory Bateson drew on systems thinking, in *Steps to an Ecology of Mind* (1972), to establish synthetic cognitive paradigms cutting across psychology, behavioral biology, evolution, systems theory, and cybernetics. The German sociologist Niklas Luhmann linked autopoiesis to social systems ("Autopoiesis"). Modeled on the life cell, on the construct of a self region patrolled by an autonomous boundary (filtering environmental stimuli to enable a distinct identity to self-create), autopoiesis in its very name suggested a migration of systems theory into poetics, or the reverse, the movement of Romantic aesthetic irony—a self-referential, closed system—into systems theory. For Luhmann, meaning itself was a system that structurally resembled Romantic irony. "Meaning systems," he wrote in 1984, "are completely closed to the extent that only meaning can refer to meaning and that only meaning can change meaning" (*Social Systems* 37).

Luhmann's emphasis on systems closure stands in contrast to an earlier tradition in the 1950s and 1960s in which the open system was the dominant paradigm. With an emphasis on how systems interacting with the environment evolve into new hierarchical structures of organization, the open system was applied to organismic exchanges between matter and environment and to instances of negative entropy. Cybernetics led to a further opening of the open system, onto vistas of genetics and language. Feedback loops, swarms, adaptive and random response models, input-output, complexity, cost-benefit-risk calculations, information spread, allometry, entropy, morphogenesis, pattern recognition, space-to-surface algorithms, autocatalytic networks, world dynamics—each concept yielded formal systems governed by structural logics that often applied across disciplines. There was even, one could argue, a principle of pantranslatability holding among living cell, graphic image, linguistic sign, and programming code.

With its taste for totalizing rubrics, systems theory formed part of a general postwar trend of "grand theory in the human sciences," dominated by Hans-Georg Gadamer, Thomas Kuhn, Jürgen Habermas, Louis Althusser, Claude Lévi-Strauss, and the *Annales* historians (see Skinner). This said, the more functionalist systems theorists, especially in the social sciences, distanced themselves from grand theory, advocating descriptive modeling over explanation. In the estimation of Hauke Brunkhorst, sociological systems theory

> reconciled itself to its virtual inability to provide causal explanations along with strongly empirical concepts, oberservability, etc. It explains the imprecision and circularity of its functional explanations, however, not by the ontological peculiarity of its symbolically structured object domain, or, like *verstehende* sociology, by the impossibility of escaping the hermeneutic circle, but by the complexity and opacity of system structures which are in principle not amenable to causal analysis. Autopoietic (self-forming) systems alter themselves by discovering completely new structures in an unpredictable manner. (678)

While functionalist differentiation and autopoietic systems theory in the social sciences could be seen as reconcilable with, say, chaos and complexity theory in the sciences (based on their common investigation of unpredictable, self-evolving structures), their aboveground approach to structure risked neutralizing the political. By contrast, world-systems theory, particularly in its Wallersteinian iteration, maintained political critique as its principal objective. Coming directly out of Marxist sociology, it extended class analysis to conditions of hegemony among nation-states.

There was and is no easy extrapolation of either systems or world-systems theory to literary criticism, though it could be argued that world literature, as a fulcrum of literary comparatism, constituted literary world-systems theory *avant la lettre*. Shaped by Renaissance humanism; Hegelian aesthetics; Goethe's notion of *Weltliteratur*; the Marxist ideal of an "Internationale" of letters; or, more recently, transnational and postcolonial literacy networks focusing on the circulation of hyper- and counter-canonical works, translation markets, and modes of reading, world literature is by nature a "systemic" construct continually remaking itself diachronically and dialectically (Damrosch 45). As Michael Denning has shown, the proletarian novel gave way to magic realism, which in turn yielded the contemporary globalization novel:

> Like "world music," the "world novel" is a category to be distrusted; if it genuinely points to the transformed geography of the novel, it is also a marketing device that flattens distinct regional and linguistic traditions into a single cosmopolitan "world beat," with magical realism serving as the aesthetic of globalization, often as empty and contrived a signifier as the modernism and socialist realism it supplanted. There is, however, a historical truth to the sense that there are links between writers as unlike as Gárcia Márquez, Naguib Mahfouz, Nadine Gordimer, José Saramango, Paule Marshall, and Pramoedya Ananta Toer, for the work of each has roots in the remarkable international literary movement that emerged in the middle decades of the twentieth century under the slogans of "proletarian literature," "neorealism," and "progressive," "engaged," or "committed" writing. (703)

Denning reveals the cozy commercial fit between "world lit" and "world beat" in the culture industry but leaves untouched the broader issue of what constitutes "systemic" thinking in literary criticism. This problem is brought to the fore by A. S. Byatt's analysis of Balzac, whose readers are made uneasy, Byatt conjectures,

> because they feel, as Proust also did, that Balzac writes down whatever comes into his head. This is true, but as I have hoped to show— with flowers and weeds and meadows, or with paper and books and minds and lovers—he connected everything to everything else, sometimes at considerable distances in the texts. His heir in this regard is the George Eliot of *Middlemarch* who used the metaphor of Bichat's idea of "primitive tissue," spiderwebs, and the nature of optics to bind all her text together—science and mythology, love and death, little England and larger Europe. (407)

Are spiderwebs evidence of systems? Are there systems writers par excellence (Honoré de Balzac, Gustave Flaubert, Marcel Proust, Herman Melville, Edgar Allan Poe, Henry James, Thomas Pynchon, Don DeLillo) who thematize the mindful design of novels? Byatt's comment exemplifies what one might call weak systems theory—that is to say, a use of systems that is all too easily reducible to figural pattern recognition. There is nothing logically wrong with this ascription, but it has the disadvantage of applying to almost any work of literature and thus to virtually all interpretation. For this kind of systems think to perform something new, it needs to be allied with something more—a reading, say, of the novel as case study of paranoia or model of cognitive system. Thomas LeClair's *In the Loop: Don DeLillo and the Systems Novel* (1987) does this reading by identifying the systems novel as a distinct genre that historicizes the impact of systems theory on postwar American fiction. Katherine Hayles's *Chaos and Order: Complex Dynamics in Literature and Science* (1991) and *How We Became Posthuman: Virtual Bodies in Cybernetics, Literature, and Informatics* (1999) take a different tack, treating literature as a medium of technoscientific theory.

Media theory may be at an advantage over literary history when it comes to experimenting with systems approaches. Literary history has been beset by what Christopher Prendergast, following Arjun Appadurai, calls the "Eurochronology problem," a problem arising from the fact that critical traditions and disciplines founded in the Western academy contain inbuilt typologies—"epic," "classicism," "renaissance," "genre," "world history"—adduced from Western literary examples ("World Republic" 4). It is impossible, for instance, to disengage the genre of epic from Homer's the *Iliad* and the *Odyssey* and from the idea of ancient Greece as the foundation of Western civilization. Developmental narratives of literary history that structure the unfurling of national literary traditions privilege the works of canonical authors as peaks in a world literary landscape. They tend to naturalize parameters of comparison that exclude certain kinds of cultural production from the realm of art, or assign the term *art* only to certain kinds of objects. So, for example, when European nineteenth-century art history invented "Chinese art," it treated China as a totalized cultural essence; calligraphy and painting were anointed as art, while temple architecture was consigned to lower-status sacred building.[4] Similarly divisive categorizations govern Western classification of works as either literature or folklore. British and French literatures carry the prestige of print culture (heightened by a special claim on the modern novel) while anglophone and francophone literatures, subject to Eurocentric standards of literariness and readability that class them closer to folklore and oral culture, tend to occupy a more tenuous position in world literature. Clearly, the nations that create the critical lexicon are the nations that dominate the literary world-system.

The coincidence of high concentrations of literary capital in metropolitan capitals has had a decisive impact on the politics of world literature, according to Pascale Casanova's *The World Republic of Letters*. First published in French in 1994, the book emphasizes how the rise of capitalist modernity intersected with national strategies of cultural self-legitimation. Prizes, translation, incorporation into the academic curriculum—these forms of accreditation are revealed as mechanisms for assigning universality to elected authors and texts. Europe (France in particular) is shown to claim the lion's share of universal world literature, because, so Casanova's narrative goes, it was instrumental in establishing the criteria according to which symbolic capital was rated and distributed. The unequal playing field between Western and non-Western nations meant that "small" literatures—that is, those hailing from peripheral territories or written in minority languages—had difficulty gaining visibility. Having less access to translation and literacy networks, nonmetropolitan literature was locked into a marginalized position in the "world republic of letters."

Whether Casanova's French-centered critique of power and translatability ultimately reinforces or challenges Eurocentric conceptions of the global literary field remains open to debate, but certainly she is not alone in recruiting systemic approaches to the cause of a more worldly sociology of literature. In hewing to a metropole-periphery cartography of global literary markets, Casanova joins the company of Moretti. When Moretti writes, for example, in *Atlas of the European Novel*, that provincialism and centralization "are two sides of the same coin," he defers to a kind of systems theory loop explicable in terms of Marxist dependency theory:

> Provincialism is not so much a matter of difference from the center, but of *enforced similarity*: the conviction that "real" life is only to be experienced in Paris (or London, or Moscow)—while life in the provinces is merely a shadow. And the novels that arrive from the center, with provincial malaise as one of their favorite themes, reinforce the circle of dependence over and over again. (152)

Moretti's world history of the novel, his seminal article "Conjectures on World Literature," and books—*The Modern Epic: The World-System from Goethe to García Márquez* (1996), *Atlas of the European Novel, 1800–1900* (1998), and *Graphs, Maps, Trees: Abstract Models for a Literary History* (2005)—aimed to show how genres, styles, and subgenres (the picaresque, sentimental novels, oriental tales, war stories, minor historical novels, village stories, the bildungsroman, naturalist fiction, decadent poetry, modernist narrative, New Woman novels) might be taken as literary units of value equivalent to units of economic capital. The mention of "abstract models" in the subtitle of *Graphs, Maps, Trees* confirms an unabashed admiration for quantitative history, geographic maps, and topological schemata. This love of system, often alien to humanists, is traced back to the scientific spirit of Marxism, acknowledged by Moretti as crucial to the motivation of his method. He marshals science in the service of understanding literature as a socialization process responsible for cultural power structures, class hierarchies, the bourgeois domestication of consciousness, and the revolutionary potential of intellectual labor. In *Graphs, Maps, Trees,* the political purpose of literary history seems less evident than his scientific ends. "[W]hile recent literary theory was turning for inspiration towards French and German metaphysics," he writes, "I kept thinking there was actually much more to be learned from the natural and the social sciences" (2). Neo-Darwinian calculations of how a literary tree selects for maximizing its survival supplant his earlier emphasis on global narrative economy.

Though Moretti's rehabilitation of evolutionary theory has been criticized as a throwback to nineteenth-century theories of natural selection (with their eugenicist baggage), his modeling of literary life cycles, seasoned with quirky examples, opens up new directions for systems theory in the marriage of biogenetics and philology, some of them already announced in the neovitalist materialism of Gilles Deleuze. The afterword to *Graphs, Maps, Trees,* contributed by the evolutionary biologist Alberto Piazza, explores the possibility of literal analogies between linguistic and DNA codes. When Moretti asserts, for example, that the bildungsroman emerged after the French Revolution "in response to a precise social need," that is to say "mediation of the conflicting demands of freedom and stability," Piazza reads his argument as illustrative of how "even literary genres cannot survive without cultural variety" (99). The open or closed status of a literary world-system is thus defined in terms of the system's ability to mutate like a microorganism or species. "Literary writing," Piazza alleges, "can be construed as a system that is not bound by the particular instruments it has itself created, and is therefore capable of metabolizing metaphors and ambiguities belonging to several systems of knowledge" (95).

In pushing analogies between biological and literary metabolism, Piazza fixes on translation as the literary process most proximate to natural selection, random genetic drift, and migration:

> *Graphs, Maps, Trees* does not tell us how far translation of the same
> novel into different languages may alter the reception and success of a

literary genre in the country where it is translated, but Moretti's findings in the third chapter of *Atlas of the European Novel*, on literary
diffusion and the correlation between literary models and geographical space, suggest an important role for migration, not of people but
of "forms," at least in Europe. (104)

Though translation, in Piazza's estimation, affords an imprecise measure
of literary survival, it nonetheless emerges as a crucial variable in the de-
termination of a literary form's capacity for migration and mutation. Im-
plicitly capitalizing on the common derivation in *genus* (type or species)
of the words *genre* and *gene*, Piazza assigns translatability a signal role in
biogenetic and literary evolution.

For Moretti, translatablity is defined both in market terms (by mapping or graphing a genre's circulation, influence, imitation, marketability,
election to the canon, congeniality to cultural comparatism and appropriation) and in evolutionary terms (as when he hypothesizes that "morphological novelty" results from "spatial discontinuity"). He writes:

> Take a form, follow it from space to space, and study the reasons for its
> transformations: the "opportunistic, hence unpredictable" reasons of
> evolution, in Ernst Mayr's words. And of course the multiplicity of
> spaces is the great challenge, and the curse, almost, of comparative
> literature: but it is also its peculiar strength, because it is only in such
> a wide, non-homogeneous geography that some fundamental princi-
> ples of cultural history become manifest. (*Graphs* 90)

Here, it would seem, as critics from Georg Lukács and Erich Auerbach to
George Steiner and Edward Said have repeatedly contended, texts must
experience the condition of exile. Transplanted from their native soil and
forced to encounter extreme cultural and linguistic difference, literary
forms jump the line into morphological innovation. This innovation happens, according to Moretti, when a form like free indirect discourse (associated with the postrevolutionary nineteenth-century European novel,
famous for bringing unruly subjective consciousness into line with bourgeois *idées reçues* via the conceit of a covertly inserted omniscient narrator) travels to Russia and confronts an alien discursive mode. As Flaubert
becomes Fyodor Dostoevsky, as *Madame Bovary* turns into *Crime and
Punishment*, the supposed passivity of free indirect style gives way to an
active stream of consciousness delivered as riposte in the second-person
singular voice. The conclusion one is meant to draw from this example is
that substantive generic modification occurs not because difference is

reconciled in hybridity (that would be a dialogic free indirect discourse) but rather as a result of the absence of mediation. Born of Dostoevsky's genius, dialogism emerges as the equivalent of genetic drift—that is to say, a new morphology or literary form.

The evolutionism of Moretti-style comparative literature leaves its footprint all over contributions to *The Novel*, especially in the section organized around polygenesis (defined as the plurality of forms over and against "[man-made] monogenesis" [Hägg 125, 129]), or in Henry H. Zhao's essay on how Lu Xun's character without lineage foiled genetics and generic hierarchy typical of traditional China (91–93), or in Catherine Gallagher's brilliant analysis of the nominalist shift in mid-eighteenth-century British fiction such that proper names, instead of referring to specific individuals, began to refer to species or the "morphophonology of names in the everyday world" (e.g., "Tom Jones," "Clarissa Harlow") (352).

Whether or not one is convinced by Moretti's literary examples, Moretti's focus on the diversification and speciation of literary forms highlights critical issues and questions for the study of world literature: Are new genres made by virtue of translation failure? Is the lack of a common ground of comparison a spur to literary evolution? Does differentiation (in the species sense) necessarily come at the expense of hybridity models of cultural difference? Is the interdependency of narrative markets—crucial to a Wallersteinian model of literary world-systems—now simply the economic symptom of literary survivalism? Is a genre's travel the measure of its aliveness, its drift the gauge of force required to break open the bounds of a closed world-system?

When Moretti speaks in *Graphs, Maps, Trees* of "a materialist conception of form" that would reveal "form as force" (92), he seems to be reimagining the literary world-system as a universe of competing national galaxies, each combating the other for title to possession of the maximum number of novelty genres; each rivaling the other to become the universal form of a homogenized, capitalized global lit. A competitive model of literary world-systems drafted from Moretti's evolutionary teleology might at the very least prove useful in addressing the need for viable paradigms of East-West comparatism. As Asia and Euro-America increasingly position themselves as bipolar models of one-worldedness, each vying to outflank the other in becoming the sole arbiter or default mode for the terms of cultural comparison, survivalism comes back into play, albeit in a rebarbatively Malthusian mode. Two empires, one could say, are engaged in mimetic rivalry, exacerbated by high walls of linguistic untranslatability and divergent conceptions of the citizen-subject. Two world-systems, locked into an agon for linguistic hegemony pitting, say, global Chinese against global English. As many see it, twenty-first-century language politics will increasingly underwrite the future of literary historiography, especially intra-Asia and Euro-America literary world-systems.

Even if one rejects this competitive model, it seems increasingly evident that intra-Asian literary relations are being increasingly theorized as a literary world-system that refuses an East-West comparatism privileging genres and styles with a Eurocentric, orientalist inflection such as decadence, abstraction, chinoisierie (transferred from the decorative arts to literary description), and *japonisme*. *Japonisme* has been particularly privileged as such a system in international modernism. Stéphane Mallarmé, Victor Segalen, Lafcadio Hearn, Ernest Fenellosa, Ezra Pound, W. B. Yeats, Henri Michaud, and Wallace Stevens contributed to a first-wave aesthetics of *japonisme* identified with haiku-esque brevity, blank spaces, ellipsis, understatement, and imagism. California *japonisme,* as inflected by the regional-ecological-spiritual poetics of the California beat poets Kenneth Rexroth, Robert Creeley, Gary Snyder, Philip Whalen, and Cid Corman, emerged as a second wave. Now, often synonymous with a purist international style—or with subtractive aesthetics, distinguished by veneration for the blank canvas, the white page, white achitecture, and decorative minimalism—*japonisme* functions on the order of what Lydia Liu terms a "super-sign," a "hetero-cultural signifying chain that crisscrosses the semantic fields of two or more languages," camouflaging the foreignness and internal split of a verbal unit (13–14).

In recent years, the critique of orientalism in international modernism has occasioned efforts to restitute cultural specificity and theoretical density to Asian modernisms. Attention has increasingly been devoted to the multiple imperialisms of modernism, and in particular to the impact on style of the Japanese occupation during World War II. In the context of intra-Asian world-systems, Western modernism continues to figure strongly as a lexicon of avant-garde techniques and genres, but the emphasis is on how that lexicon enabled Asian modernisms to redefine what modernism is. Dislodged from its periodized framework as a designation for early-twentieth-century American and European experimental writing with global sway, *modernism* becomes the name for slippages between modernity and modernization, nationalism and westernization, cosmopolitanism and anti-imperialism, individualism and militant collectivism, bourgeois and proletarian culture. It also serves to designate a complex aesthetic dischronology during the interwar period, which saw the co-existence of art for art's sake (typified by the poetry of China's Li Jinfa and Korea's Kim Ok); realism (defined by the Chinese writers Lu Xun and Mao Dun); Japanese new-sensibility writers (fascinated by the avant-garde New Woman, urban spectacle, and technology); pan-Asian nationalist fiction (Sato Haruo's 1938 *Son of Asia*); and anti-Western, proletarian narratives (by China's Zhao Shuli or Korea's Lin Hua). This heterodox modernism does not wane the way modernism in Europe and America arguably did with World War II but continues in the wake of Deng Xiaoping's 1978 reforms as an omnibus term designating the desire for democracy, avant-garde conceptualism, humanism, structuralism, global imagism, and much more.

At its most promising, literary world-systems theory enhances non-Eurocentric area studies in comparative literature and shuttles creatively between chronotope and genotype, history and evolution, topography and topology, graph and tree, media theory and cognitive science. In his recent book *Archaeologies of the Future: The Desire Called Utopia and Other Science Fictions*, Fredric Jameson takes systems theory in the direction of cognitive science when he discerns shape-shifting capabilities in Emile Zola's experimental novel and Ursula Le Guin's science fiction, both of which, in his estimation, "provide something like an experimental variation on our own empirical universe" (270). He argues:

> As antiquated as Zola's notions of heredity and as naïve as his fascination with Claude Bernard's account of experimental research may have been, the naturalist concept of the experimental novel amounted, on the eve of the emergence of modernism, to just such a reassertion of literature's cognitive function.

Le Guin's comparable "thought experiment" is the result of what Jameson calls "world reduction, in which "what we call reality is deliberately thinned and weeded out through an operation of radical abstraction and simplification" (271).

Jameson's cognitive turn toward a science fiction of brain waves and breakthroughs hints at future versions of systems theory that encompass sociocybernetics, autopoiesis, blending, and genetic drift.[5] We find examples of such systems aesthetics here and there among essays in Moretti's *The Novel*, as when Ato Quayson, analyzing magic realism in a comparative frame, identifies the uncanny with

the conversion of the perception of a systemic disorder into a negative af-
fect. In the face of persistent physical or social violence brought on either by acute political chaos or the collapse of the social order there is
an internalization of these perceived disorders in terms either of guilt,
an inexplicable terror, or a general sense of disquiet which does not
seem to have a clear source. (730)

Invoking expressions like "systemic disorder," "chaos," and "negative
affect" (an objective correlative to negative entropy?) in the general context of a "generic blurring" of *fabula* and war, Quayson gestures toward
marrying social and scientific world-system approaches (729, 730, 735).

What we discover here is systems theory that is at once weak and
strong. It is weak insofar as systemic disorder, used semimetaphorically as
a synonym for broken figuralism and civil disorder, bears little more than
a superficial or topological relation to systems theory proper. But it is
strong inasmuch as the concept of generic blurring inclines literary criticism toward cognitive blending—the idea that the mind reaches around
what is ungraspable by dynamically projecting a third concept that blends
source and target (as in the figure of the talking animal). More explicit in
his recourse to classic systems theory, Andreas Gailus avails himself of a
Luhmannesque rhetoric of autopoiesis. The German novella is characterized as a "genre of crisis," its "internal differentiation" aligned with the
"system' of the individual," whose "traditional patterns of ordering [have]
become unstable" (740). Goethe's novella becomes symptomatic of the
autoimmune syndrome, a form of systems breakdown whereby a subject
becomes its own pathogen and programs its own destruction. Gailus
writes, "Whereas Boccaccio's protagonists deploy cunning and deceit to
ensure their *self-preservation* and increase their enjoyment, the heroes of
the modern novella are characterized by compulsive self-destructive tendencies" (745). The novella, then, is "the blend" that enters contingency
into traditions of idealist narration, thereby producing itself as genetic
novelty, a new "*modern* symbolic form" (776).

There is an obvious risk, in work like Gailus's, directly grafted from
sociological or scientific systems theory, of criticism's becoming a carica-
ture of fearful symmetry: a perfect loop between neuronal function and
narrative formalism, a fantasia of cognitive mapping in the ecosphere, an
algorithmic utopia or paranoid vision of omnivorous networks that extend from galaxies to nanoworlds. There is an equally strong risk of producing a facile globalism in which distinct literary worlds are flattened to

fit homogenous paradigms or laws of comparability. These concerns aside, and despite stigmas inherited from the cold-war period when systems theory was a reigning orthodoxy of the behavioral sciences, the theory promises an interdisciplinary field of interest to the humanities as a branch of media theory or literary technics (*technics* is a term drafted from Heideggerian *techne* to refer to intersections of literary genetics, grammatology, technologies of translation, problems of semiotic iterability, program). Located at the nexus of economics, cybernetics, biogenetics, information, network, organization, probability, complexity, and chaos theory, literary technics explores the boundaries of literary world-systems by interrogating the conditions of mediality as such.

Notes

1. Among Wallerstein's principal sources are William McNeill, a world historian of human history's systolic and diastolic rhythms; Nikolai Kondratieff, an economic theorist who wrote in the 1920s on long-wave production cycles; Fernand Braudel, the *Annales* school historian who analyzed large, complex swaths of geopolitical territory such as the Mediterranean region; Marian Malowist, the Marxist economic historian of early modern European money markets; Gregory Bateson, author of the epistemologically synthetic work *Steps to an Ecology of Mind*; Giovanni Arrighi, whose notion of long centuries stretched historical continua beyond the bounds of periodizing convention; and Ilya Prigogine, a theorist of dissipative structures or the laws of self-organizing systems as defined by temporality, chaos, and uncertainty. See Prigogine, *From Being* and "Order"; Prigogine and Stengers, *Nouvelle alliance* and "Postface." David Porush extends Prigogine's theory into literary analysis. Finally, Elizabeth Grosz draws on Prigogine's notion of being and becoming in her Deleuzian reading of temporality.

2. References to systems theory proper are curiously absent from Wallerstein's theoretical pieces on world-systems theory, though Wallerstein draws heavily on Kondratieff's definition of cycles (especially B-phase). In *Unthinking Social Science: The Limits of Nineteenth-Century Paradigms* (1995), Wallerstein seems more interested in establishing world-systems theory as a paradigm shifter within the social sciences.

3. Other key figures in systems theory are Warren McCulloch, who did mathematical modeling of neural networks; Claude Shannon and Norbert Wiener, both founders of information theory and cybernetics; and John von Neumann, innovator in the fields of game theory, quantum mechanics, and cloning. The British neurospsychiatrist William Ross Ashby inaugurated complexity theory in the 1940s; Russell Ackoff developed management operations research in the 1950s; and in the same period the engineer Jay Forrester, inventor of core memory and random access magnetic storage in computing, extended systems theory to world dynamics, using biofeedback models to examine the organization of industries, cities, and environmental situations.

4. Craig Clunas suggests, "The question 'What is art in China?' could really be rephrased as 'What has historically been called art in China, by whom and when?' " (10). The French scholar Victor Segalen (1878–1922), author of a pioneering work called *The Great Statuary of China*, refused to deal at all with Buddhist sculpture in China (which forms the bulk of the surviving work in all media) "on the grounds that it was 'not really Chinese,' but rather an 'alien' import from India" (Clunas 12).

5. On blending, see Fauconnier; Turner. On the general issue of scientific theory in comparative literature, see Saussy, "Exquisite Cadavers."

Works Cited

Abu-Lughod, Janet. *Before European Hegemony: The World System A.D. 1250–1350*. New York: Oxford UP, 1989. Print.

Bateson, Gregory. *Steps to an Ecology of Mind*. Chicago: U of Chicago P, 2000. Print.

Brunkhorst, Hauke. "System Theory." *The Blackwell Dictionary of Modern Social Thought*. Ed. William Outhwaite. Oxford: Blackwell, 2003. Print.

Byatt, A. S. "The Death of Lucien de Rubempré." Moretti, *Novel* 2: 389–408.

Casanova, Pascale. *The World Republic of Letters*. Trans. M. B. DeBevoise. Cambridge: Harvard UP, 2005. Print.

Clunas, Craig. *Art in China*. Oxford: Oxford UP, 1997. Print.

Damrosch, David. "World Literature in a Postcolonial, Hypercanonical Age." Saussy, *Comparative Literature* 43–53.

Denning, Michael. "The Novelists' International." Moretti, *Novel* 1: 703–25.

Derluguian, Georgi M. *Bourdieu's Secret Admirer in the Caucasus: A World-Systems Biography*. Chicago: U of Chicago P, 2005. Print.

Fauconnier, Gilles. *The Way We Think: Conceptual Blending and the Mind's Hidden Complexities*. New York: Basic, 2002. Print.

Frank, Andre Gunder, and Barry K. Gills, eds. *The World System: Five Hundred Years or a Thousand?* New York: Routledge, 1993. Print.

Gailus, Andreas. "Form and Chance: The German Novella." Moretti, *Novel* 2: 739–76.

Gallagher, Catherine. "The Rise of Fictionality." Moretti, *Novel* 1: 336–63.

Grosz, Elizabeth. *The Nick of Time: Politics, Evolution, and the Untimely*. Durham: Duke UP, 2004. Print.

Hägg, Tomas. "The Ancient Greek Novel: A Single Model or a Plurality of Forms?" Moretti, *Novel* 1: 125–55.

Hayles, N. Katherine, ed. *Chaos and Order: Complex Dynamics in Literature and Science*. Chicago: U of Chicago P, 1991. Print.

———. *How We Became Posthuman: Virtual Bodies in Cybernetics, Literature, and Informatics*. Chicago: U of Chicago P, 1999. Print.

Jameson, Fredric. *Archaeologies of the Future: The Desire Called Utopia and Other Science Fictions*. London: Verso, 2005. Print.

LeClair, Thomas. *In the Loop: Don DeLillo and the Systems Novel*. Urbana: U of Illinois P, 1987. Print.

Liu, Lydia H. *The Clash of Empires: The Invention of China in Modern World Making.* Cambridge: Harvard UP, 2004. Print.

Luhmann, Niklas. "The Autopoiesis of Social Systems." *Sociocybernetic Paradoxes.* Ed. Felix Geyer and Johannes van der Zouwen. London: Sage, 1986. 172–92. Print.

———. *Social Systems.* Trans. John Bednarz, Jr. Stanford: Stanford UP, 1984. Print.

Moretti, Franco. *Atlas of the European Novel, 1800–1900.* London: Verso, 1998. Print.

———. "Conjectures on World Literature." Prendergast, *Debating* 148–62.

———. *Graphs, Maps, Trees: Abstract Models for a Literary History.* London: Verso, 2005. Print.

———. *The Modern Epic: The World-System from Goethe to García Márquez.* Trans. Quintin Hoare. London: Verso, 1996. Print.

———, ed. *The Novel.* 2 vols. Princeton: Princeton UP, 2006. Print.

Piazza, Alberto. Afterword. Moretti, *Graphs* 95–114.

Porush, David. "Fictions as Dissipative Structures: Prigogine's Theory and Postmodernism's Roadshow." Hayles, *Chaos* 54–84.

Prendergast, Christopher, ed. *Debating World Literature.* New York: Verso, 2004. Print.

———. "The World Republic of Letters." Prendergast, *Debating* 1–25.

Prigogine, Ilya. *From Being to Becoming: Time and Complexity in the Physical Sciences.* San Francisco: Freeman, 1980. Print.

———. "Order through Fluctuation: Self-Organization and Social System." *Evolution and Consciousness.* Ed. E. Jantch and C. H. Waddington. Ontario: Addison, 1976. 93–126. Print.

Prigogine, Ilya, and Isabelle Stengers. *La nouvelle alliance: Métamorphose de la science.* Paris: Gallimard, 1974. Print.

———. "Postface." *Hermès: Literature, Science, Philosophy.* By Michel Serres. Ed. Josué V. Harari and David F. Bell. Baltimore: Johns Hopkins UP, 1982. 94. Print.

Quayson, Ato. "Fecundities of the Unexpected: Magical Realism, Narrative, and History." *Novel* 1: 726–58.

Saussy, Haun, ed. *Comparative Literature in the Age of Globalization.* Baltimore: Johns Hopkins UP, 2006. Print.

———. "Exquisite Cadavers Stitched from Fresh Nightmares: Of Memes, Hives, and Selfish Genes." Saussy, *Comparative Literature* 4–42.

Skinner, Quentin, ed. *The Return of Grand Theory in the Human Sciences.* Cambridge: Cambridge UP, 1985. Print.

Turner, Mark. *Reading Minds: The Study of English in the Age of Cognitive Science.* Princeton: Princeton UP, 1991. Print.

Wallerstein, Immanuel. *Geopolitics and Geoculture: Essays on the Changing World-System.* Cambridge: Cambridge UP; Paris: Maison des Science de l'Homme, 1991. Print.

———. *The Modern World-System I: Capitalist Agriculture and the Origins of the European World-Economy in the Sixteenth Century.* New York: Academic, 1977. Print.

―――. *The Modern World-System II: Mercantilism and the Consolidation of the European World-Economy, 1600–1750*. New York: Academic, 1980. Print.

―――. *The Modern World-System III: The Second Great Expansion of the Capitalist World-Economy, 1730–1840's*. San Diego: Academic, 1989. Print.

―――. *Unthinking Social Science: The Limits of Nineteenth-Century Paradigms*. 2nd ed. Philadelphia: Temple UP, 2001. Print.

―――. *World-Systems Analysis: An Introduction*. Durham: Duke UP, 2004. Print.

Wallerstein, Immanuel, et al. *Antisystemic Movements*. London: Verso, 1989. Print.

Zhao, Henry Y. H. "Historiography and Fiction in Chinese Culture." Moretti, *Novel* 1: 69–93.

Zhang Longxi

What Is Literature?
Reading across Cultures

Once in an undergraduate comparative literature course, I introduced a passage from the Chinese philosopher Zhuangzi and asked my American students to read it along with a passage from one of Plato's *Letters*. In that letter, Plato speaks of his distrust of language, particularly the written language. By using the example of a circle in five different categories—circle as a name, a description, an image, a concept, and finally as a pure idea, which Plato considers to be the only "actual object of knowledge which is the true reality"—the philosopher argues that no language can adequately describe or express that true reality:

> Hence no intelligent man will ever be so bold as to put into language those things which his reason has contemplated, especially not into a form that is unalterable—which must be the case with what is expressed in written symbols. (1590)

By differentiating the five categories of an object, Plato's argument moves in the disciplined route of logical reasoning familiar to my students, while his critique of language here and of poetry in *Republic* X, I thought, should be clearly understood by students of literature so that they could learn how to respond to the philosopher's challenge.

The Zhuangzi passage, however, was not familiar to my students, though it happens to speak also about a circle (or, more precisely, a wheel) and the inadequacy of language. Zhuangzi says something rather similar to Plato when he complains:

> What can be seen in looking at things are shapes and colors; and what can be heard in listening are names and sounds. It is sad that the world should suppose that shapes, colors, names, and sounds are sufficient to reveal the true reality of things.

As these external markers are not sufficient to reveal truth, Zhuangzi claims, following the Taoist philosopher Laozi, that "the one who knows does not speak; the one who speaks does not know." Instead of an elaborate taxonomy of categories and deductive reasoning, however, he tells the story of a wheelwright who happens to work in front of a hall where Duke Huan is reading. The wheelwright tells the duke that the book he is reading contains "nothing but the dregs of the ancients!" (217; my trans.). The duke is not amused and demands an explanation. The wheelwright then remarks that the art of making a wheel, presumably a matter much simpler than the wisdom the duke wants to absorb from old books, is something quite beyond language. "I can't even teach it to my son, and my son can't learn it from me," says the wheelwright. "The ancients and what they could not pass on to posterity are all gone, so what you are reading, my lord, is nothing but the dregs of the ancients!" (218). The Zhuangzi text is full of such charming anecdotal stories, which my students, with the help of some explanations, can understand without much difficulty, but the form of Zhuangzi's argument is so different from that of Plato that a student asked me in genuine perplexity, "You mean this is philosophy?"

To shake up students with their conventional ideas is of course one of the intended effects of reading across cultures or across boundaries of cultural and literary forms, because it is important and useful for students to question received notions, to expand their horizon of understanding and learn to appreciate different forms of expression, which can nevertheless be brought together in a meaningful dialogue about something interesting and significant, a common theme or shared concern. The question that the student raised does not so much challenge the legitimacy of the Zhuangzi text as a form of philosophy as it does the conventional notion of philosophical discourse, of what counts as philosophy. I had no doubt that after reading Zhuangzi and Plato in the context of a philosophical critique of language, the students would emerge from such cross-cultural readings with a new perspective, an expanded vision, and an open-minded appreciation of the diversity of forms that a particular theme or topic might take in the rich treasury of world literature.

Zhuangzi and Plato are both saying that the truth of things is not easily accessible through language, that words are pointers inadequate to the task of leading you to a reality that lies beyond language. The Chan (Zen) Buddhists have a famous metaphor for this idea in mapping the domain of language and reality onto the relation between a finger and the moon that the finger points to. The *Lankāvatāra Sūtra*, an important Mahayana Buddhist scripture, speaks of a foolish man who looks only at the finger but not the moon it points to. The same metaphor appears in another Buddhist text, the *Sūrangama Sūtra*, in which Buddha tells Ānanda:

> You are still using your clinging mind to listen to the Dharma. . . . This is like a man pointing a finger at the moon to show it to others who should follow the direction of the finger to look at the moon. If they look at the finger and mistake it for the moon, they lose (sight of) both the moon and the finger. (Luk 31)

D. T. Suzuki explains:

> According to Zen, there is no struggle in the fact itself such as between the finite and the infinite, between the flesh and the spirit. These are idle distinctions fictitiously designed by the intellect for its own interest. Those who take them too seriously or those who try to read them into the very fact of life are those who take the finger for the moon. (19)

Looking at the finger but ignoring the moon thus becomes an unmistakably Chan Buddhist metaphor for the ignorance of those who cannot understand the undifferentiated nature of things beyond the phenomenal world with all its superficial distinctions.

In a totally different context, that same metaphor takes on a surprisingly Augustinian coloring when it is used to illustrate problems in understanding the Holy Scriptures. At the beginning of his treatise *On Christian Doctrine*, Saint Augustine makes the disclaimer that he should not be held responsible for any lack of understanding on the part of some readers. "I am not to blame because they do not understand," says Augustine:

In the same way, if they wished to see the old and the new moon or some very small star which I was pointing to with my finger and they did not have keen enough sight even to see my finger, they should not on that account become angry with me. And those who have studied and learned these precepts and still do not understand the obscurities of the Holy Scriptures think that they can see my finger but not the heavenly bodies which it was intended to point out. But both of these groups should stop blaming me and ask God to give them vision. Although I can lift my finger to point something out, I cannot supply the vision by means of which either this gesture or what it indicates can be seen. (3–4)

The similarity here is remarkable, for Augustine's use of the metaphor has no relation to that same metaphor in Buddhist sutras. Yet the coincidence is not totally fortuitous, because the metaphor of the finger and the moon serves the purpose of emphasizing the spiritual object of contemplation as opposed to a physical one, which is of course a point shared by many religious writers, be they Buddhist or Christian.

For our purposes here, I offer yet another reading of this interesting metaphor or image. Those who approach this finger-and-moon image only in the context of Eastern writings may think that it is specifically Buddhist, while those who find it in Saint Augustine and in the limits of Western writing may consider it uniquely Christian. From the broader perspective of reading across cultures, however, both these approaches are too narrow; both look only at the finger, as it were, without realizing that the specificity of the finger is only partial and limited understanding, whereas the moon shining above both and all fingers is much more encompassing and should lift our eyes toward the liberality and capaciousness of the mind that truly understands the full range of human creativity.

To be able to see beyond the limitations of local and parochial views is always a joy and valuable in itself; it opens our minds to the numerous possibilities of different literary forms, forms that, although different, come together to reveal extraordinary affinities of the imagination. Such cross-cultural and cross-disciplinary readings should also open our minds to forms of writing that may challenge a narrow definition of literature. I have so far quoted Plato, Zhuangzi, Buddhist sutras, and Augustine—that is, philosophical and religious texts—but these texts all question the efficacy of language or the use of a metaphor, ideas that are crucial to what we normally think of literature. These philosophical and religious texts all have a certain literary quality, and they provide important background that can shed light on many works of literature. To be sure, the idea of literary quality is difficult to define precisely, but it makes effective use of metaphors and other rhetorical devices, and its force of persuasion relies on logical cogency or emotional appeal or both. Such a quality does not exclusively reside in a narrowly defined literary text like a poem, a novel, or a play, but great works of literature, especially great poetry, are exemplary of good writing. Traditionally in China, anthologies of literary prose normally include excerpts from histories, pieces of argumentation, travelogue, and other kinds of writing, and the only reason they are put together thus is the quality of good writing they all share.

Thus philosophy, religion, history, and literature are not mutually exclusive, as literature takes all these and many other aspects of life as objects of representation. Stéphane Mallarmé told Edgar Degas, "Ce n'est point avec des idées, mon cher Degas, que l'on fait des vers. C'est avec des mots" (qtd. in Valéry 141). It may be true that one writes poems with words, not with ideas, but Degas also has a point in seeking ideas in art and literature, whereas Mallarmé's poems are certainly not meaningless babble. Thematic substance or ideas in a literary text become particularly important on the level of world literature, which, as David Damrosch argues, necessarily lifts a literary text out of its local moorings and makes it "circulat[e] out into a broader world beyond its linguistic and cultural point of origin" (6). That is to say, what appeals to the reader in a work of world literature is not just linguistic ingenuity, either in its original form or conveyed to various degrees in translation, but the attractiveness of its thematic content, the idea that manifests itself in felicitous language and exquisite poetic expressions.

The metaphor of the finger and the moon is interesting because a philosophical and religious idea is conveyed in a beautifully simple image, in which the idea and its metaphoric expression, matter and form, or thought and language are so closely intertwined that it becomes almost pointless to make a distinction. As George Lakoff and Mark Turner argue, "[M]etaphor resides in thought, not just in words" (2). With the finger and moon, we have what they identify as "the basic UNDER-STANDING IS SEEING metaphor: what enables you to see is metaphorically what enables you to understand" (94). They also maintain that such basic metaphors "are part of the common conceptual apparatus shared by members of a culture" (51). But what adds to the attractiveness of this particular metaphor is precisely the uncanny coincidence of its presence not just in one culture but across cultures, in works from the East and the West that are otherwise radically different. When such unexpected coincidence occurs, there is indeed a sense of pleasure in the discovery.

If culturally and not just geographically, East and West are thought to be at opposite ends of the world, the unexpected commonality in thematic substance and linguistic formulation gives us an idea of human capability on a global scale, of what truly deserves the name of world literature. Perhaps that is why Claudio Guillén speaks of East-West studies with such enthusiasm as an area of potential growth for comparative literature, where comparative work becomes all the more exciting despite or, rather, because of enormous cultural differences. "This lack of genetic relations, of mutual influences," says Guillén, "is precisely what stimulates a whole series of practical and theoretical perplexities of great interest" (16). Reading literature across cultures East and West is therefore not merely about going beyond Eurocentrism or replacing the Western canon with non-Western works; it is, more, to reach a global vision of human creativity, to appreciate literary works and forms in all their diversities, and appreciate them not as isolated monads sealed off from one another but as expressions of themes and ideas that are deeply connected, even though manifested in different languages and literary forms.

To illustrate the point with literary examples, let us look at a basic conceptual metaphor that compares the experience of life to a journey with its twists and turns, which Lakoff and Turner have also discussed with reference to Western literature (9–15). One of the best-known examples in European literature is the beginning of Dante's *Divine Comedy*:

> Halfway in the journey of our life,
> I found myself in a dark forest,
> for I had lost the right road ahead. (my trans.)

The image of a man lost in "a dark forest" because he has taken a wrong turn on the road is Dante's metaphoric way of saying that one is likely to be led astray by dangerous temptations in life, symbolized by the three wild beasts that confront him in the forest at the beginning of the poem. In fact, the entire *Divine Comedy* is structured as a long journey, both physical and spiritual, leading from Inferno to Purgatory and finally to Paradise.

Many great narratives, particularly those dealing with the archetypal theme of a quest, have the journey as their basic structural metaphor. In the Western tradition, there are many stories of spiritual quest in the form of a physical journey, such as Saint Augustine's *Confessions*, John Bunyan's *Pilgrim's Progress*, legends about the Holy Grail, and what Northrop Frye sees as the two concentric quest myths in the Bible: first, Adam's fall out of Eden, the wandering in "the labyrinth of human history," and his final restoration by the Messiah; second, the loss of Israel, the wandering in "the labyrinths of Egyptian and Babylonian captivity," and the final restoration in "the Promised Land" (191). Both narratives, the symbolic and the historical, are conceived as a quest, a journey leading from captivity to freedom. History, like life, can be seen as a long journey. It is perhaps this basic metaphor that gives Milton's poetry a particularly moving pathos and rhetorical power when he ends *Paradise Lost* with the depiction of Adam and Eve's being driven from the Garden of Eden and embarking on the difficult journey of an uncertain future, confronted with death and the challenge of a fallen life:

> The World was all before them, where to choose
> Thir place of rest, and Providence thir guide:
> They hand in hand with wandring steps and slow,
> Through *Eden* took their solitarie way. (10.1537–40)

Not only Dante and Milton but poets and writers in many other traditions have used the metaphor of life as a journey. In Chinese literature, a famous example is *Journey to the West* (Wu Cheng'en), which describes, on the literal level, the physical journey taken by the Tang monk Tripitaka, accompanied by his three disciples, chief among them the Monkey King, to fetch Buddhist sutras in India. On the metaphoric or allegorical level, this sixteenth-century Chinese novel tells the fascinating story of a spiritual quest, the search for understanding and enlightenment couched in the language of Buddhism, old myths, and popular legends.

From the basic life-is-a-journey metaphor, many related ideas have developed to expand the range of metaphoric mapping: to be born can be thought of as setting out on a journey, death as reaching the journey's end, and life can be conceptualized as a temporary stay at a roadside inn. Here is a poem from the famous *Rubáiyát* by the Persian poet Omar Khayyám (in Edward Fitzgerald's translation), in which the brevity of life is vividly expressed by using the metaphor of a roadside inn, for life is a momentary visit, and then the traveler is gone, never to return:

And, as the Cock crew, those who stood before
The Tavern shouted—"Open then the Door!
You know how little while we have to stay,
And, once departed, may return no more." (lines 9–12)

In book 3 of *Palamon and Arcite*, John Dryden also uses the image of a tavern or inn as a temporary dwelling in the metaphor of life as a journey:

Like pilgrims to the appointed place we tend;
The world's an inn, and death the journey's end. (lines 887–88)

In a poem by Li Bai (701–62), one of China's greatest poets, we find a remarkably similar expression:

Those who live are passers-by,
Those dead are back at home.
Heaven and earth are but an inn,
All to dust will mournfully come. ("Twelve Poems" 1099)

Like all good writing in classical Chinese, with these words the poet alludes to earlier works, reaching back to illustrious predecessors in an intertextuality of poetic images and metaphors. Li Bai's first two lines here recall a metaphor in the Taoist book *Liezi*: "The dead are those who have returned home, so those alive are travelers" (Yang Bojun 16). The idea that heaven and earth serve as an inn for the traveler alludes to a group of famous, anonymous texts dating back to the Han Dynasty (206 BCE–220 CE), known as *Nineteen Ancient Poems*, in which the metaphor of life as a journey is prominent. Poem 3 has these lines:

Men living between heaven and earth
Are transient as travelers on a long journey. (Liu Fu et al. 24)

In poem 13, we find the same idea expressed with a similar metaphor:

The sun and the moon are on constant move;
Like dew we come and are quickly gone.
Life's like staying in a temporary shelter
And never endures like metal or stone.   (46)

Li Bai writes elsewhere:

Heaven and earth are the inn for all creatures, and time is a passer-by of all generations. Fleeting life is like a dream, of which how many are truly happy moments? So it was with good reason that the ancients would hold candles and go out during the night. ("Prefatory Remarks" 1292)

In the last sentence, he alludes to poem 15 of *Nineteen Ancient Poems*, in which the sorrowful recognition of the brevity of life leads to the strong desire to make the best of every moment, and thus the poet encourages a kind of desperately joyful carnival spirit, similar to the carpe diem theme in many Western works:

> A man's life does not reach a hundred,
> But filled with a thousand years' worry.
> The day is too short and the night long;
> Why not go with a candle and be merry? (Liu Fu et al. 49)

The tone of this poem is celebratory, sharply different from that of works that are strongly religious in intent and treat life as a sort of miserable sojourn, tolerable only in view of the final salvation in God's grace. Thus Henry Vaughan's traveler in "The Pilgrimage" stays sleepless in the tavern, "full of tossings too and fro" (line 10), and appeals to God to sustain him till the final moment:

> O feed me then! and since I may
> Have yet more days, more nights to count,
> So strengthen me, Lord, all the way,
> That I may travel to Thy mount. (lines 24–27)

Such a strong religious sentiment is rarely found in classical Chinese literature, in which the poet tends to accept life and death with a tranquil mind, without appealing to a divine validation. Here we do find one of the important cultural differences between Chinese and Western literatures, but again, this is a difference in degree, not in kind, of religiosity, and such differences are not distributed along the geographic or cultural borderlines of East and West.

Consider the works of Tao Yuanming (365–427), whose poetry is distinguished by its richness in simplicity, as his language is always simple but elegant and his imagery natural but sophisticated. In poem 7 of his "Twelve Miscellaneous Poems," the metaphor of life as journey is further developed, with the implication that death is the final destination:

> Home is but a room in a small inn,
> And I, a mere departing guest.

Whither am I when I leave? You ask—
An old house on southern hills to rest. (352)

Here "a room in a small inn" alludes to a phrase in the book of *Liezi* that "living at home is like staying in a room of a small inn" (Yang Bojun 81). Tao Yuanming has a peculiar piece entitled "Self-Obituary," in which he imagines his own death, saying that "Mr. Tao is about to leave the small inn he stays in and return permanently to his own home" (555). From these allusions and textual evidence, commentators have concluded that the "old house on southern hills" in the lines quoted above is a tomb, the final resting place in death. Here the sojourner's voice is calm and content, and the tranquillity in having made peace with death is achieved without a religious conviction.

The acceptance of death expressed here may remind us of the song in Shakespeare's *Cymbeline*:

Fear no more the heat o' the sun
Nor the furious winter's rages;
Thou thy worldly task hast done,
Home art gone and ta'en thy wages.
Golden lads and girls all must,
As chimney-sweepers, come to dust.

Fear no more the frown o' the great,
Thou art past the tyrant's stroke;
Care no more to clothe and eat;
To thee the reed is as the oak:
The sceptre, learning, physic, must
All follow this and come to dust. (4.2.329–40)

Thus the basic life-as-a-journey metaphor may have a variety of formulations, each in some way different from the others. Those differences, however, do not fall neatly along the lines of a simple East-West divide or the borderline of cultural identities. In fact, members of the same culture may hold very different views and argue with one another, while agreement may sometimes come from people faraway or long ago, living under very different cultural and social conditions. Indeed, sometimes we may find Shakespeare closer in spirit to the Chinese poet Tao Yuanming than to his fellow countryman Henry Vaughan enveloped in an intense Christian spiritualism. Of course, recognizing similarities in the use of metaphors by poets from East and West does not compel us to ignore cultural difference, but reading across cultures does enable us to appreciate world literature with a spirit of openness and sympathetic understanding and to acquire a broad perspective for discerning thematic affinities and patterns of literary imagination beyond the gaps of languages and cultures.

Teaching world literature with appreciation is by no means an easy task, but the potential benefit, as Geoffrey Lloyd observes, is the acquiring of better knowledge about ourselves as well as others, for we can at least "learn more about the parochial quality of some of our most cherished assumptions" (10). That benefit, I would argue, is worth all our efforts at reading and understanding.

Works Cited

Augustine. *On Christian Doctrine.* Trans. D. W. Robertson, Jr. Indianapolis: Bobbs, 1958. Print.

Damrosch, David. *What Is World Literature?* Princeton: Princeton UP, 2003. Print.

Dryden, John. *Palamon and Arcite.* Project Gutenberg, 1 Feb. 2005. Web. 18 Jan. 2008.

Frye, Northrop. *Anatomy of Criticism: Four Essays.* Princeton: Princeton UP, 1957. Print.

Guillén, Claudio. *The Challenge of Comparative Literature.* Trans. Cola Franzen. Cambridge: Harvard UP, 1993. Print.

Lakoff, George, and Mark Turner. *More than Cool Reason: A Field Guide to Poetic Metaphor.* Chicago: U of Chicago P, 1989. Print.

Li Bai. *Li Taibai quanji* [Li Bai's Complete Works]. 3 vols. Beijing: Zhonghua shuju, 1977. Print.

———. "Prefatory Remarks on Gathering Relatives for a Spring Night Banquet in the Peach-Blossom Garden." Li Bai, *Li Taiabi quanji* 3: 1292–93.

———. "Twelve Poems in Imitation of Ancient Works." Li Bai, *Li Taibai quanji* 2: 1092–101.

Liu Fu et al. *Gushi shijiu shou jishi* [Nineteen Ancient Poems, with Collected Annotations]. Taipei: Shijie shuju, 1997. Print.

Lloyd, G. E. R. *Ancient Worlds, Modern Reflections: Philosophical Perspectives on Greek and Chinese Science and Culture.* Oxford: Oxford UP, 2004. Print.

Luk, Charles, ed. and trans. *The Surangama Sutra.* London: Rider, 1966. Print.

Milton, John. *Paradise Lost.* Renascence Eds. U of Oregon, Dec. 1997. Web. 18 Jan. 2008.

Omar Khayyam. *Rubaiyat of Omar Khayyam.* Trans. Edward Fitzgerald. *Middle East and Islamic Studies Collection.* Cornell U Lib., n.d. Web. 7 Apr. 2008.

Plato. Letter 7. Trans. L. A. Post. *The Collected Dialogues of Plato, Including the Letters.* Ed. Edith Hamilton and Huntington Cairns. Princeton: Princeton UP, 1963. 1574–98. Print.

Shakespeare, William. *Cymbeline [and] Timon of Athens.* Booklovers Ed. New York: Univ. Soc., 1901. *Google Book Search.* Web. 18 Jan. 2008.

Suzuki, Daisetz Teitaro. *Essays in Zen Buddhism*. New York: Grove, 1961. Print
First Ser.

Tao Yuanming. "Self-Obituary." Tao Yuanming, *Tao Yuanming ji jianzhu*
555–63.

———. *Tao Yuanming ji jianzhu* [Tao Yuanming's Works, with Commentaries
and Annotations]. Ed. Yuan Xingpei. Beijing: Zhonghua shuju, 2006. Print.

———. "Twelve Miscellaneous Poems." Tao Yuanming, *Tao Yuanming ji jianzhu* 338–62.

Valéry, Paul. "Poésie et pensée abstraite." *Variété V*. Paris: Gallimard, 1945.
140–43. Print.

Vaughan, Henry. "The Pilgrimage." *The Poems of Henry Vaughan*. Ed. E. K.
Chambers. 1896. N. pag. *Google Book Search*. Web. 18 Jan. 2008.

Wu Cheng'en. *Journey to the West*. Trans. W. J. F. Jenner. Beijing: Foreign Langs.,
1993. Print.

Yang Bojun. *Liezi jishi* [Liezi, with Collected Annotations]. Hong Kong: Taiping
shuju, 1965. Print.

Zhuangzi. "The Way of Heaven." *Zhuangzi jishi* [Variorum Edition of the
Zhuangzi]. Ed. Guo Qingfan. Beijing: Zhonghua shuju, 1954. 204–18. Print.
Vol. 3 of *Zhuzi jicheng* [Collection of Distinguished Philosophical Works]. 8
vols.

Anuradha Dingwaney Needham

The Place of Difference in Cross-Cultural Literacy

My interest as a teacher and, in some ways, as an activist, is to build for difference; in other words, to think of what we might be doing or saying strategically, sometimes tactically within a very powerful institutional structure.

—Gayatri Chakravorty Spivak

The central issue, then, is not one of merely acknowledging *difference; rather, the more difficult question concerns the kind of difference that is acknowledged and engaged.*

—Chandra Talpade Mohanty

Analyzing "translingual practice," Lydia Liu avers that a

cross-cultural study must examine its conditions of possibility. Constituted as a translingual act itself, it enters rather than sits above the dynamic history of relationship between words, concepts, categories, and discourses. One way of unraveling the relationship is to engage rigorously with those words, concepts, categories, and discourses beyond the realm of common-sense dictionary definition, and even historical linguistics. (29)

In my essay on teaching cross-cultural texts, I examine *difference*, one such word-concept-category-discourse that occupies a contested place in discussions of cross-cultural texts or, more accurately, texts considered central to a multicultural or culturally diverse curriculum in the Anglo-American academy. By *difference* I mean minority racial, ethnic, or gender difference. In its varied manifestations difference has played a significant role in my teaching and writing on cross-cultural texts—literary texts written in or translated into English from languages spoken and written in the so-called Third World (see esp. Dingwaney and Maier; Dingwaney and Needham; Needham, "At the Receiving End" and "Reimagining").

At first glance, it seems counterintuitive to foreground difference while talking about cross-cultural texts. For whereas *cross-cultural* implies overlapping or connected spaces that exist between or across boundaries that are otherwise seen as separating or marking off one culture from another, difference functions, in many of the discussions I am drawing on, as a marker of separation, of incommensurate cultural spheres, of boundaries not amenable to being crossed. Nevertheless, I argue that deploying difference matters in the pedagogical and cultural work I want these texts to perform in the classroom. But its effectivity depends primarily on how and what kind of difference is deployed. First, however, it is important to specify some of the understandings of difference that matter for this essay.

Even a quick glance through the literature on difference, by now considerable, reveals a formidable dossier against deployments of difference. This dossier includes several stringent critiques by minorities—people of color and women, the subjects, as it were, of this difference. A number of these critiques view difference as continuous with—both cause and product of—colonial constructions of the colonized people's alterity and thus as inextricably linked to hierarchical modes of thinking and exclusion, violence and power. Deployments of difference by or on behalf of a minority or subjugated people are thus viewed as participating in "the very instrumentality of [one's own or their] subjection" (Gates 606). Colonial powers are not the only kind implicated. "Rethinking difference" in the context of Africa, Aili Mari Tripp notes, "In countries such as Uganda, Sudan, Rwanda, or South Africa, the politicization of difference has resulted in civil war or violent conflict based on ethnic, religious, and other differences." The challenge, therefore, has been "to minimize difference" (649).[1]

Underwriting the politics of difference is a politics of identity, which has also been castigated for its investment in an authenticity that can yield only essentialist notions of identity, notions forcefully at odds with the far more porous and impure processes through which identities are actually constituted. What's more, it's argued, identity politics in its insistence on the radical incommensurability (or unique particularity) of a given group's experience prevents the possibility of communication and relationships between and across differently constituted groups. Difference conceived this way seems deeply inhospitable to commonsense notions of cross-cultural understanding and knowledge production.

A more stringent criticism of the insistence on the radical incommensurability of a given group's experience suggests that this incommensurability, which is made to support what is in effect a politics of difference, is manufactured or deliberately cultivated so as to authorize certain "visibly different" identities over others when it comes to analyses of, or projects related to, ethnic, racial, or gender difference (Bahri 279)—namely, it is tied to questions of "turf and territoriality" (duCille 597).[2]

Yet other sharply critical assessments are not directed against deployments of difference per se but speak instead to the institutional constraints in which difference operates or is allowed to flourish: at the behest primarily of, or in complicity with, the dominant (Spivak, "Marginality"; C. Mohanty; and Bahri). Not surprisingly, one of the ways in which institutional constraints operate in the Anglo-American academy is by framing diverse histories, experiences, and perspectives as "benign variation" in the interests of an "empty pluralism" defused of the threat of "conflict, struggle, . . . [and] disruption" of institutional common sense (C. Mohanty 181). Here insistent, pious claims about respecting the heterogeneity of race, ethnic, gender, class, and other identities are made to stand for substantive engagement with such heterogeneity.

Without diminishing the force of these critical assessments, with which I am in broad agreement, I want to redirect the discussion of difference to extract some of its significance for the study and analysis of cross-cultural texts. I ground my argument for difference primarily in my pedagogical practice, where difference (or different deployments of difference) is made to serve what are most often strategically defined goals in producing certain understandings related to the study of texts coming out of or dealing with cultures that exist in asymmetrical relations of power with and in Anglo-America. My argument is inflected by the critiques of difference above; it is also inflected by my substantive investment in the importance of the social location of subjects of (or marked by) difference and of those who undertake to interpret or access them.

Social location both determines and is itself determined by one's identity and experience;[3] it informs our perspective; is able, as Satya Mohanty puts it, to "facilitate or inhibit knowledge by predisposing us to register and interpret information in certain ways."[4] "Our relationship to social power," he adds, "produces forms of blindness just as it enables degrees of lucidity" (73). In this regard, Fabienne Worth is right when, drawing on bell hooks's comment on "potentially inaccessible locations," she notes that "certain spaces cannot be understood from certain positions" (9).[5] But I also believe that social location, while determining, does not entirely determine our interests, commitments, and ways of apprehending our experiences. Our "consciousness and will," in turn, as Maivân Clech Lâm points out, "modify the relevance of [our] social [location]" (891).

The meanings of difference that I work with, then, exist in a finely wrought tension between specifying degrees of inaccessibility and accessibility of the subjects of difference. The intensity with which this tension is felt and addressed depends on the contexts and on the specific pedagogical imperatives thrown up by these contexts, which are difficult to know and work out in advance. Thus there is always an ad hoc quality to the nature of the intervention on behalf of or against difference.

I turn to some of my uses of difference in the classroom by giving an extended example that focuses on two essays with which I tend to open my course on anglophone literatures of the Third World: Fredric Jameson's "Third World Literature in the Era of Multinational Capitalism" and Aijaz Ahmad's riposte, "Jameson's Rhetoric of Otherness and the 'National Allegory.'" But first, a brief remark on the pedagogical imperatives of this course.

Part of a group of offerings organized by historical period, genre, and national affiliation, my course, like others in the group, seeks to introduce students, mostly sophomores, to different kinds of literature in English; like others in the group, it also seeks to make students self-conscious and critical in their reading and understanding of these literatures. To this end, I explicitly address my selection of texts, critical assumptions, and pedagogical methods so as to encourage critical reflection about what is being read and discussed, how, and why or to what end. My course intersperses discussions of eight or nine novels from or about various sites in the so-called Third World with theoretical essays that enable me to foreground not only questions pertaining to definitions of this body of work but also privileged topics and writers that turn up in the scholarship on this work.[6] Difference occupies a significant place in my theoretical selections, but I focus on its interaction with identity and identification, on its amenability (or lack thereof) to its translation into the familiar or same.

Apart from discussion of significant issues—definitional, theoretical, political, and rhetorical—that the essays by Jameson and Ahmad enable with respect to the category called Third World literature, they are also remarkably productive for examining varied and provocative deployments of difference in several ways. Their value, furthermore, derives also from the inconsistent uses of the difference they each embrace or abjure, which can then provide an instructive site for learning.

Jameson's essay is organized around a series of claims designed to demonstrate the "radical difference of [Third World] texts," his focus primarily on the novel. Starting from the view that nationalism, "long since liquidated [in the United States] and rightly so," is "fundamental to the third world" (65), Jameson argues that "what all third world cultural productions seem to have in common and what distinguishes them radically from analogous cultural forms in the first world" is the use of allegory: "All third world texts are to be read . . . as national allegories" (69). This definition is elaborated and buttressed by oppositions that argue for the First World's investment in the "private . . . the poetic . . . the domain of sexuality and the unconscious" as opposed to the Third World's investment in "the public . . . the political . . . the . . . world of classes, of the economic, and of secular political power"—"Freud Versus Marx" (69).

It has always struck me with considerable ironic force that the very students who are invested in absolute notions of Third World difference balk at (indeed, are deeply critical of) Jameson's claims. Partly, this resistance could be a result of having read Ahmad's strong refutation alongside or even before Jameson's essay. Thus students come primed to take Jameson to task for his many homogenizing generalizations that imperil, as Ahmad so insistently points out and my students concur, the densely structured particularities and heterogeneities of diverse Third World cultures and their literatures that Jameson seeks to theorize.[7] But, more, their resistance to Jameson's claims and to the conduct of his argument coheres with a conception of difference that is tied to the question of who does or does not have the right to speak for the Third World. Thus their criticisms of his claims get enfolded in or may even be fueled by who he is not: a Third World subject. Concomitantly, Ahmad's critique acquires force because Ahmad is (and identifies himself, I think intentionally, early on in his piece as) someone my students and Jameson would have no hesitation calling a Third World subject ("born in India . . . a Pakistani citizen, I write in Urdu" [4]).

What should be recognized, however, is that Jameson is enlisting difference to accomplish specific ends: "to rethink our humanities curriculum in new a way—to examine the shambles and ruins of all our older 'greater books,' 'humanities,' 'freshman introductory,' and 'core course' type traditions" (67). In this rethinking, "some specific engagement with the question of third world literature" is called for as part of a larger engagement with the study of "world literature," which he finds necessary for this "new situation" (66). Engagement with difference, at one level, has to do with cultivating "a wide range of sympathies with very different people [and texts]" (66). But the insistence on "the radical difference of [Third World] texts" also carries a specific pedagogical charge not entirely covered by this view of difference: namely, to cultivate radically different practices of reading and interpretation—different habits of mind, possibly, and of ways of being in the world—from those countenanced by what Jameson simply refers to as the canon.

Thus much of what Jameson seems to value in literature and in interpretations of literature—the investment in "the political," in collectivities, in "the . . . world of classes, of the economic," in a view of the writer as public and "political intellectual . . . who produces both poetry and praxis" (74–75)—is assigned to Third World literature (which, incidentally, is labeled "non-canonical" [65]) and presented as constituting the "radical difference" that its readers are then enjoined to take on board. But since readers don't necessarily sequester different or differently developed modes of reading and analyses from one another, the expectation is that the radical difference framing their reading of Third World literatures will infiltrate their reading of canonical texts and transform it. "The purpose of the canon is to restrict our aesthetic sympathies" by "discourag[ing] us from reading anything else *or from reading those things in different ways*" (66; emphasis added). Difference is being enlisted strategically here to help cultivate new or a wider range of sympathies and, more significant, radically different habits of reading and interpretation.

But difference operates in another, perhaps even opposing, way in Jameson's argument, whereby it is subjected to a strategy of domestication.[8] It is instructive, for instance, that Jameson never couples difference—radical difference, even—with incommensurability. The claims he forwards, the intricate readings that he offers of Lu Xun and Ousmane Sembène, seem to proceed from the assumption that these literatures are substantially accessible to him as a First World reader. What's more, the effect of his proceeding this way has even a stringent critic like Ahmad observe that he "wholly admire[s] the knowledge, the range of sympathy [Jameson] brings to the reading of texts produced in distant lands" (3). Jameson's refusal to equate difference with incommensurability, one could say, enables Jameson to speak authoritatively of this literature in the first place. Analogously, his argument at various points suggests that the radical difference of Third World texts need not close them off from First World readers, inasmuch as this difference is that "of *our own* cultural past and its now seemingly old-fashioned situations and novelists" (66). First World readers, that is, already have more proximate access to the interpretive tools they need; all they need do is recuperate them.

What are we to make of the (deliberate?) slippage between the two apparently conflicting designations of "radical difference," whereby it is simultaneously a distinct property of distant cultures and also of "*our own* cultural past"? Drawing on responses mooted in class discussion, I would say that the slippage is meant to provoke estrangement from the dominant models of reading and analysis that the former designation directs us toward and, at the same time, to mediate this estrangement through recourse to the familiar, what Jameson calls the "already-read" (66) though now forgotten or repressed past. One could call this a model for cross-cultural analysis that wants to disrupt canonical common sense and also restrict or ameliorate the consequence, so that cross-cultural study is not refused on the grounds of its absolute unfamiliarity or alienation.[9]

Ahmad's refutation of Jameson's brief for the radical difference of Third World texts is, to a significant extent, of a piece with the rich, by now substantial tradition of critiques of colonial and Western discourses about the (formerly) colonized world, a tradition inaugurated by Edward Said's *Orientalism*. These critiques view the mobilization of Third World difference as continuous with processes of othering that entrap the subjects of this difference in stereotypes, homogeneities, monolithic essences. Difference per se, we should note, is not being abjured here, only those deployments of it that forgo "the fecundity of real narratives in the so-called third world" (9). Thus, Ahmad notes, "[a]s for the specificity of cultural difference, Jameson's theoretical conception tends . . . in the opposite direction, namely, that of homogenization." Against a difference that "absolutis[es]" the "otherness" of the Third World, then, Ahmad posits an understanding of difference that recognizes "the enormous cultural heterogeneity of [its] social formations." This heterogeneity, it seems, is best (or can only be) spoken for by someone from the "so-called third world" (10).

Students in class discussions have often remarked on how Ahmad draws attention to Jameson's location while not really addressing his own. They are on the mark and right in sensing that Ahmad's location matters in the way Ahmad suggests Jameson's does.[10] For a great deal of the passion that animates Ahmad's critique, the kinds of claims he takes issue with, and the counterarguments he offers all derive substantially from his location, which includes but is not restricted to the few autobiographical references he supplies at the outset. For example, the viscerally felt force of his critique of what he views as Jameson's procedures of othering derives from his self-identification as being from among those who are being theorized as a civilizational other. A comparable, also viscerally felt critique of the objectification of blackness-otherness by Frantz Fanon helps us realize that Ahmad's status as former colonial and now Third World subject feeds into our assessment of the justice of his critique, much as it feeds into Ahmad's own sense of its necessity: "I had always thought of us, Jameson and myself, as birds of the same feather"; however, five pages into Jameson's essay, "I realized that what was being theorized was . . . myself" (3–4). Here location produces defensiveness that leads to a disavowal: "we live not in three worlds but in one" (9) and, again, in his conclusion: "Jameson's text is not a first-world text, mine is not a third-world text. We are not each other's civilizational Others" (25). Ahmad's refusal of difference is itself premised, paradoxically, on his location as a subject of Third World difference.

Location works in other ways in Ahmad's argument. His counterclaims regarding "the enormous cultural heterogeneity" of the Third World are, for instance, substantiated through an erudite meditation on the "history of Urdu literature" that constitutes a valuable expansion of the First World reader's cultural literacy, not least because a First World reader is not likely to encounter it, given the rarity of "a major literary theorist in Europe or the United States who has even bothered with an

Asian or African language" and given, also, that translations from Asian and African languages are infrequent, if not altogether absent, in the First World (5). Here location operates in productive ways—initiating new knowledge, prodding the First World reader to acquire a more informed understanding.[11] The "specificity of cultural difference" that Ahmad's comments on Urdu literature reflect and bring to the fore, and the pointed reference he makes to languages that are seldom translated in the First World, I think, could only have come from someone situated like Ahmad. I mean not that this information could not be in the possession of a First World subject but rather that its disposition in Ahmad's argument, the need to provide it, signals the kind of investment that comes from intimacy with the literatures he writes about and values, and for that reason he feels the sting of their exclusion from the Third World Jameson writes about.

Both Jameson's and Ahmad's arguments are inflected (infected) with what each writer refuses. Jameson's assertion of the "radical difference of [Third World] texts" is destabilized by his recourse to the same: the identification of this difference with that represented by *"our own* cultural past." Difference, as he deploys it, is not or cannot be absolute; the attempt to appropriate it necessitates the use of familiar terms and thus its inscription in the same. Concomitantly, Ahmad's assertion of sameness is destabilized by the necessity to invoke his (Third World) difference to create the critical distance from Jameson's argument from which to launch a persuasive critique.

These instabilities become especially evident when the two arguments are read in tandem, when they are read as mutually dependent on and therefore as mutually illuminating of each other rather than as antagonistically framed either-or arguments. Reading the two in tandem allows us to see not only the inconsistencies in their arguments on behalf of or against difference but also how each marks the limits of the other, including the blind spots to which their differing emphases commit them. Difference, as Jameson's and Ahmad's deployments of it make clear, is a double-edged sword—valuable but open to critiques of difference. The two essays demonstrate that often the identical deployment of difference is valuable and problematic simultaneously, functioning in terms of Spivak's memorable deconstructive formula "for good or for ill. As medicine or as poison, perhaps always a bit of both" ("Burden" 278).

Nonetheless, the value of deploying difference remains: difference offers the possibility of interpretation and understanding that counters the force of canonical common sense. A possibility released by reading cross-cultural texts, difference remains crucial to their interpretation. Beginning with difference, my students are likely to be cautious in their judgments, and modest, even self-critical about the interpretive skills they already possess to read the cultures that are the subjects of these texts.

Notes

1. Many feminist interventions in the deployment by various fundamentalisms of racial, ethnic, and gender difference (and its correlate, a politics of identity organized around race, ethnicity, and gender) also seek to minimize difference. On such minimizing, see especially the essays in Moghadam.

2. Mario Biagioli argues that claims about incommensurability are associated with "instances of trespassing professional or disciplinary boundaries and violating socio-professional hierarchies," and they "play a crucial role in the formation and preservation of a group's cohesion and socio-professional identity" (183, 186–87).

3. Since each of these terms, concepts, or categories is open to a great deal of contention, let me specify the definitions I draw on. Following Stuart Hall ("Cultural Identity"), I think of identity as both assigned and actively constructed in specific contexts and constraints and in response to particular individual and collective needs. Identity is always mediated by social and theoretical constructs—"social narratives, paradigms, even ideologies" (S. Mohanty 47). Thus there is no self-evident or pregiven truth of experience that inheres in an identity and gives it voice. What we have are events, interactions, political and other identifications made available at certain historical junctures that are then worked through in the process of constructing an identity. However, to say an identity is constructed is not to accede to the voluntarism that inheres in certain elaborations of identity's constructedness (223–31). This ignores, as Hall also notes, "certain conditions of existence, real histories in the contemporary world, which are not exclusively psychical, nor simply journeys of the mind"; thus it is incumbent on us to recognize that "every identity is placed, positioned in a culture, a language, a history" ("Minimal Selves" 44–45). (For a more sustained discussion of these terms, see Dingwaney and Needham.)

4. For location (and the identity it produces and is produced by) as a powerfully enabling and disabling source of one's perspective, consider the following comment on Edward Said by Asha Varadharajan: "The inspiration and disillusion that Palestine signifies for Said become both 'the splinter in [his] eye' and 'the best magnifying glass' . . . ; Palestine functions as the incomprehensible violence of a history that blots out all else even as it provides 'a different set of lenses' . . . through which to illuminate all else. In a telling moment [in his *Reflections on Exile*], Said writes enigmatically of 'how perspective in the Nietzschean sense is *less a matter of choice than of necessity*' . . . , attesting, thereby, to the manner in which a 'scrupulous subjectivity' . . . invests historical events and philosophical categories with shape, meaning, and desire" (emphasis added).

5. For Ien Ang, for example, one such space or location has to do with having or not having "subjective knowledge of what it means to be at the receiving end of racialized othering" (60). Maivân Clech Lâm provides anecdotal evidence for a similar claim (865–70).

6. Inasmuch as Jameson's essay focuses on the novel, his specific examples deriving from China (Lu Xun's *Diary of a Madman*) and Africa (*Xala*, by the Sengalese writer and filmmaker Ousmane Sembène), it has proved particularly useful in a course like mine, which privileges the novel over other literary forms. Including Jameson's and Ahmad's essays, some of the other critical-theoretical essays I consider are Spivak's "The Burden of English," selections from Frantz Fanon's *Black Skin, White Masks*, essays by Timothy Brennan and by Bruce Robbins on cosmopolitanism, Ranajit Guha on subaltern historiography, and Henry Schwartz's "Provocations toward a Theory of Third World Literature."

7. At various junctures in his argument, Jameson precedes his claims with disclaimers, which also include more substantial qualifications regarding his use of the term "third world" (67) and his deployment of the "radical difference of [Third World] texts," that he recognizes may be reproducing the "strategy of otherness which Edward Said . . . called 'orientalism' " (77).

8. The term *domestication* should not be negatively assessed here as signaling merely a form of ideological containment. Rather, I am drawing on Lawrence Venuti's use of it in his comments on translation: "Translations inevitably perform a work of domestication," because "most literary projects are initiated in the domestic culture, where a foreign text is selected to satisfy different tastes from those that motivated its composition and reception in its native culture. And the very function of translating is assimilation, the inscription of a foreign text with domestic intelligibilities and interests" (10–11).

9. Venuti's use of the concept of remainder, which he gets from Lecercle, provides another, related way of understanding the relation between Jameson's two uses of *difference*. The remainder is that variable in language use that occupies the status of the minor at a particular historical moment or juncture, which nonetheless "subverts the major by revealing it to be socially and historically situated" (10–11). The remainder also is a "domestic" term that has been defamiliarized, by having become, to allude to Jameson's terms, part of "*our own* cultural past" that now needs to be resuscitated. Translations (which, for Venuti, are always domesticating) are most powerful in re-creating cultural values when they have recourse to the remainder (5).

10. Ahmad is more categorical about some of the determinants of Jameson's location than of others. "Jameson's," he says, "is a *gendered* text . . . it is inconceivable to me that this text could be written by a US *woman*." Similarly, "it is determined also by a certain *racial* milieu. For it is equally inconceivable to me that *this* text could be written by a *black* writer in the US." About Jameson's First World location Ahmad is more qualified, focusing more on Jameson's investments as "a US intellectual of a certain kind" (24).

11. This meditation on Urdu literature performs a task analogous to what Anthony Appiah calls "thick translation," which "seeks with its annotations and

accompanying glosses to locate the text in a rich cultural and linguistic context" and thereby transmutes the "easy tolerance" of a pluralism celebrating "[cultural] variousness" into an undertaking geared to "the harder project" of an informed and knowledgeable understanding, which is liable to produce "genuine respect" for difference (427).

Works Cited

Ahmad, Aijaz. "Jameson's Rhetoric of Otherness and the 'National Allegory.'" *Social Text* 17 (1987): 3–25. Print.

Ang, Ien. "Comment on Felski's 'The Doxa of Difference': The Uses of Incommensurability." *Signs: Journal of Women in Culture and Society* 23.1 (1997): 57–64. Print.

Appiah, Kwame Anthony. "Thick Translation." *The Translation Study Reader.* Ed. Lawrence Venuti. London: Routledge, 2000. 417–29. Print.

Bahri, Deepika. "Marginally Off-Center: Postcolonialism in the Teaching Machine." *College English* 59.3 (1997): 277–98. Print.

Biagioli, Mario. "The Anthropology of Incommensurability." *Studies in History and Philosophy of Science* 21.2 (1990): 183–209. Print.

Brennan, Timothy. "Cosmopolitans and Celebrities." *Race and Class* 31 (1989): 1–19. Print.

Dingwaney, Anuradha, and Carol Maier. "Translation as Method for Cross-Cultural Teaching." *Between Languages and Cultures: Translation and Cross-Cultural Texts.* Ed. Dingwaney and Maier. Pittsburgh: U of Pittsburgh P, 1995. 3–15. Print.

Dingwaney, Anuradha, and Lawrence Needham. "The Difference That Difference Makes." *Socialist Review* 26.3–4 (1996): 5–47. Print.

duCille, Ann. "The Occult of True Black Womanhood: Critical Demeanor and Black Feminist Studies." *Signs: Journal of Woman in Culture and Society* 19.3 (1994): 591–629. Print.

Fanon, Frantz. *Black Skin, White Masks.* Trans. Charles Lam Markmann. New York: Grove, 1967. Print.

Gates, Henry Louis. "Significant Others." *Contemporary Literature* 29.4 (1988): 606–23. Print.

Guha, Ranajit. "The Small Voice of History." *Subaltern Studies IX: Essays on South Asian History and Society.* Ed. Shahid Amin and Dipesh Chakrabarty. Delhi: Oxford UP, 1994. 1–12. Print.

Hall, Stuart. "Cultural Identity and Diaspora." *Identity: Community, Culture, Difference.* Ed. Jonathan Rutherford. London: Lawrence, 1990. 222–37. Print.

———. "Minimal Selves." *Identity.* Ed. Lisa Appignanesi. London: ICA Document 6, 1987. 44–46. Print.

Jameson, Fredric. "Third-World Literature in the Era of Multinational Capitalism." *Social Text* 15 (1986): 65–88. Print.

Lâm, Maivân Clech. "Feeling Foreign in Feminism." *Signs: Journal of Women in Culture and Society* 19.4 (1994): 865–93. Print.

Liu, Lydia H. *Translingual Practice: Literature, National Culture, and Translated Modernity—China, 1900–1937.* Stanford: Stanford UP, 1995. Print.

Moghadam, Valentine, ed. *Identity Politics and Women: Cultural Reassertions and Feminism in International Perspective.* Boulder: Westview, 1994. Print.

Mohanty, Chandra Talpade. "On Race and Voice: Challenges for Liberal Education in the 1990s." *Cultural Critique* 14 (1989–90): 179–208. Print.

Mohanty, Satya P. "On the Epistemic Status of Cultural Identity: On *Beloved* and the Postcolonial Condition." *Cultural Critique* 24 (1993): 41–80. Print.

Needham, Anuradha Dingwaney. "At the Receiving End: Reading 'Third' World Texts in a 'First' World Context." *"Turning the Century": Feminist Theory in the 1990s.* Ed. Glynis Carr. Spec. issue of *Bucknell Review* 35.2 (1992): 38–46. Print.

———. "Reimagining Familiar Dichotomies in Reading 'Alternative' Texts." *Journal of the Midwest Modern Language Association* 25.1 (1992): 47–53. Print.

Robbins, Bruce. "Comparative Cosmopolitanism." *Social Text* 31–32 (1992): 169–86. Print.

Schwartz, Henry. "Provocations toward a Theory of Third World Literature." *Mississippi Review* 49–50 (1989): 177–201. Print.

Spivak, Gayatri Chakravorty. "The Burden of English." *The Lie of the Land: English Literary Studies in India.* Ed. Rajeswari Sunder Rajan. Delhi: Oxford UP, 1992: 275–99. Print.

———. "Marginality in the Teaching Machine." *Outside in the Teaching Machine.* New York: Routledge, 1993. 53–76. Print.

Tripp, Aili Mari. "Rethinking Difference: Comparative Perspectives from Africa." *Signs: Journal of Women in Culture and Society* 25.3 (2000): 649–75. Print.

Varadharajan, Asha. "Indigent Dwelling, Itinerant Thought." *Politics and Culture* 1 (2004): n. pag. Web. 19 Jan. 2008.

Venuti, Lawrence. *The Scandal of Translation: Toward an Ethics of Difference.* London: Routledge, 1998. Print.

Worth, Fabienne. "Postmodern Pedagogy in the Multicultural Classroom: For Inappropriate Teachers and Imperfect Scholars." *Cultural Critique* 25 (1993): 5–32. Print.

Lawrence Venuti

Teaching in Translation

Whatever theoretical or critical significance is attached to the term "world literature," it will be applied to courses that gather texts originally written in various foreign languages, archaic and modern. And when teachers in the Americas (as elsewhere) undertake these courses, they will rely on translations out of sheer necessity. The factors that prevent us from assigning foreign texts start with the limits of our own educations. But even if we've been fortunate enough to master several languages and literatures, we must still confront the unevenness of foreign language preparation in any given class and the improbability that many undergraduates will have attained advanced reading proficiency in more difficult languages like Chinese, Classical Greek, and Russian. The possibility of a bilingual student body in places like Canada and Puerto Rico may lead teachers to expect a class to read French, Spanish, or English texts in the original languages. But here too the difficulty of assuming a uniform level of linguistic and analytic skills, particularly among undergraduates, militates against any such expectation. Teaching world literature means teaching most, if not all, required texts in translation. Yet this inevitability need not be lamented as a distortion or dilution of foreign literatures. It can rather be seen as enriching literary study in unexpected ways.

Translation broadens the range of questions that students might ask of languages, texts, traditions, and cultures as well as of the relations among them.

Nonetheless, teaching in translation is not the same as raising the issue of translation in the classroom, which must be done in a systematic way to be productive and therefore requires a rationale and a methodology. Perhaps the first reason to introduce this issue is to deepen students' knowledge of languages, native as well as foreign, while improving their skills in linguistic and literary analysis. A detailed comparison between a translation and the foreign text it translates can work toward these goals by focusing attention not only on lexicon and syntax but also on patterns of meaning, and not only on denotation and connotation but also on dialect and register, style and genre, intertextuality and intercultural relations. To conduct this sort of analysis, the instructor needs to present translations of passages that are central to the form and theme of the foreign text. Supplementary materials can be useful here, starting with the most basic: dictionaries. I sometimes bring in entries from various dictionaries in the foreign and translating languages, monolingual and bilingual, including historical dictionaries like the *OED* and more specialized ones like the *Dictionary of American Slang*. When dictionaries are used to analyze a translated passage against the corresponding passage in the foreign text, students can see how foreign author and translator each make verbal choices that produce literary effects, although always with suggestive differences. At the same time, students can learn a great deal about the interpretive dimension of translation as well as about literary interpretation in general.

To develop and illustrate these points, I explore a particularly rich case that might well appear on the syllabus of a course in world literature: the Argentine writer Julio Cortázar's short story "Las babas del diablo" ("The Devil's Drool," in a close rendering) and Paul Blackburn's English version, "Blow-Up." Cortázar's text is narrated by a translator, interestingly enough, who is also an amateur photographer. One day he comes upon a couple that piques his curiosity, an older woman and a teenaged boy, and he decides to photograph them while speculating about their relationship in a most self-conscious way, aware that he is "guilty of making literature, of indulging in fabricated unrealities" (Blackburn 124). Cortázar's text is relentlessly self-reflexive: it problematizes the representation of reality in literature through various linguistic and stylistic devices that put into question the narrator's reliability. These devices include constant shifting between first- and third-person points of view, the use of the conditional tense for the narrator's speculative comments, and explicit criticisms of the accuracy of his descriptions.

Suddenly the narrator notices a man sitting in a nearby car, and he revises the sexual scenario he initially saw unfolding between the woman and the boy:

> Y lo que entonces había imaginado era mucho menos horrible que la realidad, esa mujer que no estaba ahí por ella misma, no acariciaba ni proponía ni alentaba para su placer, para llevarse al ángel despeinado y jugar con su terror y su gracia deseosa. El verdadero amo esperaba, sonriendo petulante, seguro ya de la obra; no era el primero que mandaba a una mujer a la vanguardia, a traerle los prisioneros maniatados con flores. El resto sería tan simple, el auto, una casa cualquiera, las bebidas, las láminas excitantes, las lágrimas demasiado tarde, el despertar en el infierno. (69)

> And what I had imagined earlier was much less horrible than the reality, that woman, who was not there by herself, she was not caressing or propositioning or encouraging for her own pleasure, to lead the angel away with his tousled hair and play the tease with his terror and his eager grace. The real boss was waiting there, smiling petulantly, already certain of the business; he was not the first to send a woman in the vanguard, to bring him the prisoners manacled with flowers. The rest of it would be so simple, the car, some house or another, drinks, stimulating engravings, tardy tears, the awakening in hell. (129)

A classroom analysis of Blackburn's translation might begin with this key passage, scrutinizing his use of English dialects and styles that occasionally deviate from the Spanish text. The English version is cast mostly in the current standard dialect, but some choices are distinctly colloquial, whereas the Spanish is consistently written in the standard. Thus Blackburn pointedly renders "el verdadero amo" as "the real boss" and "la obra" as "the business." A Spanish-English lexicon like *Simon and Schuster's International Dictionary*, edited by Tana de Gámez, or María Moliner's *Diccionario de uso del español* shows Blackburn's hand by indicating a wide spectrum of possible meanings for "amo": they include "master (of the house); head (of the family); owner, proprietor; boss, foreman, overseer." With "obra," a word that can signify such meanings as "work" or "product" and "act" or "deed," Blackburn's use of "business" is more free but not so much as to constitute a wholesale revision of the Spanish text. Both his choices reveal an effort to cultivate a strain of colloquialism, and this strategy is confirmed in yet another shift from the Spanish, his insertion of the slangy "tease," which has no corresponding word in Cortázar's text. The word "tease" may not need any lexicographical analysis for anglophone students, but a consultation of the *OED*, especially an entry like "cock-tease," can easily document its sexual resonance. Even with this rapid and selective analysis, it becomes evident that Blackburn's English is doing things that Cortázar's Spanish doesn't do. The shift to a colloquial register introduces what amounts to underworld argot, edging the translated passage toward a noir style. Blackburn's choices exaggerate, even sensationalize the suggestion of a sex crime in the Spanish text, where the boy is assumed to be fifteen years old.

In an undergraduate class that contains students proficient in Spanish, this analysis can be turned into a collaborative activity and extended. Once the instructor has pointed out a few shifts between the Spanish and English, students can locate others on their own and consider the stylistic implications. Colloquialisms occur throughout the translation. Cortázar refers to the teenager variously as "el chico," "el muchacho," "el muchachito," and "el adolescente," whereas Blackburn not only resorts to standard English equivalents like "the boy" and "the young boy" but also lowers the register by using "the kid" repeatedly (124, 126, 127). The phrase "el pobre" ("the poor [boy]") becomes "the poor kid" (65; 125). For "la mujer rubia" ("the blond woman") Blackburn similarly substitutes "the blond." The colloquializing tendency sometimes results in free renderings that are tailored to the immediate context but still maintain a noir style: "resumiendo" ("in a word") is turned into "to cut it short," "a disimularlo" ("to dissimulate it") into "to play it cool," "para acertar con la verdad" ("to guess the truth") into "to hit the bullseye," "socarronamente" ("craftily") into "on the sly," "la salida" ("the exit") into "the way out" (62, 64, 65, 66; 121, 123, 124, 126). At one point, Cortázar's text seems to invite this colloquializing with an image drawn from a sport long associated with the criminal underworld: boxing. The sentence "el chico había agachado la cabeza, como los boxeadores cuando no pueden más y esperan el golpe de desgracia" (68) might be translated closely as "the boy had lowered his head, like boxers when they can do no more and wait for the coup de disgrace." Blackburn's version sacrifices Cortázar's witty play on *coup de grâce* for a more hard-boiled lexicon and syntax: "the kid had ducked his head like boxers do when they've done all they can and are waiting for the final blow to fall" (128). Words like "kid" and "ducked," the use of "like" for "as," and the contraction are noticeably nonstandard usages.

When students are shown how to perform this sort of translation analysis, they will quickly see that Blackburn's style is actually more heterogeneous—even without comparing his choices to the Spanish text. In the passage I quoted above, the narrator's language turns poetical as he speculates about the man's sexual designs on the boy. Blackburn's choice of "tardy tears" seems to be partly a literalism for "las lágrimas demasiado tarde" ("the too late tears"). But with the aid of the *OED* an instructor can demonstrate that "tardy" is one of several poetical archaisms that include "tousled hair" (for "despeinado" ["uncombed" or "mussed"]), "manacled" (for "maniatados" ["hands bound or restrained"]), and "stimulating engravings," where "stimulating" is a rather genteel choice for "excitantes" as compared to the stronger sexual connotation of an alternative like "arousing." The deliberateness of Blackburn's choices here, as well as their stylistic significance, can be underscored by referring to earlier passages where he renders two of these same words with colloquialisms: "despeinarlo" is turned into "muss his hair" and "maniatar" into "handcuffing" (62, 63; 121, 123). The poeticizing tendency might be described as a Victorian lyricism that works to euphemize what the narrator imagines to be the reality he is witnessing: the woman's seduction of the boy to serve as the object of the man's pederasty.

This analysis rests on several theoretical assumptions that are worth formulating in the classroom as methodological principles. The aim is to read translations as texts in their own right, which are obviously imitative of the foreign texts they translate but relatively autonomous from those texts because of differences that are both linguistic and literary, structural and cultural. Hence we must abandon notions of equivalence as a one-to-one correspondence, in which a translation is judged acceptable when it apparently reproduces a univocal meaning assumed to be inherent in the foreign text. Several possibilities can be proposed for most words and phrases in any foreign text. Phrases like "the real boss" and "the business," furthermore, do in fact establish a semantic correspondence to the Spanish text based on current dictionary definitions, what might be called a lexicographical equivalence. To dismiss Blackburn's choices as incorrect or inaccurate is not only to ignore this fact but also to substitute another, unstated criterion of equivalence, perhaps one that gives preference to the current standard dialect of English or to a particular shade of meaning. Blackburn, however, was undoubtedly applying his own criterion, as translators typically do, and it involved the creation of analogues with English-language literary styles. Translations, even those that closely adhere to the lexical and syntactic features of the foreign text, produce effects that exceed a lexicographical equivalence and work only in the translating language and culture. It won't do, then, to insist that Blackburn's English should match the Spanish in every respect, barring the structural differences between the languages. The English "tardy" is a calque for the Spanish "tarde"; they share a basic meaning as well as an etymology, but the former has become a poetical archaism while the latter remains a current standard usage. This effect of "tardy" is part of the gain that a translation always inscribes in the foreign text while losing or deviating from textual features specific to the foreign language.

If a world literature course includes a theoretical component, another kind of supplementary material might be introduced at this point to increase students' critical sophistication in reading translations: essays in translation studies that take up the topic of equivalence. To theorize the ratio of loss and gain in Blackburn's translation, Eugene Nida's concept of dynamic equivalence can be fruitfully juxtaposed to Jacques Derrida's concept of iterability. Nida argues for an "equivalent effect," wherein the translator

> is not so concerned with matching the receptor-language message with the source-language message, but with the dynamic relationship, that the relationship between receptor and message should be substantially the same as that which existed between the original receptors and the message.

To achieve a dynamic equivalence, the translator "tries to relate the receptor to modes of behavior within the context of his own culture" (159).

Yet how can an equivalence be achieved, we might ask, if the translating is so ethnocentric? Won't the equivalence be compromised by the replacement of the foreign cultural context with the receiving culture? Blackburn's stylistic analogues are not present in Cortázar's text, and because they are specific to English-language literary traditions, they ensure that the anglophone reader's response to the translation will differ from the response that the hispanophone reader has toward the Spanish text. We can better understand Blackburn's work by turning to Derridian iterability, the idea that the meaning of any sign can change, because a sign "can break with every given context and engender infinitely new contexts in an absolutely nonsaturable fashion" (320). Translation partakes of iterability: it is a recontextualizing process that can never produce an equivalent effect, because it transforms the form and theme of the foreign text, although any transformation is guided fundamentally by structural differences between languages as well as cultural differences between literary traditions. It is these differences that any translation analysis must describe and examine insofar as they endow a translated text with significance.

As a result, we must qualify—if not jettison—the communicative model of translation, which is still widely held by readers, whether professional or popular, scholarly or student. To read a translation simply as the communication of a univocal meaning collapses the translation into the foreign text and conceals the translator's labor of transformation. A translation communicates not so much the foreign text as the translator's interpretation of it, one interpretation among others, to be sure, but nonetheless an interpretation that should be articulated for students, not dismissed as arbitrary or irrelevant or displaced by a competing interpretation that the instructor has constructed or culled from specialists in the foreign literature. Blackburn's translation provides ample evidence that he applied what is effectively an interpretant to guide his verbal choices, a stylistic analogue that signifies beyond the Spanish text but is designed to interpret its form and theme. If we treat Blackburn's verbal choices as interpretive moves, if his lexicon and syntax are seen as inscribing meanings in the Spanish text, his translation does reflect a careful reading. The mixture of noir and poeticism shapes the characterization of the narrator, indicating his preference for a particular image of what he sees, at once salacious and sensationalizing, threatening and repressively euphemistic.

Here a more general point about literary interpretation might be made for students—namely, the idea that interpretation, like translation, is essentially a recontextualizing process, an application of an interpretant to fix a meaning in a text whose meanings can vary with different interpretants, whether formal (e.g., a theory of interpretation or equivalence) or thematic (e.g., a code or ideology). To make this point, an instructor might note the similarities and differences between the acts of translation performed by Blackburn and by the translator-photographer who is the narrator. For the narrator also applies an interpretant in his speculations, turning the visual images into a narrative on the basis of a psychoanalytic

concept. The Oedipus complex is the *combinatoire* or underlying structure that generates his two conflicting explanations of the interactions
among the other characters. He moves from a heterosexual to a homosexual version of what is basically the oedipal triangle, made explicit by
the references to the woman and boy as "mother and son" (118, 123). In
effect, the narrator invents scenarios in which he identifies with the emotions that he imputes to the boy, first a masculinist desire for the maternal
woman, then a homophobic fear of the paternal man (it is important to
keep in mind that he fantasizes the man's homosexuality). The stylistic
mix of Blackburn's translation, the combination of hard-boiled noir and
Victorian poeticism, might therefore be seen as an interrogation of the
narrator's unconscious, perhaps his Latin American machismo: the translation highlights his transgressive excitement and his sexual anxiety, his
sense that the boy would feel "his manhood diminished" if he fled from
the woman and that the man is trying to commit an "abusive act" beneath a quaintly seductive cover (127, 129).

Thus far the analysis has been a close reading of translation strategies,
assessing their significance in relation to the form and theme of the foreign text. In the classroom, the analysis might be deepened by situating it
in a broader context, of the translator's other projects, for instance, or of
the translation tradition in which those projects emerge. Translation
strategies can form fairly continuous traditions, in which translators adopt
similar verbal choices and interpretive moves over long stretches of time
or introduce variants and innovations. Blackburn's strategies reflect the
modernist experimentalism that characterizes his other projects, including translations of the Provençal troubadours, and these strategies were
influenced by Ezra Pound (see Venuti, *Translator's Invisibility* 194–232).

In his essay "Guido's Relations" (1929), Pound advocates a translating style derived from English-language poetic traditions so as to re-
create effects that he perceives in the foreign text. To render Guido
Cavalcanti's thirteenth-century Italian verse, he recommends the use of
"pre-Elizabethan English," the language of early-sixteenth-century poets
such as Sir Thomas Wyatt and Gavin Douglas; and to explain his choice
he asserts that these "writers were still intent on clarity and explicitness"
(199). Yet Pound underestimates the interpretive dimension of his translating. He believes that the effects he seeks through an early-sixteenth-
century language are comparable with effects inherent in the Italian
texts, when in fact he is inscribing those texts with his own modernist
poetics, applying a formal interpretant that consists of linguistic precision

(see Venuti, *Translator's Invisibility* 166–67). His stylistic analogue recontextualizes both the Italian and the English poetries with a modernist difference, laying the groundwork for their reinterpretation and revaluation.

A similar point can be made of Blackburn's analogues, but because Blackburn is translating a contemporary foreign literature, the question of international literary relations comes into play. Here too supplementary materials can be useful to create an interpretive context for the translation. Consider Franco Moretti's controversial effort to reconceptualize comparative literature on the model of world-system theory. He hypothesizes asymmetrical patterns of influence between a "core" represented by the literatures of France, the United Kingdom, and the United States and a "periphery" consisting of other literatures worldwide (56). From this hypothesis a "law of literary evolution" follows: the modern prose narrative (the novel, for Moretti) "first arises not as an autonomous development but as a compromise between a western formal influence (usually French or English) and local materials," which he ultimately specifies as "*foreign plot*; local *characters*; and then, local *narrative voice*" (58, 65). This theory might provoke various questions during a translation analysis, although perhaps the case of Blackburn's Cortázar gives special urgency to one in particular: What happens when a narrative from the global periphery is translated into a core language like English with an English-language stylistic analogue?

Cortázar's text does indeed seem to exemplify the often unstable structural compromise at the heart of Moretti's theory, which, however, might need to be qualified because of the textual effects of Blackburn's translation. The narrator, one Roberto Michel, is identified as French Chilean, and the plot that structures his speculations about the woman, man, and boy, insofar as it involves an element of suspense and criminality, derives from the British and American detective stories that began to circulate in Argentina in the late nineteenth century and were also used in innovative ways by Cortázar's countryman Jorge Luis Borges. The noir style in Blackburn's translation, then, exposes the hybrid literary conditions of Cortázar's text, its anglophone formal roots made more self-conscious by Borges's experiments. Yet Cortázar's text comes back to worry Blackburn's stylistic analogue by defamiliarizing it: the psychoanalytic representation of gender and sexual roles interrogates the masculinism typical of noir, exposing its psychological conditions.

A translation strategy, especially if it inscribes a rich intertextual network, can be seen as initiating a critical dialectic between the foreign and translated texts, a mutual interrogation, whose significance can be articulated by reconstructing the literary traditions, cultural situations, and historical moments in which those texts are produced and circulate. Blackburn's translation belongs to the so-called Boom in South American literature during the 1960s and 1970s, the wave of translations that formed a new canon of foreign literature in English and altered contemporary fiction in the United States, encouraging writers like John Barth to develop related narrative experiments (see Payne, ch. 1). Translation complicates Moretti's theory by opening up another level of potentially unstable structural compromise, one that enables literary texts from the periphery to destabilize a core literature.

I have tried to sketch a pedagogy of translated literature on the basis of a single translation, but other approaches are possible, perhaps desirable in some cases. Archaic texts that are repeatedly retranslated offer an opportunity to juxtapose different versions of the same passage, revealing different strategies and interpretations (see Venuti, "Pedagogy" 99–102). The notion of translation might be construed with latitude to include various derivative forms and practices, so that interlingual translations are studied alongside imitations and adaptations in different media. Cortázar's text also became the basis of an intersemiotic translation, *Blowup*, Michelangelo Antonioni's 1966 film adaptation. Whatever the media, however, the pedagogy must include a detailed comparison of the prior and the derivative works so as to locate shifts or variations, the significant differences from which strategies, interpretations, and values can be inferred and subsequently contextualized in cultural and social terms. What may most recommend raising the issue of translation in the classroom is the renewed emphasis it places on reading closely and carefully.

Works Cited

Blackburn, Paul, trans. "Blow-Up." *"End of the Game" and Other Stories.* By Julio Cortázar. New York: Pantheon, 1967. 114–31. Print.

Cortázar, Julio. "Las babas del diablo." 1959. *Las armas secretas.* Barcelona: Planeta, 1984. 56–71. Print.

de Gámez, Tana, ed. *Simon and Schuster's International Dictionary: English/ Spanish, Spanish/English.* New York: Simon, 1973. Print.

Derrida, Jacques. "Signature Event Context." *Margins of Philosophy.* Trans. Alan Bass. Chicago: U of Chicago P, 1982. 307–30. Print.

Moliner, María. *Diccionario de uso del español.* Madrid: Gredos, 1994. Print.

Moretti, Franco. "Conjectures on World Literature." *New Left Review* 1 (2000): 54–68. Print.

Nida, Eugene. "Principles of Correspondence." *Toward a Science of Translating, with Special Reference to Principles and Procedures Involved in Bible Translating.* Leiden: Brill, 1964. 156–71. Print.

Payne, Johnny. *Conquest of the New Word: Experimental Fiction and Translation in the Americas.* Austin: U of Texas P, 1993. Print.

Pound, Ezra. "Guido's Relations." *The Literary Essays of Ezra Pound.* Ed. T. S. Eliot. New York: New Directions, 1954. 192–200. Print.

Venuti, Lawrence. "The Pedagogy of Literature." *The Scandals of Translation: Towards an Ethics of Difference.* London: Routledge, 1998. 88–105. Print.

———. *The Translator's Invisibility: A History of Translation.* 2nd ed. London: Routledge, 2008. Print.

Part II

Program Strategies

Introduction

The broad scope of world literature far exceeds any individual's scholarly grasp, and mounting even a single world literature course often entails bringing together a group of faculty members to pool their expertise, with the result that the shape of a given course will be strongly influenced by the interests and skills of those available to teach it. Even more than individual survey courses, programs in world literature are shaped by the opportunities and constraints offered by their institution. The essays in this section present a variety of strategies for mounting successful courses and programs, at both the undergraduate and graduate levels.

Kathleen Komar highlights the close relation that can be built up between a world literature course and a diverse population of students in a major urban center whose immigrant communities give an unusual base for student contributions to discussion of linguistic and cultural questions in a wide range of texts. Political and racial turmoil in Los Angeles, for example, has provided surprising new contexts for reading a work such as Kleist's *Michael Kohlhaas*. By contrast, Oscar Kenshur discusses the disciplinary constraints on curricular change. In comparative literature departments, the long-standing emphasis on reading texts in the original comes into conflict with the growing need to use translations, while beyond the comparative literature department, national literature departments may resist encroachment on their home turf—resistances that Kenshur's program has had to work carefully to overcome.

The next two essays underscore the value of active participation by undergraduates in shaping the courses they take. Jane Newman discusses the development at her institution of world literature courses emphasizing modes of reading and canon formation, courses that markedly improved as students became involved in their planning. Carol Luther discusses the formation of a learning community engaged in the joint study of Western literature and Western civilization, a community that included not only the teachers who team-taught the courses but also the students, who worked in groups to synthesize and present material.

The next four essays discuss program designs intended to broaden comparative literature programs from their typically European base to a more global scope. Michael Palencia-Roth describes a pioneering program developed at his institution in the mid-1980s at both the undergraduate and graduate levels, the graduate courses emphasizing instances of cross-cultural contact in colonial settings. John Burt Foster discusses a flexible, region-based approach that has enabled him and his colleagues to mount global courses in a single-semester format. Caroline Eckhardt presents a range of strategies by which graduate programs can give students more exposure and training in world literature even while maintaining the emphasis on studying works in the original languages. Finally, Colin Meissner and Margaret Doody describe the process of inventing a global program de novo, in an institution that had no existing PhD programs in any literature other than English, so that the turf concerns that Kenshur describes didn't arise. Meissner and Doody's program sought to give graduate students a solid grounding in a national tradition while at the same time emphasizing international circulation and interdisciplinary approaches.

None of these approaches can simply be mapped onto programs at other schools, but readers at many institutions will find ideas here that can fruitfully be adapted in a wide variety of circumstances.

Kathleen L. Komar

Teaching World Literature in a Microcosm of the World

Across the country, many colleges and universities are enrolling an increasingly diverse student population. Many students are the children of immigrants or themselves immigrated as children, while others are international students. These diverse student bodies offer particular opportunities for teachers to utilize students' linguistic and cultural knowledge in the classroom, as we have found at the University of California, Los Angeles, which has one of the most diverse student bodies in the country. The local newspaper is fond of pointing out that Los Angeles has more Koreans than any city but Seoul. Similar points could be made about Armenians, Russians, Iranians, several East Asian and Southeast Asian groups, Latin American groups, and many more. This diversity exists in addition to the sizable Hispanic American and African American populations of the area and a large citizenry of Asian Americans (in all their many ethnic variations). We have almost 25,000 undergraduates and over 11,000 graduate students. Many of our students speak more than one language; many have parents whose first language is not English. Teaching "world literature" to such a group presents a special challenge—and some genuine opportunities.

Because of the availability of multilingual students, several years ago UCLA was able to mount an undergraduate comparative literature major in which students take courses offered by the various national literature departments in the original languages along with comparative literature courses on theory and primary texts.[1] This major allows students to do cultural and literary comparisons based on the original texts and to read with a sophisticated understanding of the languages involved. All our comparative literature undergraduate majors are therefore working in more than one language to fulfill their course requirements. Some of the work in our own comparative literature courses is inevitably done with texts in translation, because the languages that students have mastered range from Armenian to Spanish, Korean to German, Chinese and Arabic to Ancient Greek, and many more. In any of our courses, therefore, the array of languages open to the students cannot be expected to match the languages of the primary texts in the class. Given this fact, when we order texts for a course on the upper-division level, we double-order the texts in the original language and in translation. Any student who can read a text in the original language is expected to do so. When students do not have access to that particular language, they read in translation. So at any given moment, we have some students reading the Japanese or Spanish text and some reading the translation. While this arrangement may sound chaotic, it allows for discussion of issues of translation and the difficulties of conveying certain cultural assumptions in the translated text. If we can obtain facing-page translations of poetry or other short texts, we do so. This strategy too aids in discussions of the linguistic fine points of the original texts, even for students who may not know the language well.

I encourage my students who can read in the original to point out passages in which the translator has run into problems or failed to convey an important cultural point. This practice does two things. First, it makes us all more sophisticated in our understanding of texts to which we do not have direct linguistic access. Second, it encourages those students who have direct knowledge of multiple cultures to use that experience in a way that both assists their peers and makes the students appreciate the complexities of their own multicultural heritage. Although students are shy at first about contributing in this way, they eventually begin to exchange cultural information and to gain respect for cultures very different from their own backgrounds.

I have watched students from a Buddhist background explain that the cobra is a protective symbol, unlike the iconographic snake that the

Blessed Virgin may be standing on in the Christian Garden of Eden. This kind of explanation and resulting interaction become a learning opportunity for all of us in the class. Each of my undergraduates may be an expert on some cultural information unavailable to others in the class. Everyone learns. The exchanges that this kind of discussion triggers among my students have been among the most fruitful in my decades of teaching experience. They also make rapidly evident that any one culture's claim to superiority becomes difficult to sustain when placed in a context that reveals the richness of many cultures. Binary assumptions about East and West, north and south, European and other, and male and female become problematic when students see the range of possible attitudes and cultures explored in a particular course.

In case you have been wondering about the linguistic competence of the instructor in these courses, let me say that I too must read texts in translation. Teaching world literature necessitates humility—and the willingness to become an eternal student. I am only too happy to be a student. When I am using a text that I cannot read in the original (e.g., Japanese or Brazilian), I try to find a student in the course to report on the linguistic or cultural issues the text raises that are not evident to me. If that is not possible, I ask graduate students in the Comparative Literature Department if they'd be willing to give a guest talk in my class. The graduate students have the benefit of an additional teaching opportunity and an admiring audience. Some have received a standing ovation at the end of a presentation. One student was an Africanist who gave a talk on the number of languages, ethnic groups, and political complexities subsumed under the term *African literature*. Intra-African issues became comparative in a whole new way for those of us in the class.

If you are lucky enough to have wide-ranging graduate students, they can be extremely helpful in designing a world literature course. For those of us who were trained in the traditional German-French-English configuration of comparative literature but who want to teach much more broadly, well-informed, intelligent, and forthcoming graduate students are a godsend. When we decided that our Euro-American great-books offerings were incomplete in a contemporary global setting, I was charged with designing a lower-division, introductory course with a non-Euro-American base. I turned to my colleagues in other fields but received even more detailed help from our graduate students in comparative literature. They provided me with annotated bibliographies of texts from dozens of cultures, indicating what major issues each text presented, whether it was available in translation, and what problems I should anticipate in teaching it. Happily this course, Great Books from the World at Large, is now taught with much more sophistication by my younger colleagues, who work in Middle Eastern, East Asian, Caribbean, Latin American, African, and other literatures and cultures. We should not be afraid to venture beyond our comfort zone—both linguistically and historically—in attempting to expose our students to literatures and cultures they would otherwise never experience. I am delighted to be taught by my students. They are currently teaching me about the wonders of electronic literature of various kinds.

Some version of our lower-division introductory great-books courses has been taught at UCLA for the past four decades. Following an approach related to the "great books" tradition at Chicago, Columbia, and Harvard but long before "world literature" became a popular concept, UCLA had broadly introductory, general education literature courses taught under the rubric of humanities. Early on, these were very large lecture courses with readers. My senior colleagues in comparative literature revised their format by adding more discussion sections and specialized composition work. This move proved to be a crucial moment both for our undergraduates and our graduate students, as I outline below.

These early humanities courses were largely Euro-American-based for many years. As the cultural competence of our faculty expanded with new colleagues and as our student body grew ever more culturally diverse, we expanded our courses to include many more areas of the world. While extending the geographic and cultural scope of our introductory world literature offerings, we tried to maintain historical scope. Our lower-division world literature courses are divided roughly into historical periods, beginning with the course Antiquity to the Middle Ages, which often begins with *Gilgamesh*. The second course in the sequence is entitled Middle Ages to the Seventeenth Century, and the third is Age of Enlightenment to the Present. All contain non-Euro-American material, but our final course, Great Books from the World at Large, concentrates on major literary texts usually overlooked in courses that focus only on the canon of Western literature. Texts from at least three of the following areas are read in any given term: African, Caribbean, East Asian, Latin American, and Middle Eastern literature.

These lower-division introductory courses are designed to fulfill general education requirements for the UCLA college and are thus taught using texts originally in English or in English translation. Some of these courses are lecture-and-discussion (three hours of lecture, one hour of discussion section); others include a composition component and are taught as two lectures and two discussion sections per week so that students can get more individualized help with their writing skills. Both kinds of courses provide opportunities for our graduate students to learn teaching skills, to broaden their own knowledge of world literature, and to interact with undergraduates who may become comparative literature majors. This teaching experience provides both needed financial support for the graduate students and more help for the undergraduates. By tying the lecture version of these introductory courses to the teaching of composition, we were able to work more rigorously on the writing of our undergraduates while at the same time supporting our graduate students and giving them more extensive training in the teaching of both literature and composition.

The world literature and composition courses are designed to use great literary texts to teach writing skills in addition to cultural and literary-critical understanding. As one of my colleagues, Arnold Band, put it, "The courses taught good writing through good reading." The sections for these courses are limited to twenty students so that we can better work with undergraduate students on their composition skills. The writing assignments in this series are designed to fulfill a number of different—and increasingly sophisticated—purposes. In the initial, short assignments, students learn to recognize the major ideas and themes of an argument or narrative. They begin to understand literary techniques and how language and writing are used strategically in the text. As the assignments progress and get longer, students are given the experience of analyzing literary genres (poetry and drama in addition to narrative). They learn to trace some of the course's central concepts across national boundaries to see how those concepts change in differing cultural situations and become embodied in different metaphors or symbols. Students get some idea of how literary movements develop and move through both geographic and historical dimensions. Most crucially, they use these literary models to analyze rhetorical strategies in texts so that they can learn how to use them in their own writing. They see examples of clarity and precision in literature, which they can try to imitate. They experience the ways in which writers use metaphor, repeated imagery, and symbols to build arguments. Students also see how narrative, dramatic, or poetic strategies differ in different cultural settings.

Students receive extensive comments by the instructor and teaching assistants; they also do some peer evaluations, which help them understand that it is not just the stuffy academic establishment that has trouble understanding their writing. If their colleagues cannot understand them, students know they must improve their arguments, style, and grammar. In our world literature and composition series we constantly link great literature to the students' developing composition skills. Students thus are introduced to major literary texts and the practice of interpreting them and in the process get a rigorous course in writing.

These introductory world literature courses may be the only literature courses our nonliterature majors will take at UCLA. We feel it is important, therefore, to introduce them to texts from several cultures written in different languages and genres. We want to give our undergraduates the tools they need to read critically and write clearly and insightfully. We also want to keep in their view the incredible cultural variety that surrounds them now and will do so even more in their future lives. It is a great deal to ask from one or two quarters of course work. But it is a beginning. And not infrequently, some students who set out to be doctors suddenly realize that their real passion lies in the direction of language, literature, and culture. While parents are not always delighted at such a shift, it is gratifying to see for those of us who teach the introductory courses.

But are these courses still necessary in a world in which technology is overtaking every part of our daily lives? Does reading dusty old books or even contemporary popular ones really contribute to our students' future lives? Let me close with a reality-teaching experience, which I hope shows why teaching literature—and in particular world literature—remains a crucial task and also makes clear how texts from one culture can speak to the issues and problems of another culture and another historical moment. In the wake of resource-centered management and business models that swept higher education in the last decade, demonstrating why the teaching of any kind of literature was worthwhile became ever more difficult. In addition, those of us at public institutions still partially supported by state legislatures were being asked why the state should fund such apparently unnecessary activities as the teaching of literature and the arts. I began to despair of convincing people of the value of our teaching when a rather idiosyncratic occurrence indisputably reaffirmed its fundamental necessity.

In April 1992, I was teaching part of a lower-division great-books course that happened still to be focused on European literature—in this case, on German texts. The fifty students in the class and I had made it into the early nineteenth century when the Los Angeles riots exploded. As was typical of my classes at UCLA, this class was very multicultural and multiethnic, including African Americans, Chicanas and Chicanos, Latinas and Latinos, Korean Americans, and several other Asian American groups. Some of my Korean American students had been wearing flak jackets and defending their homes or their parents' stores; others of my students were on the opposite side, protesting the injustices they felt were exemplified in the beating of Rodney King by Los Angeles police. The lecture hall was extremely tense.

Quite fortuitously, we had just finished reading Heinrich von Kleist's *Michael Kohlhaas* (1808) and were in the middle of Georg Büchner's *Woyzeck* (1836). The first of these texts portrays a man who resorts to violence when he feels justice is being denied him by a corrupt political system; the second depicts a man abused and in abject poverty, who ends up destroying what is nearest and most precious to him. When the class met in the midst of the upheaval, one student began a discussion by admitting that he thought these books we were reading were pretty "old and out of it" but that, to his surprise, they had suddenly become very relevant. It was a small revelation that issues of justice, corruption, and exploitation in a far-off time and a foreign country could seem so close to what we were in the middle of in Los Angeles. We then had a wonderful discussion of the social, economic, and legal implications of *Kohlhaas* and *Woyzeck*, with the riots firmly in mind and literally in view.

For *Kohlhaas*, we discussed issues of resorting to violence in order to gain justice—and what or who might get hurt in the process. For *Woyzeck*, we discussed what happens to a man who is reduced to living like an animal and whose frustration can be vented only on those closest to him and least deserving of his rage. We discussed in both texts what happens to a society when the very legal and political systems that are supposed to uphold justice and equality become polluted and corrupt. When I say "we" here, I really mean my students, who suddenly had a number of epiphanies that I would have been hard put to induce with quite the intensity that the riots produced.

Suddenly those of my students who could not confront one another directly because of racial and ethnic distrust had found a way to talk about their personal feelings and how they experienced the injustice of their various positions. I had students occupy the roles of different characters in the texts and argue their case from the point of view of each character. It was often instructive to them to find that they could indeed see how one would resort to violence—even a violence that destroyed one's immediate neighborhood—when pushed too far. The role-playing was later spun out into papers for the course, which gave students another opportunity to reflect on the issues attached to justice, violence, and bureaucratic abuse. They were among the best papers I ever received—not in their polish but in the depth of their insights. They were extremely personal yet also about the literary texts; the personal was possible only because of those mediating texts. Students came to realize that our predicament is not exclusively American and that problems of class, ethnicity, and exploitation are unfortunately universal. But they also understood much more clearly how other students in the same city could feel so differently. They began to see how the reserve and diffidence of one culture might be read as disdain and disrespect by someone with another cultural background.

After this experience I was quite sure that the teaching of literature was still vital to society at large. I do not mean to imply here that literature is valuable only when it is relevant to current affairs. On the contrary, literature's capacity to reach across two centuries to make my students think critically and feel contemporary injustices more profoundly is evidence rather of the enduring and timeless power of the texts. I have argued with administrators and legislators for the value of aesthetics itself and for the importance of our teaching students to appreciate it. But the fact that Kleist's and Büchner's portrayal of human suffering and injustice can trigger epiphanies centuries after Kleist and Büchner wrote certainly belongs among the reasons we find literature indispensable to the development of human understanding and culture.

I realized that with a little forethought I could encourage similar interactions among students in all my classes. The riots provided an extreme case—as our current experiences of terrorism, surveillance, and civil rights might—but other experiences could also be played out through world literature by giving students enough distance to discuss critically what is too painful in their lives to discuss directly on a personal basis. The teaching of world literature is, among many other wonderful things, a forum for working out some of our contemporary cultural conflicts. It allows students to interact with one another and to explore their personal issues and experiences in a context less threatening than the streets. The apparent distance that is created when students read a text that they know comes from a distant country and is written in a strange language makes possible discussions that they would hesitate to have if they felt they were confronting one another directly about personal experiences. If we can get students to occupy those "foreign" perspectives for the length of a class, I believe the insights they gain will be carried back to the streets.

Great literature, foreign and domestic, is often about societies in crisis. I'm afraid our students will have increasing need of precisely such texts in the immediate future. We who teach world literature may not contribute directly to our state's economy by creating new nanotechnologists or computer scientists, but we certainly contribute to the state's ability to exist as a functioning democracy: we help create citizens who can think critically and who acquire an ability to occupy cultural positions different from their own. That contribution just might be worth our tax dollars after all.

Note

1. Our English department also mounts a "world literature" concentration as part of the English major. It consists of nine upper-division courses in English or American literature and four upper-division courses in foreign literatures, at least one of which must be taught in the original language. The intense focus on English and the lack of emphasis on work in any other language mark this program as very different in requirements and philosophy from the comparative literature major, which requires students to take at least four upper-division courses in a language other than English and another course either in a third language or in another discipline.

Works Cited

Büchner, Georg. *Woyzeck*. Trans. Nicholas Rudall. Chicago: Dee, 2002. Print.
Kleist, Heinrich von. *Michael Kohlhaas: A Tale from an Old Chronicle*. Trans. Frances H. King. New York: Mondial, 2007. Print.

Oscar Kenshur

Habits of Mind: Comparative Literature Meets the World

When I was asked to write about the kinds of institutional constraints that might have affected the teaching of world literature in my department, my first reaction was to think that I had nothing to write about, that there had been no institutional constraints. Indeed, in a university that allowed Alfred Kinsey to teach courses on human sexuality in the 1930s and to establish the Institute for Sex Research in the 1940s, it would be surprising to find institutional constraints impeding twenty-first-century curricular developments in the Comparative Literature Department. Moreover, since the discipline of comparative literature takes as its point of departure the study of literature across cultural boundaries and since our department in particular has a long history of curricular innovation beyond its Western European starting point, courses in world literature might seem to be a natural outgrowth of the very idea of comparative literary study as well as our own institutional history.

A glance at the courses and programs that have been developed in my department over the past half century would seem to reveal a continuous history of outward movement from Europe to the larger world. Starting with the most conspicuous and influential European literatures, the Comparative Literature Department at Indiana University developed pioneering courses in Asian-Western and Arabic-Western literary relations, and in African literatures. More recently, we began offering courses exploring relations among cultural areas outside Europe—for example, Caribbean literature in relation to African and black American literature, South American literature in relation to North American. Even in the European context, we have witnessed the redefining of cultural geography in such a way as to highlight supranational and subnational objects of study such as literatures of stateless minorities (Yiddish literature, for example) or the literature produced by immigrants or exiles. Most recently, we have added to our curriculum the undergraduate course World Literature before 1500, which brings together texts from Europe, South Asia, and East Asia. By the time these words appear in print, we will have offered a graduate version of this course.

Some of these courses were pioneering efforts, while others paralleled contemporaneous developments at other universities. It might nonetheless seem as if they could all be placed on a historical continuum that moves gradually from a traditional Eurocentric "great powers" conception of comparative literary study to an increasingly broader approach that culminates in the world literature courses. However, a closer look reveals that the movement has not been so smoothly incremental. A significant gap separates the world literature courses from other courses dealing with non-European literatures, and something of a chasm separates the undergraduate world literature course from the graduate version. The gaps are not cultural or geographic; they are the result of what has been allowed and what has been disallowed by disciplinary norms.

What sets the world literature courses apart is the fact that the colleague who has developed and taught them is unable to read several of the assigned texts in their original languages. This limitation, of course, is inherent in the undertaking; it comes with the vastness of the territory. But this inherent feature of the teaching of world literature has a special significance in a comparative literature department. To understand this significance and the significance of the difference between the undergraduate and the graduate world literature course, we must shift our attention from overt institutional constraints to other kinds of constraints.

While world literature might seem to be the logical outcome of the boundary crossing that lies at the heart of the enterprise of comparative literature, there are countervailing principles of comparative literary study that give rise to logics other than the global one. And although these alternative logics may currently find expression only *sotto voce*, in occasional murmurs of disapproval, it is important to recognize that opinions that fail to prevent certain things from taking place can still count as constraints, constraints that may have had more institutional muscle in the past and that could conceivably regain their strength in the future. Moreover, the disciplinary constraints that can work to inhibit curricular change may themselves profitably be understood as subtly mediated outcomes of larger institutional pressures. In a word, not all institutional constraints take the form of deans saying no.

The species of constraints that concern me here are those that arise from what I'll call disciplinary protocols. Paradigmatic examples might be the protocols that give scientific experiments prima facie legitimacy: control of variables, double-blind testing, replicability, and so on. The humanities have their own, less rigid protocols: the number and kind of footnotes that are needed to establish sufficient mastery of the secondary literature on a given topic, for example, or the demonstration that one is using the appropriate or most reliable edition of a given text.

Self-imposed disciplinary protocols may, however, have their origins in institutional constraints, such as an initial or ongoing need to justify the presence of the discipline in a university structure. In some cases these underlying pressures do not lie very far from the surface. For example, when a scholar presenting a so-called theory of comparative literature wrote that comparing an Anglo-Saxon text with a text in modern English lay outside the disciplinary parameters of comparative literature, it was easy to see that this attempt to theorize about the nature of the discipline had been carried out with one eye fixed on the institutional structures in which comparative literature units sought to find a place for themselves. Thus theories of comparative literature tended to insist, however subtly, on the nonthreatening nature of the discipline, the ability of comparative literature programs to locate themselves among existing units without intruding on neighboring turf.

But to say that a comparison between *Beowulf* and Virginia Woolf lies beyond the disciplinary boundaries of comparative literary study does not in itself obviate institutional suspicion. After all, strictly speaking, comparative literature is not an interstitial discipline but one that, by its nature, infringes on the turf of other disciplines; in a large research university, it almost always infringes on the territory of other units. If comparatists, instead of comparing *Beowulf* with Virginia Woolf, bring a comparison between Woolf and, say, Proust into a university's curriculum, they are not working in the empty space between two other units but straddling a space already occupied by two other units.

When the occupation of territory cannot be justified on the ground that the territory was previously uninhabited, the occupation is often justified on the ground that the new arrivals are bringing progress and enlightenment. And while we have every reason to be leery these days of the *mission civilisatrice* in the geopolitical world (especially when it is being engineered by people who are themselves not paragons of civilized values), the arrival of comparatists on the pedagogical terrain of other disciplines does not wreak havoc; it may provide perspectives that are of value to students of individual national literatures.

The disciplinary protocols of comparative literature, of course, spell out not only the kinds of courses and the kinds of research that are specific to the discipline but also the kinds of scholarly rigor that are required to endow this research and these courses with intellectual respectability. The protocol that arguably has the greatest impact on comparative literature's disciplinary identity and that has, I suspect, done the most to impede the addition of world literature courses to curricula is the insistence on studying each text in its original language. Whatever its origin, this protocol has no doubt served to deflect institutional pressures that might have been inspired by the suspicions of practitioners of neighboring disciplines. If scholars claim to be able to throw light on texts from two or more national traditions and claim that they are doing so in a rigorous and systematic way, they must be prepared to demonstrate that while being recontextualized, the texts in question are being read and taught no less competently than they would be by scholars in the individual national literature departments. This claim cannot be convincingly made unless the comparatists read each key text in its original language.

The protocol that militates against analyzing a text that one cannot read in the original language is not only a deeply entrenched feature of comparative literature's disciplinary identity but also an eminently justifiable principle for people whose job is to explicate texts. What concerns me here is the extent to which this research protocol impinges, or ought to impinge, on the teaching of world literature.

Of course if *world literature* were still, as it was only a couple of decades ago, a misnomer that referred to canons of the literary great powers of Western Europe, then even the most rigorous application of the original-language protocol would not prevent some comparatists from teaching modern Western great works under the world literature rubric.

But precisely because such world literature courses were being taught elsewhere by people who did not know the original languages, there was little incentive for comparatists to employ a label that they associated with dilettantism. Today, world literature has come to include an increasingly wide range of cultures and languages, and even comparatists steeped in Old World erudition would be hard pressed to range from European languages (ancient, medieval, and modern); to Biblical Hebrew and the other languages of the Ancient Near East; to Modern Hebrew, Arabic, and Persian; to Sanskrit and South Asian vernacular languages, Chinese, Japanese, African languages, Mesoamerican languages; and so on.[1] From the perspective of the original-language protocol, this development would open the gates to a larger world of dilettantism. Comparatists teaching a world literature course would have the advantage of knowing some of the European languages and, ideally, one or more of the non-European ones.[2] This knowledge would allow them to make students aware of what is sometimes lost or transformed in translation. But the original-language protocol does not accommodate itself to different degrees of linguistic and cultural competence. Thus, paradoxically, the very people whose linguistic and cross-cultural training should put them in the best position to teach world literature are inhibited from doing so by the very same disciplinary protocols that place high value on linguistic and cross-cultural competence.[3]

The easiest way to deal with tensions between conflicting principles or tendencies within a given system of beliefs is to ignore them. The world literature courses being taught in my department came into being after a faculty member asked the department chair whether such a course could be offered and the chair (who happened, at the time, to be me) responded enthusiastically in the affirmative. Since my department's world literature offerings initially entered our course schedule by fiat rather than as a result of any elaborate procedure or any formal or explicit justification, it might seem unduly scrupulous of me to worry about providing a rationale after the fact. But there are moral imperatives that come under the general heading of "a decent respect to the opinions of mankind," and there is, in addition, an intellectual challenge that confronts anyone who feels that actions taken by fiat are justifiable—a challenge that has engaged theologians and, on occasion, former department chairs. Finally, there are pragmatic reasons to try to reconcile the original-language protocol with the teaching of texts that an instructor cannot read in the original.

Whereas the undergraduate version of our World Literature before 1500 course has now gone through all the bureaucratic procedures to become part of the curriculum, the graduate version of the course is being offered for the first time and on an ad hoc basis. Before the course can be given its own number and its own place in the *Graduate School Bulletin*, some colleagues may need to be convinced that the protocol regarding knowledge of original languages does not apply.

In fact, the case of graduate courses in world literature poses the most formidable challenge—which is why I indicated above that there is a chasm between the undergraduate and the graduate version of the world literature course. When applied to teaching, the protocol does not require that students read each foreign language text in its original language, since even the most polyglot graduate students may not read the same languages as the instructor in a given course. Nor does the protocol prevent instructors from including in an undergraduate course certain key texts that they may be unable to read in the original. For example, a Greekless instructor might include Homer in a course on narrative or Aristophanes in a course on satire. But the protocol does require that instructors be able to clarify exegetical issues by recourse to the original text—in most cases in an undergraduate course and in virtually all cases in a graduate course. It is at the graduate level, where instruction is traditionally defined as professional training, that there is supposed to be no gap between research and teaching protocols. How then can a comparative literature department justify offering graduate courses with a heavy dose of texts that the instructor cannot read in the original?

The answer does not lie, I think, in setting forth an alternative model of scholarship, one that configures literary study in terms of extensive rather than intensive analysis. Such models are, to be sure, available, stretching from the venerable example of Northrop Frye to the more recent work of Franco Moretti, whose manifestos call for "distant reading," "where distance is . . . not an obstacle but a specific form of knowledge: fewer elements, hence a sharper sense of overall interconnection" (1).

The problem with using a version of distant reading as a research paradigm to justify teaching world literature courses—and I'm using Moretti's term to refer to all approaches that sacrifice close reading in favor of a broader perspective—is that the great majority of literary scholars still employ techniques of close reading in preference to grand overviews. And since graduate training in the humanities is generally understood as the inculcation of techniques that the teachers themselves actually practice or are qualified to practice, it would seem that the mere existence of a research protocol that emphasizes distant reading instead of close reading would not provide sufficient justification for the teaching of world literature by members of the nondistant majority.

But graduate education is not strictly a matter of techniques; it also involves the acquisition of knowledge. Although the literary disciplines originally set up shop by prescribing the body of knowledge—starting with the classical canon and moving on to canonical national literary traditions—that counts as the context for specific sorts of expertise, contemporary scholars are familiar with disciplinary protocols requiring systematic knowledge that stops short of expertise. To justify the study of world literature, we need only recognize that there are countervailing protocols that would limit the scope and force of the original-language protocol.

Even among practitioners of close literary analysis, research protocols often require some familiarity with texts that lie beyond one's expertise and perhaps beyond one's linguistic competence. That is to say, there are texts that one needs to have read even if one cannot read them in the original. It is precisely for this reason that graduate students take courses in which they read texts in translation. While one may not be qualified to write a learned article or book about a given text unless one can read it in the original language, one may, precisely in order to be qualified to write about other texts that one knows in the original language, need to be acquainted with texts that one can read only in translation. For example, students of the English novel, especially the early novel, need to know Cervantes and the Spanish picaresque tradition. There are many other examples, but, for reasons that will become clear, I offer one that is hypothetical.

Imagine a scholar of eighteenth-century French literature who is working on Voltaire's philosophical tale *Micromégas*, a satiric narrative in which interplanetary travelers whose size is proportional to the vast size of their home planets visit Earth, a planet whose inhabitants are, from the perspective of the space travelers, microscopic creatures. Voltaire's conceit is obviously indebted to Swift, and even if our imaginary French scholar does not read English, the disciplinary protocols of literary scholarship would require the scholar to have read *Gulliver's Travels*, if only in translation.

Now, it might be objected that the need for a Voltaire scholar to be familiar with *Gulliver* depends on the fact that Voltaire and Swift are part of a single European satiric tradition. World literature, the objection might continue, is different precisely because its authors are often not part of a single tradition and therefore do not know one another's work. In the absence of a coherent tradition, is there a disciplinary protocol that would require the Voltaire scholar to know *Gulliver*? What if there were no question of historical influence? What if *Gulliver's Travels* had been written, say, in Persian and had not been translated into French or any other European language until very recently? What if Voltaire had no inkling about the existence of *Gulliver's Travels* and the similarities between the two works were purely coincidental? Would this coincidence, once it came to light, oblige the Voltaire scholar to read the book?

Well, if one thinks cynically about the workings of disciplinary protocols in the humanities, one might answer that the Voltaire scholar would feel obliged to read the Persian *Gulliver* only if other Voltaire scholars had been writing about it. But if one took a more high-minded stance and posed the question in terms of the obligation to obtain the deepest and most complete knowledge of the object of one's research, the answer would be more relevant to our purposes. Would the Voltaire scholar's understanding of *Micromégas* be enhanced by a familiarity with the Persian *Gulliver* or with any other esoteric work that used differences in scale to satiric effect? I think there would be fairly general agreement that it would: such familiarity would give the scholar an insight into the realm of possibilities that are contained in the literary genre or mode that the disparate writers are using and into the way an individual text takes its place in that array of possibilities.

Treated this way, genre becomes more of an anthropological than a historical concept. But following a genre across two or more of the separate traditions that make up world literature does not require a scholar or teacher to be anthropological in the distant mode of, say, Frye. That our Voltaire scholar was obliged to know *Gulliver*, even if only from a distance, does not transform the scholar from a close reader to a distant reader, any more than being able to place a given work or author in a specific historical tradition would transform a scholar into a distant reader. One could place the *Iliad* in the context of the Western epic tradition; one could also place it in the context of national epics or oral epics around the world. Neither contextualization requires one to be less focused on the analysis of the individual work; each enhances one's ability to carry out a close analysis.

It should be clear that the force of our hypothetical example is not that it provides a model of someone who needs to fill gaps—accomplished scholars and their acolytes can fill gaps on their own, without a formal course. On the contrary, the example demonstrates that there is a middle ground between filling gaps, on the one hand, and attaining expertise, on the other. We recognize, and have always recognized, the need for a systematic contextualization that falls short of anyone's expertise. What we haven't recognized is that courses on world literature can provide that sort of contextualization.

The book that we know as *Gulliver's Travels* was first published in 1726 as *Travels into Several Remote Nations of the World*. The remoteness of the strange worlds that Gulliver discovered is, of course, illusory. The satiric effect comes not only from the differences in scale between Gulliver and the Lilliputians and between Gulliver and the Brobdingnagians but also from the shock of recognition when one realizes that the exotic creatures are "just like us," that their smallness or greatness or (especially in the case of the Yahoos) bestiality renders our weaknesses and vices all the more ridiculous or contemptible. The tiny size of the Lilliputians and their empire, for example, makes their pride all the more absurd. Like-wise, in *Micromégas*, the enormous size of the extraterrestrial visitors and of the universe itself makes a mockery of the human pride that is encountered on earth.

But even if the device of having Englishmen or Earthlings appear small from the perspective of prodigiously large outsiders lends itself to satire against pride, the difference between Swift's work and Voltaire's tells us not only about the difference between their cultural situations but also about the range of satiric possibilities that inheres in the same perspectivist conceit. Whereas Swift's satire is grounded in the Christian tradition, according to which pride is the chief sin and source of all vices, Voltaire's satire mocks—among other things[4]—the pride, embedded in Christianity itself, that places humankind at the center of divine creation:

> un petit animalcule en bonnet carré . . . dit qu'il savait tout le secret, que cela se trouvait dans la *Somme* de saint Thomas; il regarda de haut en bas les deux habitants célestes; il leur soutint que leurs personnes, leurs mondes, leurs soleils, leurs étoiles, tout était fait uniquement pour l'homme. A ce discours, nos deux voyageurs se laissèrent aller

l'un sur l'autre en étouffant de ce rire inextinguible qui, selon Homère, est le partage des dieux. (ch. 7)

a little animalcule in a square hat [a doctor of the Sorbonne] . . . said that he knew the secret, which was to be found in the *Summa* of Saint Thomas Aquinas; he scanned the celestial travelers from head to toe; he informed them that they and their planets, their suns and stars, were all made solely for the sake of humankind. In response to this speech, our two travelers doubled over and began choking with the inextinguishable laughter that, according to Homer, is the prerogative of the gods. (trans. mine)

The similarities and differences between Swift's and Voltaire's use of the same satiric device would be of interest to Voltaire scholars (and to Swift scholars), I submit, even if the two authors were not part of the same European tradition. And the value of reading them both would override the disadvantage of having to read one of the texts in translation. To be sure, in a university course on world literature the relation between my hypothetical Persian *Gulliver* and Voltaire's Enlightenment *Micromégas* might be examined in terms of the nature of the genre rather than in terms of the history of European satire. Likewise my department's actual course World Literature before 1500 is organized on the basis of genre—lyric and epic—and I imagine that genre would be the organizing principle of most world literature courses. The study of a genre is by nature open-ended and subject to continual revision: each newly discovered instance can alter our understanding of all the others. Such an open-ended approach to genres, as opposed to one that treats genres and traditions as strictly definable phenomena—as the hypothetical example of the Persian *Gulliver* reveals—is in fact an established research protocol, that is readily applicable to the study of world literature.

It is easy to imagine that, ranging across the world, one might find other examples of the same device being used to mock other varieties of pride or parochialism. Each new example would give us the perspective of another culture, while altering our understanding of the genre. Perhaps there would even be a tale of divine beings who encounter a race of diminutive creatures, not in *bonnets carrés* but in tweedy or posttweedy attire, a race whose convictions about what deserves its attention seem, from an outside perspective, more than a tad parochial and whose stern pronouncements would, in the denouement of the tale, be met with the inextinguishable laughter of the gods.

Notes

I am grateful to Paul Losensky for insights and observations that helped me formulate the issues addressed in this essay.

1. For an overview of the evolution of world literature from the great-powers paradigm to one that is open to works from non-European and even nonliterate cultures, see Damrosch, ch. 3 ("From the Old World to the Whole World").

2. The colleague who has spearheaded the development of the world literature courses in my department represents such an ideal, since he has linguistic and cultural expertise outside the Western tradition. But for the purposes of the discussion that follows, I am not assuming that world literature courses should be taught only by those with such optimal credentials.

3. The resistance to world literature courses is not entirely attributable to the original-language protocol. One needs to acknowledge the persistent notion that canonical European works are intrinsically better than noncanonical or non-European works and therefore more worthy to be taught. Since this prejudice is not specific to comparative literature and since the present essay is not the place for a foray into the culture wars, I sidestep the issue of literary merit.

4. For an analysis of *Micromégas* that focuses on Voltaire's ideas about intellectual method, see Kenshur, ch. 4.

Works Cited

Damrosch, David. *What Is World Literature?* Princeton: Princeton UP, 2003. Print.

Kenshur, Oscar. *Dilemmas of Enlightenment: Studies in the Rhetoric and Logic of Ideology.* Berkeley: U of California P, 1993. Print. The New Historicism: Studies in Cultural Poetics 26.

Moretti, Franco. *Graphs, Maps, Trees: Abstract Models for a Literary History.* London: Verso, 2005. Print.

Swift, Jonathan. Travels into Several Remote Nations of the World, *by Lemuel Gulliver; or,* Gulliver's Travels, *by Jonathan Swift.* Comp. Lee Jaffe. Jaffe Bros., n.d. Web. 25 Jan. 2008.

Voltaire. *Contes en vers et en prose.* Ed. Sylvain Menant. *Gallica: Bibliothèque numerique de la bibliothèque nationale de France.* Bibliothèque Nationale de France, 1998. Web. 7 Apr. 2008.

Jane O. Newman

The Afterlives of the Greeks; or, What Is the Canon of World Literature?

An Afterlife

In fall 2002, Wole Soyinka published "The Isle of Polyphemus," a short essay in which he describes traveling to the West Bank to visit Bir Zeit University. Crossing a checkpoint into Ramallah, he observes a shepherd, who instead of using the road moves his herd through a gully "of stone and scrub," thereby avoiding the "deep gutter that had been cut across the tarmac" to prevent easy passage to the other side. In a "flash," Soyinka writes, the image of "Ulysses among the Cyclops, trapped in the cave of the one-eyed Polyphemus" sprang to mind. He goes on to read both the shepherd's detour and the political standoff between Ariel Sharon and Yasir Arafat through the lens of the Homeric hero's wily deeds. Soyinka's use of a scene from the Western canon as an "irresistible metaphor" of contemporary political conditions in the Middle East should come as no surprise. His *The Bacchae of Euripides: A Communion Rite* (1973) is, as Chantal Zabus has argued, an elegant "de-Aryanizing" revision of the Attic tragedy. The aptness of the collocation of the ancient and the modern in "The Isle of Polyphemus" may be debated nevertheless. Aren't these two cases of resistance really too different to be juxtaposed? The conundrum of Homer's Odysseus is after all an ancient fiction, and the Palestinian shepherd must circumvent all-too-real barriers in the here and now. Moreover, for whom is Soyinka's juxtaposition of Polyphemus and Sharon legible in the first place? Is it not only—and too narrowly—for those educated in the Western tradition? Yet even if students do understand the reference, they may find Soyinka's rereading of Homer too political and thus irrelevant to their classroom concerns. Conversely, activists could find the reference to the canon merely opportunistic, the occasion for an already world-famous author to display his literary expertise. How, then, is the afterlife of the Greeks to be read responsibly and compellingly in our fraught world?

World Literature and the Canon in the Undergraduate Classroom

The challenge of reading "The Isle of Polyphemus" exemplifies some of the issues involved in developing a methodology for studying world literature in the undergraduate classroom. Often identified with Eurocentrism, world literature has recently been redefined by Vilashini Cooppan, David Damrosch, Sarah Lawall, and Kristin Ross,[1] all of whom assume that an updated version of the subject will allow the interrogation of "literature and cultural production in a global context" (Ross 667) in richer ways than comparative literature, for example, a discipline also often dismissed (perhaps too quickly) as an outmoded artifact of only European concern (see Spivak; Pratt; and Lionnet). In the light of such critiques, many United States programs in comparative literature began at the end of the 1990s to rethink the shape of their curricula. Comparative literature at the University of California, Irvine (UCI), did likewise between 2000 and 2002.[2]

The new undergraduate curriculum at UCI did indeed move away from the European literatures–based model of a chronological survey by stressing instead several alternative ways to study global literature. A required three-quarter sequence of sophomore-level courses introduced students to the study of a geographically and chronologically broad selection of texts by teaching them to read literature and other forms of cultural expression in three modes:

> intertextually: texts in dialogue with other texts originally written in different languages and from different cultures and periods (e.g.,

Homer, Vergil, and Dante; Dante, Gloria Naylor, and Nuruddin Farah)

comparatively in a historically intensive way: the in-depth study of a single period or of similar periods in at least two different cultures (e.g., Chikamatsu, Lessing, Prévost, and Saikaku)

using the lens of genre: comparative approaches to autobiography, for example (Augustine, Rousseau, and Alice Partnoy)

Students were also required to take two upper-division courses in literary theory. The prior foreign-language literature requirement (two upper-division courses in a single non-English literary tradition, taught in the language) was made more flexible in order to accommodate not only students presenting European languages but also those presenting Chinese, Japanese, or Korean. A third year of language study and two upper-division courses in translation in the same tradition may now be offered to fulfill the requirement, when that language is an Asian language. (Only the first two years of Arabic are taught at UCI; it and other languages could nevertheless be accommodated in this model.) The major was rounded out by a series of topic-variable lectures and seminar courses that must deal with texts from more than one language tradition and that are theoretically organized or interdisciplinary in nature. Study abroad in the junior year is actively encouraged. A capstone seminar in which majors investigate the comparative method in a single set of issues and texts was also required.

While the new curriculum reflected nearly two years of faculty-based discussion, there was little input from the undergraduate population at UCI in the course of these deliberations. We also did not spend sufficient time discussing the capstone seminar. Most important, however, and perhaps as a result of the absence of undergraduate voices, we failed to consider the possible reception of our faculty-initiated innovations by twenty-first-century students, whose familiarity with the polemics of the canon wars of the end of the twentieth century, which motivated our desire to reinvent the major, de facto differed from our own. How could we teach them where the world of comparative literature had traditionally been, and why did we feel compelled to redefine it? In turn, could teaching them to understand the serial construction of such diverse worlds in the discipline be part of the curriculum for advanced students?

To address these questions, I proposed a course entitled The Afterlives of the Greeks; or, The Challenge of "Global Literature." Following

Soyinka's lead, the course took as its central question the implications of comparison between texts by the stalwarts of the traditional canon—in this case, the ancient Greeks—and the reworking of those texts by postmodern and global writers. A series of twinned texts was assigned: Homer, Sophocles, and Euripides, on the one hand, and Soyinka, Derek Walcott, and Seamus Heaney, on the other.[3] My purpose was to study both the individual dialogues constructed between these texts and the broader theoretical question of whether analyzing such dialogues was a means to understanding the politics and poetics of canon production in comparative literature. The challenge with respect to this second issue was to steer clear of a "happy" model of curricular inclusionism that Edward Said associates with an unthinking capitalism—"free markets, open and unregulated competition . . . [and] decentralized or deemphasized planning" (Said, "Globalizing" 66)—as we expanded our range. Such an approach would replace the old Eurocentric canon, to be sure, but would also run the risk of masking the relations of power on which such "progressivist" knowledge projects are based (Chow 73; Shih). The Afterlives course was thus intended to involve the students in thinking through the politics of text choice in ways that would allow them to make sense of the comparative literature major, while also avoiding what René Wellek already in the 1940s dismissed as a "vague sentimental cosmopolitanism" associated with the "easy" opening out of the reading list (qtd. in Cooppan 14).

The complexity of these questions addressed the challenge of giving the exceedingly complex texts their due, but because we had no more than one academic quarter, the Afterlives course only partially succeeded. That is, we ended up privileging the comparative reading of the individual texts in terms of their respective embeddedness in a welter of local political contexts and sociocultural traditions, spending a great deal of time researching both the role of the ancient Athenian ephebate (young male military class) in Sophocles's *Philoktetes*, for example (see Vidal-Naquet; Winkler), and the position of the poet as commentator on political, religious, and economic conditions in an equally militarized Northern Ireland in Heaney's powerful reworking of Sophocles's play, *The Cure at Troy* (see Denard; Brazeau). As fascinating as these parallels were, our concern with them left little time to focus on the relevance of our case studies for developing a general model for the comparative study of world literature. A subgroup of the students from the class thus signed on for an independent study the following quarter to continue our work.

The Participants

The Students. The group working on the second course consisted of three women and one man, ranging from sophomore to junior status. Although ethnically diverse, their intellectual commitments and institutional backgrounds were similar; all had attended large public high schools and had graduated between 1999 and 2002. Two were declared English majors in their freshman year. Of the two others, who were undeclared, one describes knowing from the outset what he did *not* want to study—namely, a curriculum that "reminded [him] of a heavy, tattered old tome that was [his] literature book in [his] eleventh-grade English class." Another remarked that she wanted to shy away from courses that "were all too reminiscent of [her] Advanced Placement English literature course" taken in her senior year. Three of the students had chosen the comparative literature major after taking the new introductory sequence, citing in particular the "international" and "interdisciplinary" dimension of the classes as contributing to the appeal of the major.

The Instructor. I hold a PhD in comparative literature and specialize in sixteenth- and seventeenth-century European literature and culture. I was comfortable working with the ancient texts in the original Greek in the first course. In both quarters of this project, however, I had to research new areas—Nigerian, Caribbean, Irish, and Argentinian literature and history—along with the students. This challenge provided a significant pedagogical benefit by upsetting the hierarchical professor-student relationship that normally characterizes the undergraduate classroom.[4]

Teaching the Canon, Teaching the World

In the second course, I introduced the historical background of the changes in the undergraduate curriculum in comparative literature at UCI by locating them in the context of developments in the discipline in the United States in the post–World War II and post-cold-war periods by assigning the guidelines for programs and departments developed by the American Comparative Literature Association (ACLA) in a sequence of reports from 1965, 1975, and 1993 (available in Bernheimer, *Comparative Literature*). I asked the students to analyze our new curriculum in the light of disciplinary developments over the past nearly half century as they were articulated in these reports. The students' commentary on the history of comparative literature at both the national and local levels reflected their ability to understand the historicity of disciplines in general as well as the specific changes that United States comparative literature had undergone. Although most had not thought previously about the historical constructedness of their majors or about the university's relation to extracurricular political and social factors and events, they were intrigued by the claim, made in the 1993 report in particular, that there was a link between their studies and political and social forces outside the classroom. In this context we had a fascinating discussion about school reform in post-Hussein Iraq, which then led the students to consider the political and historical context of their own schooling in the new American empire.

The students noted with special interest the argument that comparative literature had been in crisis since its very inception, on the one hand, and the claim that it was now entering, just prior to and during their college years, a new period of crisis in connection with the era of globalization, on the other (see Bernheimer, "Introduction"; Wellek; and Saussy). One student suggested that this crisis would be permanent because of the "permeability of the discipline" and that this permeability was a good thing, as it meant that students could be involved in shaping their studies. Another pointed out that the shift to a more inclusive canon of domestic multicultural texts recommended by many in the Bernheimer volume appeared to have been accompanied by "decreasing the emphasis on . . . linguistic aptitude," a trend that represented an ironic loss, she said, as it would eventually lead to a monolingualism at odds with the international aspirations of the field. Indeed, all the students remarked on the need to restore to the discussion of comparative literature the international component that had so appealed to them in the first place.

There was nevertheless surprisingly little reaction at this stage to the resounding silence of the 1993 ACLA report in particular on the study of the older canonical texts that the students had read in the earlier class. That internationalism seems more important than domestic multiculturalism and the here and now more in need of attention than the long ago is understandable for this generation of students, whose college careers began just before or at the time of the events of September 11 and were continuing during the wars in Afghanistan and Iraq. It may well have been both the pressure of world events and the persistently presentist hue of most recommendations to globalize the curriculum that made the question of whether to study the classics from any culture nearly invisible (on presentism, see Biddick). Cooppan observes that developing a "new pedagogy" is "not just a question of recognizing the modern emergence of a transnational, transregional, global literature" but that one must read "older works and older categories of belonging . . . in global ways" as well (18).[5] When I proposed that we might consider ancient Greek tragedy as also international and indeed as a culture of the world, the students responded that many of the authors of the materials on changes in the discipline of comparative literature we had read would not define the globe in this way. A complex mechanism of canon formation was thus already in play here, with only select texts counting as global.

In the next phase of the second class, I assigned readings that took the question of curricular reform and methods of teaching world literature as their focus. Although our main interest was in the college-level curricula covered by Damrosch, Cooppan, and Ross, I included one article about the teaching of world literature at the high school level (Reese) in order to encourage the students to reflect on their own secondary school experiences. In these essays, the students identified several models that appeared to guarantee more inclusive courses but that ultimately did not address the questions of canonicity or internationalism in satisfactory ways.

Two models that resembled each other in their discussion of how to create the conditions for a more inclusive comparison were Damrosch's description of a new literary geometry ("Literary Study" 128 and "World Enough") based on the ellipsis and Cooppan's discussion of the relational thinking that guided the curriculum of the new world literature course at Yale ("World Literature"). Damrosch argues that every case of literary study should have "two foci." Studying the culture of the metropolitan center of London, for example, should always involve the consideration of "the wider waxing and waning [of] Empire," as these two spaces overlap ("Literary Study" 128, 130).[6] Subsequently, he extended the figure of the ellipsis to accommodate "multitemporal comparison" ("World Enough" 284) in a way that the students now began to appreciate. Similarly, Cooppan describes the "lateral networks" behind the constellations of texts assigned at Yale, introducing the *Ansatzpunkt*, or point of engagement for reading developed by Erich Auerbach, as an organizing element (15). In that course, specialist lecturers first "embed each text in a highly particular culture"; a generalist lecturer then moves out from each beginning "point" in centrifugal fashion, to show how the text had been subject to "expansion, transmission, and exchange" (20).

Both these models appeared to encourage, if not guarantee, the internationalism that originally attracted the students to comparative literature, even as the models also began to reveal some constraints with which the students took issue. Damrosch's definition of the canon of world literature produced by his elliptical model, for example, as containing texts that become "world literature by being received into the space of a foreign culture" ("World Enough" 282) and that "gain in translation" (288), on the one hand, and his corresponding honesty about the limits imposed on scholars and students precisely by reading most texts "only in translation" and thus not fully connected to its "culture of origin" (285, 295), on the other, exposed the limits of his method.[7] Cooppan's equally candid admission that the Yale course "had little place for" what Franco Moretti "identifies as the 99.5% of non-canonical literature" (19) struck the students as equally problematic, especially when I reminded them of the limitations of our first course, in which the expansion to the globe similarly occurred only through Nobel Prize–winning authors and texts.

Ross's allegorical model of comparison initially seemed most attractive to the students, because it appeared to guarantee more fully the expansion of the canon. According to Ross, at the heart of the canon wars of the 1980s and 1990s was the limitation set by conceiving of the issue of text choice as one of representation. If coverage were really the issue, how could enough specialists possibly be hired to teach the world of world literature? Citing the work of Walter Benjamin and Paul de Man, Ross rejects "symbolic notion[s]" of both coverage and field expertise that suggest that works of literature must be the parts that embody the whole of a particular literature and culture and history; she recommends, rather, an allegorical approach that "preserves the differences of each historically situated and embedded experience" and text while also "drawing a relation between those experiences" (672). One tradition is to be read in terms of another precisely not in order to establish sameness between the two cases; the purpose instead is to make the specificity of both cases legible. The allegorical model made sense to the students, because it provided the opportunity for addressing multiple cultures and issues, thus accounting at a theoretical level for how to accommodate missing elements in the curriculum while also permitting in-depth research. Yet it seemed unsettlingly centrifugal and also did not guarantee an international perspective. Indeed, by offering no mandate at all concerning the terms of the allegory, courses could have an all-local focus all the time.

After reading these essays, the students realized that both the obligation to read a countercanon (which was *the* question of the 1980s and early 1990s) and a recourse to theoretical models of reading (which begged the question of internationalism) had yielded models that strangely enabled both more traditional and more random courses than ever before. Any and all—or just a single set of—texts, periods, and cultures could become the object of study in a world literature course so defined. In the face of an anticanon that seemed both infinitely expanding and ever the same, were there actually any constraints? This was an important issue for this group of students in particular, all of whom planned to pursue graduate study. What did it mean to become a competent professional in a discipline (comparative literature) that had few if any discernible principles of competency? And how could an international perspective be guaranteed?

We turned to a case study of comparative reading—namely, Sophocles's *Antigone* (fifth century BCE) and the Argentinian playwright Griselda Gambaro's *Antígona furiosa* (1986)—in order to consider what it might mean to acquire competency in comparative methods in a more inclusive global comp lit course.

Another Afterlife: Sophocles and Gambaro

I initially assigned not only Sophocles's and Gambaro's plays but also the French playwright Jean Anouilh's *Antigone*. In so doing, I hoped to remind the students of how wide the range of historical, geographic, and linguistic coordinates for the study of world literature could be. We later zeroed in on the Sophocles and Gambaro texts. After the students read both plays, I assigned essays on the reception of the ancient play by the nineteenth-century German philosopher Georg Wilhelm Friedrich Hegel—essays written by two accomplished UCI graduate students (see Miller; Rust). Sharing my graduate students' essays with the undergraduates was designed to introduce the undergraduates to the nature of the graduate work to which they all aspired. I also assigned an article about how Sophocles's *Antigone* was taught in nineteenth- and early-twentieth-century United States colleges, where it was recommended for its "peculiarly female story of religious obligation, family duty, and martyrdom to true womanhood" (Winterer 88).

We then tracked the perhaps inadvertent but nevertheless consistent penetration of both these readings into two further discourses. The first discourse had characterized the students' high school classrooms; we accessed it through an analysis of the California Department of Education guidelines for the Language Arts curriculum in grades 9 through 12 (*Grades*), where *Antigone* appears as one of the mandated texts in the Language Arts curriculum. While the suggested CDE approach to ancient tragedy recommends that students learn how to "read and respond to historically or culturally significant works of literature that reflect their studies of history and social science," the students noted that in their experience the play had been taught only in terms of the universal themes also recommended for study by the CDE and thus with little attention to its historical specificity. The significance of the play was most often assessed in terms that appeared indebted to both Hegelian and domesticizing interpretations.

To trace how difficult it is to shake this dominant reception of Sophocles's play, we turned in a second set of assignments to a more localizing analysis of the text, by William Blake Tyrell and Larry J. Bennett (1998), which situates it in the context of fifth-century BCE Athenian colonial politics. We then juxtaposed Tyrell and Bennett's reading to a wide range of post-1998 criticism on the tragedy that I had asked the students to locate and share with one another.[8] By placing the most recent criticism on *Antigone* in dialogue with Tyrell and Bennett's reading, we were able to see how a broad spectrum of readers and critics, including classicists, literary-historical generalists, feminist theorists, and secondary school teachers, continued to read *Antigone* as the students had in high school— namely, as a text that addresses citizenship, ethics, tragic recognition, and gender roles in universalizing terms. The localizations of this play in particular (in Tyrell and Bennett's reading) and of ancient Greek tragedy in general available in reputable historical scholarship from the 1990s could thus be easily ignored, it appeared.[9] These assignments allowed one side of the process of canon formation to become visible to the students, since they were able to track the persistence of approaches to the ancient play that made it into a poster child for timelessness.

Gambaro's *Antígona furiosa* was not a text that the students had encountered previously. Having familiarized themselves intimately with Sophocles's text, they were easily able to provide excellent close readings of the Argentinian play, not only insofar as it presents a shortened version of the story as told posthumously by Antigone but also in terms of the

play's avant-garde staging techniques, such as suspending the title character in a cage above the stage and identifying the figure of Creon by a kind
of portable shell that several of the actors wear in turn. After engaging in
a bibliographic research project like the one they had done for Sophocles's
play, the students discovered that even as critics acknowledged the consis-
tency of theme (the relation of the individual to the state) between the
ancient and the modern plays, the smallish body of criticism that addressed Gambaro's text nearly always read it only in the context of Argentina's devastating Dirty War (1976–83) and thus as a political allegory.
The critical response to this lesser-read modern text thus situated it in a
canon of its own—namely, that of political literature, as evident in the
work of Fredric Jameson and in Ahmad's critique of Jameson's category of
"national allegory." (I had the students read both Jameson and Ahmad to
introduce them to these terms.) If one ignored the aesthetic and drama-
turgic issues that had jumped out at the students in their first readings,
this kind of canon formation suggested that readers could find in Gambaro's play issues of only local significance.

In the Sophocles-Gambaro example, the students witnessed the creation of an abyss between the two plays in the history of their critical reception and saw how canonical works are often read, well, canonically, as
articulating universals, as opposed to how their successors are often read
and perhaps also taught—that is, as only local works. The students won-
dered whether studying precisely the mechanics of such bilateral canon
formation of both literature and method might not be central to professional comparatism. They proposed designing the capstone seminar for
comparative literature majors along the lines of that approach.

Teaching World Literature and the Canon

The students proposed canon formation as a key issue to be covered in
the capstone course. Since they were not sure that the bibliographic work
they had done could be achieved in a single quarter, they suggested that
an analysis of several different editions of anthologies, such as the *Norton
Anthology of Literature in English* or the *Norton Anthology of World Literature*, be assigned instead, so that students could see that the canon
does indeed shift. They also recommended assigning a pair of texts like
the Sophocles-Gambaro plays for closer examination, in order to introduce what they came to call the familiarity-unfamiliarity dyad. One text

should come from the so-called traditional canon, the other from what they variously described as the "underrepresented," the "culturally other," and the "unfamiliar" canon. In an attempt to guarantee the international dimension, they declared that the second text should "culturally dislocate" the first in an explicit way and, if possible, should force students to cross "geographical and temporal borders," thereby creating "discomfort" with the idea of a single location of writing and reading. The pairing of a text that had received broad reception and could thus function as what one student called an "axis of reference" for how critical orthodoxies get constructed over time with a text that had been narrowly received would require students to study precisely the fact of their own learned familiarity and unfamiliarity with various traditions and methods of reading. Such pairing would thus dispel the idea that there is only one canon or one correct reading of a text. Finally, essays on the disciplinary development of comparative literature should be assigned. Students must understand that they are "part and parcel of their discipline's development," one student stated.

At the end of her play, Gambaro has her protagonist, Antígona, declaim in metatheatrical fashion that she will "*always* want to bury Polyneices" (158). The line captures nicely the ability of scenarios from the ancient canon, like hers and like the Ulysses-Polyphemus standoff that Soyinka describes, to remain uncannily consistent even as they circulate into new contexts. Antigone will always want to bury Polyneices, just as Ulysses will always outfox the Cyclops, regardless of the places and ways in which they do so and regardless of the reasons why. Yet it is precisely the dialogue between these continuities and the specificity of their various locations that is significant in all cases. Reading a diverse canon—Sophocles with Gambaro, Homer with the Middle East—allows this dialogue and the problematics of canonicity to emerge.

Notes

This essay is the product of a close collaborative effort by the author and four undergraduate students: Michele Goffeau, Kristin Noone, Jenny Sohn, and Martin Vega. Selections from papers by Noone, Sohn, and Vega are quoted in the essay. Without the students' commitment to and assistance in working though the issues discussed, the project described here would not have been possible. The students should thus be considered true coinvestigators in every sense of the word.

1. The easy conflation of world literature with a Eurocentric worldview has of course been the object of debate by comparatists since the mid–twentieth century, when Friederich, for example, dismissed the world literature course as merely so many anthologized "snippets" of "NATO literature" (30–31). See also Pizer; Moretti; and Baucom. For a reading of the original Goethean trope of *Weltliteratur*, see Auerbach; Pizer; and Strich.

2. Since this essay was written, the Department of Comparative Literature at UC Irvine has further redesigned its undergraduate curriculum. Please consult the departmental Web site for details.

3. The selection of primarily anglophone moderns was a problem, of course, as was the fact that Heaney, Soyinka, and Walcott are all winners of the Nobel Prize for Literature and thus not at all marginalized even if they are global. On the problems of promoting a new kind of hypercanonicity even as the range of texts expands, see Damrosch, "World Literature"; Cooppan.

4. Ross examines the "myth of pedagogy" that often hinders the development of new curricula (669). The students were fascinated by Ross's explication of this myth, and we discussed at length how to design an undergraduate course that would work against infantilizing students, by training them in research techniques (bibliography and online research, for example) and by involving them in curriculum design. On the need for good "sites of pedagogy" that teach students to produce knowledge on their own, see Di Leo, Jacobs, and Lee.

5. For an intriguing addendum and method for reading texts in and as belonging to "deep time," see Dimock.

6. The formulation is reminiscent of Damrosch's late colleague Edward Said's notion of contrapuntalism. See Said, *Culture*.

7. Damrosch clearly states that language learning is crucial to the study of world literature and strongly advocates that it be more diverse and better ("World Enough" 290–91). But he makes a virtue of the necessity of accepting that sufficiently broad and deep "improvement[s] in . . . language study" will not occur by veering off into a discussion about the interesting claims that translation theorists make.

8. Each student located citations to no fewer than ten articles or chapters on *Antigone* that were written after Tyrell and Bennett's book. This assignment yielded references to twenty-seven additional critical readings. Each student read and reported to the class on six or seven of these interpretations. This bibliographic work proved popular with the students, as they both improved their library research skills and learned how to track critical trends.

9. See Loraux; Vidal-Naquet; and Vernant, all works to which Tyrell and Bennett's work is indebted methodologically. Also see Easterling; Winkler; and Zeitlin and Winkler. For a critical assessment of these trends, see Griffin.

Works Cited

Ahmad, Aijaz. "Jameson's Rhetoric of Otherness and the 'National Allegory.'" *Social Text* 17 (1987): 3–25. Print.

Auerbach, Erich. "Philology and *Weltliteratur*." Trans. Edward Said and Marie Said. *Centennial Review* 13 (1969): 1–17. Print.

Baucom, Ian. "Globallit. Inc.; or, The Cultural Logic of Global Literary Studies." *PMLA* 116.1 (2001): 158–72. Print.

Bernheimer, Charles, ed. *Comparative Literature in the Age of Multiculturalism.* Baltimore: Johns Hopkins UP, 1995. Print.

———. "Introduction: The Anxieties of Comparison." Bernheimer, *Comparative Literature* 1–17.

Biddick, Kathleen. "Bede's Blush: Postcards from Bali, Bombay, Palo Alto." *The Shock of Medievalism.* Durham: Duke UP, 1998. 83–101. Print.

Brazeau, Robert. "Thomas Kinsella and Seamus Heaney: Translation and Representation." *New Hibernia Review / Iris Éireannach Nua* 5.2 (2001): 82–98. Print.

Chow, Rey. "How (the) Inscrutable Chinese Led to Globalized Theory." *PMLA* 116.1 (2001): 69–74. Print.

Cooppan, Vilashini. "World Literature and Global Theory: Comparative Literature for the New Millennium." *Symplokê* 9.1–2 (2001): 15–43. Print.

Damrosch, David. "Literary Study in an Elliptical Age." Bernheimer, *Comparative Literature* 122–33.

———. "World Enough and Time." *What Is World Literature?* Princeton: Princeton UP, 2003. 281–303. Print.

———. "World Literature in a Postcanonical, Hypercanonical Age." Saussy 43–53.

Denard, Hugh. "Seamus Heaney, Colonialism, and the Cure. Sophoclean Re-visions." *Performing Arts Journal* 66 (2000): 1–18. Print.

Di Leo, Jeffrey, Walter Jacobs, and Amy Lee. "The Sites of Pedagogy." *Symplokê* 10.1–2 (2002): 7–12. Print.

Dimock, Wai Chee. *Through Other Continents: American Literature across Deep Time.* Princeton: Princeton UP, 2006. Print.

Easterling, P. E., ed. *The Cambridge Companion to Greek Tragedy.* Cambridge: Cambridge UP, 1997. Print.

Friederich, Werner. "Great Books versus 'World Literature.'" *"The Challenge of Comparative Literature" and Other Addresses.* Ed. William J. DeSua. Chapel Hill: U of North Carolina P, 1970. 25–35. Print.

Gambaro, Griselda. *Antígone furiosa.* Trans. Marguerite Feitlowitz. *Information for Foreigners: Three Plays.* Ed. Feitlowitz. Evanston: Northwestern UP, 1992. Print.

Grades Nine and Ten: English-Language Arts Content Standards. Adopted 1997. California State Board of Educ., 16 Oct. 2007. Web. 2 Feb. 2008.

Griffin, Jasper. "The Social Function of Attic Tragedy." *Classical Quarterly* 48.1 (1998): 39–62. Print.

Heaney, Seamus. *The Cure at Troy: A Version of Sophocles' Philoctetes.* New York: Farrar, 1961. Print.

Jameson, Fredric. "Third-World Literature in the Era of Multinational Capitalism." *Social Text* 15 (1986): 65–88. Print.

Lionnet, Françoise. "Spaces of Comparison." Bernheimer, *Comparative Literature* 165–74.

Loraux, Nicole. *The Children of Athena: Athenian Ideas about Citizenship and the Division between the Sexes.* Trans. Caroline Levine. Princeton: Princeton UP, 1993. Print.

Miller, Nichole E. "Blood and Beyond: *Antigone*, the Sublime, and Sacrifice." 2001. TS.

Moretti, Franco. "The Slaughterhouse of Literature." *Modern Language Quarterly* 61.1 (2000): 207–27. Print.

Pizer, John. "Goethe's 'World Literature' Paradigm and Contemporary Cultural Globalization." *Comparative Literature* 52.3 (2000): 213–27. Print.

Pratt, Mary Louise. "Comparative Literature and Global Citizenship." Bernheimer, *Comparative Literature* 58–65.

Reese, James D. "Learning for Understanding: The Role of World Literature." *English Journal* 91.5 (2002): 63–69. Print.

Ross, Kristin. "The World Literature and Cultural Studies Program." *Critical Inquiry* 19.4 (1993): 666–76. Print.

Rust, Jennifer. "Forensic Dramaturgy: Greek Tragedy as Legal Theory in Hegel and Benjamin." 2001. TS.

Said, Edward W. *Culture and Imperialism.* New York: Knopf, 1993. Print.

———. "Globalizing Literary Study." *PMLA* 116.1 (2001): 64–68. Print.

Saussy, Han, ed. *Comparative Literature in an Age of Globalization.* Baltimore: Johns Hopkins UP, 2006. Print.

Shih, Shu-mei. "Global Literature and the Technologies of Recognition." *PMLA* 119.1 (2004): 16–30. Print.

Sophocles. *Antigone. Sophocles I.* 2nd ed. Trans. and ed. David Grene and Richmond Lattimore. Chicago: U of Chicago P, 1991. 159–212. Print.

———. *Philoktetes.* Trans. Carl Philipps. Oxford: Oxford UP, 2003. Print.

Soyinka, Wole. *The Bacchae of Euripides: A Communion Rite. Collected Plays.* Vol. 1. Oxford: Oxford UP, 1973. 233–307. Print.

———. "The Isle of Polyphemus." *Nation.* The Nation, 29 Apr. 2002. Web. 25 Jan. 2008.

Spivak, Gayatri Chakravorty. *Death of a Discipline.* New York: Columbia UP, 2003. Print.

Strich, Fritz. *Goethe and World Literature.* London: Routledge, 1949. Print.

Tyrell, William Blake, and Larry J. Bennett. *Recapturing Sophocles'* Antigone. Lanham: Rowan, 1998. Print.

Vernant, Jean-Pierre. *Myth and Society in Ancient Greece.* Trans. Janet Lloyd. New York: Zone, 1990. Print.

Vidal-Naquet, Pierre. "Sophocles' *Philoctetes* and the Ephebeia." *Myth and Tragedy in Ancient Greece.* By Jean-Pierre Vernant and Vidal-Naquet. Trans. Janet Lloyd. New York: Zone, 1990. 161–79. Print.

Wellek, René. "The Crisis of Comparative Literature." *Concepts of Criticism.* By Wellek. Ed. Stephen G. Nichols. New Haven: Yale UP, 1963. 282–95. Print.

Winkler, John J. "The Ephebes' Song: *Tragôidia* and *Polis*." *Representations* 11 (1985): 26–62. Print.

Winterer, Caroline. "Victorian Antigone: Classicism and Women's Education in America, 1840–1900." *American Quarterly* 53.1 (2001): 70–93. Print.

Zabus, Chantal. "The Yoruba Bacchae: Wole Soyinka's De-Aryanization of Greek Civilization." *(Un)Writing Empire*. Ed. Theo D'haen. Amsterdam: Rodopi, 1998. 203–28. Print.

Zeitlin, Froma, and John Winkler, eds. *Nothing to Do with Dionysus? Athenian Drama in Its Social Context*. Princeton: Princeton UP, 1990. Print.

Carol J. Luther

Western Voices:
Western World Literature
in a Learning Community

When one teaches literature, it is often necessary to spend time on historical background in order for students to fully appreciate and understand a
work. Similarly, in history courses, literature is often discussed to enrich
students' understanding of a period. It only makes sense, then, that a
course that combines the two subjects should enhance students' study of
each.

At Pellissippi State Technical Community College, the decision was
made to experiment with a learning community format that would combine the courses Western World Literature and Western Civilization. The
learning community is considered not an advanced or honors class but
rather a double course that will help the average student integrate two
related subjects. Students register for both classes, which are scheduled
consecutively.

The learning community was developed to give students a more holistic learning experience and to remedy some problems uncovered in departmental reviews and discussions. Offering the courses together would,
we believed, encourage students

> to take their history and literature sequence at the same time. In this way, they could more easily connect the ideas and concepts presented in each of the courses. Students tend to take the history course in their first year, the literature course in their second.

> to take a history and literature sequence in which each subject complemented the other. Students usually prefer to take the American literature survey courses for the literature requirement, believing that they are more familiar with the material, but most majors require the Western civilization course.

> to achieve more in both courses. Our students generally have little high school background in these subjects. They are also often several years out of high school. Teaching the subjects together reinforces facts and ideas. The combination also encourages retention: students are reluctant to drop six hours, and the commitment motivates them to work harder.

A learning community is not simply a team-taught course. The two subjects are integrated under an overall theme, tests and assignments are jointly constructed, and students are expected to do a major project that shows that they have synthesized the material studied. Each instructor is responsible for a different subject rather than a different part of one subject. However, as in a team-taught course, the instructors must carefully integrate their approaches. I focus on the second-semester course that Toni McDaniel of the history department and I developed.[1]

The semester before the course was to be taught for the first time was allotted for planning. The overall title of the learning community was Western Voices. The texts were volume 2 of *The Norton Anthology of World Masterpieces* (Lawall et al.), Mary Shelley's *Frankenstein*, and Jackson J. Spielvogel's *Western Civilization* (comprehensive ed.). We supplemented the texts with handouts. The history instructor and I decided to focus on three overall questions as guides for our study throughout the semester:

> What do we mean by progress? Has the West progressed?
> Where does reason lead us?
> Are we essentially rational?

Students would explore answers offered by thinkers and writers of different periods. They were to collect quotations and examples from the literature and history. We also asked them to ponder the following question: Where should reason lead us?

Working out the day-to-day schedule was time-consuming, so those wishing to try this approach should allow ample preteaching time for planning. We divided the learning community into four periods: Enlightenment, French Revolution and Romanticism, Age of Ideology, and Twentieth Century. We scheduled some class periods entirely to history, some entirely to literature, and some to both. The history classes, being mostly lecture, were fairly predictable as to time needed to cover the material. Literature classes were more difficult to predict—more or less discussion might be needed—so we built some flexibility into the schedule. We also decided to include an experiential component by asking the dance instructor to teach students a dance from three of the major periods, because dance also reflects the zeitgeist and dances are fun to learn. (Students were not graded on that skill!)

During the planning semester, the minor projects and major project, both involving group work, were outlined as well, although some specific decisions were left to the teaching semester, when we would be able to take the measure of the class. For the minor project, each student had to select one activity from a list that we suggested. Minor-project presentations were spaced throughout the semester to coincide with the appropriate period. Students who chose the same topic worked together to develop a presentation. For the major project, which required the synthesis of ideas central to the course, students formed groups of their own to develop presentations for the last week of class.

We decided that the tests would be in three parts: identifications on history and literature, a take-home essay, and an in-class essay. At least one essay would connect literature and history; the other might focus on either history or literature or both as needed. In addition, students wrote a paper that involved some research, either on *Frankenstein* or on the poetry of World War I. One time we taught the course, students had the additional choice of compiling an annotated bibliography on a non-American author of the late-nineteenth or twentieth century. All grades counted for both classes except for the separate reading-quiz grades for literature and history.

During the first semester that the course was taught, the history instructor and I met about once a week to discuss issues; after the first semester, we did not need to meet so often. We met to write the tests and grade assignments. Usually we graded separately, then discussed to reach a consensus when we disagreed.

In selecting which works of literature to use, I had to make few changes in what I would normally have assigned, even though, in a sense, the history was driving the literature. The most change came in the twentieth-century section. The literature I had been using did not particularly reflect the topics to be covered in history: rise of fascism, communism and the Cold War, Vietnam, the Reagan years. The history of this period also had a more American focus. In the literature course I usually try to avoid American works, because students have the opportunity to take an American literature survey course, and I do not want to repeat material. Thus, several new works were substituted for the ones I ordinarily used. We also wanted to include films in the twentieth-century unit, as examples of the new art form of the century.

I do not mean to imply that the literature was presented only as an illustration of the history, but naturally we did consider the history connection more thoroughly than I would have in a separate course. I also presented the literature as literature, commenting on literary techniques, devices, themes, and so forth.

So we launched the course. Molière's *Tartuffe* and Voltaire's *Candide* were the literary selections for the Enlightenment period, the focus on satire and the struggle between reason and passion. The minor-project choice was to present selected scenes from *Tartuffe*. Students learned the minuet, a stately dance reflecting the control and order of the period. The connecting essay question on the test asked them to discuss *Candide* as advancing reform ideas of the Enlightenment.

The French Revolution and Napoleon were the emphasis for the Romantic period, which included English Romantic poems, selections from Rousseau's *Confessions*, and Shelley's *Frankenstein*. One choice for minor projects in this period was to debate whether Napoleon carried on the ideas of the Enlightenment or opposed them. Another was to review four or five historical-literary films from a list that we compiled. The connecting question on the exam asked students to compare and contrast Napoleon and Victor Frankenstein. The prompt for the question had students assume the persona of Robert Walton, the explorer who attempts to rescue Frankenstein in the Arctic and hears the story of his creature. We posited the idea that Walton later encounters Napoleon on Saint Helena and is struck by similarities (and contrasts) between the two men. Students wrote Walton's perceptions. For the dance in this unit, they learned the waltz, which calls for emotion: the partners focus more on each other than on the pattern of steps. Students are surprised to learn that the waltz was considered shocking when it was first introduced.

The age of ideology in history was reflected in the literature choices: sections of Marx's *Communist Manifesto;* Heine's poems; and Ibsen's *Hedda Gabler,* which previews the women's issues to be discussed in the twentieth century. Students could choose as the minor project to debate women's suffrage using arguments of the period. The connecting essay was to point to things in the history and literature that might have been the basis for Marx's ideas.

Modern consciousness and the twentieth century were represented by Sigmund Freud's "Dora," some World War I poems, Eliot's "The Love Song of J. Alfred Prufrock," Yeats's "The Second Coming," and Kafka's "Metamorphosis." Camus's "The Guest" illustrated existential ideas. Tadeusz Borowski's "Ladies and Gentlemen, to the Gas Chamber" reflected the horrors of the Holocaust, and Alexander Solzhenitsyn's "Matryona's Home" revealed life in Stalinist Russia. The last reading assigned, Tim O'Brien's "The Things They Carried" and some poems relating to the Vietnam War, helped students focus on decolonialization and America's role in Vietnam. The minor-project choices in this section asked them to collect oral histories on life during the Depression, World War II, or the period of social change in the 1950s and 1960s. Students were often able to interview parents, grandparents, or other people they knew, an opportunity that made for some enthusiastic and vivid projects. For example, one student's grandfather had been in a famous sea disaster in World War II. She had newsreel footage of the incident as well as newspaper accounts; she shared these with the class. Another student interviewed a faculty member who had been in a Vietnam War protest. For the dance experience, in one semester that we taught the course, students learned the Charleston and other dances of the 1920s; in another semester, they learned the dances of the 1960s. Both sets of dances showed the movement away from structure toward individualism and improvisation characteristic of the twentieth century.

The take-home essay for the twentieth-century test required students to consider the changes in warfare in World War I and in attitudes toward the war, using both the history and literature we had read. The in-class essay asked students to explain the historical context for one of the following stories and to discuss what comment the story was making on events of the time: "Ladies and Gentlemen, to the Gas Chamber," "Matryona's Home," and "The Things They Carried."

As students by now were working on their major thematic projects, we showed two films during class. One was Stanley Kubrick's *Dr. Strangelove* as the quintessential cold-war film, which we related back to the satire of the eighteenth century. The other was Tom Tykwer's *Lola rennt (Run, Lola, Run)*, a postmodern German film whose telling of a story suggests three different plots, depending on whether Lola is early, on time, or late for an important rendezvous with her boyfriend. While the characters exemplify alienated antiheroes with solipsistic values, they retain a love for each other that would please a Romantic.

The major project was a twenty-to-thirty-minute group presentation in which students attempted to answer the thematic questions posed at the beginning of the course through the words and ideas of the historical and literary figures studied. They also had to give their own answers to the questions from the perspective of the twenty-first century. They were asked to choose at least three figures from literature and history and answer the thematic questions from the figures' viewpoints. There had to be at least one literary figure and one historical figure. The format could be an interview show, a series of dramatic monologues, a *PowerPoint* presentation, a video presentation, clips from videos with analysis, a play, or some other format approved by the instructors. There had to be a visual, audio, or dramatic component; we did not want a simple lecture. Students were also required to have three sources in addition to their literature and history texts. For the written portion of this project, they submitted their scripts to the instructors, an analysis of why they chose the figures and the format that they used, an annotated works-cited page, and a program. Copies of the program were distributed to the class. Group members also submitted group and self-evaluations of the project, which were included as part of the grade.

Several groups presented videotaped projects, which varied in sophistication; some groups used music and special effects to enhance the video. Videotaping gave students the ability to correct errors or try different versions before submitting the final version. Other groups did live presentations in a talk-show format. One group assembled a very effective *PowerPoint* presentation. Some examples of the character combinations chosen by students one semester are Jean-Jacques Rousseau, Gregor Samsa, and Herbert Spencer; Sigmund Freud, his patient Dora, Mary Wollstonecraft, and Hedda Gabler; Rousseau, Frankenstein's creature, and Sigmund Freud.

At the beginning of the semester, students complain that there is a great deal of reading, so they have to be reminded that they are taking two classes: the reading load is what it would be if they were taking the classes separately. The great advantage to them is the tests and projects are combined.

I was concerned about jointly grading the tests and projects, foreseeing that a history instructor and I, an English instructor, might have different expectations. The problem turned out to be not great. We discussed our expectations on joint questions ahead of time. On matters of history, I deferred to my colleague; on matters of literature, she deferred to me. Usually, however, our assessment of the grade that an answer deserved was almost the same.

Another problem area was overlapping material. I was accustomed to giving background lectures on the history and ideas of various periods in my literature class, but most of that would be covered in the history sections of the course. Similarly, the history instructor was accustomed to speaking about literary movements. We worked to modify our approaches so that they would be complementary and not repetitive. As an example, my colleague presented almost everything related to philosophical ideas and background of the Enlightenment, which left me more time to discuss the literature. I dealt with most of the Romantic movement, leaving her free to concentrate on historical aspects of the period.

The whole experience contributed to our professional development in classroom management and in knowledge. It is important to discuss classroom management issues before they arise and have a sense of what one's colleague might do. Students have a tendency to divide instructors. One instructor may be perceived as more accommodating or available, for example. Students may need to be told that a decision cannot be made before the other instructor is consulted. If a unilateral decision must be made, the other instructor should be informed as soon as possible. Since good communication guarantees that instructors work effectively together, regular if brief meetings are desirable.

More important, we each had the experience of being in the classroom with a colleague from another subject area day after day. We watched how each other taught and how each other dealt with students. What we observed tended to reaffirm our own strengths. I had the valuable experience of thoroughly reviewing Western civilization from the seventeenth century onward. I sat in class and took extensive notes, as though I were one of the students, and my colleague did the same when I was conducting class. Our attention helped model student behavior. In addition, the historical review has helped me in teaching Western world literature by itself and in other classes when I deal with this period. We were both able to refer to things each other had said as we discussed our own sections, thus reinforcing the connections for students. Sometimes we disagreed in our interpretations, but it was valuable for students to witness a difference of opinion handled professionally. Moreover, they need to realize that there is more than one possible interpretation.

While this learning community has not been taught often enough for conclusions about its effectiveness to be drawn analytically and in detail, general observation and anecdotal evidence from this and from other learning communities at Pellissippi State suggest that students gain a more comprehensive, integrated view of history and literature than those taking the separate courses and that their grades are as good as and actually slightly better than those of students in the regular courses. Retention, particularly compared with that of regular sections of Western Civilization, is greater.

In the learning community, the students' journey takes students from Voltaire to Vietnam, from the Sun King to the cold war, emphasizing the many voices that contribute to our concept of Western culture. We instructors take the journey as well, challenged to transform our approaches and adjust our perspectives, led to reconsider our teaching styles, and given an enriched appreciation of the subjects we teach.

Note

1. Laurie Stapleton's advice was of great value in designing the learning community. I would also like to thank her for reading parts of this essay and making suggestions that have assisted me in improving it. McDaniel likewise gave me the benefit of her helpful comments on parts of this essay.

Works Cited

Kubrick, Stanley, dir. *Doctor Strangelove; or, How I Learned to Stop Worrying and Love the Bomb*. Columbia, 1964. Film.

Lawall, Sarah, et al., eds. *The Norton Anthology of World Masterpieces*. 7th ed. Vol. 2. New York: Norton, 1999. Print.

Shelley, Mary. *Frankenstein*. New York: Pocket-Simon, 2004. Print.

Spielvogel, Jackson J. *Western Civilization*. 4th ed. Comprehensive ed. Belmont: Thomson, 2000. Print.

Tykwer, Tom, dir. *Lola rennt*. X Filme Creative Pool, 1998. Film.

Michael Palencia-Roth

Pioneering Cross-Cultural Studies and World Literature at Illinois

In fall 1985, I sat down with two of my colleagues at the University of Illinois, Janet Smarr and Girdhari Tikku, to reshape and refocus the Program in Comparative Literature.[1] Our intention was to rethink the way we taught comparative literature on the graduate and undergraduate levels as well as the place of our discipline in the university and in the profession. Our conversations were driven by several factors. First, we were determined to maintain academic rigor in both our undergraduate and graduate programs and to resist the dumbing down of our discipline in an effort simply to increase enrollments. Second, we refused to become an omnium-gatherum program, in which almost any course of study would be deemed acceptable as long as a student could get a faculty member to sign on to it. Third, we wanted to pay attention both to the traditional center of the discipline and to its more recent developments. While we did not believe that there was a "crisis in comparative literature" (the title of René Wellek's famous essay on the subject), we did believe that the discipline was changing and that those changes presented both challenges and opportunities.

Key to rethinking our discipline was our attempt to anticipate the future of comparative literature nationally and internationally in a changing global environment. Although in the 1980s literary theory was widely considered to be the future of the discipline and although several comparative literature departments in other universities seemed to be becoming theory departments first and literature departments second, we did not want to go that route and diminish the importance of knowing one's literatures and their histories in their original languages. We did increase the work in literary theory required of our graduate students, and we did continue to require expertise in literary theory of the faculty members we hired. However, we believed that the long-term future of our discipline lay in reducing its Eurocentric bias and in creating theoretically informed and disciplined yet flexible means of studying literatures across cultures, not merely across the traditional national and linguistic boundaries. In effect, we became the first cross-cultural and world literature program in the nation *by design,* anticipating by a number of years both the discipline's development nationally and the increasing commitment of the University of Illinois to multicultural, cross-cultural, and global studies.

In 1985, those ideas were not even on the table in our university and in most of academia. It was another sixteen years, for instance, before the MLA responded to this paradigm shift in comparative literary study by publishing a special issue of *PMLA* in January 2001 on the topic "Globalizing Literary Studies." Being so far ahead of the curve caused the program some difficulties at first, for the university did not immediately appreciate what we were doing, why it was significant, why comparative literature couldn't just be replaced by a loose and voluntary federation of national literature departments, why cross-cultural studies couldn't be entirely done in translation, and what sort of animal global studies was anyway. As the university came gradually to understand and adopt global paradigms, in time those difficulties diminished or disappeared.

What did we do? We created new core courses on both the undergraduate and graduate levels as well as new sets of requirements. On the undergraduate level, we balanced our traditional two-semester Western literature sequence with a new two-semester sequence in non-European literatures, dividing that sequence into a classical phase and a modern phase. Here we insisted that each semester's syllabus contain texts from three or four major cultural areas and that the ordering logic be chronological, thematic, and topical. We also created a more specialized cross-cultural course at the advanced undergraduate level (with variable content, depending on the expertise of the instructor) and made the cross-cultural academic experience a requirement of all our majors and minors in both comparative literature (the traditional model, emphasizing foreign languages) and world literature (a general education model, emphasizing literatures in translation). On the graduate level, we created a required seminar in the issues and practice of cross-cultural comparison and instituted the further requirement of another cross-cultural seminar. When hiring additional faculty members, we favored candidates with expertise and interests in cross-cultural issues. At first, qualified candidates who fit the profile of our redesigned program were relatively rare, but they have become more common in recent years. Finally, we renamed ourselves the Program in Comparative and World Literature in order to more accurately reflect our intentions, our methods, and our scope.

Early on, we decided to remain committed to literary history and to pay sufficient attention to the cultural contexts of specific traditions. One may ask why, among all the different ways that one may structure a world literature curriculum, we chose to emphasize literary history rather than, say, a great-books approach or a foundational literary classics approach. After all, these approaches offer enormous pedagogical freedom, for they permit instructors to focus on great ideas, on great works or authors, or on superb examples of this or that genre. But we chose what we chose because of our history as teachers. Each of us, toward the beginning of our careers and in different institutions, had taught courses that compared great works of world literature regardless of their cultural or historical contexts, as if they were disembodied entities existing somehow in the ether of eternal verities and universal literary themes. Each of us had been encouraged to do so by our respective department heads as a way of generating student interest, and we each believed that we had been successful in that regard. The students seemed to have enjoyed our courses, and we had enjoyed high evaluations. However, when we met those same students a year or so later in more advanced courses, we realized that they had little sense of literary history, of each literary generation's ongoing conversation with prior texts and authors. Simply put, our students were unprepared for advanced work, and it was not their fault but ours. This realization was sobering, and, as we reflected on what we had done, we became aware that we had inadvertently crossed the line from teaching to entertainment.

In 1985, conscious of our initial missteps as teachers, we were resolved to create a curriculum that was intellectually coherent and pedagogically responsible, so that the more advanced courses built on the knowledge and skills gained in the less advanced ones. The less advanced courses were to be contextually grounded in both literary and social history and were to be taught with attention paid to chronology and geography. It was important to us to create a structure that would function in this manner no matter which one of us, or which one of our future colleagues, taught the prerequisite courses.

It was fairly easy to ensure this structure in both the European and non-European components of our undergraduate majors. Here we had two years to work with: one year with historical literary surveys was followed by another year of more advanced issues in comparison, methodology, and history of ideas, and those two years were followed by the far more specialized undergraduate seminars.

We faced a somewhat different challenge on the graduate level. On the one hand, our students come from all over the world and have quite different levels of literary expertise, both as interpreters of texts and in literary theory. On the other, like most graduate programs in comparative literature, we have very few universal course requirements; each student's track to the PhD is individualized as far as possible. Therefore, beyond the obligatory course in literary theory and the introduction to comparative literature as a discipline, we instituted two new requirements. The first is a course to be taken by all our first-year graduate students. It highlights the two dimensions of our program that in 1985 we considered would become distinctive: its cross-cultural emphasis and its world literature reach. We decided that this course, taught in the students' second semester, would be followed in a subsequent year by another cross-cultural seminar but one closer to the student's own areas of interest. Every graduating PhD, then, no matter how specialized in the dissertation or in the other coursework, would thus be trained to pay attention to contexts, to literary and cultural history; to be at ease with cross-cultural comparison and world literature; to be at home in literary theory in general and in cross-cultural issues in literary theory in particular; and to be aware always of the broader dimensions of any particular comparison. The students' work as teaching assistants in our four large undergraduate survey courses was also meant to reinforce this training.

The centerpiece of our cross-cultural initiative on the graduate level is the course that I briefly describe here: the spring-semester cross-cultural studies course. It follows the fall offering, which is the introduction to literary theory and to the discipline of comparative literature for our new graduate students. Both courses, as I have said, are required of all our graduate students. I have taught both over the years, but I have generally been drawn toward the spring semester cross-cultural course, which I taught for the first time in 1986, in collaboration with other faculty members and then—for most of these twenty years—usually alone. Occasionally I team-teach the course with newer faculty members. When that happens, I ask that the other teacher's specialization be far from mine (I have taught with specialists in China, Japan, and India) so that our differences can illuminate the material from different cultural perspectives. In my view, team teaching is the best way to give such a course, but budgets in our institution have not permitted that as a permanent policy or pedagogical strategy.

Early on in the teaching of this cross-cultural course, I realized that if I were to be responsible both to chronology and to geography, I would have to pay particular attention to history. And if I were to be responsible to the foundations of cross-cultural analysis, I would have to pay attention to situations in which two or more cultures came into actual contact. I wanted to train our graduate students to acquire an attitude that would become second nature to them: comparisons should not be invented by the interpreter but rather should arise from the authors themselves and from the historical and cultural contexts that shaped them. This interpretive attitude has proved to be particularly difficult to teach to graduate students who, in their undergraduate years, were allowed and even encouraged to seek the most original comparison, even if it existed only in the mind of the student.

After several years of experimentation, my colleagues and I chose colonization as the skeleton on which to attach the flesh of comparative cross-cultural study at the University of Illinois. Herbert Lüthy once wrote, "the history of colonization is the history of humanity itself" (29). Today one might present the issue without using the term *colonization* and in the form of a question, "What is the history of the humanity if not the history of cross-cultural encounters?" Whether one uses *colonization* or the more general term *encounter*, the fact remains that much so-called history is the result of one culture's coming into contact with another, often through invasion, the intention being to overcome, control, and shape the invaded society politically and culturally. This notion of history as comparative colonizations or encounters is as applicable to the study of the Greek colonization of the Mediterranean or to Alexander's wide-ranging conquests as it is to Roman imperialism, Chinese or Arabic expansionism, the Mughal invasion of India, the Spanish conquest of the New World, and so on. Moreover, much subsequent comparative literary history, originating as it does from such cross-cultural contacts, registers the effects of less violent encounters between and among authors and intellectuals from different cultures and traditions.

I address the following sorts of questions in the required cross-cultural course: What happens when widely different cultures or civilizations come into contact with one another? How is the other viewed by the one, and how are both changed by the encounter and by continued contact? How are the new cultures, concepts, or customs conceptualized, categorized, made familiar? Why do some comparative literary histories seem to change and evolve across generations, even centuries, while others exhaust themselves rather quickly? How does literature reflect and sometimes even create what Michel de Certeau has called the heterological?

These and other questions are approached from several angles: a theoretical angle, a literary history angle, and a practical angle. Let me briefly address these angles in order.

I sometimes use Certeau's *Heterologies* as a critical resource throughout the semester. I have also used other texts: for instance, Samir Amin's *Eurocentrism,* Johannes Fabian's *Time and the Other,* and David Spurr's *The Rhetoric of Empire.* I have sometimes relied on my own essays (e.g., "Comparing Literatures, Comparing Civilizations" and "Contrastive Literature") to complement the in-class discussions. More recently, I pointed students to selections from Charles Bernheimer's *Comparative Literature in the Age of Multiculturalism,* Gayatri Spivak's *Death of a Discipline,* and David Damrosch's *What Is World Literature?* These materials are supplemented by a twenty-page bibliography on cross-cultural comparison that I hand out at the beginning of the semester. In the theoretical dimension of the course, which is present throughout the semester, my main concern is to give students the terminology to deal with the phenomena of imperialism, colonization, and decolonization and thus with a number of current controversies in cultural studies, postcolonial studies, and deconstructive issues in general.

That these issues are not new is part of the message of the literary history angle of the course. I generally begin with examples of encounters between the Greeks and Romans and their respective barbarians.[2] Using the language of cultural alterity, I ask how one culture may impose its terms on another or seek to create analogies where none existed. I begin with the stories of encounters found in Homer, especially in books 9 and 10 of *The Odyssey,* and in Herodotus, especially book 4 of *The History.* I then turn to excerpts from Julius Caesar's *Gallic Wars,* from Vergil's

Aeneid, and from Saint Augustine's *The City of God.* Each of these five texts presents, from quite different perspectives and with quite different intentions, issues of cultural classification and even, when those issues are taken to their logical extreme, questions of human identity. Some standard texts from medieval travel literature follow—for instance, "The Letter of Prester John," the *Travels* of Marco Polo and of Mandeville.

The worldviews behind all these texts, from Homer to Mandeville, become the framework I use to interpret both the European discovery of the New World (Columbus, Vespucci, Cortés, Montaigne) and European explorations of the Orient (Vasco da Gama, Camões). Camões I teach as the first literary work of the age of historical globalization. In most semesters, I also analyze what I would call the second phase of colonization—when institutions are being established, legal and educational systems put into place, and the principal structures of commerce and government erected. Though I have at times considered the European colonization(s) of Africa, for the past several years I have looked at the English in India through the prism of two very different Englishmen and two very different essays and their effects: Sir William Jones's inaugural essay establishing the Asiatic Society of Bengal in 1784 and Thomas Babington Macaulay's "Minute on Indian Education" of 1835. The literary-historical part of the course takes about eight or nine weeks in a fourteen-week semester.

The remainder of the course is given over to the graduate students themselves, in three assignments that constitute the practical dimensions of the course. First, I select several cross-cultural teams of students. Our graduate program is so international that I almost always succeed in having students from Latin America, Europe, India, Russia, China, Japan, and Korea be represented on most of the teaching teams, along with American students. These teams are then asked to teach narratives from the twentieth century that in some way are shaped by, or respond to, the issues unfolded in the first eight or nine weeks of the course. I will have chosen the texts beforehand, depending on the composition of the entering graduate class: three or four twentieth-century novels that are thoroughly cross-cultural—for example, Mario Vargas Llosa's *The Storyteller,* V. S. Naipaul's *The Enigma of Arrival,* Italo Calvino's *Invisible Cities,* and Shusaku Endo's *The Samurai.*[3] The dialogues in class are always interesting, as students from different cultures and different interpretive traditions try to achieve a unified, if complex, presentation of the text, the author, and the issues.

The second assignment is to prepare a cross-cultural syllabus on an author or issue. Each student undertakes this work in consultation with me, and generally we talk about it continually throughout the semester. This syllabus must come from the student's own area of study and be based on texts read in the original. Each syllabus must also be historically grounded so that the grounds for comparison can never be questioned or criticized as arbitrary. Sometimes, however, to vary this assignment, I require a conventional research paper. Here, too, I insist on a topic that is cross-cultural and on grounds for comparison that are incontrovertible. Finally, each student is asked to write a ten-page review essay on a scholarly book relevant both to the student's professional interests and to cross-cultural studies. Most students choose a book from the cross-cultural bibliography that I handed out at the beginning of the semester, though some choose to review a book not on the list.

In addition to the above workload, students are asked to keep a journal of their intellectual journey during the semester and to hand in that journal every two weeks for comments from me. The first journal submission thus begins a series of individual dialogues with each student that continues throughout the semester. Gradually, almost every student acquires greater intellectual and moral sophistication, as well as a more fluid and interesting writing style. Several even discover their dissertation topic through these journal assignments.

All this is an unusual amount of work to ask of a seminar and an extraordinary responsibility as well, but our students seem to thrive on the hard work and the trust that is placed in them.

Every decade or two, it seems, professors of comparative literature call the discipline to account, examine it, question its raison d'être, and recommend changes in response to whatever is happening in the humanities in general and in literary study in particular. Perhaps these initiatives are undertaken because ours is an introspective and anxious discipline, unusually alert to the winds of critical or pedagogical fashion and always open both to reflecting and shaping those paradigm shifts that define humanistic study. We are in such a paradigm shift now and have been in it for some time. Multiculturalism, globalization, and postcolonial studies, for instance, are but aspects and instances of the paradigm shift toward world literature, a shift once dreamt of by Goethe that is now a reality far more complex and vital then even he could have imagined.

Notes

1. We are designated a program rather than a department. For all practical purposes, however, we have existed as a department since our founding in the mid-1960s and so have not sought a name-change designation from the state of Illinois—a cumbersome and time-consuming procedure. We have our own budget, dedicated faculty lines as well as shared lines and courtesy nonbudgeted appointments, the common administrative structure of a department head reporting to a dean, and both undergraduate and graduate programs with the full range of support for our students. What is sometimes problematic, however, is the thoroughly interdepartmental nature of our activities: all students do a significant amount of their work in other departments, either as students in the classroom or as teaching assistants. The faculty's responsibilities are generally split as well. These characteristics of our program and our discipline are not generally a problem, but they do mean that each change of administration (new dean, new provost) requires that we "educate" the higher administration in what we do and how we do it.

2. Students sometimes ask me why I go out from Europe rather than into Europe—say, from China, India, or Africa—in my course and if my procedure does not actually reinforce the Eurocentrism that I seek to revise. The criticism is well taken. My response is twofold. First, I tell them that, as far as possible, one must teach texts that one can control in the original and that I have read in the original all the Western literary texts taught in this course. I respond in this way in order to encourage them to learn more than the two or three languages they learned before enrolling in our graduate program. Second, I tell them that one must begin from where one is standing but not do so naively or blindly; that is, one must acknowledge one's standpoint and perspective—I was trained as a Europeanist—and account for it in the interpretive process. I address these issues in a theoretical sense when I discuss the phenomenology and hermeneutics of understanding in cross-cultural analysis.

3. Over the years, our students have worked on a variety of novels: Chung-shu Ch'ien's *Fortress Besieged*; Salman Rushdie's *Midnight's Children*; Raja Rao's *The Serpent and the Rope*; Tayeb Salih's *Season of Migration to the North*; Chinua Achebe's *Things Fall Apart, No Longer at Ease,* or *Arrow of God*; and Ngũgĩ wa Thiong'o's *A Grain of Wheat*.

Works Cited

Certeau, Michel de. *Heterologies: Discourse on the Other.* Trans. Brian Massumi. Minneapolis: U of Minnesota P, 1986. Print.

Damrosch, David. *What Is World Literature?* Princeton: Princeton UP, 2003. Print.

Lüthy, Herbert. "Colonization and the Making of Mankind." 1961. *Imperialism and Colonialism.* Ed. George F. Nadel and Perry Curtis. New York: Macmillan, 1964. 26–37. Print.

Palencia-Roth, Michael. "Comparing Literatures, Comparing Civilizations." *Comparative Civilizations Review* 21 (1989): 1–19. Print.

———. "Contrastive Literature." *Comparative Literature in the Nineties.* Spec. issue of *ACLA Bulletin* 24.2 (1993): 47–61. Print.

Wellek, René. "The Crisis in Comparative Literature." *Concepts of Criticism.* By Wellek. Ed. Stephen G. Nichols. New Haven: Yale UP, 1963. 282–95. Print.

John Burt Foster, Jr.

Cultural Encounters in Global Contexts: World Literature as a One-Semester General Education Course

A major issue in designing world literature courses today is to find effective ways to move beyond a focus largely on the West. The problem of global coverage becomes particularly acute when, as at George Mason University, the introductory world literature course is only a single semester long and serves to fulfill a general education requirement. This essay describes the creation of a fundamentally new course—really, a menu of course options—designed to give George Mason's students an introduction, in one semester, to world literature that has genuinely global scope. It is a course that the instructors can actually teach, that uses their existing expertise while also helping them learn and teach new things.

Unlike the large-lecture format of many of our general education courses, the introduction to world literature is taught in small, discussion-oriented classes of about twenty-five students. These classes are designated as writing-intensive, meaning that students must write three or four papers during the semester as well as a variety of other, less formal assignments. Eighty to ninety of these sections are offered every year, and instructors have a lot of leeway in designing syllabi. Under a grant from the National Endowment for the Humanities, our team of five faculty members has just introduced six world literature courses for sophomores. The team is composed of me; Associate Professors Amal Amireh, Joel Foreman, and Alok Yadav; and Assistant Professor Tamara Harvey.

The basis for this project was our department's growing but hardly unique sense of the inadequacy of an already existing world literature course that probably dated back to the founding of our university in the 1960s. This course was typical for the time: a two-semester survey of Western literature from Genesis and Homer to Kafka and Sartre (in the 1960s) or to García Márquez and Soyinka (by the 1990s). Our version's only unusual feature was that it was limited to works in translation, so that the anthology best suited to the course was the so-called continental edition of *The Norton Anthology of World Masterpieces* (Mack et al.), which omitted the English-language works in the standard edition while adding a handful of others and which emphasized fiction and drama because of the well-known difficulties in translating poetry. Over the years, as criticisms of Eurocentrism escalated in the profession, we saw ever more clearly that this course, despite its value in expanding our students' horizons beyond the literatures of the English-speaking peoples, left out huge expanses of the world.

Meanwhile, the nature of our student body was, if anything, outpacing what the profession was telling us. Since the 1960s, George Mason has undergone a dramatic shift that reflects the changing demography of northern Virginia, whose growing variety was the subject of a 2001 feature article in the *National Geographic* (Swerdlow), which described it as exemplary of a trend nationwide. George Mason, as a result, now ranks at or near the top on diversity lists compiled by college guides like the Princeton Review's *The Best 361 Colleges*. The once obvious assumption of Norton's continental edition that readers would immediately recognize the continent in question as Europe came to seem ever more dubious as we taught more and more first-generation American students whose parents came from every inhabited continent, foreign students who themselves had arrived from all these continents, and returning older students who had lived all over the world. Outside the classroom, moreover, we faced the familiar situation of an administration that wanted all units in the university to globalize.

Desiring, as a result, to prepare some wider-ranging world literature courses for our sophomores, we settled on two main criteria: regional multiplicity and interculturalism (cultural encounters). Regional multiplicity meant a decisive turn away from curricula that would remain dominantly Western in coverage even if they introduced a scattering of works from around the world. This mostly Western model is the one generally followed by the world literature anthologies now on the market. As an MLA session revealed several years ago (From the Old World), such anthologies are required by publishers to be at least two-thirds Western in content—not that courses using these anthologies need to hew to that proportion, since no instructor could possibly teach everything in them.

Our own, contrasting approach was to allot no more than one-third of any course's time to literature from any one geocultural region, such as the West. We devised this one-third rule bearing in mind that doctoral programs in comparative literature commonly require at least two languages in addition to English. Whatever the initial motives for this practice among comparatists, we proposed an equivalent representation of at least three regions. The hope was that this arrangement would discourage the tendency to make invidious comparisons and dualistic oppositions between the two geocultural regions, a danger in courses where only two traditions are in play and especially where one of the regions would be the West. Moreover, when the West was one of three traditions in a course, students would get a better and more direct sense from the other two of how much variety is masked by such blanket terms as *foreign*.

In selecting the geocultural regions to be represented, we decided to emphasize units that were comparable to the West in extent and distinctiveness. Several models proved helpful as we proceeded. One was the only world literature anthology that seemed, at least in its volume on the modern world, to make some attempt to go beyond the two-thirds Western rule: *The HarperCollins World Reader*, edited by Mary Ann Caws and Christopher Prendergast. This anthology was of interest also because it organized its materials by region. The only problem was the sheer number of regions that it identified: nine larger units and seven smaller ones, which, however true to the world's literary diversity, were far too many for the single-semester courses we needed to design. So we also turned to a recent book by two geographers—Martin W. Lewis and Karen E. Wigen's *The Myth of Continents*—and to Fernand Braudel's thought-provoking proposal for a world history curriculum in 1960s France that unfortunately was never adopted, published in English as *A History of Civilizations*. After thinking through their broad cultural schemes for understanding the regions of the world and then cross-referencing these ideas with the Caws-Prendergast anthology, we arrived at five major geocultural regions besides the West, each with its own distinctive literary and cultural traditions, which of course included major internal tensions on the order of familiar Western ones that go back to biblical and Greco-Roman models.

These regions were East Asia, South Asia, the Middle East and North Africa, sub-Saharan Africa, and Latin America and the Caribbean. We buttressed Latin America's status as a separate region by including pre-Columbian America, whose surviving traditions and contributions to a sense of regional identity offered a venue for Native American verbal arts. Treating Latin America and the Caribbean as a region in its own right also reduced the problem of Western sprawl, which if not addressed could swallow up both Americas, Australia, Asian Russia, and Europhone Africa as well as Europe. Witness, for example, the already mentioned inclusion of García Márquez and Soyinka in the final version of Norton's continental edition.

We considered adding the region of east central Europe and Russia and that of Southeast Asia and Oceania to the six already mentioned. Like Latin America, east central Europe and especially Russia could claim, and indeed have at times asserted, their distinctiveness vis-à-vis the West, based in this case on Eastern Christianity, on closer connections eastward or marginality with regard to the West, and on the old First World–Second World divide. Likewise, Benedict Anderson has argued cogently in favor of the cultural specificity of Southeast Asia and the neighboring Pacific world. But in the end we decided to stick with the six regions already delineated, because of pressing practical concerns. In our fourteen-week semesters, which must allow for an introduction to the course, for several meetings devoted exclusively to student writing, and for a conclusion, the most ambitious format, which would give equal time to all five regions plus the West, could easily be divided into six two-week segments. The minimal three-region version could, by the same token, allot four weeks to each of the regions chosen by the instructor.

Our second criterion was interculturalism, on the assumption that a world literature class needs to do more than just use literary texts as a convenient vehicle for introducing students to other cultures on a global scale. To be sure, *world literature* is an ambiguous term, since it can variously and even simultaneously suggest the excellence of works whose worth is recognized worldwide, the sheer diversity of the writings that have become canonical in specific parts of the world, and the representational value of verbal art that confronts readers with differences in the world's cultures. In this fluid domain, we decided to focus on literature that would reflect our awareness of the complex constitution and continuing porousness of cultural boundaries, associated with theorists like Mikhail Bakhtin, critics like Edward Said, and fields like cultural and postcolonial studies. Instead of keeping to the older and still current idea that cultures are distinct, bounded, and autonomous wholes, we wanted to expose students, in their reading experience, to the overlapping, interacting, and syncretic dynamics through which distinctive cultures are constituted and continually modified both across and within the world's geocultural regions. From this perspective, works of world literature are not windows on particular, self-enclosed cultures but are themselves sites of and embedded in larger dynamics of intercultural encounter and negotiation.

Yet the nature or provenance of the works on a syllabus does not exhaust the possibilities we envision for these general education courses. On a more immediate level, the emphasis on cultural encounter overlaps with the day-to-day lives of our students, both on campus and off, throughout the Washington metropolitan area. Over a decade ago, in fact, a group of students who felt that our Board of Visitors was insufficiently informed produced a video that was meant to show just how varied their undergraduate world was: it opened with an international student wearing a stylish headscarf and showing a truly exceptional command of American slang. We were intrigued by the possibility of making good educational use of this lived diversity in a classroom that along with Americans of various ethnicities might include a foreign service brat just back from Japan, an Indian, a Pole, a Greek, a Shiite Muslim, a Sunni Muslim, a Nigerian, and a Peruvian woman who has walked the road to Macchu Picchu. Facing such an array of students, we wanted to assemble a world literature curriculum of cultural encounter that would have the power to spark discussions that, in a manner that was both vibrant and pedagogically sound, could draw on the variety already in the classroom. Up to now in our general education literature classes, this variety was usually limited, given the need to master a body of Western literature. Wouldn't a broader selection of texts encourage greater openness, resulting in livelier discussions, more interesting papers, and a cultural literacy better suited to both local and global conditions?

Let me make it clear that we do not aim to encourage a literary version of identity politics; we would simply value contributions from students possessing particular knowledge relevant to the readings. I think here of the student with an Indian mother and Pakistani father who, in one of our more advanced classes, reported on the tensions between Hindus and Muslims that surface toward the end of Tagore's *The Home and the World*. What we really have in mind, however, are the kinds of cross-cultural and interregional insights advanced, for example, by an Argentine student for whom the ominous mood that Naipaul evokes so vividly in the unnamed African nation in *A Bend in the River* recalled political repression in her homeland. Or by the Korean American who found that the Italy of Stendhal's *The Charterhouse of Parma*, with its arbitrary borders and its abrupt swings between Austrian and French domination, resonated with parental stories of her divided peninsular nation. These examples point up the cross-cultural opportunities that can arise and spark valuable exchanges in our small, discussion-oriented classes.

The small-course format also made it possible for us to launch a variety of world literature classes. As I write at the end of our project's first year, we have just finished testing six pilot courses, each of which takes a distinctive approach to world literature within the intercultural and broad regional parameters just outlined. As an additional commonality, we agreed that we would all teach Soyinka's *Death and the King's Horseman*, on the assumption that the play's variety of styles, the kinds of conflict that it dramatizes, and the interpretive questions that it raises would all make it an excellent benchmark for gauging our students' progress as readers of world literature. As might be expected given the constraints of a single semester, none of the courses that we developed could make any claim to broad coverage. We had to limit ourselves to thematically defined case studies. It is easy to imagine a course on ancient literacy with works from East Asia, South Asia, and the Middle East, but none of our courses featured any readings prior to the literature of New World contact; our earliest selections were Aztec poetry and Sor Juana Inés de la Cruz's *loa* to *The Divine Narcissus*. At least one course, however, did give some attention to the issue of orature, building on Prendergast's point that "both historically and geographically, the oral vastly exceeds the written," thus indicating that "world" in its ideal inclusiveness must overrule the relative exclusivity of "literature" (4).

Despite these limitations, the following list of pilot courses, whose syllabi will be posted at www.culturalencounter.org, suggests the variety of topics and geocultural breadth that we were able to address:

Literature and the Politics of Language: works from Brazil, Nigeria, and Ireland (the instructor is Yadav)

World Literature with a Feminist Accent: works from New Spain and Latin America, colonial and postcolonial Africa, and the current Middle East (Harvey)

The Literature of Emancipatory Struggle: works from colonial Africa, colonial India, Maoist China, the Arab-Israeli conflict, and the Vietnam War era (Foreman)

World Literature in Postcolonial Perspective: works from the Middle East, Africa, and the West (Amireh)

World Literature Online: a reconfiguration of The Literature of Emancipatory Struggle that makes use of streaming video materials, ranging from interviews with authorities on particular texts to pictorial dramatizations of key questions and concepts, materials that the instructor has assembled for works like Soyinka's *Death and the King's Horseman* and Mahfouz's *Miramar* (Foreman)

World Literature and Global History: works from all six geocultural regions in a linked arrangement with a history course whose main text, *Worlds Together, Worlds Apart* (Tignor et al.), singles out the changing relations among those regions (Foster)

Perhaps the greatest challenge in planning and teaching these courses centered on faculty development. What kind of guidance would we be in a position to give our students during a semester that moved them relentlessly from work to work and from one geocultural region to another? One possible solution, that of importing experts in each region to talk to students, simply would not work with our small, discussion-oriented classes. In any case, such an approach might tend to set each region apart from the others. It might also leave the students to their own devices in trying to accomplish an impossible task of synthesis. It would clearly not be suitable for courses that proposed to emphasize cultural encounters within and between regions. What we needed were instructors well enough prepared to be able to intervene helpfully at opportune moments in discussions that grew out of the dynamics of a specific class. Rather, we needed to *become* such instructors.

Thanks to the NEH grant, we didn't have to take the leap into the totally unknown that many first-time teachers of world literature find so daunting. As laid out in our proposal, we began by identifying experts in each of our five non-Western regions who in addition to their expertise as scholars had experience in presenting the literatures of their region to general student audiences. Then, after a semester that the team spent

reading and discussing a short list of representative texts from these regions, we met with each expert in a day-long session that considered such
practical issues as choice of texts, course design, and teaching strategies
along with questions of intercultural and cross-cultural exchange and of
comparability on a global scale. Joining us were representatives from six
other universities (Illinois, Ohio State, Virginia Commonwealth, North
Carolina State, Georgia, and Alabama) with world literature programs of
different kinds, who could give us the benefit of their experiences while
themselves drawing fresh insights from the experts leading the sessions.
In the future we hope to keep this network alive, since there is much to
be gained by exchanging ideas for courses, sharing syllabi, and identifying teachable and readily available texts with colleagues elsewhere.

The most immediate challenge that we had to face with our courses
was how best to choose texts that would deliver our individualized approaches to world literature to students. One solution was simply to
make do with an existing anthology, to assign many of its sometimes
scattered selections from around the world but to be more selective with
its richer assortment of Western works. In our one-semester courses,
however, this approach generally meant limiting the course's temporal
scope, since teachers could hardly ask students to buy more than one or
two volumes of today's six-volume anthologies.[1] Another approach was
to organize the course around five or six individual works. In this regard, the Norton Critical Edition of *Death and the King's Horseman*
worked especially well as our shared text. But many works of world literature that are currently in print lack the extensive apparatus provided by
the Norton editions. In this situation, teachers can turn to the Internet
as a resource for student research, since it can often provide a surprising
amount of detailed information about other cultures and environments.
Several of us built Internet assignments into our classes. Yet another approach is the photocopied course reader, which has the advantage of allowing for a totally customized, culturally wide-ranging syllabus but the
disadvantages of permission fees, occasional restrictions on length, the
absence of introductory material, and an inconvenient format for in-class
discussions. General education sophomores, we found, do not get the
cutting-edge thrill from reading matter of this kind that graduate students might.

Another challenge was learning to teach world literature in a literature requirement that has other major goals, like promoting skills in ex-
pository writing or instilling a lifelong interest in literature. New kinds of

paper assignments had to be devised to meet these broader goals while also advancing the students' understanding of unfamiliar geocultural regions, of the intercultural dynamics that underlie cultural differences, and of the difficulties in interpreting these dynamics. The sheer number of papers to evaluate in these writing-intensive courses was itself a significant amount of work to add to the challenge of fielding a new and broader array of texts, yet reading these papers did give us a clearer sense of the students' knowledge and capacities.

A single semester is too little time to learn how to orchestrate a course that will make optimum use of all the possibilities in one's syllabus while leaving room for the interests and knowledge of the students. In my experience, it took five or six years just to approach this goal when teaching a general education course in Western literature, and that was the field in which I was trained. Yet world literature is often assigned either to graduate students with no background in the field and little experience even in teaching literature or to adjunct faculty members whose heavy teaching loads keep them too busy to do justice to the subject's exciting intellectual challenges.

Despite these difficulties, world literature can play an important role in general education. Obviously literature in our own language and tradition will continue to do much to enlarge our sense of human possibility, to add nuance to our inner map of geocultural assumptions, and (above all) to nourish our imagination in new and valuable ways. But literature from around the world, with its richly textured representations of people in varied settings, can broaden students' horizons even further and in ways that complement courses in world history, international relations, and anthropology. World literature can promote a more intimate understanding of specific cultures, catalyze insights into underlying similarities and differences, and sharpen awareness of communication among cultures. It can also illuminate the intercultural dynamics through which these cultures are shaped and transformed in the first place. In general, it can give more substance and depth to a worldwide perspective on human experience.

No one would argue that people should stop reading their native literature, but it would be foolish to insist that they never read elsewhere—or to suppose that they can really understand their own literature and culture without a broader awareness of how interactions on a global scale have helped shape them. Viewed in this way, world literature can contribute much to a more globally conscious general education.

Note

1. A fuller list of both multicultural and world literature anthologies has been compiled by Alok Yadav and can be accessed at mason.gmu.edu/~ayadav/anthologies.

Works Cited

Anderson, Benedict. *The Spectre of Comparisons: Nationalism, Southeast Asia, and the World.* London: Verso, 1998. Print.

The Best 361 Colleges. Princeton Rev. New York: Random, 2006. Print.

Braudel, Fernand. *A History of Civilizations.* Trans. Richard Mayne. New York: Penguin, 1995. Print.

Caws, Mary Ann, and Christopher Prendergast, eds. *The HarperCollins World Reader: The Modern World.* New York: Harper, 1994. Print.

From the Old World to the Whole World: Anthologies Today. MLA Annual Convention. San Diego. 29 Dec. 2003. Session.

Lewis, Martin W., and Karen E. Wigen. *The Myth of Continents: A Critique of Metageography.* Berkeley: U of California P, 1997. Print.

Mack, Maynard, et al., eds. *The Norton Anthology of World Masterpieces: Fifth Continental Edition.* New York: Norton, 1987. Print.

Prendergast, Christopher. "The World Republic of Letters." *Debating World Literature.* Ed. Prendergast. London: Verso, 2004. 1–25. Print.

Swerdlow, Joel L. "Changing America: A High School Melting Pot." Photographs by Karen Kasmauski. *National Geographic* Sept. 2001: 42–61. Print.

Tignor, Robert, et al. *Worlds Together, Worlds Apart: A History of the Modern World from the Mongol Empire to the Present.* New York: Norton, 2002. Print.

Caroline D. Eckhardt

World Literature and the Graduate Curriculum

Aliter enim cogitamus Carthaginem, quam nouimus, aliter Alexandriam, quam non nouimus.

We think in one way about Carthage, which we know; in a different way about Alexandria, which we do not know.

—Augustine, *De Genesi ad litteram*[1]

The world literature movement has captured the allegiance and imagination of many practitioners of comparative literature, along with colleagues in humanities, English, and foreign language fields. I am not naively ignoring the extent to which world literature is still a contested intellectual category, always stretched between ideologies of assimilation and ideologies of differentiation, as David Damrosch has demonstrated in rich detail and as others in this volume have discussed. Augustine acknowledges that the way he thinks about the place he knows inevitably differs from the way he thinks about the place he does not know: the two places cannot have the same conceptual presence in his mind. As practitioners of world literature we inevitably begin with our own Carthages. Aware that we regard other places differently, we can be afflicted with guilt, because we are appropriating someone else's cultural production; because we are not appropriating enough of it, choosing only what happens to fit our own agendas; or because we are not appropriating it as well as it deserves. We can also be afflicted with anxiety and exhaustion, because there is so much literature in the world while our talents and time are so limited: *ars longa, vita brevis*, as the ancients knew ("the lyf so short, the craft so long to lerne," in Chaucer's translation [line 1]). But despite the risks of guilt, anxiety, or exhaustion, there is also exhilaration, and in many institutions world literature has arrived in full and unembarrassed vigor in the undergraduate classroom.

At the graduate level, however, world literature has not been widely admitted into the curriculum.[2] Thus we are participating in one of our profession's many engaging paradoxes: we may believe that undergraduates should study world literature as part of their education in the humanities, but in our own professional formation, at least in United States graduate programs, we do not often encounter world literature course work. Many of us who are teaching world literature to undergraduates have not taken such a course since we were undergraduates ourselves, if we took one then (and if we did, its design was probably very different). In the classroom, then, we and our students may be amateurs together. This is not necessarily a bad thing: as I have noted elsewhere (Eckhardt 151), those who retain the etymological linkage of the amateur's condition to the motivations of love and desire may be in an excellent position to convey the pleasure of reading, which should always be one of the crucial aims of any literature course. But aesthetic pleasure need not be the only aim, and amateur devotion need not be our only posture in relation to world literature texts.

Does this paradox derive from a healthy division between the characteristics of undergraduate and graduate education, or an outmoded curricular gap that we should work to remedy? I suggest here that we are already remedying it, in part, by a variety of strategies; and yet the gap itself, though sometimes bridged, should also be allowed to stand.

There are at least two reasons why world literature as such is not more widely represented at the graduate level. First, as a concept that often celebrates breadth, world literature resists being implemented as a specialization, while graduate education continues to be devoted primarily to the development of deep knowledge and new understandings within specializations. Second, if graduate work in literature is understood to include research on texts in their original languages (a viewpoint I endorse), then it is natural to resist constructing wide-ranging courses or degrees in which faculty members as well as students may be reading virtually everything in translation. Even the most polyglot instructors can know only a tiny fraction of the world's nearly seven thousand living languages (*Ethnologue*), not to mention the many literary languages of the past. In the undergraduate curriculum, and especially in general education courses, expectations are different and the daunting question of language expertise is less likely to predominate.

Nevertheless, despite the small number of official graduate degrees or courses, I propose that world literature often constitutes an implicit curriculum, where it takes multiple guises and uses various strategies, each of which can provide a powerful opportunity to achieve critical aspects of the intellectual agenda associated with the worlding of literature.

Theorizing World Literature for Graduate Students

Graduate curricula in literature often require a methods proseminar or a course on theory (for one example and discussion in a comparative literature context, see Arens and Richmond-Garza; Emerson, Neubauer, A. Dharwadker, V. Dharwadker, Eckhardt, and Froula). Some of these courses have become capacious enough to allow space for discussing the nature of world literature. A two-week unit in such a course might be based on the chapters in part 1 of the present volume, along with sections of David Damrosch's *What Is World Literature?* Alternatively, the topic of world literature can be addressed as one of several ongoing foci throughout such a course—as I have done, assigning a chapter or two of *What Is World Literature?* each week to allow theoretical questions to emerge through the book's astonishing plenitude of literary case studies, ranging from ancient to contemporary and from every continent except Antarctica. Also useful are collections such as *Debating World Literature*, edited by Christopher Prendergast, and, a decade earlier, *Reading World Literature: Theory, History, Practice*, edited by Sarah Lawall.

The theory or methods seminar should of course make students aware that not all critics have welcomed the expanded interest in world literature. As verb or adjective, *world* implies the results of a full spectrum of practices, from the long overdue recognition of the world's immense array of literatures, past and present, to nearly the opposite, the effacement of local literatures as megaliteratures spread over the world. Although as an advocate of world literature in the first sense, I use the term positively, it should be acknowledged that much of what is now globally marketed (in anglophone packages) as world literature has been determined primarily by academic Westerners, disproportionately from the United States. More than one voice has objected that the entire enterprise, far from being praiseworthy for expanding the range of writers and texts that are widely read, can instead become another form of exploitation in which literary works from many cultures are appropriated, packed up according to Euro-American expectations, and sold for the United States domestic market and for anglophone readers worldwide. Productive discussions of this controversy, in addition to those in this book, have been offered by Emily Apter, Vilashini Cooppan, Djelal Kadir, Franco Moretti ("Conjectures," "Evolution," and "More Conjectures"), and Gayatri Chakravorty Spivak. Moretti's propositions—including his application of world-system theory, with its concept of locations at the core from which literary phenomena are diffused in waves to the semiperiphery and periphery; his recourse to evolutionary biology, with its model of a branching tree; and his notion of distant reading to capture broad transcultural patterns, as a counterpoint to close reading to capture individuations—have continued to provoke both endorsements and objections, as in the responses by Eileen Julien and by Hui-sok Yoo in Gunilla Lindberg-Wada's volume. A theory or methods course in which graduate students were assigned to read several of these position statements would provide a strong basis for understanding why world literature is an endlessly fertile but always contested territory.

Further, the graduate theory or methods course can emphasize that the world literature movement exists not in isolation, but in conversation with an expansion of other discourses about *world* and *worlding*. In the domains of landscape and material culture, for example, UNESCO's World Heritage project, which has identified 830 sites that "belong to all the peoples of the world, irrespective of the territory on which they are located" (UNESCO World Heritage Committee), calls upon concepts of transnational circulation, canonicity, and the juxtaposition of presumed world values with local conditions. In the social sciences, similarly, studies such as those of Jan Jindy Pettman on "worlding women" in feminist international politics, or Herman van der Wusten on "political world cities" (cf. Simone), offer opportunities to compare our own concerns with the assumptions and anxieties associated with notions of "world" and "worlding" as used in other disciplines.

Worlding a Literature

An implicit step toward a world literature framework that respects the linguistic specialization associated with graduate education occurs when the worldwide circulation of specific languages and their literary cultures is recognized. Where English literature faculties once tended to see themselves as divided primarily between specialists on British and on American literature, now their departments also pursue fields such as transatlantic studies and world literature in English. Several French departments, such as those at UCLA, Penn State, the University of Nottingham, Macalester College, Carleton College, and Hobart and William Smith Colleges, have recently reconfigured themselves as Departments of French and Francophone Studies (see Lionnet), in recognition not only of the interdisciplinarity implied by the "studies" label but also of the fact that *francophonie* is a condition that exists worldwide. Graduate students in such programs can often construct a well-grounded transnational education through taking a geographically diverse set of departmental seminars, even if each seminar remains more narrowly defined. Similarly, Wang Ning, among others, has pointed out that there are many Chineses and has argued for a global conception of "literature in Chinese" wherever it is produced. The modest syntactic shift from "X literature" to "literature in X" (e.g., from "Spanish literature" to "literature in Spanish") entails a fundamental revision of the paradigm, as it opens out into the wide-lens view.

This shift is no quick fix, however. As Francesco Loriggio points out in his critique of "proposals to internationalize departments of English, to transform them into departments of literatures written in English," significant losses can result if we decontextualize each literature from its "cultural intimacies" or obscure the fact that many such literatures come from "multilingual societies with a multilingual literary production" (73–74). But to affiliate all literatures in English (or in Chinese or any other language) with one another need not entail disaffiliating them from their local selves or siblings. The pan- and transcontinental literatures of the Middle Ages, such as those in Latin, Arabic, or Hebrew, may provide useful examples here: in addition to their situatedness within widespread reading communities—dispersed across parts of Europe, Africa, and Asia—medieval Latin, Arabic, and Hebrew texts were also inflected by their situatedness in a local context, as can often be seen in the physical materiality and textual variations of individual manuscript copies.[3] Similarly, a graduate program engaged in worlding a modern language and literature can include historical and contextual readings that deploy multiple frames of reference. The new MLA book series World Literatures Reimagined, which aims to "consider particular literatures in an international context" (*Guidelines*) and whose first volume addresses Brazilian narrative (Fitz), will provide an increasing array of resources for the graduate teaching of individual literatures reconceptualized to include their transcultural relations. The transnational literary productions of large regions, such as the Americas, can also be worlded in the sense of being examined, in their multiple spatial and geopolitical relations, through the exchange of ideas among scholars worldwide, as in the agenda of the International American Studies Association, founded by Djelal Kadir (www.iasaweb.org) (cf., with a narrower scope, Dimock and Buell).

Listening to Each Other's Voices from Afar

Even a single work or writer can be presented in graduate courses according to a world literature framework by displaying the transcultural itineraries of both texts and critics. A ready example is Shakespeare: recent scholarship on "international Shakespeare" or "global Shakespeare" invites us to teach *Hamlet, Macbeth, Lear*, and the other plays not only from the perspective of Anglo-American literary history, theory, and criticism, or their general "universal" appeal (a very ambitious term indeed), but also in their specific, localized manifestations worldwide. A great array of resources is available at Stanford's *Shakespeare in Asia* Web site (sia .stanford.edu), while the online *World Shakespeare Bibliography* offers "coverage extending to more than 118 languages and representing every country in North America, South America, and Europe, and nearly every country in Asia, Africa, and Australasia" (Introduction).

Beyond individual authors, graduate courses or clusters of readings can use models such as diaspora to address the literary productions associated with peoples, cultures, religions, and so on, wherever they may be found. In addition to the more widely taught subjects of the African and the Jewish diasporas, resources such as Everett Jenkins's *Muslim Diaspora* (a reference compilation), Emmanuel Nelson's *Reworlding: The Literature of the Indian Diaspora* (a collection of essays), Dale Olsen's *The Chrysanthemum and the Song: Music, Memory, and Identity in the South American Japanese Diaspora* (a study in ethnomusicology), and the journal *Diaspora* (published by the Univ. of Toronto Press since 1991) are making it easier to locate materials for teaching a widening range of diasporic literatures and listening to critical voices from afar.

The point of representing such voices in graduate courses is not to see what, or whether, scholars elsewhere can contribute to our critical discourse; it is to understand what their own discourses are saying. If they express critical modes that we ourselves are not pursuing, students will see that the critical positions predominant in their graduate programs, positions whose rightness sometimes seems self-evident, may not enjoy a similar centrality elsewhere. Inserting that observation into any graduate course redirects students' attention back to the texts with new questions to ask about cultural circulation.

Listening to Each Other's Voices Right Next Door

A greatly underestimated resource in many graduate programs, moreover, may be closer at hand: our students, who bring with them languages and cultural traditions that can expand the range of literatures our graduate programs include. The graduate students in Penn State's comparative literature department in 2007–08 (and our situation is probably not unusual) represented thirteen countries and many languages, including eight or so of the more familiar classical and modern Western languages along with Arabic, Cantonese, Catalan, Chinese (Mandarin), Hebrew, Japanese, Korean, Krio, Luo, Mandé, Navajo, Portuguese, Swahili, Swedish, Turkish, Ukrainian, and Urdu. A seminar session on the formation of canons, for instance, or on literary periodicities, or on the options for translating humor can become a great world literature moment if all students are asked to deploy their linguistic and literary knowledge as an asset for the class as a whole. Tanya Agathocleous and Karin Gosselink, focusing on the concept of "going into debt to others" in teaching world literature, recommend engaging students in collaborative reading and group work (471). Though they address undergraduate teaching, projects such as their group translation exercise may work even better at the graduate level.

Another greatly underestimated resource for many graduate programs consists of our colleagues, often just down the corridor or in the next building. Institutional cultures may make team-teaching either easy or difficult—some schools, mine among them, provide funding to encourage such ventures—but whatever the administrative rules, faculty members and graduate students can usually find ways to overleap departmental boundaries. The building in which my office is located houses some three hundred faculty and graduate student members of five language and literature departments, including many who have studied and lived abroad; we meet at the coffeepot, the sandwich shop, a weekly interdepartmental lunch series, and other venues. Cross-listings of seminars, or concurrent scheduling (where two or more classes meet together, but students remain registered in their own departments, thus avoiding problems about credit flows or degree requirements), can enrich the scope of graduate offerings while pooling and enhancing expertise. Graduate students could also be required to take some part of their course work in another literature department (comparative literature degree programs standardly do this) or to take a course in history, philosophy, art, women's studies, and so on that incorporates international or global perspectives. In the long run, reciprocity should alleviate logistical concerns about lost enrollments. Nothing is really lost and intellectually a great deal can be gained by these short local journeys into one another's classrooms.

Teaching to Teach

Many literature departments that offer graduate degrees also offer undergraduate world literature courses in which graduate students serve as graders, tutors, discussion leaders, or sole instructors. Where these arrangements include faculty supervision through mentoring or a pedagogy course, such a context offers an excellent opportunity to teach, and teach about, world literature. This present volume, along with a collection of previous local (and other) syllabi, would provide material for discussion.

Teaching to teach is now likely to include the use of instructional technology. Interactive teleconferencing, for example, permits instructors at different locations to visit each other's classes or to teach entire courses together. A recent Penn State "hybrid" course on French culture and politics involved four Penn State instructors and four from the Sorbonne. All instructors initially met face-to-face on our Pennsylvania campus, and the class sessions then continued transatlantically, using technology rooms at both locations. At the end of the course several of the Penn State graduate students traveled to meet their counterparts in France. A project of that sort requires additional funding, but even with low-key uses of technology, graduate students teaching world literature can use passages of texts recorded in original languages, online contextual materials such as maps, and e-mail or conference phone exchanges among interlocutors in various parts of the world. In the process of learning how to teach this way, with the classroom understood not as a closed space but as a site of potential access to other spaces, graduate students' own knowledge of ways to negotiate the domains of world literature will surely expand as well.

Going to School When School's Out

Summer institutes, workshops, and seminars at conferences can expand the graduate curriculum and advantageously blur the line between graduate students and faculty members when both participate. A few years ago my department offered a summer institute on world literature that brought together graduate students from several institutions. An analogous current project is the NEH-funded summer workshop on the teaching of world literature in general education English courses, held at George Mason University.[4] Though it focuses on faculty, some aspects of this workshop are adaptable to a graduate student context.

A similar option to bring together graduate students from different institutions is the seminar structure of the annual meetings of the American Comparative Literature Association (ACLA), where eight to twelve faculty members and graduate students meet in morning or afternoon sessions over three days and can thereby come to constitute a working group. Some of these ACLA groups have addressed the nature of world literature or have dealt with topics in that framework; some groups have continued over several years. Student participants occasionally find that this extramural, voluntary, ungraded, untranscripted annual seminar has become a crucial part of their graduate formations.

Other summertime or conference-time opportunities of course exist as well; they are often easy to initiate and can quietly disappear when their usefulness has passed. The challenge for a world literature agenda may be to make more of these projects broadly international (global?) in subject and in personnel. One could envisage an ongoing summer world literature institute with a dozen or more participants from as many countries, perhaps hosted at a different site each year, in which graduate students would engage with their counterparts who have been educated in a wide range of intellectual traditions, conversing either (preferably) in person or through technological mediation.

None of these strategies is broad enough in itself to constitute graduate study in world literature. Some represent only a modest stretching beyond national or monolingual forms of graduate education. Further, these projects do not necessarily all cohere conceptually, as they represent different instantiations of what happens when we world the literature that we write about and teach. Yet each is a gesture in the direction of world literature, and several such gestures together can form a responsible and challenging implicit curriculum at the graduate level. Many are already in place, especially in graduate programs in comparative literature. Others could be implemented even without the infusion of additional funds, which are chronically hard to find. Given some combination of these strategies and others that may be available, no student need graduate with an MA or PhD in a literature field without at least a fundamental understanding of the importance of world literature, the underlying theorizations for (and against) teaching it, and a range of interpretive methods and critical tools with which to address this literary paradigm in an informed and self-critical way.

The Ethics of World Literature

Finally, whether through an explicit curriculum or the implicit curriculum that accompanies it, the education of graduate students also needs to emphasize that how (or whether) they engage with world literature represents an ethical posture. Thinking about world literature or doing something about it is a conceptual and ideological practice, not only a response to the realities of academic job descriptions. The position that the role of teacher and scholar entails the ethical imperative of moving beyond our own comfortable intellectual parish (Miner 10), lest we be parochial ourselves and inculcate parochialism in our students, has been stated in many ways. The opposite position—a rejection of the viewpoint that staying close to home entails parochialism while traveling is inherently an ethically superior act—is less commonly articulated but can sometimes be perceived, for example, as a subtext in arguments against using translations in the classroom, in warnings against dilettantism, or in reminders that we should not stray too far from our areas of expertise. A triangulating opposite position of a different sort is that to participate in world literature as presently practiced is not so much an alternative to parochialism as complicity in the harmful aspects of globalization. My own sympathies, clearly, lie with the first of these positions, but I recognize that this position is not always invulnerable.

In preparing this essay, I happened to notice that the copyright page of Prendergast's collection *Debating World Literature* includes, along with the typical publication data, this statement: "The moral rights of the authors and the editor have been asserted." On investigation I realized that this sentence is a formula relating to intellectual property rights (Oppenheim), but for a moment its forthright reference to morality seemed especially apposite here. Either to embrace or to shun the teaching of world literature, in any of its plausible or implausible forms, is to exercise an ethical choice; and this choice requires that graduate students, like other learners and teachers, be cognizant of the implications. To return to Augustine's formulation: it is true, as he said, that we cannot think of unknown places, our counterparts to his Alexandria, in the same way that we think of the place we know and mentally inhabit, our counterparts to his Carthage; but ethically in our era we have outlived the option of not thinking about our Alexandrias at all.

Notes

1. Since Augustine is speaking of himself (12.6), the translation can read "I" rather than "we," as Taylor's translation does (2: 186); cf. Lozovsky 42.

2. At least in North America, there seem to be very few graduate degrees called "world literature" or offering a specialization or requirement with that name. Internet and database searches in May 2008 (I thank Annika Farber for her assistance) turned up only a handful or so of such programs: Case Western Reserve University offers an MA in world literature; the Web site of the literature program at the University of California, Santa Cruz, mentions "world literature and cultural studies" among the program's strengths; the Web site of the Department of Comparative Literature and Foreign Languages at the University of California, Riverside, refers to its "graduate degrees based on the comparative studies of world literatures and cultures"; the Web site of the MA in literature offered by Northwestern University's School of Continuing Studies (an evening program) lists "comparative and world literature" among its optional specializations; the MA in English at North Carolina State University includes a world literature concentration; the home page of the literature PhD at the University of Notre Dame discusses *Weltliteratur* (I note in passing that the term *Weltliteratur* sometimes retains an evocative status denied to *world literature*); the PhD in comparative literature at the University of Alberta includes an examination field called world literature; and so on. There is a somewhat larger representation of individual graduate courses called World Literature, such as the Studies in Modern World Literature course in Sam Houston State University's English

department; while some of these courses aim to read a worldwide selection of literary texts, others focus on the phenomenon of literary globalization.

3. In pointing to medieval literatures as pertinent here, I disagree with Moretti's position that there are "*two distinct world literatures*: one that precedes the eighteenth century—and one that follows it" and that "the past and the present of literature should be seen . . . as *structurally so unlike each other* that they require completely different theoretical approaches" ("Evolution" 120–21). Instead, I would argue that graduate-level preparation in the criticism and pedagogy of world literature should not institutionalize that presumed dichotomy.

4. This project, entitled "Cultural Encounters in Global Contexts: Teaching World Literature in General Education English Courses" and directed by Joel Foreman and John Foster, is designed to prepare faculty members "trained in some aspect of North American or European literary studies to grapple effectively with the global terrain" ("Faculty").

Works Cited

Agathocleous, Tanya, and Karin Gosselink. "Debt in the Teaching of World Literature: Collaboration in the Context of Uneven Development." *Pedagogy: Critical Approaches to Teaching Literature, Language, Composition, and Culture* 6 (2006): 453–73. Print.

Apter, Emily. "Afterlife of a Discipline." *Comparative Literature* 57.2 (2005): 201–06. Print.

Arens, Katherine, and Elizabeth M. Richmond-Garza. "The Canon of Theory: Report on an Institutional Case." *Comparative Literature Studies* 34.4 (1997): 392–413. Print.

Augustine. *De Genesi ad litteram.* Ed. J. Zycha. Vienna, 1894. Print. Corpus Scriptorum Ecclesiasticorum Latinorum 28.1.

———. *The Literal Meaning of Genesis.* Trans. John H. Taylor. 2 vols. Mahwah: Paulist, 1982. Print.

Chaucer, Geoffrey. *The Parlement of Foules. The Riverside Chaucer.* 3rd ed. Gen. ed. Larry D. Benson. Boston: Houghton, 1987. 383–94. Print.

Cooppan, Vilashini. "Ghosts in the Disciplinary Machine: The Uncanny Life of World Literature." *Comparative Literature Studies* 41.1 (2004): 10–36. Print.

Damrosch, David. *What Is World Literature?* Princeton: Princeton UP, 2003. Print.

Dimock, Wai Chee, and Lawrence Buell, eds. *Shades of the Planet: American Literature as World Literature.* Princeton: Princeton UP, 2007. Print.

Eckhardt, Caroline D. "Old Fields, New Corn, and Present Ways of Writing about the Past." *Comparative Literature in an Age of Globalization.* Ed. Haun Saussy. Baltimore: Johns Hopkins UP, 2006. 139–54. Print.

Emerson, Caryl, John Neubauer, Aparna Dharwadker, Vinay Dharwadker, Caroline D. Eckhardt, and Christine Froula. "Responses." *Comparative Literature Studies* 34.4 (1997): 414–27. Print.

Ethnologue: Languages of the World. 15th ed. Ed. Raymond G. Gordon, Jr. Dallas: SIL Intl., 2005. Web. 5 May 2007.

"Faculty Earn NEH Grant for World Literature Workshop." *Mason Gazette.* George Mason U, 27 Sept. 2005. Web. 15 Feb. 2008.

Fitz, Earl E. *Brazilian Narrative Traditions in a Comparative Context.* New York: MLA, 2005. Print. World Lits. Reimagined 1.

Guidelines for the Series World Literatures Reimagined. MLA, 7 Sept. 2006. Web. 15 Feb. 2008.

Introduction. *World Shakespeare Bibliography Online, 1962–2008.* Johns Hopkins UP, 6 Dec. 2007. Web. 15 Feb. 2008.

Jenkins, Everett, Jr. *The Muslim Diaspora: A Comprehensive Reference to the Spread of Islam in Asia, Africa, Europe, and the Americas.* 3 vols. Jefferson: McFarland, 1999–2006. Print.

Julien, Eileen. "Arguments and Further Conjectures on World Literature." Lindberg-Wada 122–32.

Kadir, Djelal. "To World, to Globalize—Comparative Literature's Crossroads." *Comparative Literature Studies* 41.1 (2004): 1–9. Print.

Lawall, Sarah, ed. *Reading World Literature: Theory, History, Practice.* Austin: U of Texas P, 1994. Print.

Lindberg-Wada, Gunilla, ed. *Studying Transcultural Literary History.* Berlin: de Gruyter, 2006. Print.

Lionnet, Françoise. "National Language Departments in the Era of Transnational Studies." *PMLA* 117.5 (2002): 1252–54. Print.

Loriggio, Francesco. "Disciplinary Methods of Memory as Cultural History: Comparative Literature, Globalization, and the Categories of Criticism." *Comparative Literature Studies* 41.1 (2004): 49–79. Print.

Lozovsky, Natalia. *"The Earth Is Our Book": Geographical Knowledge in the Latin West, ca. 400–1000.* Ann Arbor: U of Michigan P, 2000. Print.

Miner, Earl. *Comparative Poetics: An Intercultural Essay on Theories of Literature.* Princeton: Princeton UP, 1990. Print.

Moretti, Franco. "Conjectures on World Literature." *New Left Review* 1 (2000): 54–58. Print.

———. "Evolution, World-Systems, *Weltliteratur.*" Lindberg-Wada 113–21.

———. "More Conjectures." *New Left Review* 20 (2003): 73–81. Print.

Nelson, Emmanuel Sampath, ed. *Reworlding: The Literature of the Indian Diaspora.* New York: Greenwood, 1992. Print.

Olsen, Dale A. *The Chrysanthemum and the Song: Music, Memory, and Identity in the South American Japanese Diaspora.* Gainesville: UP of Florida, 2004. Print.

Oppenheim, Charles. "Moral Rights and the Electronic Library." *Ariadne: The Web Version* 4 (1996): n. pag. UKOLN, 15 July 1996. Web. 15 Feb. 2008.

Pettman, Jan Jindy. *Worlding Women: A Feminist International Politics.* Sydney: Allen, 1996. Print.

Prendergast, Christopher, ed. *Debating World Literature.* London: Verso, 2004. Print.

Simone, AbdouMaliq. "On the Worlding of African Cities." *African Studies Review* 44.2 (2001): 15–41. Print.

Spivak, Gayatri Chakravorty. *Death of a Discipline.* New York: Columbia UP, 2003. Print.

UNESCO World Heritage Committee. *World Heritage*. UNESCO.org, June
    2007. Web. 13 June 2007.
van der Wusten, Herman. "Political World Cities: Where Flows through En-
    twined Multi-state and Transnational Networks Meet Places." *Cities in Glo-
    balization: Practices, Policies and Theories*. Ed. Peter J. Taylor et al. London:
    Routledge, 2007. 202–18. Print.
Wang Ning. "Global Englishes and Global Chineses: A New Framework for
    Comparative Literature." Comparative Lit. Luncheon Presentation. Pennsyl-
    vania State U, University Park. 17 Oct. 2005. Address.
Yoo, Hui-sok. "A Little Pact with the Devil? On Franco Moretti's Conjectures on
    World Literature." Lindberg-Wada 133–43.

Collin Meissner and Margaret Doody

"The World's Story": Teaching Literature in the Twenty-First Century

It is perhaps best to begin by deflating the volume of this essay's title. For if we've learned anything through the study of literatures and cultures, let alone the examination of literatures and cultures more broadly, even globally, understood, it is that definition exceeds our grasp, our conceptual abilities. "Story" is by its very nature protean and metamorphic. Strictly speaking, it is always disabling, always metastatic, always taking away as much as it gives. Henry James once described reality as that which "represents to my perception the things we cannot possibly *not* know, sooner or later, in one way or another" (1062–63). The World's Story is also the title of the inaugural world literature seminar in Notre Dame's new PhD in Literature Program, and it serves also as an articulation of the program's underlying rationale.

The seminar and the program both rely on a foundation as flexible as James's remark. To avoid imposing a conceptual framework for understanding this or that text, this or that culture, and to avoid falling victim to the prejudices of a particular methodological training or cultural inheritance, The World's Story (as well as the program in literature) relies on an undogmatic openness. Only, however, to the extent possible. Our deflating has to do with this "to the extent possible" admission. While the program's goals were conceived with the grandest ambitions about reconceptualizing the study of literature, they have been anchored by an acceptance that knowledge and interpretation are always already culturally controlled and informed. Part of The World's Story, then—the easier part—is coming to recognize how the study of literature and culture is shaped by modes of belief whose visible and invisible influences determine almost every aspect of how and what it is we understand when we understand at all. The ambitious part, the program-building component, is in trying to get beyond that culturally influenced position and bring about an atmosphere in which study of literature allows for the production of new scholars who can function in the academic community as agents of change.

In 2001, Margaret Doody and a group of her faculty colleagues at Notre Dame began a series of discussions around the idea of a new doctoral program in the study of literature. Reasons behind this idea were multiple. Some were institutional: despite an increasingly distinguished faculty, the university did not have a doctoral program in any language or literature other than English. Some reasons were more ambitious and idealistic: at no moment in American history has it seemed more important that a free and rigorous presentation of other cultures and literatures take place. This discussion group not only enjoyed full institutional support of the idea, but it was charged by the dean of Arts and Letters to develop a doctoral program that would bring together the various language and literature constituencies as well as the Department of Theology and the Department of Philosophy. Briefly stated, the PhD in Literature Program is based on the acceptance of the idea that discrete national cultures and identities have long since given way to a more porous universalism in which the individual, the place, and the country are not only collectively cultured but also globally composed. In other words, while discrete national literatures exist—as they always have—we now recognize that their production and interpretation have never been sovereign but rather have invariably relied on all manner of cultural cross-fertilization.

The design committee of the PhD in Literature Program, because of its composition, was well disposed to embrace this perspective. In addition to Doody, the committee included the chairs of the German and Russian Languages and Literatures Department, the Classics Department, the Irish Language and Literature Department, the East Asian Languages and Literatures Department, and the Romance Languages and Literatures Department. This committee had to approach any discussions about a new doctoral program in literature from the position that interpretation is transliterary and transnational, that the study of literature in the twenty-first century takes as a given our invariable tendencies to bring multiple valences to bear on any text (as broadly defined as possible), no matter how far that text may be in the past or how close to the present, no matter how deeply embedded in a national culture or how worldly and intercultural.

It's not without irony that while this perspective was the guiding principle of the committee that convened to develop the program, the perspective was almost always under attack whenever discussion moved from theory and ideas to the practicalities of implementation. Again, the need to let a little air out of this essay's title. Since the PhD in Literature Program is a doctoral degree by committee, its success and failure rest on the capacity for the program's constituent partners and, even more important, constituent faculty members to see beyond disciplinary boundaries—to get up in the air, so to speak, and see the world globally. Literature often achieves this kind of transcendence, but its study often falls short. For all our embrace and discussion of indisciplinarity and multicultural, globalist study, true cross-cultural understanding is not only exceedingly elusive and difficult, it's also often unwelcome. William Wordsworth's remark about murdering to dissect ("The Tables Turned") comes to mind when we think about the kind of constraints that stand in the way of the goals the PhD in Literature Program has set itself.

To get beyond disciplinary categories, the program decided to take both-and positions with regard to curricular development, program of study, admissions, and general competencies. Again, to the extent possible, the program has tried to address the present realities and prefigure the future of literary study. To this end, the committee agreed that the program must be built up from the principles of disciplinary expertise and that mastery of a national literature's disciplinary integrity should serve as the foundation that supports truly interdisciplinary and translinguistic research. Our broadly conceived literature seminars must both support and undermine the foci of traditional area, field, and national literary models. The big questions we encourage our students to ask must be posed from a firm grasp of a national language and literary tradition.

To this end, the PhD in Literature Program utilizes the traditional goals of a literature PhD as the point of departure and overlays those with study that encourages the flexibility to relate literary material across disciplinary divisions and national boundaries. Stated another way, by adopting a both-and strategy, the program defers to the inevitable prejudices that accompany all forms of inquiry, even going so far as to embrace those prejudices as hermeneutic tools, but demands as well that those interpretive tools be redeployed in an interanimating dynamic that reaches beyond borders and nationalities.

In practical terms, the program demands that students satisfy all the competencies one would expect in a national literature PhD program. But this expertise should serve as the point of departure for a larger research project that escapes a nationality's narrow definitions and raises questions that entertain, bring about, and promote a more free and unfettered (without being sentimental) understanding. We want students to explore the complex reality of difference. The program is asking that we develop scholars who are and scholarship that is bigger and broader than we've had in the past; scholars who understand both a literature's organic connection to place and its organic relation to humanity; scholars who are perhaps not so sure of themselves as they have been traditionally, not so willing to murder to dissect, more willing to mine the riches of what we cannot not know, sooner or later, in one way or another. To speak of scholars and scholarship this way is to speak of agents of change.

The program's most significant contribution to the larger study of world literature today has been the creation of dynamic world literature seminars and a theory-based course that serves as an introduction to a global notion of literary understanding. This course is titled Philology and *Weltliteratur* and was conceived and designed by Joseph Buttigieg. The seminars, spearheaded by Doody, have been a gateway into the program that all incoming students are required to take in their first semester; the theory course follows as the core requirement in the students' second term. The seminars have always been team-taught by faculty experts who work in the original language (although practicalities determine that course material is often presented in translation) and who bring into the classroom their refined knowledge of the various cultures and literatures under discussion. We felt it of paramount importance that at the very outset of their studies students encounter literatures and literary traditions that would exceed their normal interpretive grasp. The courses use individual texts as opposed to anthologies, are broadly designed, but must always include selections of classical literature, of Arabic literature, of oriental literature (customarily this has been Chinese), and of postclassical European literatures. Each course must offer some exposure to these literatures in their original language. The planned effect is that both faculty members and students undergo the learning experience that invariably accompanies the shock of the unexplored. The readings, both primary and secondary, are substantial and offer significant immersion, by virtue of their weight and with the knowledgeable guidance of the faculty members.

The courses' goals are to promote intellectual openness and bring students to understand that ways of interpreting and understanding one literary tradition are not necessarily portable and may even fail when applied to other literary traditions and cultures. The challenge offered by these seminars is that the material presented by faculty experts in the represented areas inevitably unsettles the paradigms most of us rely on as a means of understanding the world and how literature operates as an interpretive medium for that world. As an introduction to the PhD in Literature Program, this experience of challenge, contestation, or even failure of interpretation is absolutely foundational. It shows students why they need to get beyond their own interpretive and cultural comfort zones. The world literature seminars throw open windows on a wider, richer, more variegated world. In doing so, these courses prepare students for thinking about and teaching literature in a manner more suited to the twenty-first century.

To date, the program has created and conducted five world literature seminars (see the course descriptions in app.). The first—The World's Story: Literature of History and Ethnography—focused on how different cultures have told the same story of history. This seminar introduced the program in 2002 and has been succeeded by world literature seminars titled Love, Desire and Identity, in 2003; Life Writing: Biography and Autobiography, in 2004; Metamorphosis, in 2005; and Travel and Changing Place, in 2006. The program's theory seminar deals, as Buttigieg has articulated, with

> theories of different time and places with emphasis on the critical
> problems that arise when what we call "Literature" is investigated in a
> multicultural context. Issues that may be expected to arise include the
> following: the problems of translation, the meaning of metaphor,
> hermeneutics complexity, the meaning of the word "style" and the
> relation between oral and written literatures.

In each iteration the seminars have raised as many questions as they've answered, but a general consensus has emerged over the past four years.

To call it confusion would be playing on the histrionic; but *confusion* may be exactly the right word, except that the confusion in this case is a good thing, in the sense that our students and the participating faculty members emerge from these course less likely to suffer from the limitations of certitude, more likely to embrace the positive aspects of bewilderment. For instance, The World's Story addressed national and even global issues, offered an exposure through literature that brought the course audience to a position of greater humility with respect to other cultures. Love, Desire, Identity took the shock of The World's Story on to the level of the individual. When students followed the themes of love, desire, and identity over borders, across time, and through genders, the texts continually posed questions about how these powerful forces shape our understanding not only of what makes a human life significant but also of what makes it worth living, what makes people unique, and what makes them not always so exclusively other.

Structurally and philosophically the combination of world literature seminars and Philology and *Weltliteratur* has provoked students to pursue lines of interest that extend well beyond what one would find in traditional doctoral study. In particular, students have been increasingly ambitious in their juxtapositions of literatures, themes, and disciplines and increasingly sophisticated in their understanding of how interpretation is a contextualized and contextualizing process. Similarly, the range of reference entertained in the world literature and theory seminars has broadened the foundation from which our students have generated their research questions and sharpened the questions themselves. As our inaugural class of students has now moved through its comprehensive examinations to the dissertation stage of their studies, the program's both-and strategy is undergoing its most significant test. But at this point, insofar as the program can speak, the world's story is still being written—we hope by students who become agents of change.

Appendix: Course Descriptions

The World's Story: Literature and Ethnography

The course on world literature will focus on the way in which different cultures have told the same story of history. People, places, and religious practices have long attracted the attention of historians and travel writers (functions often combined, as in the case of Herodotus and Ibn Khaldun). History deals with problems, pain, and change, and the literature of history offers a vision of ways of approaching the world. The course, which is team-taught, deals with three major areas of history production: the Arab world, China, and the Western world (with particular focus on Ancient Greece).

Love, Desire, Identity

Themes and topics covered by various works include erotic love, filial and familial love, and love of God, but there are other loves too, such as the love of animals, pursuits, objects. Desire evokes philosophical questions about need, necessity, and the structure of the self, all of which can be and have been dealt with in a variety of ways by different cultures. Both love and desire imply a notion of identity or of identities to which the individual may be attached or which the individual may be incorporating (or rejecting). Texts studied include Ancient Greek novels and some medieval and modern fictions of both East and West (*The Tale of Genji*, *Troilus and Criseyde*, *Wuthering Heights*). The poetry we read ranges chronologically from the very early *Shih jing* (the first collection of Chinese poems) and the Song of Songs to Sappho and other Greek and Roman authors, through works by Petrarch and Dante to poems and popular songs in Asia and Europe of the present day. A variety of meditative and religious work exploring the nature of love and longing will be included.

Life Writing: Biography and Autobiography

Writing about a life, giving a shape to something called a life is a perpetual concern of writers in different parts of the world and of many different kinds of writers—historians, novelists, psychologists included. The concept immediately introduces complex aesthetic, political, and philosophical questions: What is this self about whom a narrative is spun? What is the difference between biography and autobiography? What is the relation to fiction? Life writing seems intimately related to theology, as we may see in the New Testament, in the stories of Moses and Buddha, in the meditations of Augustine of Hippo in the fourth century CE, in the work of the Sufi mystic al-Ghazali in the twelfth century, or in the narratives of the Baptist John Bunyan in the seventeenth century. Travel writing (including stories of discovery) seems largely life writing in masquerade. Poets and novelists have long played with writing lives and have presented individuals engaged in life writing. The exile or wanderer may turn to autobiography, yet such life writing is perilous for the writer, the narrator inviting us to decode the narrator while offering us various tropes and devices to both conceal and reveal. Our study includes narratives of antiquity and of modern times, of East and West, investigating various ways in which we have given meaning to the individual and the communal experience through the production of a life. Among other things, we may expect to find many clues as to our notions of the function of narrative and ways of arranging dynamic concepts such as motive, agency, affection, emotion.

Metamorphosis

This world literature course explores the concept taking Ovid's great poetic work *Metamorphoses* as a focal text. We examine the concept in relation to the arts (painting, sculpture, film) as well as to written works and consider the concept of metamorphosis in its constant challenge to concepts of identity (psychological, spiritual, ethnic, geographic, etc.). The course covers diverse genres in different periods: classical, Arabic medieval, Western medieval, early modern, Chinese classical, and modern literatures and cultures. Literary texts range from conversion narratives (such as *Deliverance from Error*, the autobiography of al-Ghazali) to fairy tales like "Sleeping Beauty" ("La belle au bois dormant"), from satiric and brilliantly poetic accounts of negative transformations (Pope's *Dunciad*) to lyric explorations of change—or resistance to change. ("Love is not love / which alters when it alteration finds / or bends with the remover to remove . . ."). But Eros is also a transformer, valued and dreaded because of its power to make its sufferer change nature and direction, as in Dante's *Vita nuova*.

Philology and *Weltliteratur*

Erich Auerbach's essay, from which this course derives its title, serves as a point of departure for exploring the possibility of developing an approach to literary history and literary interpretation that attends to the historical, cultural, and aesthetic specificity of the individual literary work and at the same time brings into relief the complex ways in which cultures interact, overlap, and modify one another. The course will focus primarily on the pertinent works of Vico, Herder and the German Romantics, Auerbach, Arnold, C. L. R. James, Raymond Williams, and Edward W. Said, as well as selections from the writings of Fanon, Ngũgĩ, Lamming, Césaire, and others.

Travel and Changing Place: Tourism, Exile, Pilgrimage, Exploration, Colonizing, and Migration

Travel is a universal experience, even though not all human beings travel. It takes many forms: individual travel for pleasure (tourism); surveying a new terrain with a scientific or commercial purpose (exploring); building a new home in a "wilderness" or among alien or hostile peoples (settling or colonizing); wandering in a group or individually to seek not only a religious site but also spiritual experience (pilgrimage); journeying under compulsion farther from an irretrievable home (exile); moving in a fragile or displaced community that seeks, often desperately, another home (migration). Travel entices and alarms us, posing questions about who we are and what counts as home as we encounter ourselves on the move. To travel is to meet strangers, to define not only space but also the self and the community in a variety of ways, both welcome and unwelcome. If we are the stay-at-homes, travelers may irritate, attract, or frighten us. Texts include Vergil, *Aeneid*; Ovid, poetic epistles from exile (*Epistulae ex Ponto*); Bartolomé de Las Casas, *Brief Report on the Destruction of the Indians*; Mme de Graffigny, *Lettres d'une Péruvienne*; Henry David Thoreau, *A Week on the Concord and Merrimack Rivers;* Charlotte Brontë, *Villette*; Wu Ch'eng-en, *Monkey* (ed. and trans Arthur Waley); Hualing Nieh, *Mulberry and Peach*; Chu T'ien-wen, *Notes of a Desolate Man*.

Works Cited

Buttigieg, Joseph. "ENGL 90904: Philology and Weltliterature." *Spring 2007 Graduate Courses*. Course Description Archives. U of Notre Dame., n.d. Web. 29 July 2008.

James, Henry. Preface to *The American*. *Literary Criticism: European Writers and the Prefaces*. Ed. Leon Edel. Vol. 2. New York: Lib. of Amer., 1984. 1062–63. Print.

Wordsworth, William. "The Tables Turned: An Evening Scene on the Same Subject." *The Complete Poetical Works*. London: Macmillan, 1888. *Bartleby.com*. Web. 15 Feb. 2008.

Part III

Teaching Strategies

Introduction

Teachers of world literature courses often find that they need to develop new pedagogical strategies to meet the challenges of conveying a wide range of materials from different periods and cultures. The eight essays in this section offer a variety of ways to approach cultural variety and difference, both conceptually and in practical terms.

The first two essays, reflecting the writers' experience in creating survey anthologies, introduce the paired issues of what to teach and how to teach it. David Damrosch describes strategies for connecting less-known writers to one another and to better-known writers, so that works less familiar to an instructor can find a place in a course and not be swamped by the presence of famous authors. Gary Harrison focuses on the value of developing dialogic modes of instruction and classroom interaction, enlisting student involvement in connecting Western to non-Western works and canonical with noncanonical writing.

The next three essays take up important instances of cultural difference. Elvira Pulitano discusses the adaptations needed to teach orally derived work in a literature course. Comparing Native American writers with aboriginal authors from Australia and New Zealand, she shows the importance of helping students attend to issues of translation and transformation as oral materials are reimagined in written form. In the process, students encounter sharp debates over issues of identity, authenticity, and hybridity, shaped by differing cultural assumptions of what an authentic native writer should be. Margaret Higonnet discusses the entry of women's writing into a traditionally male-dominated canon; she outlines ways in which gender difference makes a difference in reading and teaching, both generally and then in a particular course centered on World War I. Joseph A. Massad discusses the need to distinguish Western from non-Western ideas and assumptions about sexuality. Looking particularly at Western attempts to assess same-sex desire in the Arab world in the light of the Western discourse of human rights, he offers a cautionary tale of cross-cultural translation and mistranslation, as illustrated in the reception of Naguib Mahfouz and other writers.

The final three essays in this section give different approaches to collaboration in and beyond the classroom. Marjorie E. Rhine and Jeanne Gillespie describe their experiences in team-teaching interdisciplinary world literature courses in Louisiana, collaborating with each other, with guest artists, and with speakers of different heritages met on field trips into the rural communities outside the campus. Thomas Beebee emphasizes collaborative work among groups of students in his classes, describing the modes of "guided design" by which he prompts them to expand their learning beyond the classic triad of lecture, discussion, and paper writing. Monika Brown discusses collaborative assignments in a North Carolina campus founded to serve the local Native American population, as she works with her students both in class and online to develop communities of critics who can connect literary classics to other classics, to contemporary literature and film, and to their own lives.

These eight essayists take various issues and case studies as their examples, but their perspectives and strategies should be broadly applicable to many other institutional settings. Together, they give a general introduction to the sorts of issues of selection, cross-cultural transformation, and collaborative work that inform much teaching of world literature today.

David Damrosch

Major Cultures and Minor Literatures

Traditionally, world literature courses concentrated their attention on presenting masterpieces from a few "major cultures"—politically powerful and culturally influential countries mostly found in Western Europe, often extending also to Russia; to the United States; and sometimes to China, Japan, and India. There was a good practical reason for this emphasis: a focus on masterworks from major cultures provided a way to organize a manageable selection from the bewildering variety of the world's literatures. Often, this principle of selection was also justified on aesthetic grounds, as in a 1971 statement by the German comparatist Horst Rüdiger: world literature, he wrote, should not be "a U.N. General Assembly, in which the voices of the great powers count no more than those of the political provinces. It is the *liber aureus* of aesthetically successful and historically influential works in all languages" (4; my trans.).

As the United Nations metaphor shows, aesthetic criteria could shade fairly directly over into political terms, and it is telling that in Rüdiger's analogy, minor literatures aren't even sovereign states at all but mere "provinces." While any language could in principle contribute to the canon of masterpieces, in practice the real action was concentrated not in a general assembly of all literatures but in a sort of literary Security Council. From the 1950s through the early 1990s, indeed, the composition of many world literature courses corresponded fairly closely to the membership of the controlling body of the United Nations. Today there is much greater interest in incorporating voices from many regions of what Pascale Casanova has called "the world republic of letters." Yet within the limits of a survey course, this incorporating is a difficult goal to achieve. In the following pages I describe a variety of techniques instructors can use to expand their offerings beyond the often-taught works that still serve as staples of world literature courses, to broaden the syllabus to include works from more of the world's "minor literatures."

I use this term here in a threefold sense: to include minority-group writing such as Gaelic or Yiddish within major powers (Deleuze and Guattari's sense), the literatures of smaller countries such as Guatemala or Hungary (what Kafka meant by "kleine Literaturen" [149]), and more generally works from languages and regions rarely represented on North American syllabi. Though Indonesia has the world's fifth largest population and a rich literary tradition, its literature is rarely found on North American syllabi and so has the status of a minor literature in this third sense. In many survey courses the entire continent of South America is represented, if at all, only in a couple of short stories by Jorge Luis Borges and Gabriel García Márquez, and so the continent's rich literary traditions unfortunately compose a minor literature that hasn't found a secure place in courses oriented toward major cultures.

From an anthologist's pragmatic point of view, a major author or major culture is one that is generally well represented in world literature courses, and if a work is included in the anthology, a good proportion of users are sure to assign it without further ado. A minor literature or work may be of major importance at home and can be thought of in the highest terms by those who know the area, but it has not yet found a secure place in North American survey courses. The task then is to find ways to help the unfamiliar work get taught. Student resistance is probably not the crucial issue: the poems of Abu Nuwas and Walther von der Vogelweide are more readily accessible to students than *The Iliad*. More important is the resistance of their instructors, who are used to constructing courses grounded in Homer and who often hesitate to venture far from what they know how to teach. Unfamiliar writers are more likely to get taught if they can be brought into some clear relation to works that teachers already know they want to include.

I begin from the premise that students aren't served well by courses that flit restlessly from one brief selection to another, as it takes some time to appreciate the full force of a writer's distinctive vision and language. A constant diet of short selections is unsatisfactory even if a course stays in a single cultural tradition, and the problem worsens if we move farther afield. Students will get little real feel for epic narrative if they're given twenty pages each from Homer, Vergil, Dante, and Milton, and we can lose more than we gain if we broaden the list to include *The Epic of Gilgamesh*, the *Mahabharata*, *The Epic of Son-Jara*, and Derek Walcott's *Omeros* but then proportionately shrink all the readings, so that now we're assigning ten pages from each of these eight epics instead of an already inadequate twenty pages from four. Not only is the literary experience of each work greatly reduced but also we risk baffling students by constantly shifting frames of reference. "If this is Tuesday, it must be Belgium" is already a sorry state of affairs for a tour of Europe, where at least the tourist is still operating in a broadly shared matrix of cultural traditions already encountered in Paris and Amsterdam; it's much harder if we try to parachute down into ancient Rome on Monday, medieval Mali on Wednesday, and the contemporary Caribbean on Friday.

I have a second premise as well, and it is the converse to the first: a single sonnet or a page of haiku can open up an entire world to a student. Close focus on a few resonant lyrics can yield literary and cultural revelations as profound as can a week on an epic or a novel, whose bulk will inevitably require the teacher to discuss its episodes and themes in a highly selective manner, even supposing the students can be expected to read the entire work to begin with. Far from being opposed to each other, the two premises should ideally be seen as complementary, and at the level of the syllabus they can represent the dual imperatives of breadth and depth in a general survey course. Valuable as it is to have extended readings in individual authors, short selections also have an important role to play in survey courses, allowing for varied pacing and much greater range than would be found in courses consisting solely of a few long texts. While a course shouldn't be composed entirely of brief excerpts from dozens and dozens of writers, carefully chosen groupings or sequences of shorter works can achieve important effects, becoming greater instead of less than the sum of the individual parts.

When we editors of *The Longman Anthology of World Literature* began making our plans for the book in 1999, we devoted ourselves from the outset to helping instructors bring together works from different regions and eras. From surveys of courses in the field at that time, it appeared that many instructors were adopting anthologies that had greatly expanded their coverage of the world, but they then weren't finding ways to include many of the newly added works in their actual syllabi. It's all very well to anthologize Babylonian wisdom literature, Norse sagas, and Urdu *ghazals*, but little is gained if none of these wonderful works gets taught. In what follows, I present some examples of solutions we developed in the course of our years of work on the anthology. Each example represents a different strategy, and these strategies should be applicable to a wide variety of works in many kinds of courses.

Cultural Connections

A major emphasis in literary study in recent decades has been on the intimate connection of literature and the culture in which it is created and then read. Given their broad scope, world literature courses pose a particular problem of cultural contextualization. While it obviously isn't possible to give students the kind of contextual depth that can be provided in a course on a single country's literature, it is important to find economic ways to show how great works arise in a broader panorama of their home culture, a context essential to understanding many aspects of their meaning. Introductions and footnotes can provide a good deal of information, but it is always desirable to give students actual texts to read, so as to bring the cultural dialogue alive.

Short readings can be linked to a major text on the syllabus; one might present works that underlie the major text or works to which it responds. In *The Epic of Gilgamesh*, the hero's dying friend, Enkidu, has a grim vision of the underworld House of Dust, where even the door bolts are covered with dust and princes wait on tables, serving muddy water in place of beer. Enkidu's vision has been adapted from an earlier Babylonian poem, "The Descent of Ishtar to the Underworld." The Akkadian-language "Descent of Ishtar," in turn, is an adaptation of a still earlier Sumerian poem, "The Descent of Inanna," which is written in a haunting, oral-based incantatory style, a style very different from the later Akkadian works. By reading these two short poems along with *Gilgamesh*, students can learn much about literary evolution and rewriting in the ancient Near East, observing the dynamism of ancient poetic creation (no timeless mythic realm here) and seeing the quite different political and religious inflections the three works give to their common scene.

It is equally valuable to show how writers have always reached across borders to find resources for their work and open up new avenues not available in their own tradition. The Book of Job, for instance, builds on important texts from the dominant cultures of Babylonia and Egypt, and it is very effective to teach selections from these other texts along with it. The body of the book is an explosive expansion of a Babylonian poem known today as "The Babylonian Theodicy," a dialogue in which a suffering man asks why the gods have mistreated him and a friend tries to comfort him. Toward the end of the Book of Job (ch. 31), Job asserts his innocence in a listing of all the wrongs he hasn't committed, an adaptation of the famous "negative confession" in the Egyptian Book of the Dead. Students can have a wonderful time exploring how the Book of Job transforms its sources in deeply ambiguous and moving ways. In the process, students come to see that ancient Israel, so important in the foundation of Western culture, was not at all a major power itself but was home to a minor literature that drew on the cultures of the great powers on either side—Babylonia, the only place for a truly cultured person to live, and Egypt, the only place to die. Having had this exposure to some key Near Eastern texts stretching back into the third millennium BCE, students will also be better prepared to assess the cultural ambitions and struggles for self-definition of those other foundational parvenus on the ancient Mediterranean scene, the Greeks.

Connections across Time

To reach readers today, even well-known ancient works like the Greek classics need a triple translation: of language, culture, and era. One way to engage students with this multiple process is to pair ancient works with modern authors who have responded to both the strangeness and the immediacy of the archaic text. With Homer's *Odyssey*, it is fascinating to read George Seferis's meditation on Odysseus, "a large man, whispering through his whitened beard words in our language spoken as it was three thousand years ago." Seferis's 1931 poem, ironically entitled "Upon a Foreign Verse," succinctly shows that Homer is foreign even to Greeks today, yet at the same time his very foreignness inspires the modern poet, "conversing with the dead when the living are no longer enough" (47–48).

Ancient texts often survive only in incomplete form, and their fragmented quality can be frustrating or irritating to modern readers. Some modern poets, however, have found inspiration in the very fragmentation of the ancient works. A good example can be found in comparing some lines from Sappho with a short poem by the brilliant, troubled Argentine poet Alejandra Pizarnik (1936–72). Sappho's lyric "Honestly, I Wish I Were Dead" features passages such as the following:

> all the lovely and beautiful times we had
> all the garlands of violets
> and of roses and . . .
> and . . . that you've put on in my company,
> all the delicate chains of flowers
> that encircled your tender neck   (597)

Such damaged lines inspired Pizarnik in the years before her suicide at age thirty-six to compose deliberately broken verses. These enigmatic poems express the loss of control of someone in the throes of passion, as in her short lyric "Lovers":

> a flower
> not far from the night
> my mute body
>   opens
> to the delicate urgency of dew (599)

The poems by Seferis and Pizarnik thus serve to open up important questions of the interplay of antiquity and modernity, foreignness and immediacy, and gaps in words and in emotions. Including them as companion readings to Homer and Sappho moreover, gives Seferis and Pizarnik a place to achieve a real impact within the boundaries of a survey course that otherwise would probably not find time to include them at all.

Connections across Space

Time is never the only issue when deciding who to include in a course; equally at issue today is how to bring together traditions that aren't closely connected to each other. Seferis and Pizarnik were both reading and reacting to the classical Greeks, but a different problem is posed by the Mughal poet Ghalib (1797–1869). One of the greatest poets of the nineteenth century, Ghalib is regularly included in world literature anthologies today, yet he has rarely made his way into a syllabus. Part of the problem is that he is the only Mughal writer of his era who is relatively well known outside specialist circles, and just putting in a few pages of

Ghalib alone doesn't give teachers a critical mass of material to work with, unless he can be connected with other poets in quite different regions. Survey courses regularly include Byron, Aleksandr Pushkin, and Charles Baudelaire, and in different ways Ghalib can be compared with those poets: he is an aristocratic rebel; an outsider-insider in a court culture; and an unconventional, morally suspect figure, almost a Mughal *poète maudit*. Yet different teachers will highlight very different themes, and it doesn't do well for anthologies to adopt heavily thematic approaches, as these will likely work only for a few users.

As my coeditors and I pondered this question, we realized that all these poets and more could be considered under the general heading of national poets, an important cultural role in the age of nationalist consolidation. They could then be thought of together as public figures, either in formal terms (Ghalib was named official court poet at the Mughal court in Delhi), in their own announced ambitions (Walt Whitman heard America singing), or in their later reception as foundational for national traditions to follow them (Pushkin and Ghalib had both long been seen in this light). The category of national poet would also give us the chance to group together some shorter selections from several other poets, following the longer selections from free-standing poets, Goethe, William Wordsworth, Byron, Ghalib, and Pushkin.

So we created a grouping called "Perspectives: The National Poet," placing Whitman there, so as not to have only little-known figures in the section and also because we know that students already get a good deal of Whitman from high school onward and may not need to have as many pages of him in a world literature course. This was also a good place for selections from Dionysios Solomos (founder of modern Greek poetry in the period of Greece's struggle for independence), the Polish national poet Adam Mickiewicz, and the remarkable Vietnamese poet Nguyen Du.

In 1810, Nguyen Du published a novel called *Kim-Van-Kieu* or *The Tale of Kieu*, an adaptive verse translation of an earlier, Chinese novel. His heroine has to sell herself into prostitution to ransom her family from a group of thugs. Kieu then has a series of romantic and political misadventures, and in the process she becomes a stand-in for Nguyen Du and ultimately for Vietnam itself. Later Vietnamese poets often refer back to Nguyen Du as the founder of modern Vietnamese poetry, and we included one such poem by a poet writing amid the struggles against French colonial domination in the early 1950s. Nguyen Du's verse narrative, at once satiric and moving, makes fascinating reading next to Byron's *Don Juan*, whose hero, like Kieu, is at once a stand-in for the poet and a figure through whom Byron focalizes the political struggles of his age.

All comparative work involves the interplay of similarity and difference, and the category of the national poet must be modulated in different ways for this diverse group of poets, but it has enabled Ghalib and Nguyen Du to come into creative conjunction with each other and with Pushkin, Whitman, and the other European national poets we include. Without dictating what particular themes or issues teachers will emphasize, we hope that this grouping will catch their attention and lead to the inclusion of some of the less-taught figures along with the already well-established poets.

Ghalib poses a particular challenge, since he wrote in the lyric form of the *ghazal*. Whereas Nguyen Du's *Tale of Kieu* is a rollicking verse narrative, whose action and images come through fairly readily in translation, the beauty of the *ghazal* lies in its intricate verse form. *Ghazal*s are written in couplets, each of which must end with the same word, with a different rhyme leading into it. Ghalib has been fortunate in his translators, and the best translations are very effective, as can be seen in these lines from the poet Adrienne Rich:

> I'm neither the loosening of song nor the close-drawn tent of music;
> I'm the sound, simply, of my own breaking.
>
> You were meant to sit in the shade of your rippling hair;
> I was made to look further, into a deeper tangle.
> . . . .
> No wonder you came looking for me, you
> who care for the grieving, and I the sound of grief.   (274)

Lovely though this translation is, it can't really convey the dramatic movement of the original Urdu couplets, a series of bravura approaches to the problem of finding a surprising but apt rhyme to become the climax of each couplet. No successful English-language version has retained the original rhyme schemes; the few that do have ended up seeming stilted and ineffective. How could we convey this effect for our readers?

Our solution was to include two modern *ghazal*s by the Kashmiri American poet Agha Shahid Ali (1949–2001), as resonances to Ghalib. Ali, who made his career in the United States, was deeply interested in Ghalib, and he composed many *ghazal*s in English. He was therefore able to use rhymes effectively from the outset, and by giving examples of Ali's

English-language *ghazals*, we could suggest to readers the kinds of effects that Ghalib had achieved in Urdu, even though those can't be directly seen in translation. As an example, here are a few couplets of a poem of Ali's, entitled simply "Ghazal." The drama of the rhyme scheme is an important part of its power, even as we can see Ali boldly combining themes from Qur'anic and biblical traditions; from Ghalib; and from a great nineteenth-century American precursor, Herman Melville:

> Where are you now? Who lies beneath your spell tonight
> before you agonize him in farewell tonight?
>
> Pale hands that once loved me beside the Shalimar:
> Whom else from rapture's road will you expel tonight?
> . . . .
> In the heart's veined temple all statues have been smashed.
> No priest in saffron's left to toll its knell tonight.
>
> He's freed some fire from ice, in pity for Heaven;
> he's left open—for God—the doors of Hell tonight.
>
> And I, Shahid, only am escaped to tell thee—
> God sobs in my arms. Call me Ishmael tonight.   (282)

Situating Translations

When a work of world literature is translated from one cultural space into another, it often happens, as Lawrence Venuti has argued in *The Scandals of Translation*, that the work's foreignness is reduced in the process, becoming assimilated to host-culture values. At other times, though, a translation can exoticize the foreign work, confining it to the outlines of the host culture's mirage of the native other. In particularly tricky cases, the translation can simultaneously domesticate the foreign work and exoticize it. Attending to this process can help students see how a given work came to take the form it did as it was translated at a particular time and place. The work can thus be connected more effectively to other works of its time.

A striking example of this domesticating and exoticizing came to light as I was preparing the text of the Navajo creation story, also known as "The Story of the Emergence," for use in the *Longman Anthology* in the section "Other Americas." The fullest and most compelling version of this story was recorded in the early 1880s by a folklorist named Washington Matthews, who took down the story as recited to him by a Navajo shaman, Hathali Nez. Matthews's version is clear and highly readable, and yet it falls flat at a crucial moment in the story, when First Man slays a deer and brings it home for First Woman to cook. Once they have eaten the deer, according to Matthews's translation, First Woman "wiped her greasy hands on her dress, and made a remark which greatly enraged her husband; they had a quarrel about this, which First Man ended by jumping across the fire" (Matthews and Nez 689). First Man and the other early men start sleeping separately from their wives, and the human race almost ends before they are finally reconciled.

Just what was the remark that provoked this apocalyptic argument? The text doesn't say, but it turns out that Matthews did give the episode more fully, burying it in an endnote among the many notes at the back of his volume. We can be grateful that he did preserve the passage for diligent researchers to discover, for the argument has a hilarious, obscene content, which Matthews couldn't bring himself to retain in the text itself:

> When they were done the woman wiped her greasy hands on her dress, and said: "E'yehe si-tsod" (Thanks, my vagina). "What is that you say?" asked First Man. "E'yehe si-tsod," she repeated. "Why do you speak thus?" he queried; "Was it not I who killed the deer whose flesh you have eaten? Why do you not thank me? Was it *tsod* that killed the deer?" "Yes," she replied; "if it were not for that, you lazy men would do nothing. It is that which does all the work." "Then perhaps you women think you can live without the men," he said. "Certainly we can. It is we women who till the fields and gather food; we can live on the produce of our fields, and the seeds and fruits we collect. We have no need of you men." Thus they argued. First Man became more and more angry with each reply that his wife made, until at length, in wrath, he jumped across the fire, remaining by himself in silence for the rest of the night. (689)

This pointed passage was too good to leave out, but at the same time I didn't just want to undo Matthews's work, and so I inserted the passage in the body of the story in brackets, with a footnote explaining what Matthews had done and giving the summary lines he'd inserted in place of the argument. In this way, students have a vivid illustration of how the Navajo story's timeless wisdom reached English-speaking readers at a very specific time and place.

Further connecting the Native American story to broader American culture, I paired it with thematically related selections from John G.

Neihardt's famous *Black Elk Speaks*, in which a visionary spirit journey leads into a harrowing account of the massacre at Wounded Knee in 1890. Students can thus see how sacred knowledge was brought to bear at a moment of crisis. Yet *Black Elk Speaks* isn't a direct transcription of what Black Elk actually spoke, for Neihardt edited Black Elk's narrative as programmatically in the 1930s as Matthews had edited Hathali Nez in the 1880s. As we learn from *The Sixth Grandfather*, the more recently published transcripts of Black Elk's original conversations with Neihardt (DeMaillie), Black Elk was a more complex figure than the meditative, melancholy wise man who comes through in the published *Black Elk Speaks*.

In passages that Neihardt chose not to include in print, Black Elk speaks gleefully of trying to exterminate his white enemies, while in other dropped passages he testifies to his participation in Christian culture. Even Black Elk's name appears differently in the transcripts and in the published book. Neihardt's preface tells us that Black Elk bestowed an Indian name on him, but he never tells us that Black Elk in turn took the name Nicholas when he was baptized as a young man, and Neihardt himself called him Uncle Nick. *Conversations with Uncle Nick* would have been a rather different book from *Black Elk Speaks*.

Having signaled the complexity of the text's transcription and translation, I still wanted to respect *Black Elk Speaks* as Neihardt's highly effective poetic re-creation of his original conversations. I therefore left the text unchanged but added footnotes to give some of the most striking dropped passages, thereby offering students (and teachers!) a window into the dynamics of transmission behind the text's seemingly smooth surface. Both for the Navajo creation story and for *Black Elk Speaks*, our anthology lists both the Native informant and the Euro-American transcriber as coauthors, connecting the works to the time and place in which they took the form they have today.

All the examples given above represent attempts to heed E. M. Forster's dictum, "Only connect" (174). If we are going to succeed in giving a fuller presentation of world literature, we need new modes of connection to supplement the classic linkages provided by literary influence and reference. These connections need to work in practice as well as in theory, not only linking cultures but also giving ways to connect shorter and longer selections, major classics with writers from minor literatures—that is, literatures not well known to most American readers. Such connections can give us new and exciting ways to teach well-established works as well as to open up our syllabi to the rich variety of the world's literary traditions. Minor literatures can finally have a major presence in world literature courses today.

Works Cited

Ali, Agha Shahid. "Ghazal." *The Country without a Post Office*. New York: Norton, 1997. 40. Damrosch et al. E: 282.

Casanova, Pascale. *The World Republic of Letters*. Trans. M. B. DeBevoise. Cambridge: Harvard UP, 2004. Print.

Damrosch, David, et al., eds. *The Longman Anthology of World Literature*. 6 vols. New York: Pearson, 2004. Print.

Deleuze, Gilles, and Félix Guattari. *Kafka: Toward a Minor Literature*. Trans. Dana Polan. Minneapolis: U of Minnesota P, 1986. Print.

DeMaillie, Raymond J., ed. *The Sixth Grandfather: Black Elk's Teachings Given to John G. Neihardt*. Norman: U of Nebraska P, 1984. Print.

Forster, E. M. *Howard's End*. New York: Barnes, 2003. Print.

Ghalib, Mirza. "I'm Neither the Loosening of Song." Trans. Adrienne Rich. *Hudson Review* 22.4 (1969–70): 619. Damrosch et al. E: 274.

Kafka, Franz. *Diaries, 1910–1923*. Ed. Max Brod. Trans. Joseph Krech et al. New York: Schocken, 1976. Print.

Matthews, Washington, and Hathali Nez. "The Story of the Emergence." *Navaho Legends*. By Matthews (1890). Damrosch et al. E: 683–93.

Neihardt, John G. *Black Elk Speaks: Being the Life Story of a Holy Man of the Oglala Sioux*. Norman: U of Nebraska P, 1961. Print.

Nguyen Du. *The Tale of Kieu*. Trans. Huynh Sanh Thong. Bilingual ed. New Haven: Yale UP, 1987. Print.

Pizarnik, Alejandra. "Lovers." *Alejandra Pizarnik: A Profile*. Trans. Frank Graziano and Maria Rosa Fort. Durango: Logbridge, 1987. 45. Damrosch et al. A: 599.

Rüdiger, Horst. *Zur Theorie der vergleichenden Literaturwissenschaft*. Berlin: de Gruyter, 1971. Print.

Sappho. "Honestly, I Wish I Were Dead." *Greek Lyric Poetry*. Trans. M. L. West. Oxford: Oxford UP, 1993. 42–43. Damrosch et al. A: 597.

Seferis, George. "Upon a Foreign Verse." *Collected Poems, 1924–1955*. Trans. Edmund Keeley and Philip Sherrard. Princeton: Princeton UP, 1971. 46–48. Damrosch et al. A: 587–88.

Venuti, Lawrence. *The Scandals of Translation: Towards an Ethics of Difference*. New York: Routledge, 1998. Print.

Gary Harrison

Conversation in Context: A Dialogic Approach to Teaching World Literature

Soon after the Second World War, the American playwright Thornton Wilder presciently noted a shift in our literary imagination, a shift that has led in the last two decades to the development of courses of world literature courses in translation. In his 1950 essay "World Literature and the Modern Mind," Wilder writes, "for better or for worse world literature is at hand: our consciousness is beginning to be planetary" (219). This shift in consciousness has led to what Gayatri Spivak calls the "sea change" in our teaching of comparative and world literature (xii), which, for better or for worse, has led recently to the publication of several multi-volume anthologies of world literature, including *The Norton Anthology of World Literature* (2002), *The Bedford Anthology of World Literature* (2004), and *The Longman Anthology of World Literature* (2004). While some critics, like Spivak, are wary of the move to the study of literature in translation signaled by these anthologies, many other critics and teachers see the course in world literature as an important addition to the university and college curriculum. My remarks on teaching world literature focus on the introductory survey course in world literature, where we need make no (or perhaps fewer) apologies for the generalization involved in addressing the global and historical range such courses impose on professors and students. The aims of this course are broadly to introduce freshman or sophomore students to texts from a necessarily small but important sample of works from the world's literary traditions; to help develop in students a historical awareness of the transformations within and across those traditions; and to help students experience the rewards, while recognizing the problems and limits, of reading across time and place, cultures and languages.

Since 1988, I have been involved in the design and teaching of just such a two-semester, introductory world literature course at the University of New Mexico (UNM), and along the way I have coedited two world literature anthologies. The course at UNM had its origins in 1985, when Paul Davis, then undergraduate director in English, sought to restore a great-books, humanities type of course that had been dropped during the curricular reforms of the 1960s. Supported by an NEH grant, Davis and three other professors from the Department of English and Program in Comparative Literature planned and team-taught a pilot course that reshaped the old humanities course into a full-blown world literature one inclusive of the great traditions of China, India, Japan, the Arabic world, Europe, and the Americas from the ancient world through the present.[1] By sketching the evolution of that course, I hope to show why we have come to take a reflexive, dialogic, and contextual approach to teaching the world literature survey.

When Professor Davis and the undergraduate committee began rethinking the great-books, humanities course in 1985, they recognized that the literary space of the mid-1980s demanded a new look not only at what would be taught in the course but also at how it would be taught. As the circulation of information and communications had expanded and accelerated, we had experienced a shrinking of the globe and a flattening out of time. Not only was more of the world of the present available to us but so was more of the world of the past. The newly discovered and recently recovered texts in British and American literature; the steady flow of literary and extraliterary works written in and translated into English from around the world; and the increasing presence of hitherto neglected or undervalued works from women and ethnic writers in the United States and Europe required a remapping of readings and pedagogical strategies. With more to teach and new media to embrace, we needed a new way of teaching. As Franco Moretti more recently acknowledged, "The sheer enormity of the task makes it clear that world literature cannot be literature, bigger; what we are doing, just more of it. It has to be different" (149).

Given the increasingly multicultural and cosmopolitan archive available in English as well as the changing demographic profile of the college and university population, it was apparent that the traditional Western canon, the staple of the former course, did not meet the more diverse needs of students whose culture was more inclusive—globally, in terms of national traditions; locally, in terms of culture, gender, race, and class. Moreover, the more critically self-conscious and historically situated models of reading and teaching that resulted from the theoretical challenges to pedagogies, challenges based on New Critical models, required a rethinking of the classroom situation itself. Facing the vertigo of the global archive and meeting with considerable disagreement among themselves about how to meet these challenges, the UNM team began teaching a pilot course in 1986, and over the next several semesters it continually revised its methods, objectives, and content.

Although the great works of the Western tradition held a central place in the class, we increasingly put those works into context with canonical and noncanonical literary and extraliterary texts from China, Japan, Africa, India, the Arabic and Islamic world, as well as with multicultural works from the United States (e.g., short stories, essays, and poetry by Leslie Silko, Jimmy Santiago Baca, and Toni Morrison, among others). After several semesters of experimentation, it became clear that the teachers of world literature were not, in Davis's words, "enacting a literary Mount Sinai—bringing the ten most eternal works of the world down from the mountaintop to the students." Rather, we found that the most effective part of the pedagogical experiment was the immediate and ongoing discussion about the works that took place before, during, and after each class. Those discussions involved all the teaching team (of mixed gender and from a variety of fields of expertise) and the students.

Focusing on themes and stories with ongoing significance in cultural history—identity and difference, heroism, citizenship, religious feeling, reason and imagination, the good life—the course investigated the ways in which literary works within and outside the Western canon contributed to the ongoing negotiation of cultural identity, tradition, and value. The predominant theme structuring the course in its early years was storytelling, and we began the course talking about how stories, oral and written, serve as means for individuals, peoples, nations, and cultures to make sense of the world. Following the dynamic example of storytelling in Silko's *Ceremony* and her discussion of the power of stories in "Language and Literature from a Pueblo Indian Perspective," we hoped to show how cultures across the world draw on, modify, and recirculate stories that stem from their earliest origins in order to create a sense of identity, a sense of history, and a sense of place. We also wanted to show how stories circulating in a variety of forms—as myth, epic, lyric, fiction, drama, history, autobiography, and more—competed for legitimacy and embodied acts of survivance, to use Gerald Vizenor's phrase, as world systems clashed and competed with one another for political, economic, and cultural dominance.[2]

Importantly, we brought texts together not to initiate some preconceived resolution of differences but instead to put those differences into play. We began with a center-periphery model in which we placed a major canonical text from Europe or the United States into appositional or oppositional relation to a countertext from China, India, Japan, or Nigeria. We would introduce Laozi, for example, to the Socrates of Plato's *Apology*, aiming to point up differences between Greek rationalism and Taoism. Recognizing the dangers of Manichaeanism and essentialism in this approach, which reified such differences in the mimetic fallacy that the texts somehow represented Greece and China in the ancient world, we soon added a wider range of texts—Euripides's *The Bacchae* and Confucius's *Analects*—into the conversation. The notion of text versus countertext readily gave way to the idea of discursive clusters—a network of texts—that would put into play a variety of perspectives on a theme or issue and that would, to quote Timothy Reiss, not only make the "alien familiar, but the familiar alien" (34). We found that negotiation among cultural boundaries, *pace* Pascale Casanova, was not bound up entirely with rivalry and conflict; by placing works in context, we could find as much occasion to think in terms of conversation as in terms of conflict.[3]

As we experienced the sometimes illuminating, sometimes frustrating and puzzling results of such textual interplay, we recognized that the conversation elicited in meetings and during class discussion was embodied in the works themselves, from the earliest Sumerian stories and Chinese poems to the works of Salman Rushdie and Silko, as well as in the various readerly and ideological repertoires of ourselves and our students. Extrapolating from Mikhail Bakhtin's recognition that texts are permeated with heterogeneity and that they anticipate responses from other texts, we sought to realize, as well as to orchestrate, cross-cultural conversations in order to promote a dialogic and reflexive understanding of the works under discussion.[4]

As we agreed and disagreed among ourselves, puzzled over passages and our colleagues' and students' responses to them, we realized that the essential element of the course was to release the potential points of convergence and conflict and to pause over the inevitable collision with the inexplicable otherness of certain texts. While reading critical and historical studies on the assigned readings, inviting colleagues of various expertise to guest-lecture, and coming to class prepared to structure the discussion as we would in our Romanticism or mythology courses, increasingly we modeled and promoted a conversation in the classroom that would encourage the students to participate in the dialogue about the texts; about the cultural contexts from which they emerged; and about the importance, value, and relevance of those works from across many borders to our own culture and time.

Working within the discursive clusters (called in the Bedford anthology "In the World" units and in the Longman anthology "Perspectives"), teachers and students may well find themselves in the midst of negotiations among texts—and among readers of texts—that highlight and even heighten value clashes. But sometimes there are surprising points of agreement—as, for example, when Niccolò Machiavelli's *The Prince* meets Ibn Khaldun's *Il Muqaddimah*. Both these texts are removed from our own time by more than five hundred years, yet both speak to the critical questions about power, leadership, and authority that press on our recent historical events with great urgency. Given their often unexamined stereotypes about Islam, many of our students are surprised to find that both texts anatomize the relationship between governor and governed, often leading to similar but not precisely the same conclusions about such topics as generosity, liberality, honesty, and the use of force. What most challenges their expectations seems to be Ibn Khaldun's measured tone and emphasis on the importance of group feeling, which by contrast highlights Machiavelli's more coldly calculating approach to maintaining the prince's power at all costs.

The convergence of these texts (another example would be the treatment of the supernatural in Pu Song-ling's "The Mural," E. T. A. Hoffmann's "The Mines of Falun," and Edgar Allan Poe's "Ligeia") draws out what David Damrosch calls the meeting of the "*like-but-unlike*—the sort of relation most likely to make a productive change in our own perceptions and practices" (12). Extrapolating on this idea, Vilashini Cooppan describes this middle ground as the "literary zone" of the uncanny, which offers the most promise for a practice of reading world literature ("Ghosts"

21). Such zones of reading lead us beyond the polarities of identity and difference to a dialectical relation that is both-and. The uncanny inter-ruption of student expectations that results from bringing these texts together—and now we add into the conversation sections from Nizam al-Mulk's *Book of Government* and Doshun's *On Mastery of the Arts of Peace and War*—further complicates the theme of fashioning the prince and helps recontextualize our and our students' responses to those texts.

Like Damrosch and Cooppan, whose experiences in teaching world literature courses at Columbia and Yale Universities, respectively, have led to conclusions strikingly similar to ours at UNM, we have come to recog-nize the need to recalibrate the concept of world literature from a canon of masterworks to a way of reading that places texts from the world into con-versation with one another so that we can resist Manichaean polarities and, in Reiss's words, "try to make contact with different cultures and listen with care and tact to their voices and to their silences" (69).[5] For Cooppan, world literature is not a set of canonical works but "an episte-mology, a way of knowing and a mode of reading, that regularly places its readers in the unnerving moment in which a strange text is made at least partially familiar and the familiar canonical is made at least partially strange" ("Ghosts" 29); for Damrosch, "world literature is not an infinite, ungraspable canon of works but rather a mode of circulation and of read-ing" (5). The sea change in our teaching of world literature followed from similarly recognizing the need to emphasize dynamic, dialogic modes of reading in order to embrace the situated heterogeneity of culturally diverse writers and readers reaching across borders, whose practices challenge us to read world literature not as a static canon but as a dynamic and open-ended process—a kind of ever-shifting symphony of voices.

Our effort to capture a dialogic, contextual mode of reading and teaching diversity in a textbook that would put a variety of works into connection with one another while at the same time providing a sense of history and literary history led eventually to the publication of *The Bed-ford Anthology of World Literature* (2004). The anthology integrates our principle of the discursive cluster of world literary and extraliterary texts and emphasizes connections and cross- or transhistorical comparisons. The advent of Damrosch's *The Longman Anthology of World Literature* (2004), which also promotes resonances and thematic groupings, sug-gests that working relatively independently in New Mexico, New York, and New Haven, teachers of world literature across the country are mov-ing toward a dialogic approach of teaching world literature.

Creating a hybrid mix of canonical and extracanonical, literary and extraliterary works, the new anthologies may enable students and teachers self-consciously to experience literature in the way Octavio Paz defines that term: as a "network of relations, or more precisely a circuit of communication, a system for interchanging messages and reciprocal influences among authors, works, and readers" (218). In such a network, the cultural and historical context of the work, the text, the student reader, and teacher engage in a dialogue between the local and the global, the metropolitan and subaltern traditions. As we move in this direction, it is important to keep in mind, as Prendergast rightly cautions, that meetings among world civilizations

> do not necessarily constitute a polite get-together. The terms on which civilizations "meet," both in and out of books, are not necessarily, or even generally, those of equal parties to the encounter. Moreover, the effects of such meetings can range widely across a spectrum from exhilaration to anxiety and vertigo, as questions are raised, problems explored and identities challenged. ("World Republic" 3)

It is precisely that wide spectrum of responses that a reflexive, dialogic pedagogy aims to elicit from teachers and students.

So that students do not encounter the few works we can cover in two sixteen-week courses as a parade of universally consecrated texts yielding themselves to purely formal analysis, we need at least minimally to embed our reading of the world text in the conditions of its production and of its reception. We believe that it is important to historicize the works we present in the classroom, even as we try to bring them into a living tradition by realizing their dialogic potentials. As Damrosch succinctly puts it, "A lively awareness of a work's original context is an important safeguard against its outright assimilation to the reader's own immediate moment" (140). By assigning and discussing an introduction to each work and lecturing briefly about the national context, we hope to connect the work to its history as well as point out congruities (and incongruities) in the development of genres and form.

Moreover, historical contextualization helps students recognize that their perspectives and responses to a work are embedded in their own cultural-historical context. With a sense of both history and histories, we may use the classroom to problematize questions of genre and ideology, literary production and reception. Placing the *Iliad* or *Odyssey* alongside the *Ramayana* or *Mahabharata*, or *Beowulf* alongside the *Sunjata*, for example, challenges our definition of epic and leads us to consider the many faces of the hero, sculpted to meet the particular demands and expectations of each unique culture. We may also ask what similarities and differences obtained in the material and intellectual conditions that gave rise to these works. While we find variance in the construction of the hero among these epics, we also find discursive similarities that function to exoticize the terra incognita and demonize their others. We can also ask students how their assumptions about leaders and leadership affects their response to these figures from antiquity.

The operative principle of this kind of contextual, dialogic reading, is defamiliarization—both linguistic and cultural. To disrupt any complacency about translated texts, we regularly interrupt the flow of one translation by introducing an alternative. Our aim here is to help students recognize the hazards, if not scandals, of translation and ideally to develop in them a sense of incipient bilingualism, being receptive to the possibility of communicating otherwise, in a language outside one's own. To this end we compare alternative translations of many texts, including the Bible; the Qur'an; parts of the *Ramayana;* some Tang Dynasty poems; and selected poems by Bashō, Kabir, and Ghalib.

At the cultural level, to disrupt the (Eurocentric) familiarity of a play like *The Tempest*, we recontextualize it alongside Christopher Columbus's *Diario* and the Aztec accounts of the conquest of Mexico collected and translated from a variety of sources in Miguel Leon-Portilla's *The Broken Spears*.[6] The *Diario*, which records Columbus's Gonzalo-like wonder at the Taino of Guanahini and his Sebastian-like colonizer's gaze, broadens the historical outlines of Prospero's manifold project. Reading excerpts from the "Defense of the Aztec Religion" or from Bartolomé de Las Casas's defense of Indians from *History of the Indies* further displaces this narrative of mastery by placing Caliban's outrage and defiance in a larger chorus of native voices.

An example from the twentieth century brings Chinua Achebe's criticism of Joseph Conrad's *Heart of Darkness* ("An Image of Africa") together with George Washington Williams's "An Open Letter to His Serene Majesty Leopold II" and Mark Twain's "King Leopold's Soliloquy." While the first text attacks Conrad's apparent racism, the second two, published almost at the same time as *Heart of Darkness*, elicit the criticism of imperialism implicit in the novel by drawing a thicker description of the brutal consequences and hypocrisy of Leopold II's inhumane policies in the so-called Independent State of Congo. Bringing these multiple voices to bear on canonical texts such as *The Tempest* and *Heart of Darkness* helps students recognize the complex dynamics of identity and difference, history and art, at work in the literary texts, while also offering the perspective of the subaltern or postcolonial critic writing back to the empire.

In the role of mediator, the instructor who brings these texts together works to promote the multiple points of view that arise from this pedagogical moment and to ensure that all the interlocutors in the imaginary conversation are acknowledged and heard. The instructor should expect that students will take up argumentative positions along the full spectrum of possibilities. Some students may follow Achebe's lead in condemning Conrad for being a "bloody racist" (788); others may criticize Achebe for ignoring the attack on imperialism found in the novel; still others may seek safety in some middle ground. While I believe we must acknowledge and articulate clearly our own ideological and critical positions as teachers, the classroom should nonetheless provide a space where those who are invited to the imagined conversation among the world's writers meet on relatively equal terms. The world literature classroom—as a contact zone where at least some of the participants are as unprepared and fearful yet as full of wonder and expectation as any traveler into terra incognita—should encourage an open-minded engagement with literary and extraliterary texts that mitigates against the "inequality that structures the literary world" (Casanova 39). In the classroom, we need to handle the texts and cultural views "conscientiously," as Sarah Lawall urges us, in order to enable "a virtual dialogue that imitates a real world where dialogue often cannot take place because the interlocutors are too far apart, or too committed to an ideological position, and the issues are too highly charged" (47). It is not easy to initiate and sustain such a dialogue, but it is well worth the effort.

At UNM, we hope that teaching world literature as a dynamic process of active reading will help promote a generative, if incipient, hybridity or critical cosmopolitanism that challenges us continually to rethink and reevaluate our cultural icons—the world's great works—as they are repositioned in the play between the global and the local, the old and the new. Moreover, we hope that such reading will lead toward a more enlightened global citizenship, involving a recognition of the interdependence of nations and peoples, a respect for the cultural values and human rights of peoples and nations in the global collectivity, and a self-conscious awareness of the impact of our words and actions on others. If our students

214 Conversation in Context

leave the world literature course with a desire to study another language in order to understand better the literature, culture, and history of a particular tradition or nation, that will be all to the good. If they approach that study with a sense that national literatures and cultures are not static, essentialized entities but dynamic and heterogeneous systems participating in larger, transformative global networks of exchange and transformation, that will be even better. At the very least, a dialogic approach to world literature may offer a literary space in which, to quote Carlos Fuentes, "reading, writing, teaching, learning are all activities aimed at introducing civilizations to each other" (93).

Notes

1. The original team was Davis, David Johnson, Patricia Clark Smith, and Joseph Zavadil. Soon the course split into teams of two, and other faculty members joined the program, including me, Cheryl Fresch, and Mary Bess Whidden. I am grateful to my colleagues for helping conceptualize and put into practice the pedagogical strategies discussed in this essay, and I thank Davis, Carmen Nocentelli-Truett, and Ronald Shumaker for their helpful comments on early drafts of this essay.

2. *Survivance*, a supple remaking of story and myth to affirm one's identity in an open-ended play of similarity and difference, is Vizenor's substitute for *survival*, which suggests for him a persistence of old patterns of identity that do not adapt to the conditions of the new. See 3–5.

3. As Christopher Prendergast has argued, Casanova's sweeping account of national rivalry does not account for the multiple factors that motivate literary innovation—many of which have, in his view, little or nothing to do with national rivalry ("World Republic" 12–14).

4. Bakhtin's "Discourse in the Novel" asks us to engage "the work as a rejoinder in a given dialogue, whose style is determined by its interrelationship with other rejoinders in the same dialogue (in the totality of the conversation)" (274).

5. For descriptions of the Yale world literature course, see Cooppan, "World Literature" and "Ghosts."

6. On problems of transculturation and the belatedness of some of these materials, see Damrosch, ch. 2 (esp. 85–99).

Works Cited

Achebe, Chinua. "An Image of Africa: Racism in Conrad's *Heart of Darkness.*" *Massachusetts Review* 18.4 (1977): 782–94. Print.

Bakhtin, M. M. "Discourse in the Novel." *The Dialogic Imagination: Four Essays.* Ed. Michael Holquist. Trans. Caryl Emerson and Holquist. Austin: U of Texas P, 1981. 259–422. Print.

Casanova, Pascale. *The World Republic of Letters.* Trans. M. B. DeBevoise. Cambridge: Harvard UP, 2004. Print.

Cooppan, Vilashini. "Ghosts in the Disciplinary Machine: The Uncanny Life of World Literature." *Comparative Literature Studies* 41.1 (2004): 10–36. 22 Nov. 2004. *Project Muse.* Web. 7 Apr. 2008.

———. "World Literature and Global Theory: Comparative Literature for the New Millennium." *Symploké* 9.1–2 (2001): 15–43. *Project Muse.* Web. 7 Apr. 2008.

Damrosch, David. *What Is World Literature?* Princeton: Princeton UP, 2003. Print.

Davis, Paul. Message to the author. 4 Dec. 2003. E-mail.

Fuentes, Carlos. "How I Started to Write." *The Graywolf Annual Five: Multicultural Literacy.* Ed. Rick Simmons and Scott Walker. Saint Paul: Graywolf, 1988. 83–111. Print.

Lawall, Sarah. "Canons, Contexts, Pedagogy." *Comparatist* 24 (2000): 39–56. Print.

Leon-Portilla, Miguel. *The Broken Spears: The Aztec Account of the Conquest of Mexico.* 1962. Boston: Beacon, 1990. Print.

Moretti, Franco. "Conjectures on World Literature." Prendergast, *Debating* 148–62.

Paz, Octavio. "A Literature of Convergences." *Convergences: Essays on Art and Literature.* Trans. Helen Lane. San Diego: Harcourt, 1987. 217–26. Print.

Prendergast, Christopher, ed. *Debating World Literature.* London: Verso, 2004. Print.

———. "The World Republic of Letters." Prendergast, *Debating* 1–25.

Reiss, Timothy J. *Against Autonomy: Global Dialectics of Cultural Change.* Stanford: Stanford UP, 2002. Print.

Silko, Leslie Marmon. *Ceremony.* 1977. New York: Penguin, 1986. Print.

———. "Language and Literature from a Pueblo Indian Perspective." *Yellow Woman and a Beauty of the Spirit: Essays on Native American Life Today.* New York: Simon, 1996. 48–59. Print.

Spivak, Gayatri Chakravorty. *Death of a Discipline.* New York: Columbia UP, 2003. Print.

Vizenor, Gerald. *Manifest Manners: Postindian Warriors of Survivance.* Hanover: UP of New England, 1994. Print.

Wilder, Thornton. "World Literature and the Modern Mind." *Goethe and the Modern Age.* Ed. Arnold Bergstraesser. Chicago: Regnery, 1950. 213–33. Print.

Elvira Pulitano

Writing in the Oral Tradition: Reflections on the Indigenous Literatures of Australia, New Zealand, and North America

In her groundbreaking study *Gerald Vizenor: Writing in the Oral Tradition*, Kimberley Blaeser writes:

> Gerald Vizenor, Mixedblood Anishinaabe, comes from a storytelling people. Of the crane clan, he descends from the orators of that people. Stories form the foundation of his being, words the foundation of his career. . . . Before he ever conceived of his own power to create, young Vizenor had experienced the liberating power of oral culture, the wonderful imaginative freedom inspired by storytelling. He says, "The thing I remember mostly about stories . . . is the idea of being set free." (3–4)

Blaeser's observations on Vizenor's work might be applied in various degrees to most contemporary indigenous writers from other cultures, certainly to Aboriginal Australian and Maori New Zealanders, whose literary production this essay also considers. Like their North American counterparts, Aboriginal Australian and Maori New Zealand writers are mostly educated and ideologically steeped in mainstream academic institutions at the same time as they write out of a tradition of indigenous storytelling. The result of this mixing of cultures and worldviews is a kind of hybrid literary production in which borders are permanently crossed and paradoxical elements are consistently brought together. For the purpose of this discussion, I focus on three representative and quite diverse texts by indigenous writers in New Zealand, Australia, and North America, a novel and two autobiographical narratives: Patricia Grace's *Potiki*, Sally Morgan's *My Place*, and Gordon Henry's "Entries into the Autobiographical I."

The concept of writing in the oral tradition inevitably involves the idea of subverting Western literary genres. As the black Australian writer and critic Mudrooroo observes:

> Genres have developed as a European way of categorizing works of literature. In themselves, they are ways of manipulating the text so that the reader is led from an intuitive to a logical response to the work. Not only this, but the Aboriginal writer is led to believe that there are fixed categories of literature to which he or she must conform. If we as writers accept this we, in effect, dilute the Aboriginality of our work. (*Writing* 170)

Since the writers discussed in this essay are all challenging conventional narrative patterns, not to mention the very disposition of reality as perceived by most Western readers, rigid definitions of literary genres such as "novels" or "autobiographies" do not ultimately apply.

Historically in the Western tradition, literature (from Latin *littera*) meant the culture of letters, broadly referring to anything that had been written down. As such, oral cultures were not perceived as literary cultures, and oral literature, Arnold Krupat suggests, at least until the nineteenth century, was "simply a contradiction in terms" (97). Today such a profound misconception has been largely dismantled, and the artistic quality of indigenous forms of oral expression (including rituals and ceremonies) has been widely acknowledged. Nevertheless, a certain resistance toward such literary forms still remains, often reflected in the West's general tendency to relegate the study of oral cultural traditions to folklore and the study of indigenous literatures written in English to various disciplines from the social sciences.

All the more important in a discussion of orality and literacy are the issues of translation and transliteration of Native indigenous languages and literatures, issues that have been discussed endlessly by ethnographers and anthropologists since the eighteenth century. Today many indigenous writers are still facing the so-called translation problem, which inevitably gets intertwined with issues of authenticity. The Native

American writer and critic Craig Womack articulates the controversy rather effectively:

> The problem with the "translation problem," with its skepticism and emphasis on literary diminishment, is that it places us within a "pure versus tainted" framework that so much Native studies gets cast in . . . this locks Native studies into a system that does not allow the discipline to evolve; it is the way in which we have inherited the vanishing mentality. I might argue that the translation controversy has as much to do with the vanishing notion as with linguistic realities. (65)[1]

Womack illustrates here the kind of attitude we often encounter among Western and non-Western literary critics when they evaluate texts by indigenous writers. In North America, for instance, Vizenor has often been criticized for his excessive use of postmodern techniques and Western critical theory, strategies that would make his authenticity as an Indian author extremely dubious. For years the Santee Sioux writer and critic Elizabeth Cook-Lynn has been lambasting the mixed-blood writers Wendy Rose, Diane Glancy, Louis Owens, and Vizenor himself, among others, for losing sight of what she terms "tribal realism" and national sovereignty (69). In the Maori context, C. K. Stead forcefully criticized the awarding of the Pegasus Prize to *The Bone People* on the grounds that its author, Keri Hulme, is only one-eighth Maori. The work, he argues, "is a novel by a Pakeha [i.e., a white person] which has won an award intended for a Maori," adding that some of the Maori elements in the novel are "not entirely authentic" (104).[2]

The most notorious and controversial case of authenticity comes undoubtedly from Australia. In 1996, an article published in the *Australian Magazine* accused Mudrooroo, born Colin Johnson, of having faked his Aboriginal heritage (Laurie). On the basis of evidence from his sister, who after conducting extensive genealogical research found no trace of Aboriginal blood in the family, Mudrooroo, long established as the most famous and the most prolific Aboriginal author, was suddenly revealed to the Australian literary establishment as not Aboriginal at all.[3]

These few examples indicate the manipulation of the issue of authenticity among indigenous cultures and of the extremely complex political overtones of such debates. As Bill Ashcroft, Gareth Griffiths, and Helen Tiffin reasonably argue:

> The indigenous peoples of "settled" colonies, or "First Nations," have in many ways become the *cause célébre* of postcolonialism. No other

group seems so completely to earn the position of colonised group, so unequivocally to demonstrate the processes of imperialism at work. But indigenous groups have so often fallen into the political trap of essentialism set for them by imperial discourse. Imperial narratives such as that of anthropology in their project of *naming* and thus *knowing* indigenous groups have imported a notion of aboriginality, of cultural authenticity which proves difficult to displace. (214)

Who and what is an Indian, a Maori, or an Aboriginal Australian is indeed difficult to establish, and the establishment most certainly varies in these different contexts of writing and reception. For the most part, indigenous writers from Australia, New Zealand, and North America are constantly engaged in a battle against blood-quantum theories and essentialist definitions of identity. Their literary works become a political intervention on rigid and all the more dangerous claims to authenticity. According to Mudrooroo, "the crossblood exists at the edges of identity and his identity is always open to doubt. He is the existentialist par excellence, resting his authority on doing rather than being." On a more personal note, he states, "What has happened to me is to realize the absurdity of seeking a racial identity away from what I believe I am. Whatever my identity is, it rests on my history of over fifty years and that is that" ("Tell Them" 263–64).[4]

Existing "at the edges of identity," indigenous writers are constantly crossing ideological and essential borders between European and indigenous cultural traditions, daring to venture beyond preestablished rules of what is expected by an Aboriginal author. In the context of the oral versus written debate, all the writers discussed in this essay would agree that the oral can and should be reimagined into the written, since cultures are not static and in the oral tradition itself stories have always changed. Given the different cultural contexts and personal histories of the authors in question, how such reimagining takes place obviously varies, and I address this variation in the second part of my discussion.

Patricia Grace's *Potiki*

The enduring effects of colonialism, in its ongoing physical and cultural dispossession of the Maori populations of New Zealand, are captured in Grace's 1986 novel *Potiki*. In its straightforward plot and transparent prose, the novel tells the story of the dramatic cultural clash between the pakeha world and the Maori community. The routine life of the Tahimana family, a life made of farming, fishing, and living on their ancestral land, is suddenly disrupted when pakeha land developers, represented by Mr. Dolman (whom the Maori rename Dollarman), want to build a tourist resort on the *marae*.[5] When the Tahimana family, rejecting Dollarman's financial offers, deny him permission to build a road that would pass through sacred sites of the *marae*, the developers flood the *urupa* ("burial ground"), burn the *wharenui* ("meeting house"), and firebomb the sacred site after it has been rebuilt. Toko, the Tahimana's adopted youngest son, after whom the novel is titled (*potiki* in Maori means "the youngest son"), is in the house and dies on that tragic night.

In a perceptive reading of Grace's novel, Eva Rask Knudsen argues that *Potiki* is a "marae narrative," because the place representing the *marae*, the *wharenui*, and the open ground in front of it "is the centre of community life for the novel's Maori characters" (191). More than a simple ceremonial place, the Maori meeting house signifies the spiritual link with the tribe's founding ancestor (a likeness of whom is carved inside the walls), a corporeal embodiment of the community's history and genealogy. It is the essence of the people themselves. In *Potiki*, Grace describes the meeting house as a parent, warm and comforting in its embrace (88). The idea of the novel as a *marae* narrative opens up interesting issues in the context of reimagining the oral tradition.

In the contemporary, transnational panorama of literatures written in English, we could situate *Potiki* in a global context, even though the author, it should be pointed out, has not reached the kind of global audience that other well-established or Nobel laureate literary figures have. Maori literature and the Pacific cultures in general are still a marginalized discourse in the minds of Western academics, even more so in the minds of those who have repeatedly expressed the necessity of expanding the orthodox postcolonial canon.[6] Simply stated from a Pacific indigenous perspective, "Pacific peoples, such a small proportion of the world's population, are not accorded serious consideration in global terms." With the exception of tourist companies, military planners, and corporate elites, most of the world's population ignores "this ocean and its lands" (dé Ishtar 3), a home base to almost six million indigenous people.

Because of the strong references to the social and cultural impact of globalization on the indigenous populations of New Zealand, *Potiki* fits perfectly the discourse on literature and globalization that has characterized recent postcolonial debates. It is often taught as such. But I would argue that reducing Grace's complex narrative, epistemologically rooted in a Maori worldview, to the familiar postcolonial tale of a colonized-versus-colonizer battle may ultimately reflect the kind of Western literary colonization we unconsciously perpetuate when approaching texts originating in non-Western traditions.

Elsewhere I have written about the epistemological challenge that contemporary texts grounded in cultures other than Western, particularly those embedded in oral traditions, pose to Eurocentric readers. I have written about the importance of reading cross-culturally, of not only taking the time to learn the historical and sociocultural contexts of such novels but also—more important, perhaps—learning to acknowledge an indigenous rhetoric and epistemology, as these narratives incorporate visible strategies of orality into a written, discursive paradigm. I have stressed the importance of turning our act of reading, which often implies imposing our Western cultural assumptions on the narratives in question, into "a process of attentive listening" ("In Vain" 53). Such listening is needed for Grace's carefully woven text.

The novel's unconventional structure emerges at the very beginning. Instead of numbered chapters, we find twenty-eight sections, contained in three main parts; the sections are differentiated by the speakers. Toko, the adopted child of the Tahimana family, and his mother, Roimata, are the primary tellers. Other family members tell, such as Hemi (Roimata's husband), Mary (Toko's natural mother), and James (the Tahimana's oldest son); but Dollarman, the stories, and the *urupa* also tell. Storytelling frames the nature and content of the novel, one story spiraling into the next, clearly reflecting the epistemological tenets of the Maori universe. Part 1 is preceded by a prologue in which we find the essence of Maori spirituality:

> From the centre,
> From the nothing
> Of not seen,
> Of not heard,
>
> There comes
> A shifting,
> A stirring,
> And a creeping forward,
>
> There comes
> A standing,

A springing,
To an outer circle,

There comes
An intake
Of breath—
Tihe Mauriora. (7)

The paradox of Maori cosmogony is carved in this short poem-story, which could function, Knudsen suggests, "like a 'poem' in the original sense of the word as *'poiesis'*" (197). According to Maori belief, in the beginning there was *Te Kore* ("the Void") and *Te Po* ("the Night"), both fecund. From out of the Night arose *Ranginui* ("the Sky Father") and *Papatuanuku* ("the Earth Mother"), who lay together in a sort of cosmic embrace. They bore their children in darkness, and in darkness they remained, until their children, wishing to see the daylight, decided to separate their parents. From that separation, all creation began, including the generations of men.

After the opening poem-story, the story begins of a carver who releases preexisting figures hidden in the trees. One of the most prominent visual art forms in Maori culture, whose origins get lost in ancient myth and poetry, carving is, like storytelling, communal, a life force aimed at bringing people together, a marker of identity and kinship. By bringing this art form into writing, Grace acts as an ancient carver-storyteller retelling the old stories and experiences of the Maori people while engaging in the political act of rewriting history.

The carver of the prologue works under the rule of *tapu* (a Maori concept signifying both "sacred" and "forbidden"): he must not create anything out of living memory, and he must not blow on the shavings—otherwise his wood will harm him. By transgressing the laws of the sacred for the benefit of the community, so that the story would be remembered, the carver carved the figure of his late master, who did not have children of his own and who dedicated all his life to his work. But there is a part in the carving that is not completed, "a gap in the memory" that needs to be filled (11). By filling this gap with the story we are about to read (the story of Toko and his family), Grace makes a statement about the dynamic and ever-changing nature of storytelling, about the extraordinary power of stories to weave the past, the present, and the future in a spiral of cyclical being. As the anonymous storyteller in the section titled "The Stories" says:

And the stories continued well into the night, moving from one person to the next about the house until the circle had been fully turned. Then the people slept. But the telling was not complete. As the people slept there was one more story to be told, a story not of a beginning or an end, but marking only a position on the spiral. (180)

Sally Morgan's *My Place*

Since its first appearance in 1987, *My Place* has been perceived as a powerful condemnation of colonial history and race relations in Australia. A personal journey into the author's Aboriginal heritage, which her mother and grandmother had jealously kept secret, fearing the government policy of removing mixed-race children from their families (a policy very much in practice until the early 1970s), *My Place* has become an inspiring narrative for the descendants of the so-called stolen generation of Aboriginal Australians in search of their roots.[7] Variously classified as Western autobiography, Aboriginal life story, autoethnography, as well as a modern form of oral transmission or as-told-to autobiography, Morgan's polyphonic narrative is both a personal and social document in the way it reconstructs a significant chapter of the history of Aboriginal people. Conflating the historical and the personal, the oral and the written, Morgan weaves together three different life stories in the attempt to shed light on her own: her great-uncle's (Arthur Corunna's) story, her mother's (Gladys Corunna's) story, and her grandmother's (Daisy Corunna's) story.

The narrative opens with Sally's untitled story, which runs for more than a hundred and fifty pages and is almost uneventful, until the young protagonist hears, by accident, her sister refer to their Aboriginal ancestry. The shocking revelation creates in Sally an obsessive interest in her past and the reasons her mother and grandmother allowed her to grow up thinking that she was Indian. Morgan's growing interest in the history of Aboriginal people and of her own community in particular—the Palku and Nyamal from the Pilbara region, in the northwest of Western Australia–inevitably lead Morgan to the oral traditions.

The moment Sally decides to write a book about her family history, she realizes that the sources available to her are scant and extremely dubious. In response to her great-uncle, who more than anybody else encourages her narrative project, she states:

> Well, there is almost nothing written from a personal point of view about Aboriginal people. All our history is about the white man. No

one knows what it was like for us. A lot of our history has been lost, people have been too frightened to say anything. There is a lot of our history we can't even get at, Arthur. There are all sorts of files about Aboriginals that go way back, and the government won't release them. . . . I just want to try to tell a little bit of the other side of the story. (163–64)

With his willingness to speak, to reveal some of the atrocities committed by the white Australian government against Aboriginal people, Arthur convinces Sally of the truth and legitimacy of Aboriginal narratives over white official discourse. At one point in the story, when he tells how the white station owner Alfred Howden Drake-Brockman fathered both his sister, Daisy, and himself, he states:

By Jove he did! . . . I got no papers to prove what I'm sayin'. Nobody cared how many blackfellas were born in those days, nor how many died. I know because my mother, Annie, told me. She said Daisy and I belonged to one another. Don't you go takin' the word of white people against mine. (157)

For Aboriginal people, stories convey true facts, and oral discourse does not need scientific validation. As far back as the Dreaming, Aboriginal people have inscribed songs and stories onto the land, drawing from them a strong sense of identity as people. This reverence for language is something they share with other indigenous people around the world. Often it has been their only means of survival against the policies of systematic ethnocide and brutal displacement.

As both a writer and an artist, Morgan is particularly sensitive to the power of words and to the extremely complex task of writing down the oral tradition. Discussing the relation between her art and her writing, she states:

There is a connection in that in both of them I use dreams a lot as part of the creative process. There is a spiritual side to my writing . . . and that's true of my art. I'm also interested in not just writing oral histories, but painting oral histories, doing the same thing in a different form. ("Fundamental Question" 103)

The spiritual side to which Morgan refers is one that critics of *My Place* have not sufficiently paid attention to.[8] Even though the text does not present visible signs of orality, such as transcribed songs and myths, and the author herself has been criticized for lacking firsthand experience of the events narrated (a criticism that brings us back to the problematic question of authenticity), the narrative uncovers an indigenous subtext in which different realms of being coexist. A holistic worldview subtly emerges from the story's primary plot; it partakes of the magic of the Dreaming, a "maban reality" that, according to Mudrooroo, "is the single underlying experience of Indigenality" (*Indigenous Literature* 85). This worldview is skillfully articulated in the stories that Sally's family relatives tell and that become the fulcrum of the entire narrative.

Morgan is the main narrator of the stories told by her great-uncle, mother, and grandmother (which she taped and transcribed), but the story she tells us is communal, since the three different narrators gradually piece together a hundred years of Aboriginal history in Western Australia, embodying therefore a collective memory. Writing with a consciousness of the oral tradition, Morgan, in *My Place*, acts as an additional link in a long chain of Aboriginal storytellers approaching language as a form of spiritual cure and ultimately transforming the very process of life writing.

Gordon Henry's "Entries into the Autobiographical I"

Inspired by Vizenor's observation that "oral cultures have never been without a postmodern condition" (x), the Anishinaabe writer and critic Gordon Henry turns to trickster strategies and postmodern devices in his autobiographical narratives. In an essay subsuming various aspects of United States ethnic autobiographical writing—autoethnicity, autoethnography, autofiction, to mention a few—Henry offers a radical challenge to Ralph Waldo Emerson's universalizing subject and Western autobiography in general. Framed by an "Evocation" and "Invocation" in which the first-person narrator pays homage to "those who came before" and to "the gifts of creation" (165), "Entries into the Autobiographical I" at first appears as a postmodern collage of different narratives. As viewers to a pictorial exhibit, we are invited to open four different doors through which the narrator offers us glimpses into his multifaced self *à la recherche* of "a center around which to build." That center, one of the two epigraphs states, "is rarely an I" (165).

In "THE FIRST DOOR: I AS NOT I," the first-person pronoun makes a powerful disclaimer: "I am not: Postmodern or modern; a sign or a signifier, between signifieds; surreal or existential; neo-traditional or beat" (165); the list of ascriptions, metaphors, and stereotypical definitions continues for another page and a half and ends with the statement, "No, I am none of these. These are just some of my relatives. . . . They are my relations and for them I am grateful" (167). The postmodern I, on the verge of breaking up amid chaos and despair, finds order and balance in the family, the traditional source of tribal identification and identity. Traveling between opposites, Henry's autobiographical I takes on all the recognizable features of the tribal trickster, the mediator between worlds, the shape-shifter and natural contra dancer, ubiquitous and reluctant to be contained in the narrow definitions of social science discourse. The metaphor of the traveler becomes the most important trope in "THE SECOND DOOR: I AS TRAVELER I," a poem in which Henry's personal and family history is inscribed in the history of the Anishinaabe people:

> *I am a traveler:*
> outside White Earth, a child
> nearly dead from lack of air,
> in the heavy embrace
> of pneumonia,
> in Philadelphia projects; . . . (167)

A central figure to destabilize fixed notions of identity and culture, the traveler has become the most prominent metaphor in contemporary discussions of cultural identity.

As James Clifford has abundantly demonstrated, "everyone is on the move, and has been for centuries" (*Routes* 2). Indigenous peoples as well, he maintains, "have never been simply 'local'"; on the contrary, "they have always been rooted and routed in particular landscapes, regional and interregional networks" ("Diasporas" 309–10). In Henry's autobiographical narratives, the metaphor of travel functions on different levels: on a personal basis, it affirms a transcultural identity through which the different versions of the self actively and creatively negotiate different cultural realms; on a historical level, it serves as a reminder that the supposedly dead Native American cultures are very much alive and changing. In the concluding stanza of the poem, the metaphor of travel suggests a journey toward a home demarcated not so much by fixed territorial borders as by a sort of in-between space, one reflecting Homi Bhabha's notion of "a mode of living made into a metaphor of survival" (11). Henry writes:

> *I will be a traveler:*
> . . . .
>
> to the ceremonial center
> where we dance in place
> where we look to the center,
> the center we try to
> remember, to heal those
> others we love,
> when the idea of self
> becomes too much
> for others
> to carry; when we know
> we are truly home. (173–74)

"Home" is the concluding word, before the invocation, in "Entry Into the Autobiographical I," following a narrative section in the "THIRD DOOR," in which an "I AS ALTER I" recounts an "autobiographical meta-tale on writing" (174). Traveling in Spain, the self of the "FOURTH DOOR" longs for home, "looking forward to more stories" (181). Paralleling traditional trickster tales, in which episodes are connected by association rather than by linear progression, Henry's autobiographical narratives by spin stories within stories, forging a web of connections through which Native identity is constantly reimagined and, in typical trickster spirit, humorously liberated from the strictures of Eurocentric discourse.[9]

My brief reflections on the indigenous literatures of New Zealand, Australia, and North America have, I hope, drawn attention to some of the complex questions that reading-teaching such literary texts inevitably pose to Western readers unfamiliar with indigenous epistemological constructs. Regardless of whether they use novels, autobiographies, narrative essays, or any other Western literary genre, contemporary indigenous literatures written in English require that we engage in a different kind of reading: they require that we look beyond the surface of these texts and make an effort to learn not about but from these cultures, cultures whose worldviews are indeed different from ours but cultures that are constantly challenging us, in that difference, to reposition our cultural identities.

Knudsen's observations, at the end of her commentary on *Potiki*, neatly summarize my argument:

> Grace takes us into the bosom of this land, which is fittingly ambiva-
> lent, both new and old, and when the last page is turned the reader is
> brought back to the beginning with a greater insight into the deeper
> layers of a Maori narrative mould. We have not read just a conven-
> tional socialist-realist account of how a community fights for survival
> in contemporary New Zealand. We have been guests at Grace's *marae*.
> And that is quite a different story. (222)

As guests at indigenous writers' homes-texts, we'd better familiarize ourselves with some of the epistemological tenets (the *marae* protocol) that
will allow us to understand the richness and complexity of the cultures
beyond the touristic-consumerist approach that so often characterizes
literary studies in the era of globalization.

Notes

1. "Vanishing mentality" refers to the idea that Indians in North America,
decimated by cholera, smallpox, and other infectious diseases, appeared to their
discoverers as vanishing. Forecasting the biological extinction of Indians in the
near future, the discoverers could easily justify-legitimize taking their lands
and removing them to reservations in the name of progress. For a classical
study on the topic, see Dippie. For a more recent investigation of how anthropologists in the late nineteenth century were driven by the vanishing mentality
in their attempt to salvage a fast-disappearing Indian culture, see Deloria.

2. For an interesting response to Stead's reservations on Hulme's novel,
see Fee.

3. Mudrooroo's blackness has been traced back to African American roots,
as his sister provided evidence for a paternal grandfather born in North Carolina who later migrated to Australia in the second half of the nineteenth century. For a detailed discussion of this issue, see Oboe, Introduction; Shoemaker.

4. It is interesting to compare Mudrooroo's statement to N. Scott Momaday's understanding of Indianness as an act of self-imagination: "I think of
myself as an Indian because at one time in my life I suddenly realized that my
father had grown up speaking a language I didn't grow up speaking, that my
forebears on his side had made a migration from Canada along with . . .
Athapaskan peoples that I knew nothing about, and so I determined to find out
something about these things and in the process I acquired an identity; it is an
Indian identity, as far as I am concerned" (qtd. in Schubnell 141).

5. Both pakeha and Maori anthropologists have argued that the *marae*
stands at the center of contemporary Maori culture and identity. Whereas in the
past the term designated exclusively the open yard in front of the *wharenui*
("meeting house") and was used for the performance of ceremonies, today

marae usually designates all the buildings, including open spaces, of a Maori community facility. Often belonging to a tribal group, a clan, or an extended family, the *marae* needs to be constantly rebuilt. Its periodical maintenance allows Maori communities to keep the traditions alive and pass on skills, such as carving, to the younger generations. For a discussion of the *marae*, see Walker; Allen 47–48.

6. Elizabeth DeLoughrey's *Routes and Roots: Navigating Caribbean and Pacific Island Literatures* (2007) is the first critical study to attempt a comparative discussion in a discourse of transoceanic diasporas.

7. The practice of removing part-Aboriginal children originated from a nineteenth-century conception of white superiority. As the reasoning went, part-white children could be transformed into civilized individuals, the quantity of white blood diluting the savage nature in them. In 1995, the Human Rights and Equal Opportunity Commission (HREOC), charged by Attorney General Michael Lavarch, was established to inquire into the separation of Aboriginal and Torres Strait Islander children from their families. In 1997, a report was issued, "Bringing Them Home: The 'Stolen Children's' Report." The document publicly uncovered some of the horrific policies committed against the Aboriginal community by the white Australian government. The word *genocide*, as it is defined in the United Nation's 1948 "Convention on Punishment and Prevention of the Crime of Genocide," was used in the National Inquiry's Report (see *Bringing*).

8. See also Morgan, *Seeking* (in which Morgan further discusses the importance of dreams in her work). I have elaborated on some of these issues in an essay discussing *My Place* in the context of the Aboriginal diaspora ("One More Story").

9. In a *North Dakota Quarterly* interview, Henry said, "For me storytelling is important because it has the capacity to change, or turn, the consciousness of both the storyteller and the listener" ("Interview" 167). Henry's novel, *The Light People*, winner of the American Book Award in 1995, offers an additional example of his sophisticated storytelling technique.

Works Cited

Allen, Chadwick. *Blood Narrative: Indigenous Identity in American Indian and Maori Literary and Activist Texts*. Durham: Duke UP, 2002. Print.
Ashcroft, Bill, Gareth Griffiths, and Helen Tiffin, eds. *The Post-colonial Studies Reader*. London: Routledge, 1995. Print.
Bhabha, Homi. "Halfway House." *Artforum* 35.9 (1997): 11–12, 125. Print.
Blaeser, Kimberley. *Gerald Vizenor: Writing in the Oral Tradition*. Norman: U of Oklahoma P, 1996. Print.
Bringing Them Home: Report of the National Inquiry into the Separation of Aboriginal and Torres Strait Islander Children from Their Families. Human Rights and Equal Opportunity Commission, Apr. 1997. Web. 23 Feb. 2008.
Clifford, James. "Diasporas." *Cultural Anthropology* 9.3 (1994): 302–38. Print.

———. *Routes: Travel and Translation in the Late Twentieth Century.* Cambridge: Harvard UP, 1997. Print.

Cook-Lynn, Elizabeth. "American Indian Intellectualism and the New Indian Story." *American Indian Quarterly* 20.1 (1996): 57–76. Print.

dé Ishtar, Zohl, ed. *Daughters of the Pacific.* Melbourne: Spinifex, 1994. Print.

Deloria, Philip. *Indians in Unexpected Places.* Lawrence: UP of Kansas, 2004. Print.

DeLoughrey, Elizabeth. *Routes and Roots: Navigating Caribbean and Pacific Island Literatures.* Honolulu: U of Hawai'i P, 2007. Print.

Dippie, Brian. *The Vanishing American.* Lawrence: UP of Kansas, 1982. Print.

Fee, Margery. "Why C. K. Stead Didn't Like Keri Hulme's *The Bone People*: Who Can Write as Other?" *Australian and New Zealand Studies in Canada* 1 (1989). Rpt. in Ashcroft, Griffiths, and Tiffin 242–45.

Grace, Patricia. *Potiki.* Honolulu: U of Hawai'i P, 1986. Print.

Henry, Gordon. "Entries into the Autobiographical I." *Here First: Autobiographical Essays by Native American Writers.* Ed. Arnold Krupat and Brian Swann. New York: Modern Lib., 2000. 164–81. Print.

———. "An Interview with Gordon Henry, Jr." By Carmen Flys. *North Dakota Quarterly* 63.4 (1996): 167–79. Print.

———. *The Light People: A Novel.* Norman: U of Oklahoma P, 1994. Print.

Knudsen, Eva Rask. *The Circle and the Spiral: A Study of Australian Aboriginal and New Zealand Maori Literature.* Amsterdam: Rodopi, 2004. Print. Cross/Cultures 68.

Krupat, Arnold. *The Voice in the Margin: Native American Literature and the Canon.* Berkeley: U of California P, 1989. Print.

Laurie, Victoria. "Identity Crisis." *Australian Magazine* 20–21 July 1996: 28–32. Print.

Morgan, Sally. "A Fundamental Question of Identity: An Interview with Sally Morgan." By Mary Wright. *Aboriginal Culture Today.* Ed. Anna Rutherford. Aarhus: Dangaroo, 1988. 92–107. Print.

———. *My Place.* London: Virago, 1988. Print.

———. *Seeking the Spectacular. Context.* Context, 1 June 2004. Web. 8 Apr. 2008.

Mudrooroo. *The Indigenous Literature of Australia: Milli Milli Wangka.* Melbourne: Hyland, 1997. Print.

———. "Tell Them You're Indian: An Afterword." *Race Matters: Indigenous Australians and "Our" Society.* Ed. Gillian Cowlishaw and Barry Morris. Canberra: Aboriginal Studies, 1997. 259–68. Print.

———. *Writing from the Fringe: A Study of Modern Aboriginal Literature.* Melbourne: Hyland, 1997. Print.

Oboe, Annalisa. Introduction. Oboe, *Mongrel Signatures* vii–xix.

———, ed. *Mongrel Signatures: Reflections on the Work of Mudrooroo.* Amsterdam: Rodopi, 2003. Print. Cross/Cultures 64.

Pulitano, Elvira. "'In Vain I Tried to Tell You': Crossreading Strategies in Global Literatures." *World Literature Written in English* 39.2 (2002–03): 52–70. Print.

————. "'One More Story to Tell': Diasporic Articulations in Sally Morgan's *My Place*." *The Pain of Unbelonging: Alienation and Identity in Australasian Literature*. Ed. Sheila Collingwood-Whittick. Pref. Germaine Greer. Amsterdam: Rodopi, 2007. 37–55. Print. Cross/Cultures 91.

Schubnell, Matthias. *N. Scott Momaday: The Cultural and Literary Background*. Norman: U of Oklahoma P, 1985. Print.

Shoemaker, Adam. "Mudrooroo and the Curse of Authencity." Oboe, *Mongrel Signatures* 1–23.

Stead, C. K. "Keri Hulme's *The Bone People*, and the Pegasus Award for Maori Literature." *ARIEL* 16.4 (1985): 101–08. Print.

Vizenor, Gerald, ed. *Narrative Chance: Postmodern Discourse on Native American Indian Literatures*. Albuquerque: U of New Mexico P, 1989. Print.

Walker, Ranginui. "Marae: A Place to Stand." *Te Ao Hurihuri: Aspects of Maoritanga*. Ed. Michael King. Auckland: Reed, 1992. 15–27. Print.

Womack, Craig. *Red on Red: Native American Literary Separatism*. Minneapolis: U of Minnesota P, 1999. Print.

Margaret R. Higonnet

Weaving Women into World Literature

Over the last several decades, the world literature printed in anthologies has undergone a sex change.[1] Under the impetus of feminist criticism, along with postcolonial theory and Marxist critique, these collections reflect a revised understanding of the world, less Eurocentric and focused on social elites than before and no longer exclusively male. Such trends, reinforced by institutional distribution requirements that weight diversity rather than a universalist approach to cultures around the globe, have pointed toward the variable functions of gender in literary production and reception. A fundamental reconception of authorship, aesthetic form, and readership has led editors to include under the rubric of literature anonymous oral forms, often belonging to gendered traditions; private and autobiographical genres, part of a sphere to which women have often been relegated; and a broader range of audiences, including, for example, domestic servants, peasants, and children. As both the world and its literature have changed, then, courses in world literature have increasingly included female authors. At the same time, universalist, binary ideas of male and female, or masculinity and feminity, have given way to more complex conceptions of identity as something performed in specific social and cultural contexts, and these conceptions have fostered a richer understanding of gender as a component of literary representation and symbolic action.

One reason for this shift is that the Western canon formerly rested on a hierarchy of genres, in which excerpts from epics trumped shorter lyrics, considered to be a minor form, and the important public form of drama left no room for the private realm of diaries. Today all this has changed. As the major world literature anthologies have acknowledged the significance of short lyrics and tales in the aesthetic hierarchies of many non-Western cultures (Caws and Prendergast 681), they have given increased space to poetry lamenting loss or celebrating love, sex, and spiritual journeys—themes central to much women's writing. Bulking up into multiple volumes, anthologies now embrace the proliferation of genres across time and cultures and cut across disciplines in sections that may print a tale next to philosophy, feminist polemic, or excerpts from a conduct book. This greater inclusiveness has accommodated more women's voices.

In addition, specialized anthologies have made available in translation women's contributions to regional or national literatures, from Africa to India and from ancient times to the twentieth century (e.g., Chang and Saussy; Churchill, Brown, and Jeffrey; Daymond, Driver, Meintjes, Molema, Musengezi, Orford, and Rasebotsa; Plant; Sato; Tharu and Lalita; and Wilson and Warnke).[2] Web sites such as *Diotima* and *Perseus*, devoted to women's history and to texts in ancient Greece, further facilitate our work. These projects often represent a decade spent gathering and translating, by a collective of contributors with the support of dedicated Web administrators and editors, such as Florence Howe of the Feminist Press.

These anthologies represent a broad shift in conceptualizing world literature. Women's texts in world literature nonetheless remain daunting to teach, especially for periods before the twentieth century. Much more criticism is available devoted to the last hundred years, when access to literacy, education, and publishers permitted a broad body of women to join the republic of letters. While a world literature without any women may have seemed simpler to encompass, in today's complex multiplication of approaches and expanding notion of literature, to teach world literature by women is to take up the challenge to trace historical shifts and cultural differences for which the scholarship is still evolving. The moment is both exciting and difficult.

Gendered changes in world literature anthologies were catalyzed by a critical movement from a focus on singular woman as theme to the feminist concern with women as authors (see Finney 115). In broad terms this essay responds to that development. I begin by reflecting on a few questions raised by the incorporation of women into literary history. In turn, I point to a few reading strategies that focus on gender not only as theme but also as a factor in literary features such as genre, diction, point of view, and irony. The rise of feminist narratology in the work of critics such as Susan Lanser has been invaluable to those working on these topics.

The comparative literary history of women as authors raises numerous questions. Proverbially, "anonymous was a woman." In practice, however, we may not be able to detect from the text alone whether Anonymous is male or female. Do women differ from men in their stylistic, thematic, and narrative choices? There is considerable evidence that they do, since gendered social institutions tend to shape cultural production. Yet do women and men differ in the same ways across cultural boundaries? In cases where women such as the Brontë sisters chose pseudonyms or published anonymously in order to avoid censorship, we may be able to retrieve documentation of their authorship. The picture is complicated by the self-evident fact that artists ventriloquize the lyric or narrative voices of others. Thus the seventeenth-century Indian poet Kshetrayya wrote poems he entitled "A Woman to Her Lover" or "A Courtesan to Her Lover," assuming the female voice and role in addressing the deity (Damrosch et al. C: 25–30), a dramatic transposition of the spiritual into the erotic. Similarly, writing in the *yüeh-fu* tradition of plain folk song, the early Chin poet Fu Xuan bluntly cataloged the plight of woman in a voice that could be mistaken for that of a female poet (Caws and Prendergast 650). In the Chinese *Book of Songs* we cannot know whether the poems from the sixth century BCE that speak in women's voices were actually by women (Damrosch et al. B: 99).

We do know that women have always been verbal artists, and the channels of their art often may be culturally distinguished from those of men. One of the very earliest oral forms transmitted to us is the lullaby, typically sung by women after nursing; the nonsense features of lullabies and their child audience, however, have excluded this beautiful form from serious aesthetic consideration. Moreover, distinctions between women and men as performers of oral arts have not always been found worthy of recording, in part because in oral cultures, tales and poetry are passed across generations, so that communal memory may not celebrate the individual singer. Exceptionally, Knud Rasmussen, himself half Inuit, recorded the female shaman Uvavnuk's ecstatic Inuit song "The Great

Sea," performed after her death by her son in 1921 (Mack et al., *Norton Anthology of World Masterpieces* 2: 1792, 1798). As collecting practices have changed, emphasizing the performer and circumstances of performance, we have gained a clearer image today of the tellers of tales and a better understanding of their complex transmission processes.

In oral cultures, we now realize, women may respond to the gendered assignment of specific tasks, as in the extemporaneous yet formally intricate Greek lamentations recorded by Margaret Alexiou. Likewise in the former Yugoslavia, graveside laments (*tuzbalica*) were recited in the eight-syllable lines that typify women's songs (Caws and Prendergast 2615). Milman Parry and Albert Lord also collected women's lyrics celebrating love and marriage in the 1930s; they distinguish the metrics of these Balkan *ženske pjesme* from the ten-syllable lines of men's genres (2617). As these examples suggest, women's oral culture often celebrates thresholds in life cycles—with bridal songs at weddings, for another example. They may sing for other women or may address children. As the cyclical and locally variable practices of agriculture would suggest, ritual songs and other forms are linked to specific themes as well as to the situations that inspire the performance. Lee Haring underscores that even where "women, we know, are principal storytellers," their production of riddles, tales, and other forms is dependent on social conditions (39). In Mayotte, according to Philip Allen, Comoran "women play a more influential, even conspicuous role in public life . . . than they do in the stricter Koranic paternalism of the other islands" (qtd. in Haring 39).

By opening up space for oral forms, editors of anthologies have allowed us to glimpse a women's literary history whose continuities, such as the recurrent themes of love and lamentation, reach deep into the past. This realization interrogates our commonsense assumption that history is linear. Just as elements of the *Iliad* reach back at least four centuries before the period when the epic was written down, so too Indian lyrics by Buddhist nuns that apparently date back to the sixth century BCE were collected in the *Therigatha* anthology around 80 BCE.[3] These women found an opening at a moment of social dissent when they could cast off constraints and gain acceptance as well as legitimation by a movement that opposed discrimination on the basis of sex or caste (Tharu and Lalita 52). Their poetry of renunciation conveys the texture of daily life: one celebrates her liberation "from mortar, from pestle and from my twisted lord"; another celebrates her liberation "from kitchen drudgery, . . . from the harsh grip of hunger, and from empty cooking pots" (68–69). Over time we may observe in women's devotional poetry not only the sustained presence of their spirituality but also a shift from metaphors of healing and release to those of intensely physical ecstasy, as we find in ascetic bhakti poets of the Middle Ages. Thus the Kannada mystic Akkamahadevi (also known as Mahadeviyakka) sought union with her personal Shiva, whom she calls "lord white as jasmine," as a monsoon of love "like rain pouring on plants parched to sticks" (77). To read such devotional forms across periods and cultures complicates our understanding of cultural differences.

The comparative history woven into world literature anthologies points to many specific conditions that have enabled women's transition from orality to a female culture of writing. One is the emergence of writing in the vernacular. Since women were less likely to be educated in classical languages such as Latin, Greek, Sanskrit, and Chinese, one factor that enabled their voices to be heard was the acceptance of vernacular forms, in a turn away from languages learned only by elites. Thus the development of syllabary writing in Heian Japan gave women who lacked formal education in Chinese calligraphy access to eloquently succinct expression of emotions. The melancholy lyrics of Ono no Komachi (fl. 850), whose *waka* explore mutability and a dreamworld of romance, were anthologized in the landmark imperial collection *Kokinshū* (c. 905), the first major vernacular collection. This matrilineal culture, in which the Shinto sun deity and shamans were primarily female, welcomed such early women writers as Sei Shōnagon (c. 965 – c. 1017). Most notably, after the death in 1001 of her older husband, Nobutaka, Murasaki Shikibu (c. 978 – c. 1014), was so successful with the first sequences of her brilliant *Tale of Genji* (1010) that she was called to the court, where as lady-in-waiting she found an audience and patron in Empress Shoshi. Though proficient as a girl in Chinese, so that her father lamented she was not born a man, she would not write in characters, according to her diary, in order to avoid social condemnation as unwomanly (Damrosch et al. B: 298).

As the bhakti poets suggest, women who have sought unorthodox religious expression have also turned to compose in the vernacular, often in a fusion of erotic and spiritual genres. Even when literate, women who devote themselves to unworldly reflection have often chosen to use the language of the people. Thus, the literate thirteenth-century mystic Hadewijch of Brabant knew Latin and French but recorded her visions, poetry, and letters in Middle Dutch, ironically transposing chivalric conventions to a spiritual love whose tempestuousness may bring us "night in the daytime" (151 ["The Knight of Love"]). Similarly Julian of Norwich (b. 1342) either wrote or dictated in English her *Book of Showings* (c. 1393), which vividly praises the nurture offered by "our precious Mother Jesus," applying everyday metaphors of maternity to her subject. Atukuri Molla, an early sixteenth-century Varasaiva mystic, is the first woman poet thought to have written in Telugu, deliberately rejecting Sanskrit diction. Challenged to write a *Ramayana*, she produced one, according to legend, in five days, focusing on the divine heroine Sita. In introductory slokas about herself, Molla proclaims the importance of singing in spoken forms rather than obscure vocabulary and poetic forms: "I am no scholar / distinguishing the loanwords / from the antique stock" (Tharu and Lalita 95–96). Today she is remembered for her revolutionary use of Telugu. Perhaps Emily Brontë's humorous quotation of dialect takes on fresh meaning when set into the context of such women's innovations.

Linked to spiritual testimony, vernacular autobiography itself is an early form sought out by women. The earliest autobiography in English was by the mystic Margery Kempe (c. 1373). The early appearance of vernacular female autobiography occurs in disparate cultures. The *Kagerô Diary*, for example, by Michitsuna's Mother (936–95), is a life of "nobody," in which the author develops an ironic self-image by representing the disappointments of everyday life through the filter of romance expectations shaped by tales (Damrosch et al. B: 318). A little-known example of a woman who turned to the vernacular was the rebellious Greek autodidact Elisavet Moutzan Martinengou (1801–32). Martinengou fused the demotic Greek she heard in her seclusion at home with the poetic language she learned by reading the Bible. By combining the two in her diary, *My Story*, she forged an exemplary modern Greek that rivaled the experiments of her avant-garde contemporaries.

But the language of the people is not the whole story: court life also gave exceptional women the leisure, education, and stimulus to produce great art, as the organization of the Longman anthology makes clear. In addition to Heian Japan, where ladies-in-waiting such as Sei Shōnagon found cultivated audiences, Marie de France in the early thirteenth century wrote in Anglo-Norman for a courtly audience, albeit in the poetic transposition of a Breton folk genre, the *lai*. Just in case it was needed, religious conviction served her as a justification: "Whoever has received knowledge / and eloquence in speech from God / should not be silent or secretive / but demonstrate it willingly" (Damrosch et al. B: 905). Courtly culture encouraged dialogues between male and female poets (and sometimes actual courtship). The Turkish intellectual Mihri Khatun (1445–1512) thus celebrated chaste love in the salon of Prince Ahmad, entering a poetic exchange with the poet Nejati (Damrosch et al. D: 168–69). The Carmelite Sor Juana Inés de la Cruz (c. 1651–95) began her career as a poet while at the court of the Mexican vice-regent. Similarly, in the seventeenth and eighteenth centuries, European court circles not only witnessed the reign of several powerful queens but also tolerated women's alternative social sites of encounter, such as the salon. There aristocrats and bourgeois intellectuals could cultivate conversation and explore freedom of expression, both artistic and sexual, as exemplified by the Dutch polymath Isabelle de Charrière or the cosmopolitan Madame de Staël.

The gendered specificity of women's voices, I suggest, like the voices of the working class or of other kinds of social outsiders, springs from particular historical contexts. These might include the distinction between matrifocal and patrifocal societies or women's uneven access to social privilege and education. Even in cultures that called for young women's domestic confinement at puberty, those whose families were farmers, artisans, or merchants ironically enjoyed greater freedom and access to the public sphere. In Western Europe, women were often banned from literary societies and refused admission to universities. If Lady Murasaki could learn Chinese only by overhearing her brother's lessons, Virginia Woolf famously lamented not being taught Greek, as her brothers were. Attitudes toward gender that become internalized are shaped by forces as diverse as Confucian theories of the body and the Industrial Revolution, with its impact on the bourgeois assignment of Western women to the domestic realm. We can find the familiar fused with the unfamiliar in "Lessons for Women," a conduct book about gendered proprieties written for her daughters by Ban Zhao (c. 45–120 CE), who connects the rules of purity, self-sacrifice, and industry to the complementary constitution of husband and wife, which she compares to yin and yang (Damrosch et al. B: 92). While conceptions of gender may be universally present, a world literature course offers the opportunity to analyze the variable structures that shape characterization, voice, and narrative in quite distinct cultures.

The incorporation of women into literary history has gone hand in hand with an emphasis on the gendering of genres. As we have seen, certain forms, such as lamentation, are closely identified with women, a convention that Greek drama by male authors reflects thematically in the role assigned to Cassandra, who cries out in proleptic dismay at the gory deaths in "flame and pain" that she foresees in Aeschylus's *Agamemnon* (Damrosch et al. A: 638), or to Antigone, who takes on the duty of bury-ing, purifying, and lamenting for her dead brother, Polyneices, in the tones of a bird who has lost her young (Caws and Prendergast 238).[4] In women's writings, the voice of sorrow is heard everywhere. Sappho (7th cent. BCE) keens over rejection by a young woman, comparing love to battle. The pre-Islamic Arab poet Tumadir bint 'Amr, called Al-Khansa' (c. 575–c. 646) composed darkly pounding elegies for her warrior brother, heaping up images of loss (Caws and Prendergast 944). Li Qinzhao (c. 1084–1151) ties the gray of a chilly dawn to the loss of her husband, while Yosano Akiko (1878–1942) addresses her brother, a soldier in the bloody Russo-Japanese war, imploring him not to die in the face of the sorrows he has already left behind (1542–45). This range of textual mourning unveils the many possibilities for the application and elabora-tion of the genre: as a form of social protest, as a declaration of higher law, as an expression of thwarted desire etched in the body. The human rela-tionships are highly individualized, and even the narrative device of tim-ing gives the grief a dramatic point that differs from one text to the next.

Not surprisingly, one readerly tactic encouraged by recent antholo-gies is to juxtapose the voices of men and women. Not only genre but also features of point of view and diction lend themselves to gender analysis. When we compare the forms that mystic poetry takes across time and re-ligious differences, we can cross-read for questions such as the effect of sexual imagery in mystic poetry by men and women. Both Sappho and Ovid (in his *Amores*) compare love to war, but their points of view sharply diverge. Another tactic is to trace lines of inheritance from one woman to the next: how does a "sapphic" strain pass from Sappho herself to Louise Labé to the political satirist Mary Robinson to the lesbian couple known as Michael Field?

As for a major genre such as the novel, which is rarely visible in an anthology, the canon here too has changed as critics have recognized the importance of women authors and their realignment of stock forms. We see now that the legacy of *Don Quixote* includes many female Quixotes. Particularly evident in the nineteenth-century age of realism are differ-ences between women's and men's social conditions that affect modes of representation. Thus the gender of the protagonist redirects the female bildungsroman, which typically takes a young woman down a path that differs from the road open to a male protagonist. Whether the author is a man or a woman, the reader anticipates that the heroine's narrative trajectory will look different from the social integration that closes Goethe's seminal *Wilhelm Meister* (see Abel, Hirsch, and Langland). At the same time, a self-conscious woman writer may revise the conventionally gendered form to give it an ironic twist, as George Sand does at the end of her novel *Indiana*. While Indiana's Creole servant and double, Noun, commits suicide in a characteristic voyage in, Indiana herself eludes suicide by stepping outside the social order altogether. Nuances at the intersection of gender with class and race enable us to trace the structural functions of those parallel plots, just as the realization that masculinities and femininities form a system enables us to interrogate the masculinities of Indiana's bullying husband and her cardboard lovers Raymon and Rodolphe. The significance of such rewritings of convention has been noticed by theorists of the novel, such as Rachel Blau DuPlessis, whose notion of "writing beyond the ending" has refocused our attention on the gendering of narrative structures.

If we turn to the twentieth century, the confluence of extended women's education, an international feminist movement, and the proliferation of print media has strengthened the significance of forms such as the novel, to which women's worldwide contribution is undisputed. Here the availability of editions and translations is a less daunting problem than for the previous centuries. The broad historical record makes it possible to develop a course devoted to slices of time. As a topic saturated with gender, war has given ample room for reflection by writers of all persuasions, from all classes, and from around the globe in the twentieth century. In my own teaching of a narrowly defined period course, The Literature of World War I, the proliferation of anthologies and reprints has made it possible to address women's responses to dramatic changes in their own wartime roles as well as to men's sufferings.[5] Can women conceive of a female war hero in genres that are conventionally all about male conflicts? Do they see their own bodies at stake? How do they represent vulnerable minorities such as Jews and Armenians, who risk extermination along contested fronts? Rhetorically, do they represent men as their other, or do they other the enemy through bestial metaphors that strip away humanity and masculinity (a feature of many men's texts)?

Because so many women entered the stage of world literature in the twentieth century, a significant number of poems by the major Russian figures Anna Akhmatova and Marina Tsvetaeva can be set next to selections by little-known Czech, Polish, and Hungarian women poets. Prominent novelists, such as Virginia Woolf, Rebecca West, Willa Cather, Edith Wharton, and Katherine Anne Porter, all writing in English, poured out war narratives that can be set next to French stories by Colette, Rachilde, and Lucie Delarue-Mardrus or next to memoirs by the Danish Isak Dinesen and the Turkish Halide Edib Adıvar. Women who stayed at home can be compared with those who volunteered to work at the front or found themselves caught in a war zone with its attendant cruelties. Women write extensively on the body of the soldier, the prostitute, the nurse, the munitions worker. Because few women were in the trenches, many read war as an economy that encompasses a whole society rather than as combat along a narrow strip of land. Their social assignment finds expression in their subject matter, as well as in ironic metaphors of class, loss, and fractured communication.

One of my strategies for structuring the course has been to match women's writings with those by men. Thus readers can consider the central issue of the soldier's mutilated body by pairing Marcel Schwob's story "Les sans gueules" ("Faceless Mugs") with "The Man Whose Heart They Could See," by the Romanian avant-garde writer Hortensia Papadat-Bengescu.[6] Or readers can weigh the lingering urge of the orderly Lucien Laby to prove his masculinity with a gun against the dramatic denunciation by Mary Borden in her sketch "Moonlight" of a war that unsexes both the wounded and their nurses. In direct response to Erich Maria Remarque's *All Quiet on the Western Front* (1929), we can read Evadne Price's *Not So Quiet* . . . (1930), written to capitalize on the demand created by Remarque's instant best seller but based on women's texts, such as an ambulance driver's diary. Broadening our horizon to consider the gendered impact of imperialism, we can set Svarnakumari Devi's "Mutiny," an ironic short story about the reception of the war by English and Indian women in Bombay, next to Mulk Raj Anand's *Across the Black Waters*, about Lal Singh, a sepoy unmanned by his economic conscription to fight the master's war and by racist discrimination that strips him of his sexuality. Such dialogic readings can free readers from narrow cultural presuppositions and bring into play more than one kind of gendered interpretation.

As a "world war," the war of 1914–18 ultimately was Eurocentric, albeit with an imperial reach. The widespread notion that war is men's business left women generally out of the picture when a renewed historical interest in the colonial fronts drove interviewers to collect oral testimony. I was able to find very few women's poems and accounts from Africa, for example, to include in an anthology (*Lines of Fire*); those I did find, moreover, dramatically differed from European women's texts, not only in their political attitudes but also in their incorporation of the past into their self-representation, where issues of the body, of money, and of imperialist political agendas were curtly and effectively expressed.

Our relatively broad access to women's cultures in the twentieth century must be understood in the context of the global spread of Western genres and the indirect influence of Western publishing institutions, with their politics of translation. To weave a fuller history of women's writings, we must connect the threads of oral cultures to those of written cultures, at the same time that we trace the legacy of one woman to the next. Since women's writing so often has flourished at moments of crisis that complicate gender and that pin the symbolism of social relations onto images of the body, we must also remain sensitive to the systematic nature of gender constructions and the complexity with which gender is performed. We need to ask why certain genres remain privileged in the history of women's writings; we need to explore the connections of those genres to self-expression, resistance, performance, masquerade, and irony. Finally, the cultural instability of women's writing invites us to multiply our models of reading across the seas of social difference.

Notes

1. Do texts have a sex? When I first started teaching world literature, there were no women authors in my standard anthology. In Sarah Lawall's phrase, they belonged to "an invisible, internal rest" (in this volume, p. 26). The fifth, continental edition of the *Norton Anthology of World Literature* (1987; Mack et al.) gave Sappho, Marie de France, Marguerite de Navarre, and Sor Juana de la Cruz 74 pages out of 2,657. For a philosophically subtle analysis of the impossible relation between sex and gender, see Judith Butler. Her theory of the performative nature of gender is important to my argument.

2. My premise here is that introductory courses in world literature depend on the availability of texts in translation. Since women's literary production had suffered from neglect by editors and translators, it was especially difficult to include their work in world literature anthologies. That translation raises its own problems is acknowledged in special comparative pages in the Longman anthology's clusters of alternative translations.

3. While both male and female mystics adhering to this ascetic movement wrote about "the breath of liberty" in transcending the labors and pains of this world, the tasks they describe differ (Tharu and Lalita 69). Moreover, as the editors of the anthology point out, only the women who seek release from this earthly life in the ascetic community sing of bereavement—a theme long associated with women (68).

4. Readers must keep in mind that male actors played all the female roles in Greek plays and that men as well as women express grief at their losses, if in a different register. Thus in *Antigone*, while the heroine welcomes her own death, Creon curses himself on learning of the deaths of his son and wife. For valuable readings of women's roles and voices in Greek drama, see McClure; Zeitlin.

5. Several anthologies devoted to women's writings about World War I have appeared, edited by Dorothy Goldman, Claire Tylee, Angela Smith, and me (Cardinal, Goldman, and Hattaway; Higonnet, *Nurses*; Smith; Tylee). Svetlana Palmer and Sarah Wallis organized their anthology around complementary texts such as vividly detailed diaries of two perspicacious children, Piete Kuhr in Germany under the blockade and Yves Congar in occupied France.

6. On the cultural impact of the damaged male body, the historian Joanna Bourke's study of mutilation can be juxtaposed with Sophie Delaporte's study of facial disfigurement.

Works Cited

Abel, Elizabeth, Marianne Hirsch, and Elizabeth Langland, eds. *The Voyage In: Fictions of Female Development*. Hanover: UP of New England, 1983. Print.

Alexiou, Margaret. *The Ritual Lament in Greek Tradition*. 2nd ed. Lanham: Rowman, 2002. Print.

Anand, Mulk Raj. *Across the Black Waters*. 1940. New Delhi: Vision, 2000.

Borden, Mary. "Moonlight." Higonnet, *Lines* 373–78.

Bourke, Joanna. *Dismembering the Male: Men's Bodies, Britain and the Great War*. London: Reaktion, 1996. Print.

Butler, Judith. *Gender Trouble: Feminism and the Subversion of Identity*. New York: Routledge, 1990. Print.

Cardinal, Agnes, Dorothy Goldman, and Judith Hattaway, eds. *Women's Writing on the First World War*. Oxford: Oxford UP, 1999. Print.

Caws, Mary Ann, and Christopher Prendergast, eds. *The HarperCollins World Reader*. Single-vol. ed. New York: Harper, 1994. Print.

Chang, Kang-i Sun, and Haun Saussy, eds. *Women Writers of Traditional China: An Anthology of Poetry and Criticism*. Stanford: Stanford UP, 1999. Print.

Churchill, Laurie J., Phyllis R. Brown, and Jane E. Jeffrey, eds. *Women Writing Latin: From Roman Antiquity to Early Modern Europe*. New York: Routledge, 2002. Print.

Congar, Yves. *L'enfant Yves Congar: Journal de la guerre, 1914–1918*. Ed. Stéphane Audouin-Rouzeau. Paris: Cerf, 1997. Print.

Damrosch, David, et al., eds. *The Longman Anthology of World Literature*. 6 vols. New York: Pearson, 2004. Print.

Daymond, Margaret, Dorothy Driver, Sheila Meintjes, Leloba Molema, Chiedza Musengezi, Margie Orford, and Nobantu Rasebotsa, eds. *Women Writing Africa: The Southern Region*. New York: Feminist, 2003. Print.

Delaporte, Sophie. *Les gueules cassées: Les blessés de la face de la Grande Guerre*. Pref. Stéphane Audoin-Rouzeau. Paris: Noêsis, 1996. Print.

DuPlessis, Rachel Blau. *Writing beyond the Ending: Narrative Strategies of Twentieth-Century Women Writers*. Bloomington: Indiana UP, 1985. Print.

Finney, Gail. "What's Happened to Feminism?" *Comparative Literature in an Age of Globalization*. Ed. Haun Saussy. Baltimore: Johns Hopkins UP, 2006. 114–26. Print.

Hadewijch. *The Complete Works*. Trans. Columba Hart. Pref. Paul Mommaers. New York: Paulist, 1980. Print.

Haring, Lee. *Indian Ocean Folktales*. Chennai: National Folklore Support Centre, India, 2002. Print.

Higonnet, Margaret R., ed. *Lines of Fire: Women Writers of World War I*. New York: Plume-Penguin, 1995. Print.

———, ed. *Nurses at the Front: Writing the Wounds of the Great War*. Lebanon: UP of New England, 2001. Print.

Julian of Norwich. *A Book of Showings to the Anchoress Julian of Norwich*. Ed. Edmund Colledge and James Walsh. Toronto: Pontifical Inst. of Mediaeval Studies, 1978. *The Works of Julian of Norwich*. 16 Oct. 2007. *Luminarium: Anthology of English Lit*. Web. 14 July 2008.

Kuhr, Piete. *There We'll Meet Again: The First World War Diary of a Young German Girl*. Trans. Walter Wright. Gloucester: Wright, 1998. Print.

Laby, Lucien. *Les carnets de l'aspirant Laby, médecin dans les tranchées, 28 juillet 1914–14 juillet 1919*. Ed. Sophie Delaporte. Paris: Bayard, 2001. Print.

Lanser, Susan. *Fictions of Authority: Women Writers and Narrative Voice*. Ithaca: Cornell UP, 1992. Print.

Mack, Maynard, et al., eds. *Norton Anthology of World Literature*. Continental ed. 5th ed. New York: Norton, 1987. Print.

———. *Norton Anthology of World Masterpieces*. Expanded ed. 2 vols. New York: Norton, 1995. Print.

Martinengou, Elisavet Moutzan. *My Story*. Trans. Helen Dendrinou Kolias. Athens: U of Georgia P, 1989. Print.

McClure, Laura. *Spoken like a Woman: Speech and Gender in Athenian Drama*. Princeton: Princeton UP, 1999. Print.

Palmer, Svetlana, and Sarah Wallis, eds. *Intimate Voices from the First World War*. London: Simon, 2003. Print.

Papadat-Bengescu, Hortensia. "The Man Whose Heart They Could See." 1923. Higonnet, *Lines* 356–62.

Plant, I. M., ed. *Women Writers of Ancient Greece and Rome: An Anthology*. Norman: U of Oklahoma P, 2004. Print.

Price, Evadne [Helen Zenna Smith]. *Not So Quiet . . . Stepdaughters of War*. 1930. Ed. Jane Marcus. New York: Feminist, 1989. Print.

Sand, George. *Indiana*. Trans. Sylvia Raphael. Oxford World's Classics. Oxford: Oxford UP, 1994. Print.

Sato, Hiroaki, ed. *Japanese Women Poets: An Anthology*. Armonk: Sharpe, 2007. Print.

Schwob, Marcel. "Les sans-gueule." *La bibliothèque électronique de Lisieux*. La Bibliothèque Électronique de Lisieux, n.d. Web. 23 Apr. 2008.

Smith, Angela, ed. *Women's Writing of the First World War: An Anthology*. Manchester: Manchester UP, 2000. Print.

Svarnakumari Devi. "Mutiny." Higonnet, *Lines* 384–89.

Tharu, Susie, and K. Lalita, eds. *Women Writing in India, 600 BC to the Present*. Vol. 1. New York: Feminist, 1991. Print.

Tylee, Claire, ed. *Women, the First World War, and the Dramatic Imagination: International Essays, 1914–1999*. Lewiston: Mellen, 2000. Print. Women's Studies 30.

Wilson, Katharina M., and Frank J. Warnke, eds. *Women Writers of the Seventeeth Century*. Athens: U of Georgia P, 1989. Print.

Zeitlin, Froma. *Playing the Other: Gender and Society in Classical Greek Literature*. Chicago: U of Chicago P, 1996. Print.

Joseph A. Massad

Sexuality, Literature, and Human Rights in Translation

In Western academe, teaching sexuality in world literature courses is fraught with the same problems facing all cross-cultural comparative courses. The most salient problem is perhaps the inclination toward assimilating others into the European self under the sign of universalization as identity or, representing the other as exemplifying a radical and unbridgeable alterity, under the sign of localism as difference. The outcome of such approaches leads to the commission not only of scholarly mistakes, by reading signs through a Western grid of interpretation, but also of methodological mistakes, by risking the reification of the recently hegemonic hetero-homo binary prevailing in the West as either a transhistorical, transgeographic, and transcultural phenomenon or as a feature characterizing the superior notion of the human as defined by the European experience and its interpreters. Caution and vigilance are an immediate necessity to avoid these pitfalls.

Since the institutionalization of the homo-hetero binary in Western medicine and law in the nineteenth century and its proliferation across the surface and interstices of cultural products, cultural historians and literary critics in the United States' and West European academy have espoused the binary as a transhistorical and transcultural truism that the hand of scholarship need only reach to interpret accordingly. Eve Kosofky Sedgwick put it thus:

> An understanding of virtually any aspect of modern Western culture must be, not merely incomplete, but damaged in its central substance to the degree that it does not incorporate a critical analysis of modern homo/heterosexual definition. (1)

While Sedgwick has been careful to limit her claim to the modern West, others have been less so. Not only were figures from the constructed past of Europe and the rest of the globe (from Plato, Sappho, Catullus, Ovid, and Abu Nuwas to Oscar Wilde and Marcel Proust) brought to the present and endowed with sexual identities commensurate with the recently invented binary as definitional of their sexual desires, experiences, and identities but so were figures from the contemporary world who lie outside Western cultural definitions.

This normalizing because assimilationist move has foreclosed any possible reading of the past of Europe and the rest of the globe and the present of non-Europe outside these epistemological limitations. The error here is not merely political, where sexual liberation and a commitment to the affirmation of the identities of sexual minorities are at stake. It is, more egregiously, epistemological, where sexual desires and practices can be viewed only through a postbinarized world; such a view performs epistemic violence on those forced into assimilation.

I illustrate this error by looking first at the main site of this epistemological struggle—namely, human rights activism, especially on the issue of sexual rights.[1] I concentrate on the Arab world, which is one of the main two sites of this struggle, the other being the African continent. It is in the realm of the emergent agenda of sexual rights, which made its appearance in the United States and other Western countries in the late 1960s and began to be internationalized in the 1980s and 1990s, that talk of sexual practices in the rest of the world, including the Arab world, would be introduced to the international human rights agenda and would be coupled to notions of civilized and uncivilized behavior. As I have argued elsewhere, this incitement to discourse (see Foucault, *History* 17–35) on sexual rights outside the United States and Western Europe required human rights organizations and advocates to incorporate existing anthropological knowledge of the non-Western world. This incorporation was central for the purpose of constructing the human subjects—or, more precisely, objects—of human rights discourse. In the course of such "international" activism, two prime victims of human rights violations in Arab countries and in Africa more generally emerged or were created: women and homosexuals.

Gayatri Chakravorty Spivak recently noted that the

> idea of human rights . . . may carry within itself the agenda of a kind of social Darwinism—the fittest must shoulder the burden of righting the wrongs of the unfit—and the possibility of an alibi. Only a "kind of" Social Darwinism, of course. Just as "the white man's burden," undertaking to civilize and develop, was only "a kind of" oppression. It would be silly to footnote the scholarship that has been written to show that the latter may have been an alibi for economic, military, and political intervention. (524)

The goal, however, can also be and often is one of ethical and epistemic normalization. Spivak is clear:

> Colonialism was committed to the education of a certain class. It was interested in the seemingly permanent operation of an altered normality. Paradoxically human rights and "development" work today cannot claim this self-empowerment that high colonialism could. Yet, some of the best products of high colonialism, descendants of the colonial middle class, become human rights advocates in the countries of the South. (524)

The collusion between middle- and upper-class native informants and diasporic members of the national group in question on the one side and the Western human rights groups and organizations on the other shows that it is not only a Eurocentric culture that is being universalized but also a culture that has important class attributes. Such universalizing has serious consequences for those unfit to defend themselves. Spivak explains that "the work of righting wrongs is shared above a class line that to some extent and unevenly cuts across race and the North-South divide" (525). This native middle class,

> although physically based in the South . . . is generally also out of touch with the mindset—a combination of episteme and ethical discourse—of the rural poor below the NGO level. To be able to present a project that will draw aid from the North, for example, to understand and state a problem intelligibly and persuasively for the taste of the North, is itself proof of a sort of epistemic discontinuity with the ill-educated rural poor. (And the sort of education we are thinking of is not to make the rural poor capable of drafting NGO grant proposals!) (527)

Spivak's conclusions about the rural poor apply also in large measure to the urban poor, even though the urban poor may get more attention from international and local agents of human rights organizations, especially when the issue has to do with sexual rights.

Yet, despite the class, race, and colonial position of the fittest human rights activists who defend the unfit victims of violations, the allure of righting wrongs persists even among careful scholars and attentive advocates against identitarian oppression. Thus, Judith Butler, an otherwise exemplary scholar in her attention to detail, pushes for a universalizing of sexual rights:

> One of the central tasks of lesbian and gay international rights is to assert in clear and public terms the reality of homosexuality, not as an inner truth, not as a sexual practice, but as one of the definite features of the social world in its very intelligibility. . . . Indeed the task of international lesbian and gay politics is no less than a remaking of reality, a reconstituting of the human, and a brokering of the question, what is and is not livable? (29–30)

Butler's concern is that contemporary human subjectivity is constituted through a repudiation of what is lesbian and gay, which is therefore banished outside the perimeter of the human.

This concern may be justified in certain Western contexts, but it has no bearing on contexts in which lesbianness and gayness, let alone homosexuality as configured in the normalized West, are not the other against whom the self is constituted. In calling for the internationalization of Western sexual ontology, Butler is risking another subjective repudiation, a banishing of another other, in the formation of the Western human that is inclusive of the homosexual—namely, those cultural formations whose ontological structure is not based on the hetero-homo binary. The universalist moment here is the assimilationist moment that guarantees that the sexual subjectivity of the Western purveyors of international lesbian and gay politics itself is universal, while its racial-national-class constitution is carried out through a repudiation of the subjectivities of those unfit to defend themselves by the fittest subjectivity of all.

Butler understands the implications of international human rights work but seems to believe in the beneficial consequences of its universalization:

> International human rights is always in the process of subjecting the human to redefinition and renegotiation. It mobilizes the human in the service of rights, but also rewrites the human and rearticulates the

> human when it comes up against the cultural limits of its working conception of the human, as it does and must. (33)

She expresses much concern about imperialism but at the same time correctly rejects cultural relativism as effective or desirable resistance:

> An anti-imperialist or, minimally, nonimperialist conception of international human rights must call into question what is meant by the human and learn from the various ways and means by which it is defined across cultural venues. This means that local conceptions of what is human or, indeed, of what the basic conditions and needs of a human life are, must be subjected to reinterpretation, since there are historical and cultural circumstances in which the human is defined differently. (37)

In place of the imperialist and the reductively relativist view, she insists that "we are compelled to speak of the human, and of the international, and to find out in particular how human rights do and do not work" (37).

I am not persuaded by this argument. Butler is admirably attentive to the different configurations of including and excluding the category of woman, which has been institutionalized as a universal category at the expense of the differing local formations and legal standings of the term, informed by racial, geographic, and class positionings inter alia. Including the categories of gay and lesbian as if they were analogous to the universalized category of woman, however, is even more problematic. The categories of gay and lesbian are not universal at all and can be universalized only by the epistemic, ethical, and political violence unleashed on the rest of the world by the very international human rights advocates whose aim is to defend the people their intervention is creating. In doing so, they are not bringing about the inclusion of the homosexual in a new and redefined human subjectivity; rather, they are bringing about the exclusion of the homosexual from this redefined subjectivity altogether, while simultaneously destroying existing subjectivities organized around other sets of binaries, including sexual ones.

Subjectivities in many non-Western contexts (Africa, Asia, and Latin America) do not include heterosexuality and exclude homosexuality: that binarism is not part of their ontological structure. What the incitement and intervention of international human rights activism achieve is the replication of the very Euro-American human subjectivity its advocates challenge at home (let alone that this Euro-American subjectivity is itself racialized and classed and reflects the hegemonized experience of the white Protestant urban middle class). The new and redefined universal human subjectivity that these activists are proselytizing to the rest of the world is not that of including the homosexual but that of instituting the very binary (an assimilationist move that facilitates the tabulation of data in the databases of the human rights industry) that excludes the homosexual it created in the first place. This exclusion is carried out in the name of liberation from oppressive cultures and laws.

Talal Asad insists that the dominant view of cultures as "fragmented" and interdependent, "as critics never tire of reminding us," is not sufficient:

> Cultures are also *unequally displaced practices.* Whether cultural displacement is a means of ensuring political domination or merely its effect, whether it is a necessary stage in the growth of a universal humanity or an instance of cultural takeover, is not the point here. What I want to stress is that cultures may be conceived . . . in terms of the temporalities of power by which—rightly or wrongly—*practices* constituting particular forms of life are displaced, outlawed, and penalized, and by which conditions are created for the cultivation of different kinds of human. (153–54)

The exercise of political power to repress, if not destroy, existing non-Western subjectivities and produce new ones that accord with Western conceptions "often presents itself as a force of redeeming 'humanity' from 'traditional cultures'" (154). My point here is not to argue in favor of non-Western nativism and of some blissful existence prior to the epistemic, ethical, and political violence unleashed on the non-West, as facile critics would have it, but to argue against a Western nativism armed with a Rousseauian zeal intent on forcing people into freedom, indeed one that considers assimilating the world into its own norms as ipso facto liberation and progress and a step toward universalizing a superior notion of the human.

There is nothing liberatory about Western human subjectivity's including gays and lesbians when those non-Europeans who are not gays or lesbians are forcibly included in that subjectivity yet excluded as unfit to define or defend themselves. I am not suggesting a Derridean insistence that a binary division is always already transhistorical and exists and is constituted at the level of metaphysical ontology, as Jacques Derrida insisted in his famous critique of Michel Foucault's historicizing the banishment of madness and the constitution of reason. My point is that the historical changes brought to bear on Western ontology always already reinscribe the binary by banishing those unfit to occupy it. While I am sympathetic to the political project of an all-encompassing utopian inclusivity, I am less sanguine about its feasibility and more worried about its cruelty.

Much of this effort at producing and assimilating the entire world into the image of Europe hinges on two strategies, universalization of the West as humanity and translation of the non-West into the West. As explained above, Western sexual epistemology and ontology are universalized a priori as human and not culturally specific, although when culturally embedded sexual notions arise, translation into Europe can render them intelligible and in accordance with Western judgment of analogical notions. Hence what is presented and translated as "sexual violence against women," "homosexuals," and "children" outside the West must be held accountable to Western norms of moral and juridical judgment. Therefore translation here seems superfluous, except at the linguistic level, as all it is doing is identifying the exact correspondence in the European lexicon between words and notions in non-European languages. Translating the world into Europe becomes then an easy task of presenting the world as an extreme or more primitive form of Europe, before it was transformed by sexual liberation and sexual rights. The world therefore must be brought closer to this liberated Europe. When I speak of translation as assimilation, I am referring to the translation not only of non-European texts but also of non-European corporeal practices, ontological structures, epistemologies, and much more. Spivak's notion of translation as violation is most applicable when translation is seen as assimilation.

Let us look at how inclusivity translates into reading fiction from other cultures and languages as part of the category world literature. Aside from the processes through which novels become part of world literature, the question of interpretation when they do is most illustrative. Winning the Nobel Prize for Literature has opened the door for Naguib Mahfouz's novels to enter the category of world literature. His *Midaq Alley* is one of the most popular in courses on sexuality and literature. The novel has a male character, Kirsha, who is married but who also engages in same-sex contact and expresses a desire for younger men. Mahfouz wants to introduce the Western notion of homosexuality to his readers by using the term in its English rendering, Arabic having then no agreed-on medical or sociological term to translate it correctly, but the gist of the novel is to explain that the world in which Kirsha lives and that allows polymorphous desires with certain levels of social sanctions but without identifying their bearers ontologically, is quickly disappearing under the introduction of colonial modernity and its new epistemology, including the notion of homosexuality.

Published in Cairo in 1947, the novel received high praise and remains in print to this day. Misreading Kirsha as homosexual has led critics based in the Western academy not only to misunderstand the novel but also to misinterpret its reception in its Arab environment. *Midaq Alley* received critical acclaim by Arab book reviewers of the period. Sayyid Qutb, an Egyptian literary critic who would later become the most important Islamist intellectual of the twentieth century, expressed his dissatisfaction with the novel on account of the abundance of deviance and deviants in it (understood as general social, not sexual, deviance). He proposed that Mahfouz reduce the number of socially deviant characters from five to two (181). Nabil Matar, writing in the *Journal of Homosexuality* half a century later, misunderstood *deviance* as an Islamic term and supposed that Qutb's reference to deviance and perversion was a reference to same-sex contact. Matar interpreted anachronistically Qutb's dissatisfaction with those elements. Indeed he strangely declares that the critics, Qutb included, received *Midaq Alley* with an "outcry against the novel's inclusion of homosexual characters." He cites the Lebanese critic Adib Muruwwah's review of the novel as another example of the outcry, merely because Muruwwah stated that

> no one among writers has been able to depict these [popular] classes as they are, as Mr. Mahfuz has done. He was utterly realist and faithful, even though this reality might have contained that which would on occasion offend proper decorum (such as the sodomy of Kirshah, for example). (see Shalash 178)

Matar cites Muhammad Fahmi's review as another example, when all Fahmi stated was that he found "Kirshah's deviance . . . somewhat strange for [someone] like him; perhaps had Kamil, the sweet seller, been afflicted with it . . . it would have added not a bad atmosphere of joy to the story. . . ." This is hardly an outcry against homosexual characters (see Shalash 182). Matar's misreading is now cited by Western commentators to buttress their assimilationist missionary work (e.g., Whitaker 88, 234n).

Contrast this reception with the one that Gore Vidal's 1948 novel *The City and the Pillar* received in New York. The critical response was so violent that the *New York Times* refused to advertise the novel and, along

with all major American magazines and newspapers, had a standing policy not to review any Vidal novels for the next six years, because the novel
depicted a sexual encounter between two young, all-American athletic
types (xvi). In contrast to Vidal, Mahfouz continued to be celebrated by
the Arabic press for the rest of his career despite his continuing inclusion
of characters who desire same-sex contact—perhaps because he was vigi-
lant in depicting his characters as part of the ontologies that produced
them and not ones imposed on them from the outside.

Though these problems arise because of epistemic projections in the
interpretive work (i.e., universalizing Western sexual epistemology as human epistemology, which does away with any need for translating
non-European epistemologies), they are compounded by translations that
are also informed by the hetero-homo binary. A more recent novel by an
Egyptian author that includes a man who practices passive intercourse
with men and who is referred to as "deviant" or *shadh* in Arabic is rendered a "homosexual" in the English translation (see al-Aswani). This
problem is not merely semantic, it is decidedly also epistemological. The
Arab world has not experienced the introduction into its medical and juridical apparatuses since the nineteenth century of the centrality of the
homo-hetero binary, and therefore it has a different taxonomy of sexual
desires that are not always or necessarily endowed with identitarian dimensions, though at times they are. Translating *shadh* as "homosexual" is
therefore an assimilationist move that misinterprets the category of deviant, which was adopted by Arabic from English in the middle of the
twentieth century, in accordance with Arabic translations of European
psychology books that referred to homosexuality as a form of sexual deviance. Since then the term has had an independent momentum that has
not always been controlled by its European pedigree. *Homosexual* has
undergone a very different Euro-American institutional and epistemological journey.

As Western cultural encroachment continued, its hegemonic impact
was felt across the Arabic language, especially on matters having to do
with corporeal practices. The word *jins*, for example, meaning "sex,"
emerged in Arabic sometime in the earlier part of the twentieth century,
carrying with it not only its new meanings of "biological sex" and "national origin" but also its old meanings of "type," "kind," and "ethnolin-
guistic origin," among others. The word in the sense of "type" and
"kind" has existed in Arabic for centuries and is derived from the Greek
genos. As late as 1870, its connotation of "sex" had not yet taken place

(al-Bustani 129).[2] An unspecific word for sexuality, *jinsiyyah*, which also means "nationality" and "citizenship," was coined by translators of the works of Sigmund Freud since the 1950s (such as Mustafa Safwan [*Tafsir*] and Jurj Tarabishi [*Thalathat*]). A more specific and nonconfusing word was coined more recently by Muta' Safadi, one of the two translators of Foucault's *History of Sexuality* [*Iradat*]. Still, *jinsaniyyah* is understood only by a few, even among the literati. Words for homo- or heterosexuality were invented recently as direct translations of the Latin-derived words employed in Euro-American usage: *mithliyyah* ("sameness") in reference to homosexuality, *ghayriyyah* ("differentness") in reference to heterosexuality. Arab translators of psychology books (except for translators of Freud, who coined the term *mithliyyah* [see Freud, *Tafsir* 182, 301, 337, 390, 391, 396, 400]) as well as Arab behavioral psychologists had adopted in mid-century the European expression "sexual deviance," translating it literally as *al-shudhudh al-jinsi*, a coinage that remains the most common term used in books and the press and in polite company to refer to the Western concept of homosexuality.[3]

This discussion of terms is not to say that, given the inaccuracy of translations of novels, teachers of world literature should not teach them. Rather, when they do, they should teach them against the grain of assimilationism. *The Yacoubian Building* (the English translation of al-Aswani's novel) is one of an increasing number of Arabic novels that seek to assimilate Western norms and project them onto Arab society (hence its immediate adoption by what Pascale Casanova has termed the "world republic of letters"). In this sense, despite the continued use by its author of the term *deviant*, his novel intended to describe and categorize one of its characters (Hatem) in Western identitarian terms. Although the translator mistranslated the Arabic for "deviant" as "homosexual," his interpretive impulse of the novel was not entirely off the mark. The narrative, however, portrays this deviant identity quite differently from how a European or American novel would likely portray it. The author's ambivalence, perhaps unconscious or based on a misunderstanding, about Western taxonomies is manifested in his letting a number of characters and sexual acts identifiable as homosexual by Western taxonomies escape the identification "deviant." The collapse of passive homosexuality into deviance is indeed an important feature in this novel. The Nubian butler Idris, who has penetrative sex with the young Hatem, is a case in point, as he is never identified as a deviant in the novel. Nor is the act by Hatem's colleague, a training editor at the newspaper, who approaches Hatem from behind and presses against him to intimidate and seduce him simultaneously, identified as deviant, nor is the colleague identified as a deviant or even as having deviant tendencies. Such failures of (Western) identification abound in the novel and can be used to identify the epistemological error in the translation of "deviant" into "homosexual."

Misreading the deviant as a Western-category homosexual or, worse yet, as gay has led human rights workers to intervene in countries and cultures they insist are assimilable into the heter-homo binary prevalent in the West. That such intervention has led to unprecedented police and state action against the group identified by the Western groups has not discouraged the purveyors of Western ontologies. Using the same epistemology to inform pedagogy risks complicity with this insistence on misunderstanding Arab and African novels as depicting a familiar sexuality that is readily intelligible to Western taxonomies. The details, and therefore the repercussions, of all this are lost and gained in the translation.

Notes

1. My discussion on human rights is adapted from the introduction to my book *Desiring Arabs*.

2. Al-Bustani's dictionary dates from 1870, at which time the word *jins* had still not acquired the meaning of "sex." For medieval dictionaries that identify *jins* as "genus," see Ibn Manzur 43; Al-Fayruzabadi 738.

3. On biologically essentialist and pathologizing accounts of homosexuality, see al-Sa'dawi, especially 557–69. As'ad AbuKhalil argues that the use of the term *shudhudh jinsi* in the Arab press constitutes oppression of "homosexuals" in the Arab world today (35, 35n52). Such use is the only evidence he provides to support the charge of antihomosexual oppression. My discussion of these words is based on chapter 3 of my *Desiring Arabs*.

Works Cited

AbuKhalil, As'ad. "New Arab Ideology? The Rejuvenation of Arab Nationalism." *Middle East Journal* 46.1 (1992): 22–36. Print.

Asad, Talal. *Formations of the Secular: Christianity, Islam, Modernity*. Stanford: Stanford UP, 2003. Print.

al-Aswani, 'Ala'. *'Imarat Ya'qubyan*. Cairo: Mirit Lil-Nashr wa al-Ma'lumat, 2002. Trans. as *The Yacoubian Building*. Trans. Humphrey Davies. Cairo: Amer. U in Cairo P, 2004. Print.

al-Bustani, Butrus. *Muhit al-Muhit, Qamus Mutawwal Lil-Lughah al-'Arabiyyah*. Beirut: Maktabat Lubnan Nashirun, 1987. Print.

Butler, Judith. *Undoing Gender*. New York: Routledge, 2004. Print.

Casanova, Pascale. *The World Republic of Letters*. Trans. M. B. DeBevois. Cambridge: Harvard UP, 2004. Print.

Derrida, Jacques. "Cogito and the History of Madness." *Writing and Difference.* Trans. Alan Bass. Chicago: U of Chicago P, 1978. 31–63. Print.

Al-Fayruzabadi, Muhammad bin Ya'qub. *Al-Qamus Al-Muhit.* Vol. 1. Beirut: Dar Ihya' al-Turath al-'Arabi, 1997. Print.

Foucault, Michel. *The History of Sexuality.* Vol. 1. Trans. Robert Hurley. New York: Vintage, 1980. Print.

———. *Iradat al-Ma'arifah, Al-Juz'al-Awwal min Tarikh al-Jinsaniyya.* Ed. and trans. Muta' Safadi and Jurj Abi Salih. Beirut: Markaz al-Inma' al-Qawmi, 1990. Print.

Freud, Sigmund. *Tafsir al-Ahlam.* 1958. Trans. Mustafa Safwan. Cairo: Dar al-Ma'arif Bi Misr, 1969. Print.

———. *Thalathat Mabahith Fi Nazariyyat al-Jins.* Trans. Jurj Tarabishi. Beirut: Dar al-Tali'ah, 1981. Print.

Ibn Manzur, Muhammad bin Mukarram. *Lisan al-'Arab.* Vol. 6. Beirut: Dar Sadir, 1990. Print.

Mahfouz, Naguib. *Midaq Alley.* 1966. Trans. Trevor Le Gassick. New York: Anchor, 1992. Print.

Massad, Joseph A. *Desiring Arabs.* Chicago: U of Chicago P, 2007. Print.

Matar, Nabil. "Homosexuality in the Early Novels of Negeeb Mahfouz." *Journal of Homosexuality* 26.4 (1994): 78. Print.

Qutb, Sayyid. *Al-Fikr al-Jadid* 12 Feb. 1948: 24–25. Rpt. in Shalash 181.

al-Sa'dawi, Nawal. *Al-Rajul wa al-Jins.* Beirut: Al-Mu'assassah al-'Arabiyyah lil-Dirasat wa al-Nashr, 1986. Print.

Sedgwick, Eve Kosofsky. *Epistemology of the Closet.* Berkeley: U of California P, 1990. Print.

Shalash, 'Ali, ed. *Najib Mahfuz: Al-Tariq wa al-Sada* [Naguib Mahfouz: The Path and the Effect]. Beirut: Dar al-Adab, 1990. Print.

Spivak, Gayatri Chakravorty. "Righting Wrongs." *South Atlantic Quarterly* 103 (2004): 523–81. Print.

Vidal, Gore. The City and the Pillar, *and Seven Early Stories.* New York: Random, 1995. Print.

Whitaker, Brian. *Unspeakable Love, Gay and Lesbian Life in the Middle East.* London: Dar al-Saqi, 2006. Print.

Marjorie E. Rhine and Jeanne Gillespie

Finding the Global in the Local: Explorations in Interdisciplinary Team Teaching

Together, we have team-taught two interdisciplinary world literature courses: a summer institute for high school teachers entitled Many Neighbors, Many Voices: Films, Literatures and Cultures in Contact in Asia, Latin America, and the United States and a six-credit undergraduate course entitled European Civilizations (and Their Discontents). By describing some of our experiences here, we hope to offer a model of how to organize courses on world literatures and cultures in intriguing thematic ways. More important, we hope to encourage teachers to look for the global in the local. First, we suggest how to assess the strengths of the individual teachers and how these strengths intersect and relate to local communities and resources with global links. We also want to emphasize the need to consider the perhaps unsuspected global perspectives that colleagues can share or that field trips can provide.

When we first began to discover how much we liked talking through our ideas together, Jeanne revealed that she had been thinking of writing a proposal to teach a summer institute for high school teachers through the extraordinary grant program offered by the Louisiana Endowment for the Humanities. Other states may offer comparable opportunities through initiatives that link higher education to K-12 initiatives or through international education enhancement programs. The National Endowment for the Humanities funds similar grant programs. Jeanne suggested that we work on the proposal and class together, and we started our collaboration by thinking about how the kind of course we could offer as a team would be more wide-reaching than, as well as different in its goals and focus from, what either of us could or would do alone. This kind of collaboration seems to us particularly pertinent in a world literature context, where the range of material that might be taught can be quite daunting.

We were both at that time teaching at Southeastern Louisiana University, a regional university (in the city of Hammond). We both had a relatively heavy teaching load, four courses per semester. Jeanne is a Spanish professor trained in Latin American area studies; Marjorie, a comparatist teaching in an English department, is interested in Kafka, Japan, and East-West contact. As we looked for ways to relate these varied interests, our idea was to go not from idea to people but from people to ideas. Instead of saying, "Let's find who I can work with to pursue this idea," we asked, "I like talking and thinking with this person—what can we work on together?"

As part of our continuing exploration of how our interests intersected with the communities around us in southeastern Louisiana, we began to look at the extremely diverse colonial and postcolonial heritages of the Gulf Coast. Certainly, the African and French heritages are in the forefront, but there are many other ethnic groups and influences visible in the area close to Hammond, once a railroad town: a large Sicilian settlement (Independence), German and Hungarian towns (Des Allemandes and Hungarian Settlement), many Asian communities (including North and South Vietnamese neighborhoods, which are, respectively, Buddhist and Catholic), as well as the strong Caribbean influences from Haiti, Cuba, Central America, and the Yucatan. Havana and New Orleans were often stops for ships coming to and leaving the gulf, so many contacts were established between the two cities. One especially strong connection can be seen in the rural communities of Cuba and Louisiana whose roots lie in the Canary Islands. As part of the Spanish colonial enterprise during the late eighteenth century, colonists from the Canary Islands were brought to settle in Cuba, Venezuela, Texas, and Louisiana. One group, now called the Isleños, settled along the Mississippi River south of New Orleans. This relatively isolated group maintained its Hispanic heritage and eighteenth-century Spanish language well into the twentieth century. The Isleños have fought to keep their cultural heritage alive by establishing a museum and by collecting and documenting examples of their musical, artisanal, and linguistic culture.

The more we talked, the more connections emerged. For example, we began to focus on how a comparative study of Latin America and Asia would yield fascinating information about how both regions of the world responded to European interests and colonial efforts. Also, we saw more clearly how satellite-settler communities in Latin America, as well as the territories that eventually became the United States, became a region for mediation between Asia and Europe, culturally and economically. For example, trade goods passed from China and Japan through Acapulco and on to Europe, while missionaries operated in sometimes different, sometimes similar, ways in the two regions we wanted to study.

Eventually, the story of Columbus became our central theme in the class that the Louisiana Endowment for the Humanities enthusiastically supported. We read literature, travel narratives, and essays and studied maps, art, and music, following a loosely chronological plan. We started with accounts of Asia as the source of spices and riches that enticed Marco Polo. Here excerpts from Herodotus and a spice cookbook (Day and Stuckey), as well as a discussion of a chapter from Wolfgang Schivelbusch's social history *Tastes of Paradise*, helped set the stage. We then turned to a few excerpts from Polo and viewed maps and images of monsters believed to people the unknown margins of the world at that time. What began as one teacher's seemingly silly idea (adapting a technical writing exercise in which students draw a monster and then try to re-create another's drawing from the written description only) was parlayed by the other teacher into a discussion of how manuscript transmission affected travelers' accounts of new lands and their inhabitants. We then turned to Columbus's study of Polo and his own journey to the East. We also considered responses to Columbus, such as those by Bartolomé de Las Casas and later Latin American writers like Alejo Carpentier, José Enrique Rodó, and Roberto Fernández Retamar. Watching a scene in *The Mission* in which a young Guarani boy is asked to sing in Latin during a debate over the humanity of his people became especially poignant in this context. We included study of the Jesuits in the New World as well as in Japan. Excerpts from the film *Shogun* work nicely here, as do Shusaku Endo's novels *Silence* (about the Jesuits in Japan) or *The Samurai* (about Japanese attempts to compete with Spanish trade routes). Throughout our discussions, we found that images of the Europeans by the people with whom they came into contact were often provocative to consider.

Two good sources of such images are *The Namban Art of Japan* (Oka-mato) and the *Lienzo de Tlaxcala*. Later, we took a comparative look at Cuba's sugar industry by viewing the Soviet-produced film *I Am Cuba* and examined Vietnam's rubber production by watching *Indochine* and reading *The Red Earth: A Vietnamese Memoir of Life on a Colonial Rub-ber Plantation* (Tran Tu Binh).

Our team-teaching collaboration extended to include colleagues and other members of the community, who, although very local in their prox-imity, often have rich and intriguing connections to the global. In our relatively small city of Hammond, Louisiana, we were able to invite a lo-cal musician to discuss the roots of rhythm (and share percussion instru-ments), a Shakespeare scholar to conduct a performance workshop on Caliban, historians to talk about trade and contact in classical antiquity as well as the Opium Wars, colleagues who research the work of Robert Olen Butler and Herman Melville's portrayal of the South Pacific, a local minister and part-time philosophy professor to talk about development in the rain forest, and a local artist inspired by Hispanic themes. Far from being too busy to bother, these people enjoyed being asked to share their expertise with colleagues and students.

As the summer institute class for high school teachers concluded, the focus turned to the study of Asian and Hispanic immigrants in the United States, especially in the South. We watched the video *Displaced in the New South* and read stories by Butler about Vietnamese immigrants in Louisiana and excerpts from Sandra Cisneros's work. But the most dy-namic and memorable component of this study of contemporary immi-grant communities was the field trips. The Catholic South Vietnamese community of Little Versailles, near New Orleans, is only about fifteen miles from the Isleño towns. Our class of Spanish, French, English, social studies, and art teachers visited the two sites on the same day. In Little Versailles, the bakers at the Vietnamese restaurant and bakery produced some of the best baguettes we had tasted, as well as traditional Chinese and Vietnamese products. They showed us how they made Chinese moon cakes and shared other foodstuffs with us while they talked about their community. All the signage was in Vietnamese and English. After having read some of the stories in Butler's *A Good Scent from a Strange Moun-tain*, we understood better how a colonial power could influence native groups. We drove through the neighborhood and saw the community gardens and the women in them wearing their traditional hats, and then we went past the Catholic church.

In the Isleño communities, we visited one of their early Catholic churches as well as their cemetery. As in Latin America and New Orleans, the cemeteries are aboveground, with family crypts that have engravings in Spanish, French, and English. At the museum, the caretakers fed us traditional foods and offered us a dramatic representation of Isleño settlers. We heard traditional *décimas*, their storytelling songs (also popular in Cuba and Texas), and we watched demonstrations of boat building, trapping, and net mending. As we headed homeward, we witnessed a dramatic example of the kind of clash of communities that has happened too often throughout the history of the Gulf South. Driving through the bayou community of Yscloskey, we came to Shell Beach Canal, one of the Corps of Engineer projects that has actually increased the saltwater infiltration of the marshlands, wreaking ecological and economic havoc and destroying an entire community.

All who participated in these trips were able to relate their experiences to their fields of expertise and share their insights with others. The social studies teachers could explain the French and Chinese influences on the Vietnamese and the colonial complexity of the Louisiana experiment. The Spanish and French teachers had specific cultural and linguistic aspects they could discuss: place-names, local phrases, musical influences, literature. The English teachers addressed immigrant narratives and community diversity. Our art teacher taught us to explore beauty and design in everything we saw, as, armed with a digital camera, she recorded every aspect of the trip, from the designs stamped on the moon cakes to the mirrors of the bus that reflected the places we visited. We had experienced, in the course of a few miles, vastly different lifestyles and cultures in our own backyard; many students remarked that they had never heard of either community before. We had our sources for ethnographic inquiry readily available; we did not have to fly halfway around the world to begin to connect with these cultures.

Our other equally profound but much more accessible field trip was to the Chinese restaurant in Hammond, a four-star family restaurant constructed in Chinese style. The four brothers who owned the restaurant had followed the vision of their grandfather in building it, even bringing some of the materials from their home in China to do so. One of the brothers gave us a tour of the restaurant and its gardens and koi ponds while he explained the architecture, the ornamentations, and the ways in which the building and decor were designed in accordance with the principles of feng shui. He also talked to us about Chinese food and preparation techniques and helped us choose a variety of wonderful dishes. He showed us porcelain like the porcelain that the Spanish galleons carried to Acapulco and across Mexico to Europe. While it may seem odd to bring students to a Chinese restaurant for a field trip, the interconnectedness of world trade since Silk Road times continues to influence our lives. For instance, the Asian textiles that were part of this same trade route had a profound influence on the Amerindians, bringing silk production and various weaving styles into the American repertoire.

These visits helped us understand the many aspects and complications of world cultures as well as our own lives. We appreciated how different communities seek to preserve their heritage while also trying to better their situations, whether through immigration or preservation. Especially profound were the passion with which members of these communities explained themselves to us and the joy we felt in becoming part of their neighborhood.

As with any memorable teaching experience, there is much more to tell. We ate rum cake while we listened to someone play blues songs about working on the sugar plantations. We sampled the delicacies of the dumplings of the world as we listened to the engaging children's book *Dumpling Soup* (Rattigan). Later presentations of interdisciplinary curriculum units included a session in which an art teacher relayed her excitement over her discovery of cross-cultural circle patterns. She compared her photographs of the designs stamped on the moon cakes at the Vietnamese bakery with the designs of tortilla presses.

This team teaching was an extraordinary experience: we made a series of exciting discoveries together, many times right in the classroom, so that the students shared in the first moments when yet another connection emerged between our two fields of study. Indeed, each teacher was often astonished at what the other brought to her field of expertise: Marjorie designed a group activity on rhetoric in the debate between Las Casas and Juan Ginés de Sepúlveda; Jeanne pointed out problematic representations of Mexicans in a Japanese novel.

Our collaboration developed and expanded when we reorganized the course, in a second appearance as a semester-long undergraduate course at Southeastern, around the theme of cross-cultural obsessions (souls, gold, coffee, sugar, opium, rubber, etc.). Offered through the Department of Foreign Languages, European Civilizations was designed to be taught in two parts over two semesters, but we were able to combine both parts in one semester, requiring students to sign up for both at once. We needed to compensate the English Department for Marjorie's absence from one course there; we found funds to hire another instructor to teach one of her classes—a small victory over the departmental structures and budgets that often work against interdisciplinary and collaborative teaching. Basically, we created what is now called a learning community of linked courses, and we team-taught both, incorporating many films by making three of the total six credits an evening film-viewing requirement.

Our students' journal entries and discussions confirmed that the field trips had encouraged them to explore the cultural resources of their own towns and cities and to investigate the many heritages in their areas. We ourselves found that even an interview with a single person from "somewhere else" could offer new perspectives about our disciplines and make new connections to parts of the community of which our students were not aware. Such experiences can be sought out in many different locales. A visit to a Mexican or Indian restaurant, in which the owners help the students learn about the foods, their preparations, or social customs can be a wonderful way to make local links to world literature discussed in the classroom. A trip to a Latin or Asian market can reveal fascinating ingredients and staples that might lead to an art project or a display of handicrafts. If you are lucky to live in a more cosmopolitan area, a trip to a Lebanese or Nigerian restaurant, or perhaps a tapestry-and-rug merchant or an import-export business, would be equally fascinating. You may have students from the cultures you are studying who can invite family members or friends to speak to the group. One of Jeanne's family friends was Japanese American, and his wife was in a book club that was reading about the Japanese internment camps. The group asked him to speak about being Japanese as a young child in California, and until that time no one realized that his family had actually been sent to one of the camps. We should never forget that a human connection, a face, often provides a powerful teaching moment and a powerful human moment.

As world literature anthologies include ever more examples of artistic creation from many diverse parts of our shrinking globe, it can be difficult for many teachers—especially those with demanding teaching loads—to choose new works to teach and to find the time to prepare them. But our experiences suggest that if teachers can open up to the collaborative opportunities as close as a nearby office door or a short bus trip away, the possibilities are rich and rewarding. We cannot take all our students on a foreign study trip, but we can help them understand some of the realities, pleasures, and images of the literature we teach by exploring our immigrant neighborhoods and by connecting with the diversity just around the corner, which beckons us to find the global in the local.

Works Cited

Butler, Robert Olen. *A Good Scent from a Strange Mountain*. New York: Penguin, 1993. Print.

Carpentier, Alejo. *The Kingdom of This World*. Trans. Harriet de Onis. New York: Farrar, 1989. Print.

Columbus, Christopher. *The Four Voyages: Being His Own Log-Book, Letters and Dispatches with Connecting Narratives*. New York: Penguin, 1992. Print.

Day, Avanelle, and Lillie Stuckey. *The Spice Cookbook: A Complete Book of Spice and Herb Cookery—Containing 1400 Superb Recipes for Traditional American and Classic International Cuisine*. New York: Independent, 1964. Print.

Displaced in the New South. Prod. Eric Mofford and David Zeigler. Berkeley Media, LLC. 1995. DVD.

Endo, Shusaku. *The Samurai*. Trans. Van Gessel. New York: New Directions, 1997. Print.

———. *Silence*. Trans. William Johnson. New York: Taplinger, 1980. Print.

Fernández Retamar, Roberto. "Caliban: Notes toward a Discussion of Culture in Our America." *"Caliban" and Other Essays*. Trans. Edward Baker. Minneapolis: U of Minnesota P, 1989. 3–45. Print.

I Am Cuba. Dir. Mikheil Kalatozishvili. 1995. Image Entertainment, 2000. DVD.

Indochine. Dir. Regis Wargnier. 1992. Columbia/Tristar Studios, 2000. DVD.

Las Casas, Bartolomé de. *Short Account of the Destruction of the Indies*. Trans. Nigel Griffen. New York: Penguin, 1998. Print.

The Mission. Dir. Roland Joffé. Warner Brothers, 1986. Film.

Okamato, Yoshitomo. *The Namban Art of Japan*. New York: Weatherhill, 1974. Print.

Polo, Marco. *The Travels of Marco Polo*. New York: Penguin, 1958. Print.

Rattigan, Jama Kim. *Dumpling Soup*. Boston: Megan Tingley–Little, 1998. Print.

Rodó, José Enrique. *Ariel*. Trans. Margaret Sayers Peden. Austin: U of Texas P, 1988. Print.

Schivelbusch, Wolfgang. *Tastes of Paradise: A Social History of Spices, Stimulants, and Intoxicants*. New York: Vintage, 1993. Print.

Shogun. Dir. Jerry Logan. 1980. Paramount Home Video, 2003. DVD.

Tran Tu Binh. *The Red Earth: A Vietnamese Memoir of Life on a Colonial Rubber Plantation*. Trans. John Spragens, Jr. Ed. David G. Marr. Athens: Ohio UP, 1985. Print.

Thomas Beebee

Beyond Lecture and Discussion: The World's Oldest Approaches to Literature

This essay is in three parts. In the first, I address what I consider to be a problem in the pedagogy of literature—namely, the disconnect between the reification of analysis and the actual mechanisms of the interest in and spread of world literature. In the second part, I give some examples of exercises that attempt to bridge this divide. In the third part, I examine the pros and cons of this type of engagement from a theoretical distance.

Teaching methods usually bear some relation to course objectives, but the objectives can vary widely, not only according to the instructor's ideological stance and teaching philosophy but also according to the background and level of the students, the overall mission of the unit or institution offering the course, and so forth. Judging from the critical-theoretical corpus on the teaching of world literature that pre-dates the present volume, there would appear to be as many objectives for the teaching of world literature as there are instructors for this subject matter. For example, in teaching world literature Ajay Heble is intent on

> negotiating between, on the one hand, a genuine insistence on and
> valuing of student expression (itself an ethical move?), and, on the

other, our ethical responsibility to promote forms of inquiry and models of knowledge-production which challenge oppression, suffering, and injustice. (147)

For Lawrence Venuti, a class in world literature is not complete unless it troubles the transparency of the domesticating translations necessary for the course to be offered in the first place. And so forth. My own aporia differs from these two; it involves the fact that, unlike solving a mathematics problem or performing a physics experiment, arriving at an understanding of a literary work calls for its historical and cultural context that can seldom be replicated in the classroom. Yet the very term *world literature* seems to invite us to shed local context in favor of a global meaning and significance.

Tobin Siebers shares the insight that our attempts at teaching multiculturalism in the university classroom must always fail, because culture cannot be taught the way professors teach literature: "For all the talk of multiculturalism today, there is very little genuine multiculturalism going on, especially in classrooms" (198). Siebers outlines three crucial aspects that shape "genuine" cultural transmission but that are missing from our higher educational contexts: recitation, personal interpretation, and religious exegesis. The first two points, recitation and self-expression, both involve acts of retelling:

> Recitation in the broad sense is everywhere a central aspect of daily life. Someone tells a story, and another person responds by reciting another story. . . . Part of learning what a culture is consists of having this kind of experience many, many times every day. It produces the large cultural conversation whose webs and interstices create the context for further conversation. . . . People at cocktail parties like to swap stories about what they are reading and the films they have seen because they identify with characters and use them to talk about themselves. . . . Personal interpretation is very much a part of cultural experience worldwide and historically. Dream interpretation, prophecy, magical ritual, astrology, games, and myths provide general symbols by which individuals explain themselves to others and to themselves. (198–99)

If one deletes the reference to cocktail parties or translates them into symposia or the like, these sentences describe the oldest responses to literature. But what is missing? Siebers sees as irrelevant to the transmission of culture the need for analysis or critical thinking, which rarely accompany the transmission of stories in a culture, because the stories' purpose is to transmit the culture they form a part of and analysis and critical thinking impede the act of transmission. Conversely, classroom teachers rarely link their texts to specific ceremonial or sacred occasions (Siebers's third point), to pragmatic moral and ethical questions and situations, or to specific topographical features of the surrounding landscape—the way traditional teachers might do.

I am less concerned with Siebers's conclusion than with his suggestion that there are ways of teaching literature that will not fit in our rationalistic pedagogy's emphasis on measurable outcomes. To put it another way, lecture, discussion, exam taking, and paper writing—all of which admittedly may be pedagogically useful apart from teaching actual course content—reify literature as an objective phenomenon to be passively recognized or analyzed rather than constructed, transmitted, or made use of. How can we give our students the experience of literature as an aspect of culture? This methodology lies beyond lecture and discussion, though prepositions such as *before* or *beneath* may be more accurate than *beyond*. *Beyond* refers more to the fact that these other techniques will probably remain supplementary to the staples of lecture, discussion, testing, and paper writing we all grew up with instead of substituting them.

There is a body of pedagogical theory and practice that deals with this beyond. My experience as a teacher of languages and as a willing, if incompetent student of mathematics and the sciences has taught me the necessity of hands-on approaches for attaining understanding of a subject. To say that one knows Urdu, geometry, or particle physics implies an ability to do something with the material beyond naming it or describing it abstractly. Should we not have the same goal for literary studies? I was also inspired early in my teaching career by a pedagogy session led by Charles Wales of the University of West Virginia on the concept of guided design (see Wales; Wales and D'Amour; Wales and Stager). The basic point of guided design, or of other forms of problem-solving-based learning, is that a real-life project or problem drives the learning, not artificial exercises presented simply in order to practice techniques that have been taught. A class led by Wales might consist of groups of students considering solutions to a single problem, such as, in a roadway engineering class, the problem of deer running onto highways. As solutions are considered, the research and methodology necessary to evaluate and refine them are acquired.

While more common in engineering and the sciences, guided design has been used in literature on occasion. Laura Behling's introduction of "literature laboratories" into her American literature course is one example where the borrowing of the problem-solving approach of the sciences is particularly obvious. Bill Hutchings of the University of Manchester "advertised" his course as

> a program of the English Tourist Board aimed at attracting people back to the countryside after an outbreak of hoof and mouth disease: "The Eye of the Beholder: Landscape Description, 1700–2000." The ad called for the creation of a booklet which would present "representative examples of landscape description from the three centuries, together with commentary and notes." The booklet, the ad went on, would be aimed at a wide public, but would be "intended to be scholarly and informed." Length? 2250–2750 words including the text excerpts. ("Problem-Based" 7)

Hutchings designed this problem for his class as a replacement for the reading, lecture, and discussion format, because the

> ordinary path . . . wouldn't encourage exploratory research, wouldn't encourage students to look at a variety of different contexts of interpretation to see which they thought most appropriate, and wouldn't really encourage them to make any sort of creative engagement with the creative power in literature. (7)

The actual history of the teaching of literature provides yet another impetus for modifying our pedagogy. Before there was reification, analysis, and interpretation of literature, there was literature's *Fortleben* ("living on") through the mechanisms of retelling, rewriting, translation, parody, production, and adaptation. Perhaps the most salient example in Western literature is the *Aeneid* of Vergil, which recycles similes, events, and character types from Homer in the service of a Roman ideology that is very different from the one apparent in the Greek model it is based on. Surely this recycling began with Vergil's captivating retellings of Homer at Trimalchian-style festivities. (Gérard Genette has famously provided a vocabulary for distinguishing between various types of literature "to the second degree." Determining whether the *Aeneid* is parody, pastiche, travesty, or indeed a transposition, as I believe Genette would pigeonhole it, is not my concern here, though of course another teacher might choose to make that question a pedagogical focus of a class.) It is also worth recalling that the pervasive rhetorical training of European schools through the nineteenth century applied the methodology of rhetoric, mutatis mutandis, to sermons, letters, speeches, and poetry. Students read examples of great rhetoric and then produced their own, often with instructions to make believe they were a famous historical personage or in a particular situation, the way students today produce sentences and compositions and conduct role-playing exercises as activities for learning a language. These pedagogical approaches resemble the actual transmission of culture as Siebers describes it more than do lecture and discussion.

I present some examples drawn from classes that I teach: Literary Humor, Forms of World Literature, and Post-Renaissance Literature of the Western World. I have used many of them in other classes as well. Each semester brings more than a hundred students into the humor class, and I put them into collaborative teams to work on projects, some of which are described below, throughout the course.[1] Many of the projects they produce are entered in a competition to be voted on by the class; the winning team receives extra credit. Grading is based on consistency and coherence between parts, as in pseudo-author bio and text for the parody; on knowledge of text displayed, as in justifying actor choices for the film design; and on depth of insight in projects where an introduction or self-critique is required. (In other words, I am still grading analysis and critical thinking while asking students to go beyond these.)

Parody

My assignment of parody asks for (1) real-author biography; (2) pseudo-author biography (i.e., of a fictional author of the parody invented by the students); (3) a segment of original text; (4) a parody text that recognizably follows the original; (5) a synopsis of the remainder if the text is long; and (6) an analysis that differentiates among what carried over well from original into parody, what needed to be left behind, what readers can learn about the original from the parody, and what the parody teaches us about the original, about ourselves, and about American culture.

In the grading, more points are assigned to the analysis than to the actual parody. I look for coherence between the first five points. The pseudo-biography should relate both to the real-author biography and to the peculiarities of the parody. Ambitious teachers might change the assignment to "What if X had written Y?," where X is an author on the syllabus and Y a work. What if Lu Xun had written *Robinson Crusoe*, for example? Or what if the Frenchman Pierre Menard had written *Don Quixote*?

Film Production Design

This project provides an example of the difference between discussion and adaptation, because it began as an impromptu warm-up question for beginning or ending analysis of a work. Internet delivery methods and the use of collaborative teams allowed me to develop the exercise into a project. The question I started from was, "What actor would you cast as X in a film version of Y?," where Y is the work of literature and X a particular character in it. For example, "What actor would you cast as Emma in a film version of *Madame Bovary*?" The trick is to justify the casting by relating the persona of the actor to the characteristics of the literary figure.

Production design asks for various components of the production of the piece, five in my version: (1) a cast list for major characters (with justifications), (2) scene designs for several different locations, (3) costume designs for at least three characters, (4) an advertising poster, and (5) an overall explanation and philosophy of production. Students also like to provide sound-track choices. Each of these components asks students to produce an interpretation of the work. I emphasize the important choices to be made in envisioning the production—for example, the choice between a historicizing approach (e.g., the characters of the *Genji* are wearing kimonos) and a contemporizing one (e.g., the woods of Athens of Shakespeare's *Midsummer Night's Dream* becomes a rave fest, Oberon is a major drug dealer, Puck is his chief mule, and so forth). Overall consistency of the approach is a major concern and not easily achieved. Grading is based largely on the coherence of the various parts with one another.

In one memorable design, students used the cast of the *Seinfeld* television series to modernize and Americanize Molière's play about hypocrisy, *Tartuffe*. Newman becomes the hypocrite Tartuffe, George's father the obsessive Orgon, Jerry Seinfeld his eloquent and reasonable brother-in-law, Elaine the sassy maid Dorine, and so on. The vapid daughter whom Orgon plans to marry against her will to Tartuffe will be played by Random Silent Hot Chick, that is, by the brainless supermodel du jour. The Plaza Hotel in New York replaces Orgon's comfortable home in Paris, and Orgon hides behind a wet bar rather than under the famous table to overhear Tartuffe's seduction of his wife. New York is the ideal American setting for the play, because that city constantly questions all our pieties, which is one of the main themes of *Tartuffe*. This particular project reinforced the idea of the continuity of comic archetypes through literary history, which is a course objective in the humor class. Instructors with other objectives might ask instead for an incongruous setting for their film, as when in the film *O. T.: Our Town* the Thornton Wilder play, set in New England, is performed by students at Dominguez High School in Compton, California, where there has not been a live play performance for twenty years.

I usually assign stage plays as film projects, but it is perhaps more challenging and interesting to have students turn prose or lyrical literary forms into performative pieces. Such a process borders on the next exercise.

Transformations

Here students are asked to rewrite a text, or part of it, using a different form or genre than the one in which it originally appeared; in the process, they note what can and cannot be preserved in the transformation. At this exercise, unlike most others, students should almost always fail, since there is a reason why certain contents require certain forms or why certain forms require certain contents. Sometimes failure occurs for formal-thematic reasons (you just can't fit a novel into a lyric poem) or for ideological-historical reasons (forms that have died can no longer accommodate the thinking and reality that comes after them). Try turning a short story by Jorge Luis Borges into an epic poem, for example. It is not simply a matter of adding more words or trying to versify. The matching of texts with their new genres can be done by the instructor, by students, or by teams drawing names out of two hats.

The grade depends on how well students recognize and analyze their failure. Failure, along with fakery, is a crucial concept in literature—think of the countless "Translation is impossible" statements—and we should teach it more often. (Or, I should say, literature is one of the few subjects that deliberately teaches it.) This exercise is a wonderfully counterintuitive battle in a culture where *failure* is a four-letter word.

Debate

Think of a debate as a presentation with an edge to it, or as two presentations that dialogue and compete with each other. Literature offers many interesting topics for debate. Some of my favorites are: Is Don Quixote insane? Do Giovanni Boccaccio's or Marguerite de Navarre's women (from the *Decameron* and *Heptameron*, resp.) make better role models? Does the protagonist of Abe Kobo's surrealist novel *Kangaroo Notebook* commit suicide, or is he euthanized? In the humor class I have also had students debate the relative merits of Sigmund Freud's theory of *Witz* ("joke") versus Henri Bergson's analysis of *le rire* ("laughter").

Teams are essential for live debates; ideally, there would be as many parts to a debate as there are team members. I enforce what I believe to be the standard format: first and second constructives followed by cross-examinations of the speakers, then rebuttals. If teams are larger, students without a chance to speak can be assigned to do research.

There is also an asynchronous, message-board version of this debate format, which can be simplified for nonteam interchanges. I divide the class into three groups, assigning one group to do pro-Boccaccio constructives (for example), another to do pro-Navarre constructives, and the third to post rebuttals to the arguments of both sides.

Judge Judy

The drama of a courtroom trial has been used repeatedly in literature (not to mention against literature), and for obvious reasons. Students inherently grasp the trial structure and the kinds of arguments to be put forth, and they love to write things like, "Case dismissed," and to invent unusual and poetic punishments for the baddies of world literature. I use an asynchronous, message-board format for *Judge Judy*, though it could also be done live. The class can be divided into thirds and assigned the roles of prosecutor, defense, and judge. Or the exercise can be a team project, and the instructor can be the judge, another team can be a panel of judges, or individual students can judge for (extra) credit. The instructor usually specifies the charges and punishment, if the defendant is convicted or found liable.[2] When individuals do the exercise, they rely purely on the texts to make an argument. When teams are used, I ask for an opening argument, three witness statements, and a closing argument. Each team also has the opportunity to refute the opposing witnesses. I ask that one of the witnesses be an expert. For example, if the German medieval trickster figure Till Eulenspiegel is being tried for blasphemy for his practice of fooling priests, bishops, and the pope, an expert witness might be a historian who has written on church practice and theology in the Middle Ages.

Write It Further

This exercise refers to rewrites of literature that are not so much parodic as simply seizing the opportunity to produce a sequel. There are basically three ways to write a sequel: pick up where the original left off, expand a relatively undeveloped scene or character, or retell the story or part of it from another character's point of view.

Isaac Bashevis Singer's "Gimpel the Fool" ("Gimpel tam" in the original Yiddish) is always a big flop in my humor course. Inevitably, a student will offer the opinion that the story just isn't funny. Gimpel makes numerous decisions, with consequences that seem less humorous as the story progresses. For example, he repeatedly chooses to believe his unfaithful wife, Elke, when she tells him that she is not betraying him. He makes the decision not to feed bread made with his own filth to his fellow villagers, who have tormented him his whole life, yet such an act would have given an opportunity for scenes worthy of the most vulgar American comedy films. Or perhaps it is Singer's style, or the style of his translator, Saul Bellow, that darkens the story so. But failure is a golden learning opportunity. So rewrite the story, already, to make it funnier! Most students reverse Gimpel's bread decision and go from there. Some have him deliver the bread in this life, others in the next world.

"Gimpel the Fool" is open at its many decision points. Other texts are open at their endpoints and beg us to write them a page or two further. Henrik Ibsen's *A Doll's House* is a prime example: Describe Nora's and Thorvald's activities a year or five years after she leaves. Texts that do not seem so open-ended can be rewritten by expanding a character or scene. Jean Rhys's *Wide Sargasso Sea* is a celebrated example of this procedure. The author rewrites Charlotte Brontë's *Jane Eyre* by greatly expanding the description of Rochester's courtship of Bertha, the madwoman in the attic, and with it the description of the West Indian isle of Dominica where the courtship took place. This transculturation of Brontë's text is accompanied a retelling of the story from another character's point of view, in this case that of Bertha. Anita Diamant's *The Red Tent* retells parts of Genesis from the point of view of Dinah and gives a voice to some women of the Bible. Sumamuru, Son-Jara's great opponent in the epic of that name, has his own shrines and praise songs in West Africa (Sisòkò). Students could be asked to rewrite a portion of the epic as Sumamuru's own griot would have composed it. And if the Fa-Digi Sisòkò and John W. Johnston version of the epic is being used as a text, students can be asked to imitate its style as well.

Reality TV

I owe this idea to Elisabeth Schmitt, a graduate student in the German Department who taught some courses in comparative literature. When we compared notes in the hall on how our classes were going, she mentioned a particularly fun activity: having the students act out the *Nibelungenlied* ("Song of the Nibelungs," a medieval German epic) as a *Jerry Springer* show. I could see the appropriateness immediately—I mean, Springer is a German name, isn't it? Seriously, the *Nibelungenlied* lends itself particularly well to Springer treatment, where Gunther would be forced to confess that Siegfried substituted for him on Gunther's wedding night with Brunhilde. The course in literary humor gave me the opportunity to use the idea to full advantage. Teams are assigned a work and asked to choose the reality show that can best convey its characters and plot twists. The grade depends on how accurately students are able to preserve the characters and conflicts of the original in the new format and on how convincingly they justify their choice of show. I can report that *Lysistrata* works very well as an MTV *Real World* show. One team was clever enough to have Laura Bush and Mrs. Saddam collaborate on the sex strike against their belligerent husbands.

Problems and Perspectives

Having depleted my bag of tricks, I look back on these activities from a critical distance. The question of how to read (i.e., how best to have students read) "culturally different" texts, posed by Gayatri Spivak, remains a foremost challenge to world literature teachers. As has been noted by several scholars, teachers of world literature need to navigate between the extreme of domesticating foreign texts and the extreme of treating them as unalterably alien. David Damrosch has formulated the risk thus: "Either the earlier and distant works we read are really just like us, or they are unutterably foreign, curiosities whose foreignness finally tells us nothing and can only reinforce our sense of separate identity" (18). Those familiar with this dilemma will note that the strategies I have outlined above are appropriative and definitely fall into the first of the two camps. Does this bother me? Yes, there is something sadly limiting about students' recasting Don Quixote and Sancho Panza as a couple of stoners whose windmill is the minifridge in their dorm room. But then again, if I can appreciate the presentness of Miguel de Cervantes's mimesis of the low-down taverns and dusty roads of La Mancha—precisely as a counterweight to the dead idealism that rules Don Quixote's mind—then I should also appreciate such presentness in students' caricatures of their own lives.

The horns of this dilemma correspond to the distinction Friedrich Nietzsche draws, in *On the Advantage and Disadvantage of History*, between the critical and monumental approaches to history on the one hand and antiquarian interests on the other. Applying these categories to the study of world literature, we could say, roughly, that the antiquarian approach is more concerned with the construction and teaching of a world literary canon as an academic subject, while the critical approach is more interested in world literature as an other that exposes United States students to attitudes and ideas that challenge their own. The monumental approach cares neither about pure knowledge nor about critique; instead it looks for works that can most powerfully inspire and motivate the students in our classrooms. The antiquarian approach would construct its canon across a broad spectrum of works; the critical approach would most likely favor postcolonial situations that directly implicate the West. The monumental approach would be the least consistent, picking and choosing works according to their perceived ability to evoke response in their readers. The antiquarian approach attempts to understand each literature to the extent possible in its own context (ideally in its original language, an old debate in comparative literature pedagogy); the other two approaches care only about either the rejection of or the incorporation of works so as to enhance the lives of their readers.

Try substituting "world literature" for "the past" in the following sentence by Nietzsche, and see whether it rings true: "Whenever the monumental vision of the past rules over the other ways of looking at the past . . . very great portions of the past are forgotten and despised, and flow away like a grey uninterrupted flood" (17). Indeed, despite all my efforts and whatever my methods or objectives, students begin this forgetting and despising of large portions of the corpus I have made them read as soon as the semester ends, if not while it is still under way. Perhaps even more appropriate are Nietzsche's remarks in *The Gay Science* on the way Roman culture went about translating (i.e., rewriting) Greek literature:

> How forcibly and at the same time how naively it took hold of every-
> thing good and lofty of Greek antiquity, which was more ancient! How
> [the Romans] translated things into the Roman present! How deliber-
> ately and recklessly they brushed the dust off the wings of the butterfly
> that is called moment! . . . They seem to ask us: "Should we not make
> new for ourselves what is old and find ourselves in it?" (136–37)

I know of no study that measures the effects of the actual teaching of
world literature in any of these modes. Indeed, the simple question of
what, if anything, students will remember from a course in world literature after handing in the final exam lacks a documented answer. In other
words, those interested in the pedagogy of world literature foresee a variety of outcomes, but there is no empirical evidence I know of that any
outcome will be consistently achieved. Hence, though the projects I have
outlined above undoubtedly fall into the camp of domesticating strategies, it is difficult to say whether the lesson students learn from them is
that it is easy to fit everything into the American format or that it is amaz-
ingly difficult for Jerry Springer to interview Genji or get him to fight his
rivals, which creates an awareness of cultural and formal differences between Heian Japan and contemporary United States culture.

One can have it both ways by adding to these domesticating approaches a level of self-critique. One would then, in Gerald Graff's terms,
be "teaching the conflicts" between exoticization and domestication. For
their comprehensive essay, a piece of critical thinking assigned and graded
in traditional fashion, I could ask students to read one or more accounts
of the issues involved in the rewriting of texts and the development of
world literature—perhaps the Nietzschean categories mentioned above—
and to evaluate or categorize the parody, reality TV show, or transformation they have produced in terms of these issues.

My tentative attempt at teaching the conflict in the fall 2005 offering
of Literary Humor was the following take-home comprehensive essay
question on the power of parody:

> For this essay topic, you are asked to compare the parodies (including
> film production designs and RealiTV shows) studied AND produced
> in this course against the following definition: "Parody . . . is a form
> of *imitation* . . . characterized by *ironic inversion*, not always at the
> *expense* of the parodied text" (Hutcheon 6). (We have seen other via-
> ble definitions of parody throughout the semester, but this will be the
> only one accepted for the purposes of writing this essay.) Notice that
> this definition allows us to question three elements of parody:

1. To what extent does it *imitate* its original?
2. What are the specific sites and mechanism(s) of inversion?
3. At *whose expense* is the humor generated (i.e., who or what is the butt of the central joke of the parody)?

I have not really solved the dilemma I started with; I have only raised it one level. While the assignments listed above give, in my opinion, a more accurate view of how world literature actually came into existence through borrowing, interchange, adaptation, and imitation, we are still missing the historical and cultural factors that valorize such activities for some texts and traditions and suppress them for others. The exercises, produced only at the insistence of a teacher, give a view of parody that resembles seeing ritual masks behind the glass display case of a museum. Good thing I have a fondness for museums—not to mention for failure.

Notes

1. On the impact of team versus individual learning strategies, see Bruffee; Stein. There are of course many issues involved in the use of teams, such as the prevention of social loafing, which space does not allow me to discuss here and which are addressed in both Bruffee and Stein.

2. Of course, *Judge Judy* and other similar television trial shows do not actually convict. They, like my students, engage in a game of make-believe with the law.

Works Cited

Abe Kobo. *Kangaroo Notebook.* Trans. Maryellen Toman Mori. New York: Knopf, 1996. Print.

Behling, Laura. "The Laboratory: A Model for Teaching the Elements of Literary Studies." *Radical Pedagogy* 8.1 (2006): n. pag. Web. 27 Mar. 2008.

Bruffee, Kenneth A. *Collaborative Learning: Higher Education, Interdependence, and the Authority of Knowledge.* Baltimore: Johns Hopkins UP, 1999. Print.

Damrosch, David. "World Literature Today: From the Old World to the Whole World." *Symplokē* 8.1–2 (2000): 7–19. Print.

Diamant, Anita. *The Red Tent.* New York: Picador, 1997. Print.

Durant, Alan. *Literary Studies in Action.* New York: Routledge, 1989. Print.

Genette, Gérard. *Palimpsestes: La littérature au second degré.* Paris: Seuil, 1982. Print.

Graff, Gerald. *Beyond the Culture Wars: How Teaching the Conflicts Can Revitalize American Education.* New York: Norton, 1992. Print.

Heble, Ajay. "Re-ethicizing the Classroom: Pedagogy, the Public Sphere, and the Postcolonial Condition." *College Literature* 29.1 (2002): 143–60. Print.

Hutcheon, Linda. *A Theory of Parody: The Teachings of Twentieth-Century Art Forms.* New York: Methuen, 1985. Print.

Ibsen, Henrik. *A Doll's House*. 1879. *Four Major Plays*. Trans. James McFarlane and Jens Arup. Oxford: Oxford UP, 1998. 1–88. Print. Oxford World's Classics.

Nietzsche, Friedrich. *The Gay Science*. Trans. Walter Kaufmann. New York: Vintage, 1974. Print.

———. *On the Advantage and Disadvantage of History*. Trans. Peter Preuss. Indianapolis: Hackett, 1980. Print.

"Problem-Based Literature Course?" *National Teaching and Learning Forum* Feb. 2006: 6–8. Print.

Rhys, Jean. *Wide Sargasso Sea*. New York: Norton, 1966. Print.

Siebers, Tobin. "Sincerely Yours." *Comparative Literature in the Age of Multiculturalism*. Ed. Charles Bernheimer. Baltimore: Johns Hopkins UP, 1995. 195–203. Print.

Singer, Isaac Bashevis. "Gimpel the Fool." Trans. Saul Bellow. *"Gimpel the Fool" and Other Stories*. New York: Noonday, 1957. 3–21. Print.

Sisòkò, Fa-Digi. *The Epic of Son-Jara*. 3rd ed. Ed. and trans. John W. Johnston. Bloomington: Indiana UP, 2003. Print.

Spivak, Gayatri Chakravorty. "How to Read a 'Culturally Different' Book." *Colonial Discourse / Postcolonial Theory*. Ed. Francis Barker, Peter Hulme, and Margaret Iverson. Manchester: Manchester UP, 1994. 126–50. Print.

Stein, Ruth Federman. *Using Student Teams in the Classroom: A Faculty Guide*. Bolton: Anker, 2000. Print.

Venuti, Lawrence. "Translation and the Pedagogy of Literature." *College English* 58 (1996): 327–44. Print.

Wales, Charles E. "Guided Design: Why and How You Should Use It." *Journal of Engineering Education* May 1972: 905–07. Print.

Wales, Charles E., and Gene D'Amour. "Improving Problem-Solving Skills through a Course in Guided Design." *Engineering Education* Feb. 1977: 381–84. Print.

Wales, Charles E., and Robert Stager. "Teaching Decision-Making with Guided Design." *Journal of College Science Teaching* 12.1 (1982): 24. Print.

Monika Brown

Collaborative Assignments for World Literature Survey Courses

For two decades I have taught world literature at the University of North Carolina, Pembroke, founded in 1887 as a normal school for Lumbee Indians and now a six-thousand-student, multiethnic state university that preserves its Native American heritage. In the 1980s, every undergraduate took a Western great-books course; now students choose among twelve literature surveys. World Literature before 1660 and World Literature after 1660, courses required only for English majors, attract undergraduates from many disciplines. Amid challenges to the Western canon and humanist inquiry, our courses continue to engage students in humanist and formalist interpretation of Western classics in cultural contexts. But they are now more global and interdisciplinary, as they embrace new pedagogies, modern scholarship, critical theories, and cultural studies. Media resources—from documentaries and film adaptations to Internet sites, computer labs, LCD projectors, and *Blackboard*—have opened new contexts for instruction, including online classes. Each world literature course I teach has an overall design whose units and assignments balance coverage of Western and global texts and cultures as they develop students' genre awareness, critical vocabulary, and interpretive skills. In each course, in-class and online collaborative activities culminate in two assignments: a critical essay and a presentation by a group or individual.

Integrated and sequential course designs, collaboration, group projects, and peer teaching are pedagogies well supported by research. College literature has moved beyond the typical 1980s class, where George Hillocks found teachers explicating texts for students and "little attempt to use one work as preparation for reading the next" (qtd. in Schilb 60–61 ["Literary Texts in Classrooms"]). Some studies suggest, as a widely distributed learning pyramid shows graphically, that students retain least from lectures (the pyramid's apex) and unguided reading, more from discussions, and most (the pyramid's base) from practice, application, and teaching others. Both guided collaborative learning and course sequencing find support from the psychologist L. S. Vygotsky, who recognized the social dimension of learning and intellectual development (Roskelly 31; Doolittle), as well as from English educators like James Moffett and Kenneth Bruffee. Especially among underprepared college students, observes Bruffee, "work tended to improve when they got help from peers," and the helpers benefited as well, because collaborative learning "harnessed the powerful educative force of peer influence" that educators have overlooked (638).

Some student populations served by UNC Pembroke especially stand to gain from teacher-led group learning. Collaboration engages adults accustomed to workplace interaction, and it is compatible both with "traditional Native American values" of cooperation under the guidance of an elder (Cartledge et al. 230) and with the family-network culture of many African Americans, "predisposed toward helping, sharing, collaborating and trusting" to further group achievements (174–75). In general, group work in college, when compared with "individualistic learning experiences," correlates with outcomes like "more positive attitudes toward the subject matter, more positive attitudes toward the teacher, greater achievement motivation, and greater persistence in completing tasks" (230). Such results are evident among my students.

My World Literature I and II classes—their units, study questions, written responses (now shared *Blackboard* posts), in-class group activities, and collaborative assignments—adapt a survey course design that I describe in a pedagogical article (Brown 19–20). Each class, based on a Norton or Longman anthology, has three chronological units that overlap in time, so as to foreground cultural periods while allowing works of similar genres to be studied together. An early unit or two involves interpretation of narratives (plot, character, setting, theme, and genre features in epic, drama, fiction, and film), and one unit exposes students to close reading and analysis of poetic texts. In each course students write, in stages involving collaboration, a critical argument essay that incorporates modern criticism. Toward the end of each course, intertextual connections link periods and cultures as student groups, pairs, or individuals take teaching roles: they present reports or create study guides and lead discussion, often making use of electronic media.

In classes of twenty to thirty students that meet twice a week, I create an environment for cooperation by asking about personal information and prior knowledge. To make time for groups and limit lectures, I print color-coded handouts (online at uncp.edu/home/monika): the "Literature Guide," with reading questions and definitions of genres and literary terms; "Cultural Context," a compact outline for each period (its history and society, worldview and values, culture and arts); a Web page of links to Internet study guides and resources; and brief study guides with study questions (and occasionally plot summaries) for each set of required readings. Aided by the study guides and online resources, most students make sense of difficult and excerpted readings, read actively, mark passages, and write one-page answers to study questions for submission to me or for online posting (every week or two on a rotating schedule). During class, I lead and synthesize discussions and give brief presentations, with media support from transparencies, Internet sites, or video clips from documentaries and film adaptations. Students are active in every class, either in open discussions or debates or in self-selected (and flexible) classroom groups. Such groups meet for ten to fifteen minutes to talk about a class topic, then present their insights—orally, on overhead transparencies, or through notes that I photocopy for class. Student contributions have a role in course content and tests.

World Literature I (before 1660) is listed as "a survey of Western and non-Western literatures from the beginnings through the Renaissance considered within the cultural epochs of their creation, including the Classical Period, the Middle Ages, and the Renaissance." Based on the first volume of the *Norton Anthology of Western Literature* and recently on the *Longman Anthology of World Literature*, volumes A–C, the course foregrounds the Athens-and-Jerusalem dialectic in Western cultures: the opposition between worldviews founded on experience, reason, and critical inquiry and those founded on a future life, faith, and spiritual revelation (as explained, e.g., in Hart 3–7). The first unit centers on Ancient

Greek epics and golden age drama, reflecting the Athenian worldview, and extends to epics from Mesopotamia and India. Readings in the second unit interpret experience in a spiritual way, deriving from the Judeo-Christian Jerusalem tradition as well as other world religions: Taoist and Confucian lyrics and selections from the Bible, the Qur'an, and medieval poetry and prose from Islamic and Christian cultures. In the final unit, poetry and prose from early modern European cultures, engaged in global contacts and with their classical heritage, bring rational and spiritual strands into a creative tension characteristic of modernity. In each unit students engage in group activities and discussions, and they complete two collaborative assignments.

The opening unit on ancient epics and drama creates a context for collaboration, as groups discuss and present answers to study questions and interpret passages for *Gilgamesh* and the *Odyssey*. This unit's segment on Greek drama lays the foundation for a long-term writing assignment that involves collaboration. For the critical essay "Interpreting Greek Tragedy," each student writes, in stages, a 1,500-word argument that states an interpretive thesis about one Greek tragedy and supports it with arguments, evidence, and quotations from the play and from a few critical sources, some of which I post on *Blackboard*. The assignment invites students into communities of critics, in and beyond our classroom, by engaging the students in dialogue about the meaning and cultural significance of literary works we study (Brown 22–25). Students draft thesis ideas during class discussions, then develop the paper over six weeks. The assignment is accompanied by sample essay outlines and bibliographies, a sample student paper, and an admonition: "This is a guided essay that evolves in stages. No essay found online or from a term paper service meets these requirements."

The assignment is presented during a class that introduces Periclean Athens, Greek drama, and Aristotle's definition of tragedy. Two class sessions are devoted to *Oedipus the King* and two to *Medea*, and for each play students turn in, or post on *Blackboard*, an interpretive response. The first class session focuses on main characters and their interactions in early scenes. Groups discuss key speeches, then paraphrase or dramatize them with quotations and commentary, while I record insights and quotations on an overhead transparency or a projected page from a computer screen. The second class, about the whole of *Oedipus* or *Medea*, begins with a video performance and class analysis of the tragic fall and ending. Meanwhile I circulate a sheet that lists the questions students were given before class, and each student writes on the sheet a thesis sentence about the protagonist or another aspect of the tragedy. Some questions ask students to interpret Oedipus as a heroic figure, tragic hero, detective, case study in denial, or scapegoat; others direct attention to Medea's character, her otherness, or the psychology of her decision to murder her children. For either tragedy, students may interpret plot structure, image patterns, or performances on film. After collecting the sheets, I call on students to elicit their insights, and I lead a debate. At the end of the unit, students write, as part of their test, an argument, from five hundred to six hundred words, about either *Oedipus* or *Medea*. They used to bring extra copies; now they post essays for everyone in a *Blackboard* forum.

Students revise their essays as the course proceeds to its second unit, which features spiritual selections from world cultures: Chinese and Christian lyric poems; Arabian and Arthurian tales; and scenes from the epics *Son-Jara, Song of Roland,* and *Inferno*. Meanwhile instructor and peers read and respond to posted essay drafts that now incorporate critical texts. After a few weeks, the finalized essay, which refers to several critical sources and ends with a works-cited list, is posted on *Blackboard* and also submitted in a folder, with plans, drafts, responses, and photocopies of sources. Evaluation is by letter grade, based on features of effective literary criticism. Most students make coherent, even original arguments about a tragedy, supported with quotations and informed by collaboration, criticism, and life experiences.

In essays about *Oedipus the King*, students expressed a variety of judgments about the character of Oedipus. One student described the king as a heroic leader, refuted character weaknesses that peers noticed (e.g., defiance of oracles), and concluded that he is a good man whose flaws are beyond his control. Matthew Anderson, analyzing the Sphinx episode for an essay about Oedipus as politician, realized, "The best answer to the riddle was not man in general; it was one specific man." This man, the essay argues, was Oedipus himself, from crippled toddler to erect leader to blinded man with a stick. "When I came up with my thesis," Matt told me later, "I felt like I had discovered some great mystery." Steven Byrd identified a core psychological trait that explains the king's stubborn denial as he confronts obvious clues about his fate. Oedipus, Steven argues, is a "very externalized, extroverted figure." Confronted by Sphinx or plague, the extrovert king "uses his personality to a positive effect, in the form of concern for others and aggressive problem solving." But as unmistakable clues fall into place, this hero "is so unwilling to look inside himself" that "in Oedipus's mind, the killer simply must be someone else."

In essays about *Medea*, students often identify in a personal way with the story's depiction of elemental passions and violence, such as Medea's desire to inflict pain on Jason to avenge her betrayal by the man for whom she did "everything he asked." After exploring Medea's motives with her collaborative group, Ashley Torre declared that Medea acted not merely out of "brokenhearted revenge" but also to make her husband into "the loneliest and most agonized man in the world." One student even highlighted and quoted passages that reminded him of his mother and girlfriends. Taking an academic approach, Randy (Tony) Pringle explained Medea's revenge in psychological terms:

> As is typical of parental splits, she needs to claim power over the struggle and come out on top. The struggle spills over, causing the destruction of the parent-child relationship. Medea displays classic revenge symptoms that destroy far more than was necessary.

Sarah Blough, drawing on an article by the feminist critic Laura McClure, argued that the protagonist exploits Greek stereotypes of women even as she publicly deplores them. In the course of the play, "Medea has controlled every character she comes in contact with by manipulating their preexisting ideas about women, and garnering sympathy from each one."

My students' success with collaboration in "Critical Essays" reflects findings by social psychologists who researched how problem solving takes place in academic and workplace settings. "Creative insight" by groups or individuals, explain Mihaly Csikszentmihalyi and Keith Sawyer, results from a prolonged "extensive mental process" that moves from "conscious preparation" to subconscious "incubation" to "conscious evaluation and elaboration." "At every stage," the psychologists point out, "the process that comes before and after the insight is heavily dependent on social interaction" (358). Csikszentmihalyi and Sawyer's social model of insight, as well as my experiences with extended assignments, suggests that creative insight and intellectual growth can flourish in a literature classroom where students collaborate as they develop interpretations and write and revise papers.

The second main assignment in World Literature I is completed during the final unit, in which early modern European lyric poems and prose, including the novel *Don Quixote*, suggest intertextual connections to now familiar classical, Christian, and Islamic texts. For the "Legacy Reports," small groups (or at times individuals) work outside class on a presentation. In the final weeks, each group takes up to fifteen minutes to explain an instance where an ancient, medieval, or early modern text was appropriated for or finds a parallel in a later text or context. Students introduce topics using media resources (Web site, CD, video, poster, *PowerPoint*, or transparency) and explain connections to course readings. Each group receives a grade that is based on criteria and may be modified for individuals. Though I suggest topics, students often find their own. After all, as Jorge Luis Borges declared at Harvard in 1967, "For many centuries the tale of Troy, the tale of Ulysses, and the tale of Jesus have been sufficient for mankind. . . . People have told them many times over" (64).

For the legacy of ancient and classical literature, students may present an epic film, a modern British poem, a French neoclassical painting, a Web site like *Perseus* or *Capitolium*, or the Oedipus or Medea complex. Students have also analyzed Greek combat in the movie *Troy* and Dido's despair in Purcell's opera *Dido and Aeneas*. Of greater resonance for them is the legacy of Jerusalem—of Judeo-Christian, medieval, Renaissance, and Islamic literatures—which pervades twenty-first-century media: epic and animated films; oratorios, operas, and musicals; poems, paintings, and festivals inspired by the Bible as well as by Camelot, *Arabian Nights*, or *Quixote*; and Web sites such as *Labyrinth* or *Danteworlds*. A report may be inspired by a popular-culture phenomenon, *The Da Vinci Code* or a Disney film, or it may express a unique interest. One group's analysis of a Luke Skywalker–Darth Vader combat scene noted Arthurian motifs in the original *Star Wars* trilogy: the mystical force, the chivalric code of the Jedi, and battles between light and darkness. Other groups revealed parallels to Dante's *Inferno* in the art films *What Dreams May Come* and *Clerks*.

Additional presentation options are available to groups and individuals. International students may present features of their culture when we study its literature. A creative response is possible, such as a video or skit inspired by a poem or a scene from an epic. A student may even present a personal connection, which may range from grief about a lost loved one that parallels Christine de Pizan's "Alone in Martyrdom" to reflections, inspired by *The Prince,* on modern public and private morality. Any of these types of reports allow students to learn by teaching as they help one another review the course and prepare for exam questions.

The structure and assignments of World Literature I are modified for World Literature II:

> a survey of Western and non-Western literatures from the seventeenth through the twentieth century considered in the cultural epochs of their creation, including the Enlightenment, Romanticism, realism, modernism, and the contemporary world.

In this course, which uses the second volume of the *Norton Anthology of World Literature*, three chronological units expand outward: from French baroque and Enlightenment comedy, tragedy, and satire (with a comparable work from Ming or Qing China), to Romantic and realist European poetry and fiction, to literature of modern global cultures and conflicts. Here, also, students contribute to discussions and group activities and complete two assignments involving collaboration. I recently taught this course online, a format that fosters interaction and collaboration learning. Online students are required to post twice a week to discussion forums—one original answer to a study question and one reply to a classmate's post—and they often engage in lively exchanges. In class, noted one student, "people are careful of what they say for fear of being misunderstood or frowned on by others," whereas *Blackboard* discussions are "more open and honest."

During the middle unit of World Literature II, on European Romanticism and realism, students are introduced to both main assignments. The late-semester presentation and teaching options are presented early, so that groups or individuals can begin to work on a study guide for a modern region (explained below) or on a connection report (similar to the legacy report). The critical essays for this course, more informed by critical theory than the essays on Greek tragedy, are based on substantial texts: *Faust, Part I, Madame Bovary,* and *Things Fall Apart.* Students prepare for these challenging readings in the first few classes of the second unit, as they apply close reading strategies and critical terms to Romantic lyric and narrative poems. Each classroom group receives a transparency of a poem (shown later to the class), which one student annotates with markers as the group applies close-reading questions from our class literature guide: Identify speaker and situation; Summarize by sections; Interpret key images, figures of speech, and formal features; and Suggest themes, symbolism, and irony. Online students post their explications to a forum and build on one another's insights through replies.

Discussions of *Faust* and *Madame Bovary* take about two weeks each. Study questions that invite close reading of passages and the application of critical quotations and approaches lay the foundation for students' essays in this course. To expose students to published criticism, I refer them to introductory essays in our textbook, hand out a page of quotations from such publications as the MLA Approaches to Teaching World Literature volumes and Norton Critical Editions, and post links to Internet sites about authors and their works. The culminating class for each text becomes a debate, as students defend their interpretations.

After students read *Faust* (aided by a plot outline, my explanations of such key passages as the wager, film clips, and a page of passages from published criticism), they articulate moral and psychological interpretations of Faust's desires, decisions, and growth through experience, or suggest feminist or Marxist readings of the Gretchen tragedy. Thesis sentences of their essays focus on aspects of the three central characters: what Faust desires and what he accomplishes; Faust as Romantic hero, tragic hero, or self-centered egoist; Gretchen as tragic heroine, realist character, Christian heroine, or as Faust-like Romantic heroine; and Mephistopheles as spirit of denial and his role in Faust's decisions and development.

In classes about the novel *Madame Bovary*—its characters, social settings, narration, symbols, and themes—students, aided by film clips and a page of passages from published criticism, have suggested Marxist analyses of the agricultural show or of Lheureux's power over Emma; psychoanalytic readings of Emma's romantic encounters or of Charles's submission to women; and feminist, psychoanalytic, or Marxist perspectives on Emma's desires, frustrations, and decisions. For *Madame Bovary*, most essay topics focus on Emma herself: as a tragic heroine; a Romantic idealist in conflict with her bourgeois community; a victim of misguided romance reading; or a psychological case of failed initiation, of narcissism, of self-destruction, of manic depression, or of instability of character. I remind students to avoid passing judgment on Emma's behavior. Other topic options are the character of Charles; on the role of one or more male characters in Emma's downfall; and Flaubert's critique of bourgeois pretensions, ignorance, materialism, and subjection of women. Students may also examine accessible qualities of Flaubert's literary art, such as shifting point of view and the use of symbolism and irony.

As with the Greek tragedy essays, students write for the unit test (and now post on *Blackboard*) argument essays of five hundred to six hundred words about *Faust* or *Madame Bovary*. They later revise and expand the test essays into critical essays. Interpretations are again shaped by the students' backgrounds, collaborations, and readings in criticism. Relatively few select Goethe's multigenre poetic drama *Faust*. The fate of Gretchen as a tragic heroine was explored by a student who saw social insecurity as Gretchen's tragic flaw. Sara Haney Williams, elaborating the Norton anthology's introduction to Goethe, adeptly traced the moral growth of Faust and concluded: "With his personal evolution from selfish abandon to the realization of another's reality, Faust finds enlightenment and spiritual knowledge" that is beyond the devil's comprehension. To Gabrielle Neal, Goethe's Mephistopheles at first represented "the subconscious sitting over the left shoulder, the one who urges us to selfishness," such as the pursuit of dangerous science; but with closer reading and responses from others, she recognized that this devil facilitates "Faust's physical and emotional transformation."

Madame Bovary, as Dean de la Motte recognizes, is particularly open to modern critical perspectives (49–50), and students take up that challenge in their class debates and essays. Some student essays quote from Marxists as they show how Emma's pursuit of romantic experiences in a realist setting ironically leads her to materialism and extravagant consumer purchases. Some student writers argue, as does Julie Lark, that Emma's mood swings can be understood as classic symptoms of bipolar disorder: "Because she suffered from manic depression, Emma could only focus on the immediate things that pleased her, and tended to let everything else in her life go—Charles, Berthe, money concerns." Psychoanalytic concepts also allow students to explain why Charles Bovary is vulnerable to manipulation by women and in denial about Emma's affairs, or to argue that Rodolphe is most responsible for Emma's debt, despair, and suicide.

In unit 3, "Literature of Modern World Cultures," each week is devoted to literary selections, usually short fiction, that represent a region of the post-1945 world and a related theme, such as European alienation, West African cultures and colonization, postcolonialism in the Middle East, and women's experiences of cultural conflict in Asian and Native American communities. Class discussion of literary texts from such diverse regions and themes is founded on group-created study guides, which include excerpts from relevant theory and criticism. Modern European literature, which once dominated this final unit, is now represented only by Franz Kafka, William Butler Yeats, and Anna Akhmatova. A central text in the unit is Chinua Achebe's novel *Things Fall Apart*, which is also an option for the critical essay assignment. Topics explored in class and in essays include the protagonist Okonkwo as ambiguous cultural hero or tragic hero; cultural practices of the Igbo and stages by which their villages succumb to white colonists; and literary features of a text that draws on the realist novel, African oral narrative, and literary modernism. Postcolonial theory helps students explore how Achebe's novel challenges stereotypes of Africans: racism that views Africans as uncivilized, appropriation by a dominant culture that assumes all share its values, and idealization of African cultures. In their essays about *Things Fall Apart*, students have agreed with scholars who note that things fall apart in Igbo society even before whites arrive, and one student quoted her Nigerian husband as she explained how Achebe's novel dispels cultural stereotypes about Africans.

Students also take peer teaching roles as they complete the second main assignment for the course. Campus students have two options: group teaching and individual teaching. For the assignment "Study Guide and Teaching," each group meets and creates a study guide for a class session on literature from one region of the post-1945 world, such as West Africa: for example, "Traditional Cultures and Imperialism." Each guide, like those I hand out for earlier units, provides classmates with concise information about the history, society, values, and culture of a nation or region; brief biographical profiles of authors; study questions for one or two classes; other resources, such as links to film scenes or illustrations; and a bibliography of works consulted. I review and edit the student-created study guides before handing them out, and when the topic comes up in class, the student experts conduct all or part of a class session. In past years, groups of prospective teachers presented—using art, film scenes, and group activities—topics like love and death in Latin American magic realism or like women between traditional and modern cultures in stories from India, China, and a Native American reservation. The best study guides I share with students in later semesters, and in future I may post them online.

The "Connection Report" is the option of peer teaching and collaboration open to students in online classes and chosen by most students on campus. Either oral or posted on *Blackboard*, each report makes a connection between a literary text we studied and any related topic, such as an extraliterary or cultural text, a major Web site, a film adaptation, a personal experience, a community or workplace issue, or a concept studied in a college course. Thus reading Voltaire's *Candide* inspired a student to research Voltaire's mistress, the physics pioneer Emilie du Châtelet, while Voltaire's account of the Lisbon earthquake of 1755 sent a group of students to articles and Web sites about religious responses to the Asian tsunami of 2004. Students have presented Internet sites and online images related to their major fields of study, such as nineteenth-century roles for women and medical practices. Others introduced our class to two Faust-theme films, both titled *Bedazzled*, or described how Carmela on HBO's *The Sopranos* reads *Madame Bovary* and behaves like Emma. Students can refer to connection reports on the final examination, where questions ask for intertextual comparisons between modern works and earlier readings.

"The world is big," begins a passage from Achebe's unpublished 1996 Bates College Commencement Address, which is quoted on many Web sites and in world literature syllabi. "Diversity is not an abnormality but the very reality of our planet. The human world celebrates itself in the magnificence of its endless varieties." UNC Pembroke's world literature survey courses immerse our undergraduates in diversity—in the Western cultural heritage, among global cultures, and in our diverse students' own genders, generations, ethnicities, and nationalities. Such diversity comes at a cost. Courses lose coherence and continuity as we substitute global texts that are new to the instructor (the *Ramayana* for the *Aeneid*) and as reluctant readers struggle to engage with frequent shifts in cultural contexts and genre features (myriad verse forms arranged in tablets, books, sutras, cantos). When a diversified course enlists individuals, groups, entire classes, and an array of media technologies in experiences of collaboration and peer teaching, instructors must reduce the number of readings and students may miss the reassuring structure of the traditional classroom. With large classes, presentations may become extra-credit options rather than requirements. Still, students can take pride in meeting challenges of influential texts from many cultures, and they often find passages and characters that speak to their experiences. By the end of each course, students have extended their global and historical cultural literacy, participated in critical conversations, and used literary and critical terminology. Critical reading and academic writing do improve as students collaborate on critical essays—when they post and respond to online reading responses, then critique and quote from published criticism and essays by fellow students.

Global world literature survey courses, collaboration, and presentations by groups and individuals serve humanities education in a broader sense as well. Unusual collaborations occur, as when parallel scenes from the *Odyssey* and *O Brother, Where Art Thou* were presented as a comic routine by a tennis-team player in his twenties and a teenage hip-hop dancer. A review session in World Literature I brought surprises, when a student who had never volunteered in class summarized Dante's *Inferno* using images displayed on the *Danteworlds* Web site and another reserved student presented a *PowerPoint* that showed images for every literary selection in the course. International students provide cultural perspectives, explaining that modern Hindus learn virtues from Rama and Sita in the *Ramayana* or that *The Story of the Stone* is familiar to Chinese children from pop songs and films and that its heroine, Dai-yu, loses social standing by being an orphan. Some personal responses to readings are shared with me privately. While studying *Don Quixote*, a student had an epiphany about her psychological disorder. Another came to my office a year after taking the class to tell me about a family trauma; for months, she said, she had felt like Gregor Samsa in "The Metamorphosis."

As I was completing this essay in fall 2006, my World Literature I class read medieval Islamic texts, *Son-Jara* and *1001 Nights*, against the backdrop of a twenty-first-century conflict in Iraq. A student from Turkey, Gamze Melahat Oner Bridenstine—using maps, Web sites, videos, and a dual-language Qur'an—described features of her native country, from Istanbul mosques and Ephesus ruins to a dance of Sufi dervishes, that are associated with Judaism, Christianity, and Islam. A few days later, we learned that her countryman Orhan Pamuk received the Nobel Prize for Literature. Such experiences allow global, interactive world literature classes to leave lasting impressions and to further the cultural understanding that Achebe advocates in his commencement speech: "Civility is a sensible attribute in this kind of world we have; narrowness of heart and mind is not."

Works Cited

Achebe, Chinua. Bates Coll. 27 May 1996. Commencement address.

Borges, Jorge Luis. "The Telling of the Tale." 1967. *Atlantic Monthly* Sept. 2000: 62–65. Print.

Brown, Monika. "Joining the Critical Conversation in a Sophomore Literature Class." *CEA Critic* 62.1 (1999): 17–33. Print.

Bruffee, Kenneth. "Collaborative Learning and the 'Conversation of Mankind.'" *College English* 46 (1984): 635–52. Print.

Cartledge, Gwendolyn, et al. *Cultural Diversity and Social Skills Instruction: Understanding Ethnic and Gender Differences.* Champaign: Research, 1996. Print.

Csikszentmihalyi, Mihaly, and Keith Sawyer. "Creative Insight: The Social Dimension of a Solitary Moment." *The Nature of Insight.* Ed. Robert J. Sternberg and Janet E. Davidson. Cambridge: MIT P, 1995. 329–64. Print.

de la Motte, Dean. "Will the Real Madame Bovary Please Stand Up." *Approaches to Teaching Flaubert's* Madame Bovary. Ed. Laurence M. Porter and Eugene F. Gray. New York: MLA, 1995. 49–54. Print.

Doolittle, Peter. "Vygotsky's Zone of Proximal Development as a Theoretical Foundation for Cooperative Learning." *Journal on Excellence in College Teaching* 8.1 (1997): 83–103. Print.

Hart, Jeffrey. *Smiling through the Cultural Catastrophe: Toward the Revival of Higher Education.* New Haven: Yale UP, 2001. Print.

Roskelly, Hephzibah. *Breaking (into) the Circle: Group Work for Change in the English Classroom.* Portsmouth: Boynton, 2003. Print.

Schilb, John. "'Text,' 'Reader,' 'Author,' and 'History' in the Introduction to Literature Course." *Practicing Theory.* Ed. James M. Calahan and David V. Downing. Urbana: NCTE, 1991. 59–71. Print.

Part IV

Courses

Introduction

This section gives ten accounts of individual courses in world literature. Given the variety of the field, this selection can only begin to suggest the range of courses now being taught, but each of these writers raises issues that will occur in the designing of many other courses. Together these essays present a range of perspectives and approaches at different sorts of institutions around the country, from community colleges to research universities. Some of these courses are fully global in scope, some focus on two or three regions, and some have a principally Western emphasis—though the West itself is seen in new ways today.

Some courses take a thematic approach, as Carolyn Ayers's course on the artist in world literature, Elizabeth Horan's Internet-based course on the comic heroic journey, and Ellen Peel's course on imagining the constructed body. Others are based on genre, as with Raymond-Jean Frontain's course on heroic action and the fragility of culture in the *Ramayana* and the *Aeneid*. Some courses use larger categories that cross generic boundaries, such as Nikolai Endres's course on gay and lesbian texts across cultures and Eric Sterling's on teaching world masterpieces through religious literature. Other essayists treat broadly regional or global bodies of material: Wai Chee Dimock on American literature in relation to global Islam, Carol Fadda-Conrey on Middle Eastern literature. Kathryn Walterschied emphasizes time frames as well as regions in her course on non-Western traditions, which counterpoints ancient and modern texts from each region under consideration, while C. A. Prettiman discusses the challenges involved in drawing connections across eras and cultures for a student population made up mostly of science majors.

Many of these essays resonate interestingly with one another and with essays elsewhere in this volume: for example, in the discussions of religious issues by Frontain and by Sterling or in Endres's and Massad's discussions of sexuality. Collectively, these essays offer many valuable reflections on broad issues involved in constructing the individual courses they discuss—as well as all sorts of ideas for creative conjunctions of works that can figure in a wide variety of courses.

Carolyn Ayers

The Adventures of the Artist in World Literature: A One-Semester Thematic Approach

In a small, liberal arts institution with limited course offerings, a single semester of world literature must perform many functions, not least of which is to help students recognize how much has of necessity been left out of the syllabus, how much remains for them to explore after the semester is over. In addition to contributing to the general curriculum goals of developing skills in critical and reflective reading, analysis, and response to literature of various genres, the course provides one of only a few (though increasing) opportunities in the English department curriculum for students to experience works from outside the British and American traditions, especially works not originally written in English. That the readings in the course, as we have defined it, will necessarily have cultural contexts and often formal features outside most of our northern Midwest students' literary comfort zone is likely to pose special challenges. Approaching world literature through the lens of a theme, I find, renders the scope a little less daunting for both students and instructor, and it provides a focus that serves as a bridge to the unfamiliar.

It would be possible to suggest many themes that operate across cultural boundaries—the individual and community, ambition, the sacred and the profane, and the demonic are among those I have experimented with—but an idea that has proved especially appealing to students is the notion of the artist. Exploring how artists, poets, and storytellers have been represented or have represented themselves in literary works from a variety of genres and cultural traditions opens up many avenues for discussion about, for instance, the ways creativity and authorship have been imagined and understood at various historical and cultural moments; about varying notions of audience; and about the value and function of literature in societies. As we study various transpositions of the artist theme, these concrete examples lead us to a larger sense of literature as an ongoing, global cultural dialogue.

Even when we work with a fairly specific focus, the time constraints of a single semester prevent any sort of attempt to trace the theme through literary history from antiquity to the present around the globe. It is more feasible to develop a selective, coherent, yet flexible reading list that can both chart out some territory and point beyond itself. Normally we begin the course with a few foundational texts of different genres that represent the artist in cultural contexts far removed from our own. Plato's *Ion,* the poetry of Li Bai (Li Bo), and *The Thousand and One Nights* give us portraits of the artist that both confirm and challenge students' preconceived ideas. These ideas are often drawn from film and other types of contemporary discourse, but they also derive, I would argue, from Romantic and modernist images that continue to be reinforced in Western culture about creativity and the artist's role in society. The artist as gifted, mad, or temporarily out of control; the artist as teacher and healer; the artist in uneasy relation to the civil authorities and to the audience—these ideas show up, we find, in these remarkably dispersed, premodern representations. Yet obvious and profound differences in both cultural context and form among these three works raise issues of meaning as well. For example, in Plato's dialogue, when Ion admits that when reciting Homer, he is inspired and therefore "out of his mind," he seems to be cornered by Socrates, whose logic the dialogue clearly favors (14). Li Bai, on the other hand, seems consciously to be creating and nurturing an image of himself as a transcendent being with access to other worlds. It is here that we can begin to examine critically the universality of such more or less familiar notions and, by implication, the universality of literary themes in general. At this early point in the semester, we raise many more questions than we can answer in terms of the interplay among history, geography, culture, and the idea or image of the artist. Yet this unit of disparate readings performs an important role in setting the stage for investigations to come.

Having acquired a vocabulary and a stance for reading the artist figure—a set of qualities and issues to be alert for as well as a sense of how these qualities might be represented and understood in various cultural and generic contexts—we next examine a kind of case study in a specific tradition: the *Künstlerroman* ("artist narrative") as it developed in northern Europe. The set of readings in this unit allows us to examine in more depth at least two cultural moments: European Romanticism and modernism. We study the life of the *Künstlerroman* as a dialogue among writers and thinkers that, while certainly less than global in scope, did cross both cultural and generational boundaries. We begin with several tales by E. T. A. Hoffmann, who, though quite influential in European literary history, tends to be unfamiliar to our students, at least beyond "The Nutcracker." Given their acquaintance with the English Romantic poets, though, it is not a huge jump for students to imagine the world in which Hoffmann wrote, his engagement with music and visual art, and his explorations of the realms of reality and imagination. We study Hoffmann not only as a major representative of a major literary movement but also as a writer who had an impact outside his own culture, in nineteenth-century Russia.

When we move on to read Aleksandr Pushkin's "Egyptian Nights" and Nikolai Gogol's "The Portrait," we are able both to follow the themes represented in the *Künstlerroman* to a new and different cultural environment and to look back, with the Russians, on what aspects of Hoffmann's artist figures were appealing and meaningful to them. This concrete example of thematic transposition[1] serves as an excellent introduction to many of the issues literary mobility raises, particularly since both Pushkin and Gogol are explicit about how the situation in nineteenth-century Russia demands and produces a kind of artist figure that differs from those emerging in western Europe. Pushkin and Gogol, national writers of the highest stature, nevertheless ambivalently accord a kind of legitimacy to western Europe as the center of high art and represent their own artistic culture as peripheral. We examine this literary transposition closely, to discover what sorts of extraliterary forces might be at work in shaping the image of the artist in any given environment. Because we frame the Russian response to a western European theme as an example, students are well prepared later to approach issues of literary representation related to European colonialism and postcolonialism.

The landscape against which the artist theme is painted becomes increasingly complex in the modernist era. In Knut Hamsun's *Hunger*, in

Thomas Mann's *Death in Venice,* in Franz Kafka's "A Hunger Artist," and in the poetry of Constantine Cavafy, we encounter writers who are themselves situated variously in relation to the "central" culture. They take up and extend to various limits the dialogue begun by their predecessors. What happens with the representation of the artist in these works pushes the class to consider also the moral situation of the writer in any given society. The brevity of the readings in this series allows us to approach the dilemma of the artist in society from a number of angles to fill out the European picture. Clearly, even the "central" culture contains contrasting but interrelated perspectives (see in particular Deleuze and Guattari on Kafka). Time permitting, we can return to the Russian tradition for responses. Vladimir Nabokov embraces the image of the artist as exile to become a world citizen, while Mikhail Bulgakov, in *The Master and Margarita,* draws on foundational narratives from the Gospels to Goethe to locate his satirical artist novel firmly in 1930s Moscow. By this point in the semester, students are generally ready to confront (with the help of generous glossing) the unfamiliar, culturally specific references and features of this work, because they are also able to recognize the deep connections between Bulgakov's narrative and the *Künstlerroman* tradition (as well as his use of earlier Judeo-Christian writings, particularly the story of the Crucifixion). In this way, the artist theme acts as a bridge to a work that might otherwise present itself as simply foreign and therefore inaccessible.

The final major unit of the course is the most open and flexible but also the most crucial in pursuing issues that point beyond the reading done during the semester. We look at various examples of more recent works of non-European origin that offer challenges and alternatives to the traditional European artist figure. There is much room for experimentation here, and the theme can be expanded in many geographic and generic directions. I usually try to introduce examples both of writers who have embraced and made use of European models (e.g., Borges, Mahfouz) and of writers who consciously reject these models as imperialist and colonialist (e.g., Ngũgĩ wa Thiong'o). Because my institution sponsors an annual series of special events (films, lectures, exhibits) highlighting a different country each year, I usually include at least one author from the culture we are featuring. So, for example, while Ngũgĩ's works did not appear to be obvious choices in a course on the artist narrative, his cultural commentary and his work with the International Center for Writing and Translation proved relevant to our larger examination of cultural and thematic transposition during the year the series featured Kenya.[2] Alternatively, essays as well as poetry by Czesław Miłosz seemed fitting readings in the year of his death; our discussions were both timely and historically grounded as we recalled our earlier thematic representations of the writer and the state. The artist narrative, then, eventually provides a springboard from which we can move out into the larger waters of world literature.

This course addresses successfully most of my major instructional goals: students are exposed to some canonical and important writers but not without critically examining the whole notion of canonicity. They get some grounding in European literature, yet there is enough non-European literature on the syllabus to introduce global critical responses to the European tradition and to Eurocentrism. And I get to teach some of the Russian writers I love. Inevitably, though, issues of both content and pedagogy remain. First, the course is hardly comprehensive in time span or geography. It worries me as well that we read few works by women; this narrowness is to some extent a function of the artist theme, the historical situation of the *Künstlerroman*, and the time period in which we spend most of the semester. Again, though, we confront this issue directly, and some of our most interesting discussions have dealt with the role of the muse figure vis-à-vis the position of the female artist. My hope is that by beginning with a few foundational premodern texts, then moving to a heavily male-dominated, European tradition, and gradually moving outward to span the globe, we can in a way recapitulate the broadening of university literary studies and gain a sort of metaconsciousness of our reading.

Pedagogical challenges are less easily handled by shifting the discussion to a metalevel. Because we approach these readings as a culturally specific dialogue among writers and readers and because the cultural specifics themselves tend to be unfamiliar to our students, they must absorb quite a bit of information before they can truly exercise their interpretive imaginations. I try to meet this challenge in several ways. First, the reading assignments include, as much as possible, cultural contextual material. For the final course unit in particular, we depend on at least one volume of a multivolume anthology; and most major anthologies now provide excellent accompanying material—maps, drawings, explanatory notes. For the readings in the earlier units that do not come from the anthology, I try to order good editions with supplemental cultural background or notes. That some students inevitably will be working from a different edition provides another opportunity to address directly issues of translation and cultural transposition. Further, our concentration on a few specific cultural moments for two units allows us to build up a rich sense of one particular cultural context, again with the awareness that this is only one example. Students are thus acquiring tools as much as knowledge. Finally and most rewardingly, students engage in independent (sometimes guided) research to prepare for a series of panel discussions as we finish each unit as well as to write their major paper.

Most classes, of course, include informal discussion as we work together to sort out familiar and unfamiliar aspects of each reading and address students' questions as they come up, but a more structured discussion at the end of each unit encourages a deeper level of engagement and preparation. Students sign up in groups to present a panel on one of the major units of the course. Each group researches the authors and their situations beyond what has been covered in the classroom. I encourage the groups to expand their reading to include contemporary nonfictional writings that might be relevant to their authors. (Many of these readings—selections from psychology, philosophy, politics, and education—I select and place on library reserve for consultation as needed. This part of the research is guided.) Before the presentation day, the group circulates a statement for discussion in which they make a claim about the role of the artist, authorship, the nature of creativity, or anything related to our theme, based on their understanding of the writers and works in their unit. The group comes prepared to back their statement with examples, while the other students prepare responses and often question the panel members' readings.

These panel discussions offer an excellent chance for students to pursue at least a few authors in depth as well as to approach larger issues of cultural remove and perspective in terms of the theme. More independent work is required for the major paper, as each student chooses a world author to situate in the artist tradition in world literature. The focus on the theme is obviously key in bringing all the various elements of the course together; it also equips the students with some confidence that, when they leave the course, they will be able to deal with the next book from the world they encounter.

Notes

1. For an extensive discussion of thematic transposition in a given culture but across genres, see Emerson, esp. 9, 209–11. Emerson grounds her defini-

tion of thematic transposition in Bakhtin's theories of generic function; the concept is useful in looking at cultural exchange as well.

2. See, for example, Ngũgĩ. A visit and reading by the author himself did more to expand our global reading horizons than anything else on the syllabus.

Works Cited

Deleuze, Gilles, and Félix Guattari. *Kafka: Toward a Minor Literature.* Trans. Dana Polan. Minneapolis: U of Minnesota P, 1986. Print.

Emerson, Caryl. *Boris Godunov: Transpositions of a Russian Theme.* Bloomington: Indiana UP, 1986. Print.

Li Bai. "Drinking Alone beneath the Moon." *The Bedford Anthology of World Literature: Book 2: The Middle Period, 100 C.E.–1450.* Ed. Paul Davis et al. Boston: Bedford–St. Martin's, 2004. 335–36. Print.

Ngũgĩ wa Thiong'o. "Creating Space for a Hundred Flowers to Bloom." *The Bedford Anthology of World Literature: Book 6: The Twentieth Century, 1900–the Present.* Ed. Paul Davis et al. Boston: Bedford–St. Martin's, 2004. 150–57. Print.

Plato, "The Ion." *Literary Criticism: Plato to Dryden.* Ed. Allan H. Gilbert. Detroit: Wayne State UP, 1962. 8–23. Print.

Wai Chee Dimock

American Literature and Islamic Time

A perennial question in world literature courses is whether the syllabus should include American literature or be reserved for texts written beyond the United States borders. American literature is sometimes excluded on principle, on the ground that if a text is American, it is therefore not of the world; even when it is included, its place is often minimal. This ontologizing of difference extends the logic of most literature departments, in which a national literature is typically taught apart, as an independent field. But is this current practice justified, empirically as well as analytically? If it is not, how can we best modify it? What if we were to think of American literature as no more than a subset, not freestanding, not sovereign unto itself, and requiring a larger set—something like world literature—for its full contours to emerge? How would this set-and-subset relation change the questions that we ask and the archives that we use?

This essay proposes a decentering of American literature, a suspension of the familiar, nation-based geography and chronology, in favor of a domain of research with no default coordinates. Not organized by the sovereign form of the nation, the field here is provisional, experimental, ad hoc. Its lengths and widths simply reflect the durations and extensions variously experienced by the world's populations. This nonsovereign approach can be attempted in ways both large and small. World religions offer an especially good point of departure.

Practiced in more than one locale and more than one continent, world religions are by definition more extended than any nation-state. They are also more ancient, with a better track record of survival. Their longitudes and latitudes probably match those of the human species better than any other institution. In their longevity and in their diffusion, they have done much to integrate the globe, breaking down the separation of periods as well as the isolation of regions, spurring cultural contact across long distances. This integrative power is as true of Islam as of Christianity.

Robert Irwin speaks of the emergence of an "Islamic world system" between the years 1000 and 1500. Of hemispheric proportion, this system extended from Sumatra to Spain, from the Nile to the Volga, spilling over from its "classical borders" into Asia Minor, eastern Europe, sub-Saharan Africa, much of India, and further on to southeastern and central Asia, and even parts of China (McNeill 485). Spanning three continents, it was "Afro-Eurasian" in a way we might not fully understand (Hodgson 97). This geographic vastness meant that Islam was multilingual from the first, translated into many local tongues, becoming a civilization (and not just a religion) through the mixing of these vernaculars and through the mixing of the Islamic faith with a wealth of secular forms, from poetry and philosophy to law, architecture, the visual arts, medicine, mathematics, and the natural sciences.[1] Against this magnificent spread, Europe can be called only an intellectual backwater for hundreds of years, its centrality on the world stage a late development. The map that aligns the West with literate progress and the East with brute tyranny is a recent invention. Hemispheric Islam yields a different map.

What would American literature look like as part of this genealogy? Can we transpose some familiar figures onto this broadened and deepened landscape? The paradigm here supplements and to some extent inverts Edward Said's *Orientalism*, his account of the representations of Islam in post-Enlightenment Europe. "Taking the late eighteenth century as a very roughly defined starting point," Said discusses orientalism "as the corporate institution for dealing with the Orient—dealing with it by making statements about it, authorizing views of it, describing it, by teaching it, settling it, ruling over it" (3). This corporate institution was clearly of European vintage. To speak of orientalism is therefore to speak of a British and French enterprise, "out of whose unchallenged centrality an Oriental world emerged" (8). The analytic domain here is strictly "within the umbrella of Western hegemony over the Orient" (7).

Yet there is no reason why the focus should be solely on Western representations or why Britain and France should be the umbrella, the starting point as well as endpoint. Much might be said for "provincialing Europe" (Chakrabarty), using a different map altogether, one that begins at an earlier moment and goes back to other parts of the globe. Off-center duration is especially helpful here. Stretching much further back than the late eighteenth century, which begins Said's chronology, it also pre-dates the hegemony of Europe during that period. This *longue durée* allows us to see a prenational civilization, much more complex and consequential than it would appear when the analytic field is no more than a couple of hundred years.

That civilization would soon spread to the Americas, becoming Afro-American as well as Afro-Eurasian. Muslim slaves from West Africa were brought to the New World from the seventeenth century on (Turner 11–46). The legacy from this group is not entirely clear, but emigration from the Middle East, beginning in the 1870s, gave the United States a solid Muslim presence. By the early 1900s, Muslim communities were well established in the Midwest (Austin; Smith 50–75). The Nation of Islam came into being in 1930, beginning with W. D. Fard's preaching in Detroit, followed by the establishment of its headquarters in Chicago in 1932, under Elijah Muhammad.

It is interesting to think of this vexed formation as another instance of vernacular Islam, a folk variant, not in the religious mainstream, having only a tenuous link to the orthodox faith. Black Muslims are not usually called orientalists, but that is what they are: a new twist on that word, the latest and most controversial incarnation. As a separatist group, the Nation of Islam was especially emphatic about its eastward orientation. Its members were taught that they "were not Americans but Asiatics," that their homeland was elsewhere, on other continents (Turner 151). According to Elijah Muhammad, the planet began sixty-six trillion years ago, when an explosion separated the moon from the earth, populating the earth with the black tribe of Shabazz, the earth's first inhabitants. This original nation spoke Arabic, practiced Islam, and was ruled by twenty-four scientists. Unfortunately, 6,600 years ago, this paradise was subverted by a mad scientist, Yacub, who schemed to create a new race of devils, whites, out of the original humans. After trying for six hundred years, he succeeded (Muhammad based these calculations on Qur'an 49.15 and 76.2). For six thousand years, the white devils would be allowed to reign supreme on earth (Curtis 75).

Mythology of this sort was meant to maximize enemies, not only among whites but also among black Christian churches and other Muslim groups. If the legacy of Islam was a divided spectrum—torn between the latitude of a worldwide brotherhood and the clannishness of a tribe—Black Muslims would seem to rehearse that spectrum to the full.[2] At the two poles stand Malcolm X and James Baldwin. What these two eloquent and opposing voices represent is nothing less than the antithetical scope claimed by Islam. For Malcolm X, Islam is very capacious indeed; it belongs to the whole world; nothing is broader, nothing falls outside its rubric. This religion can accommodate every branch of the human family, as the American nation cannot:

> I only knew what I had left in America, and how it contrasted with what I had found in the Muslim world. . . . Never have I witnessed such sincere hospitality and the overwhelming spirit of true brotherhood as is practiced by people of all colors and races here in this Ancient Holy Land, the home of Abraham, Muhammad, and all the other prophets of the Holy Scriptures. . . . I have been blessed to visit the Holy City of Mecca. I have made my seven circuits around the Ka'ba, led by a young *Mutawaf* named Muhammad. I drank water from the well of Zem Zem. I ran seven times back and forth between the hills of Mt. Al-Safa and Al-Marwah. I have prayed in the ancient city of Mina, and I have prayed on Mt. Arafat. There were tens and thousands of pilgrims, from all over the world. They were of all colors, from blue-eyed blonds to black-skinned Africans. But we were all participating in the same ritual, displaying a spirit of unity and brotherhood that my experiences in America had led me to believe never could exist between the white and the non-white. (338–40)

Malcolm X is not wrong to credit Islam with a "spirit of unity and brotherhood," for this is the specific injunction in Qur'an 49.13: "Mankind! We created you from a single (pair) of a male and a female, and made you into nations and tribes, that ye may know each other (not that ye may despise each other)" (1407). For Malcolm X, the weight of that injunction is backed by the long history of Islam. Here is a religion that goes back to Abraham and Muhammad; its scriptures and rituals are ancient; it is almost as old as the primordial landscape of Al-Safa, Al-Marwah, and Mount Arafat. This *longue durée* means that Islam is coextensive with the history of the world. It is mappable onto the entire species, not exclusive to one racial group. That is why it can take in the blue-eyed and the black-skinned and have room to spare. To become a Muslim is to undergo a scale enlargement in every sense.

This inclusiveness is the very opposite of what strikes Baldwin. *The Fire Next Time* (1962) is a passionate dissent from the Nation of Islam precisely because of the scale reduction Baldwin experiences in its midst. Where Malcolm X sees an expanse of time going back to the seventh-century prophet Muhammad, Baldwin feels suffocated by a small and contracting circle gathered around Elijah Muhammad, the current prophet, a noose very much in the present:

> I had the stifling feeling that *they* knew I belonged to them but knew that I did not know it yet, that I remained unready, and that they were simply waiting, patiently, and with assurance, for me to discover the truth for myself. For where else, after all, could I go? I was black, and therefore a part of Islam, and would be saved from the holocaust awaiting the white world whether I would or no. My weak, deluded scruples could avail nothing against the iron word of the prophet. (97–98)

Is Islam capacious or stifling? Is its radius coextensive with the species, or is it locked into one particular race, its membership automatically decided by identity politics? These antithetical questions, put forth by Malcolm X and Baldwin, yield some of the terms on which American literature bursts out of the confines of the nation-state, becoming a weave of the fabric of the world.

It would be a mistake, however, to see this antithesis as a strictly twentieth-century phenomenon, affecting only African Americans. Indeed, the importance of Islam lies precisely in its ability to break down some of the standard dividing lines, turning them into surprising lines of kinship. For the scope of this religion threads it not only into African American history but also into the history of other groups. Baldwin and Malcolm X have company in the nineteenth century.

Washington Irving was struck by the splendor of Islam. Fluent in Spanish, he was in Spain for a total of seven years (Williams 297), writing *The Conquest of Granada* (1828) and *The Alhambra* (1832), dwelling on Spain's Muslim legacy. Of the Court of Lions in the Alhambra, Irving writes:

> Earthquakes have shaken the foundations of this pile, . . . [yet] not one of these slender columns has been displaced, not an arch of that

light and fragile colonnade given way, not all the fairy fretwork of these domes, apparently as unsubstantial as the crystal fabrics of a morning frost. (79)

This combination of delicacy and tenacity makes him think that Islam is at the beginning rather than the end of its career, that its history is far from finished:

> Such is the general aspiration and belief among the Moors of Barbary; who consider Spain, or Andaluz, as it was anciently called, their rightful heritage, of which they have been despoiled by treachery and violence. . . . These families, it is said, continue to sigh after the terrestrial paradise of their ancestors, and to put up prayers in their mosques on Fridays, imploring Allah to hasten the time when Granada shall be restored to the faithful: an event to which they look forward as fondly and confidently as did the Christian crusaders to the recovery of the Holy Sepulchre. Nay, it is added, that some of them retain the ancient maps and deeds of the estates and gardens of their ancestors at Granada, and even the keys of the houses; holding them as evidences of their hereditary claims, to be produced at the anticipated day of restoration. (82)

The year 1492 not only saw the arrival of Columbus in America; it was also the year that Granada surrendered to the Christian monarchs Ferdinand and Isabella, which paved the way for the eventual expulsion of Muslims from the Iberian Peninsula, leaving a bitter aftertaste for centuries to come.[3] Irving, indefatigable traveler, learned about that bitterness on-site. But travel was by no means needed for the history of Islam to register as history. As evidenced by the lists of books Bronson Alcott borrowed from the Boston Athenaeum, stay-at-home readers, boning up on comparative philology and comparative religion, also had some acquaintance with the Qur'an.[4] Nor was this only a masculine pursuit. The most serious scholar of world religions was Lydia Maria Child, who wrote a three-volume treatise called *The Progress of Religious Ideas through Successive Ages* (1855), beginning with "Hindostan," followed by "Egypt," "China," "Thibet and Tartary," and ending with a sixty-eight-page chapter "Mohammedanism," noting that its "professors are now estimated at one hundred and eighty millions; nearly one-fifth of the whole human race" (417).

The "human race" was an important idea for the transcendentalists, and Islam, one of its vital bearers, was important for that reason. So with Child (349–417), and so too with Ralph Waldo Emerson. Emerson's introduction to Islam began as early as 1819, when he was sixteen. He seems to have read the Qur'an on his own: a journal entry in October 1819 featured this quotation from George Sale's translation: "In aforetime I created *Jan* from out of a scorching fire" (*Journal* 1: 171).[5] In 1822, Emerson read Edward Gibbon's *Decline and Fall of the Roman Empire* (*Journal* 1: 131); chapters 50 to 52 of that book are devoted to Arabic culture, with high praise for its language and poetry (Gibbon 346–47). His subsequent readings (Carpenter 198) included *Oriental Geography* (1800), by Ibn Haukal; the *Annales Muslemici Arabice et Latine* (1837), by Abulfeda; Simon Ockley's *Conquest of Syria, Persia, and Egypt by the Saracens* (1708–18); not to mention Thomas Carlyle's admiring chapter on Mahomet in *Heroes, Hero-Worship, and the Heroic in History* (37–66).

What impressed Emerson about Islam (and world religions in general) was what would later impress Malcolm X: the scope, the long duration, the ability to bind people across space and time, a point he made as early as 1822, in one of his first journal entries:

> The History of Religion involves circumstances of remarkable interest and it is almost all that we are able to trace in the passage of the remote ages of the world. . . . We know nothing of the first empires which grasped the sceptre of the earth in Egypt, Assyria, or Persia, but their modes of worship. And this fact forcibly suggests the idea that the only true and legitimate vehicle of immortality, the only bond of connection which can traverse the long duration which separates the ends of the world and unite the first people to the knowledge and sympathy of the last people, is religion. (*Journal* 1: 62)

World religions are probably the most robust diachronic axis known to humans. Such durable phenomena are likely to change, to spread out, becoming mongrelized by many new contacts. A book that exemplified all these qualities was the *Akhlak-I-Jalaly*, translated from the Persian by W. F. Thompson. Cobbled together in the fifteenth century by a worldly philosopher, Molla Jaladeddin Davani (1410–88), the *Akhlak* was anything but Islamic dogma. Mixing the Qur'an with Sufi mysticism as well as the ethics and politics of Plato and Aristotle, it was a mutt, a linguistic and philosophical hybrid, with Arabic, Persian, Greek, and now English in its veins.

This mongrelization did not bother Emerson in the least. For him, world religions such as Islam are meant to become mutts. They are meant to be half parented by the vernaculars of their translators. In his journal, he copied down these lines by Goethe:

> The Koran says, "God has given every people a prophet in its own speech." So is every translator a prophet to his people. Luther's translation of the Bible produced the greatest influence, if the critics up to this day continually stipulate and cavil thereon. (*Journal* 6: 292)[6]

Religions can inhabit the world only through their translations. The Qur'an in particular had to be mongrelized—meshed with the poetry of the Persian poets Saadi and Hafiz—before it could act as a spur on Emerson, egging him on to translate in turn. Working from Joseph von Hammer's German anthologies, he included his first translation as a journal entry in 1846 and kept up the practice for the rest of his life. Over the course of the next thirty years, he produced at least sixty-four translations, a total of seven hundred lines of Persian poetry.[7] Some of these were included in his long essay "Persian Poetry," first published in the *Atlantic* in 1858, later collected in his 1875 *Letters and Social Aims* (Frank 331, 505–06). Toward the end of his life, he paid yet another tribute to these Persian poets in a long poem of his own, entitled "Fragments on the Poet and the Poetic Gift" (*Complete Works* 9: 320–34). Hafiz was one of the last names to appear in Emerson's *Pocket Diary*. From 1841 to 1879, Hafiz was never absent from the *Journals*.[8]

Emerson was struck by the poet's name. The Persian word, he noted, "signifies one gifted with so good a memory that he knows the whole Koran by heart" (*Journal* 10: 17). Is Hafiz then an Islamic poet? For Emerson, the answer is both yes and no. Hafiz is Muslim by faith, but his poetry also seems to overflow that faith, as in these lines that Emerson translates:

> Cheer thy heart with wine:
> The earth is only
> A house to which our bones
> Give the mortar.
>
> Seek not in thy friend, truth;
> Truth is dead;
> Holy fire comes not
> Out of Church lamps.
>
> Blacken thou not my name
> For my riot;
> Who knows what the lot
> Inscribed on the brow?

Turn not thy steps
From the grave of Hafiz,
Since though in sins sunken
He waits for / expects Heaven. (*Poetry Notebooks* 315–16)

Emerson's Hafiz is both Islamic and more than Islamic, precisely because he knows the Qur'an so well, by heart. Knowing the Qur'an by heart and knowing that the earth is no more than "A house to which our bones / Give the mortar," he nonetheless dreams of "Heaven," for this heaven is not spatial, consecrated around "Church lamps," but temporal, brought forth by future readers who "turn not [their] steps / From the grave of Hafiz." Some of these readers would take the Persian poet to Europe, to America, compounding his Islamic faith with Christian symbols and turning his poetry into one that speaks both within and beyond its scriptures. Vernacular Islam of this sort, extending across continents and millennia and tracing a genealogy from Malcolm X to Emerson, shows us what American literature looks like when restored to the world.

Notes

1. Algebra (an Arabic word), geometry, optics, and medicine all flourished under Islam. See Plessner; Vernet.

2. Aminah Beverly McCloud sees this divided legacy as the tension between two Arabic words, *ummah* and *'asabiya,* both of which define Islam (3–5).

3. Akbar S. Ahmed has coined the phrase the "Andalus syndrome" to describe a grievance felt by many Muslims, occasioned not only by the fate of Islam in the Iberian Peninsula but also by the fate of Islam in Hyderabad, South India (158–71).

4. On 24 March 1849, Alcott borrowed these books from the Boston Athenaeum: *Collier's Four Books of Confucius, The Vedas, The Saama Vedas, Vishnu Parana, Saadi, Firdusi, The Zendavesta, The Koran.* The list was given to Alcott by James Freeman Clarke, who would go on to write *Ten Great Religions: Essays in Comparative Theology* (Christy 243).

5. The only translation of the Qur'an then available in English was by George Sale (1801).

6. The passage is from Goethe's *Nachgelassene Werke* 262.

7. The first translation I am able to find is in his 1846 *Journal,* a translation of Hafiz's poem "Come let us strew roses" (*Journal* 9: 398). For a checklist of Emerson's translations, see Yohannan. See also *The Topical Notebooks of Ralph Waldo Emerson.*

8. The last entry was in 1879 (Emerson, *Journal* 16: 527).

Works Cited

Ahmed, Akhar S. *Discovering Islam: Making Sense of Muslim History and Society.* London: Routledge, 1988. Print.

Austin, Allan. *African Muslims in Antebellum America: A Sourcebook.* New York: Garland, 1984. Print.

Baldwin, James. *The Fire Next Time.* 1962. New York: Laurel, 1988. Print.

Carlyle, Thomas. *On Heroes, Hero-Worship, and the Heroic in History.* 1841. Ed. Michael K. Goldberg et al. Berkeley: U of California P, 1993. 37–66. Print.

Carpenter, Frederic Ives. *Emerson and Asia.* Cambridge: Harvard UP, 1930. Print.

Chakrabarty, Dipesh. *Provincializing Europe.* Princeton: Princeton UP, 2000. Print.

Child, Lydia Maria. *The Progress of Religious Ideas through the Ages.* Vol. 3. New York: Francis, 1855. Print.

Christy, Arthur. *The Orient in American Transcendentalism.* New York: Columbia UP, 1932. Print.

Curtis, Edward E., IV. *Islam in Black America: Identity, Liberation, and Difference in African-American Islamic Thought.* Albany: State U of New York P, 2002. Print.

Emerson, Ralph Waldo. *Complete Works of Ralph Waldo Emerson.* 11 vols. Boston: Houghton, 1891– . Print.

———. *Journal and Miscellaneous Notebooks of Ralph Waldo Emerson.* Ed. William H. Gilman et al. 16 vols. Cambridge: Harvard UP, 1960–82. Print.

———. *Poetry Notebooks of Ralph Waldo Emerson.* Ed. Ralph H. Orth. Columbia: U of Missouri P, 1988. Print.

———. *The Topical Notebooks of Ralph Waldo Emerson.* 3 vols. Ed. Susan Sutton Smith et al. Columbia: U of Missouri P, 1990–94. Print.

Frank, Albert J. von. *An Emerson Chronology.* New York: Hall, 1994. Print.

Gibbon, Edward. *The History of the Decline and Fall of the Roman Empire. Christian Classics Ethereal Lib.* Christian Classics Ethereal Lib., 2000. Web. 16 July 2008.

Goethe, Johann Wolfgang von. *Nachgelassene Werke.* Vol. 6. Stuttgart: Cotta'sche, 1832–33. Print.

Hodgson, Marshall. *Rethinking World History.* Cambridge: Cambridge UP, 1993. Print.

Holy Qur'an. Trans. Abdullah Yusuf Ali. Cambridge: Murray, 1946. Print.

Irving, Washington. *The Alhambra.* Ed. William T. Lenehan and Andrew B. Myers. Boston: Twayne, 1983. Print.

Irwin, Robert. "The Emergence of the Islamic World System, 1000–1500." *The Cambridge Illustrated History of the Islamic World.* Ed. Francis Robinson. Cambridge: Cambridge UP, 1996. 32–61. Print.

Malcolm X with Alex Haley. *Autobiography of Malcolm X.* New York: Grove, 1966. Print.

McCloud, Aminah Beverly. *African American Islam.* New York: Routledge, 1995. Print.

McNeill, William H. *The Rise of the West: A History of the Human Community.* 1963. Chicago: U of Chicago P, 1991. Print.

Plessner, Martin. "The Natural Sciences and Medicine." Schacht and Bosworth 425–60.

Said, Edward. *Orientalism.* New York: Vintage, 1979. Print.

Sale, George, trans. *The Koran: Commonly Called the Alcoran of Muhammed: Translated into English Immediately from the Original Arabic.* London: Malden, 1801. Print.

Schacht, Joseph, and C. E. Bosworth, eds. *The Legacy of Islam.* Oxford: Clarendon, 1974. Print.

Smith, Jane L. *Islam in America.* New York: Columbia UP, 1999. Print.

Turner, Richard Brent. *Islam in the African-American Experience.* Bloomington: Indiana UP, 1997. Print.

Vernet, Juan. "Mathematics, Astronomy, Optics." Schacht and Bosworth 461–88.

Williams, Stanley T. *Life of Washington Irving.* New Haven: Yale UP, 1935. Print.

Yohannan, J. D. "Emerson's Translations of Persian Poetry from German Sources." *American Literature* 14 (1943): 407–20. Print.

Nikolai Endres

Worlds of Difference? Gay and Lesbian Texts across Cultures

In Gay and Lesbian Literature, an upper-level elective for English majors, I assign primary texts from a variety of histories and cultures, plus secondary works on critical theory and queer studies, and nonprint materials. Throughout the semester, we challenge and define the concepts of sex and gender, masculinities and feminisms, constructionism and essentialism, oppression and empowerment, acquiescence and resistance. Students will have broadened their insight into gay men's and lesbian women's awareness of sexuality dynamics—culturally, historically, globally.

We begin with Plato's *Symposium*.[1] I divide the class into groups and assign them one speech each. The group elects a spokesperson (similar to the election of a symposiarch in Plato) and advocates why their view of Eros is superior. This exercise leads to a spirited exchange or one-upmanship, in many ways replicating the homoerotically charged atmosphere of the banquet: one speaker makes a point; the other reacts against it. Next, Diotima's speech celebrates the philosophical over the physical, but who can live up to her lofty maxims? We are also faced with a dilemma. Not only does the love between two men have to cope with homophobia in our time, it is also the illegal love of an adult for a minor. Too, many students find the *erastes-eromenos* (lover-beloved) relationship unattractive.

Finally, all these attachments seem very different from how *we* perceive a homosexual lifestyle. Of course, I have been playing devil's advocate a bit, in order to steer into (homo)sexuality as constructed. Was Plato "gay"? We draw on reserve readings[2] and conclude that Greek society classified men and women in terms of penetrator and penetrated. I end on a musical note, Leonard Bernstein's *Serenade*, a highly idiosyncratic orchestral rendering of Plato's speakers:

> If there is a hint of jazz in the celebration, I hope it will not be taken as anachronistic Greek party music but rather as the natural expression of a contemporary American composer imbued with the spirit of that timeless dinner party. (Bernstein)

Petronius's *Satyricon* strikes my students as incredibly modern. As the protagonist and narrator Encolpius realizes, "shipwreck of some kind is everywhere" (95). In groups, we turn to the shipwrecks of love and sex, reality, men and women, the military, direction, life, the body, religion, education, the self. These shipwrecks are not all that different from the shipwrecks of our time, we realize. I have been deliberately withholding the essentialist scholarship on the history of sexuality, which I now introduce (e.g., Boswell; Brooten; Richlin; Skinner). Especially Amy Richlin's argument that what we call a homosexual nowadays was in Rome a "male penetrated by choice" (the *cinaedus* or *mollis*) and at home in a subculture surrounded by homophobia provides food for thought (526). Indeed, Rome seems to hit much closer to the American sexual ethos than solemn Plato. I supplement the *Satyricon* with Juvenal's satires 2 and 9, Suetonius's *Lives of the Caesars*, and Roman homoerotic poetry (available in Hubbard), all of which complicate our understanding of the cultural similarities and differences between us and Rome. I end with a movie, *Fellini Satyricon*.[3] How did an Italian filmmaker appropriate ancient Roman sexuality? How would the class put the *Satyricon* on the screen? Would it be a porn flick, an epic, a soap opera, an art movie, a road trip? Should a movie attempt to complete Petronius's fragment? Who would be the best American actors to play Encolpius, Giton, Ascyltos, and Eumolpus?

I then introduce the sodomites in Dante's *Inferno* (Musa), Titus and Gisippus in Boccaccio's *Decameron*, and the Pardoner in Chaucer's *Canterbury Tales* and briefly lecture on medieval sexualities[4] in order to transition to two seminal Renaissance texts. First, Shakespeare's sonnets (Wells). As a treat, I play Derek Jarman's experimental *The Angelic Conversation*, where fourteen of the sonnets are being read by Judi Dench against a young man's isolation and subsequent confrontation with another man. Drawing on Bruce Smith's study, I point out the different myths for conveying homosexual desire: combatants and comrades, the passionate shepherd, the shipwrecked youth, knights in shifts, master and minion. In class, we discuss bawdy language, homoerotic allusions, the speculations surrounding Mr. W. H., or the contrast between the master-mistress and the dark lady. Second, Christopher Marlowe's *Edward II*. In groups, we analyze the mastery of (homo)sexual and political desire; the carnivalesque nature of the court; the creation of a sodomitic order with Piers Gaveston as Edward's queen; the legendary homoerotic relationships evoked in the play: "The mightiest kings have had their minions: / Great Alexander loved Hephaestion / The conquering Hercules for Hylas wept, / And for Patroclus stern Achilles drooped" (1.4.391–94); class and race; Edward's firebrand death; the iconography of Ganymede as Zeus's beloved (see Saslow, *Ganymede*); and a comparison with Jarman's movie *Edward II*. Did the Renaissance permit homosexual identity and subjectivity? Once again, student reports enhance our grasp of Elizabethan sexuality.[5]

Oscar Wilde's erotic code in *The Picture of Dorian Gray* can be understood only through a specific examination of Wilde's life, of Victorian culture, and of literary models.[6] Wilde read all the works that we have discussed in class so far. He also traveled widely (France, Italy, the United States), coming in close contact with other cultures. How can "the love that dare not speak its name" be conveyed to men who love men? As William Cohen explains, *unspeakable* is "something *incapable* of being articulated as well as something *prohibited* from articulation" (3). We draw connections to modern homoerotic models: Charles Baudelaire on the dandy, decadent literature; J. K. Huysmans's *À Rebours* (almost all available in Fone). And just what kind of life is Dorian leading? With the help of a report on Walter Pater's "Conclusion" to *Studies in the Renaissance*, we get a better understanding of Dorian's promiscuity. Here, André Gide's *The Immoralist* (Wilde and Gide were friends) complements *Dorian Gray*. Michel openly leads Dorian's secret life—but comfortably, on a different continent, in the world of the arid desert and Arab boys. I ask why travel is so popular to gay men. A writing assignment students enjoy is a journal from Marceline's viewpoint. How much did she know about her husband's (homo)sexual escapades? Is she the devoted martyr who dies so her husband comes to life? Or did she not care because she too was having a secret affair? How would Marceline have reacted to a meeting between Michel and Dorian or Lord Henry, or between Michel and Bosie, Wilde's doomed lover? Once again, though focusing on Wilde, we have strayed to Athens and Africa, Florence and France.

Thomas Mann's *Death in Venice* assimilates different cultures: Homer's *Odyssey*, Plato's *Phaedrus*, Euripides's *Bacchae*, Friedrich Nietzsche's *The Birth of Tragedy*, and the music of Richard Wagner and Gustav Mahler. Since it is paper time, I ask students to focus on one of Mann's sources and investigate its place in the novella. If they want to look ahead, they are welcome to compare *Death* to Benjamin Britten's opera *Death in Venice* or the films *Morte a Venezia*, by Luchino Visconti (1971); *Death in Venice, CA*, by P. David Ebersole (1994); *Love and Death on Long Island*, by Richard Kwietniowski (1997); and *Gods and Monsters*, by Bill Condon (1998).

In class, we find that *Death* is a perversion of the *Phaedrus*, a monologue (arguably onanistic and autoorgasmic), a total failure of Platonic intercourse. Gustav Aschenbach loves Tadzio, but Tadzio only flirts with him, if that (moreover, he is tantalizingly silent). In groups, we examine philosophic vacation and erotic knowledge, Dionysian madness (mania) and sexual outrage (hubris), Apollonian animation and petrifaction. Eventually, we correct various homophobic readings of Mann's novella— homoeroticism involving effeminacy (Aschenbach in the beauty salon), corruption (the narrator's distancing himself from the protagonist), child molestation (*Knabenliebe*), and death—for they distort the Platonic heritage and Mann's biographical record, as collected statements from his diaries, letters, and essays underline. We also pay attention to the cholera, which, like AIDS, is a plague; it comes from elsewhere. Tuberculosis and syphilis, on the other hand, are modern or atavistic diseases that individualize their bearers. All things considered, Aschenbach is no dirty old man (students' frequent first impression), while Tadzio often comes off as a flirtatious brat and, as one student dismissed him, a "lousy twit."

For Marcel Proust's *Sodom and Gomorrah*, I ask what the Bible says about homosexuality. I am of course opening a can of worms, but students find it helpful to collect the relevant passages. At the same time, why is Roman Catholicism so attractive to many gay people? Eve Sedgwick provides a provocative compendium: "the shock of the possibility of adults who don't marry, of men in dresses, of passionate theatre, of introspective investment, of lives filled with what could, ideally without diminution, be called the work of the fetish" (140). How does Proust deviate from the Bible? How does the Baron de Charlus contrast with Socrates? I show Jean Delville's painting *Plato's Academy* (in Woods 5), where we see how Platonism has become Christianized for nineteenth-century tastes. (More representations may be found in Saslow, *Pictures*.) Christopher Robinson proposes that "the Greek love / master-pupil defence of homosexuality is not one in which Proust is interested. Indeed his narrator specifically states that it is a dead concept with no relevance to modern times" (46), but this view is a nice invitation for comparison. In groups, we investigate the various theories of homosexuality in Proust: medical-pathological, aesthetic-decadent, criminal-sociological, modern-stereotypical, and so on. To give students the whole picture, I supplement our reading with other relevant episodes (Mlle Vinteuil and her friend at Montjouvain, Albertine's covert lesbianism, Saint-Loup, the brothel in *Time Regained*), assign seminal Proust criticism (O'Brien; Rivers; Sedgwick 213–51), and end with a glimpse of Proust on his deathbed: the star-studded movie *Time Regained*, which assembles in stream-of-consciousness fashion Proust's inhabitants of Sodom and Gomorrah.

How about the United States? Gore Vidal's *The City and the Pillar*, published in 1948 and revised in 1965, was hailed as the first important American gay novel. I distribute a handout with discussion questions: Where did Vidal get the idea of Jim Willard's quest for a brother or twin? (Answer: Plato's Aristophanes.) Do you find gay stereotypes in the novel? Compare and contrast *City* and the *Satyricon*. How would you describe the erotic relationships in the novel? ("Dysfunctional" is inevitably the answer, but why and how so?) Explain Vidal's belief that *homosexual* should be an adjective only, not a noun. Do you find the ending (Jim raping—killing, in the original edition—Bob) unsatisfactory, offensive, or in keeping with the depiction of (homosexual) love in the novel? For background, I assign group presentations.[7] Moreover, many students know that Vidal stands out as an irreverent critic of academia, morality, and government. What kind of sexual politics, then, does he advocate? I bring in passages from his autobiography *Palimpsest* and his essay collection *United States* and close the period with an account of my personal contact with Vidal.

Mary Renault's *The Persian Boy* again evokes various cultures—Macedonian, Greek, Persian—and could not be more relevant in our post-9/11 world. Alexander advocates a multicultural society. How are the multiple cultural differences negotiated? Then, for our emphasis on sexuality, *The Persian Boy* offers a story told by a castrated man, someone who usually has no voice, who is a slave and sex toy. Love bridges, not class as in E. M. Forster's *Maurice*, but race. How about Bagoas's love for Alexander? Bagoas will initiate Alexander into manhood: his "subject position—as narrator of Alexander's story and Renault's text—and his object position—as Alexander's boy—problematizes not only gender but sex itself" (Zilboorg 225). At the same time, Bagoas is never oblivious of his sexual flaw: "I was like one who can play for the dancers, yet not dance" (26). Here I show a clip from the movie *Farinelli*. How does a castrato deal with his handicap—more specifically, how does Bagoas? In Platonic terms, his entire narration can be seen as the dissemination of his lost seed: "Bagoas must learn that procreating dreams is as satisfying as procreating sons" (Hoberman 291). Finally, we turn to Ed Stephan's Web site, which provides a bridge to yet another culture: the relationship between Alexander and Hephaestion is modeled on Achilles and Patroclus in the *Iliad*. Students will find this connection interesting because of the recent movie *Troy*, which ludicrously depicts the men as cousins. I also compare Alexander and Hephaestion with Harmodius and Aristogeiton (*Persian Boy* 251) and with Nisus and Euryalus in Vergil's *Aeneid*. Is this relationship an ultimately unattainable ideal of erotic reciprocity? I then have a group report on Gilgamesh and Enkidu, Achilles and Patroclus, and David and Jonathan (see Ackerman; Halperin 75-87), which enhances our understanding of these cross-cultural gay prototypes.

Yukio Mishima's *Forbidden Colors* is the perfect text to finish the gay part of the course. Though a non-Western novel, it reiterates many ideas we have addressed. It begins with Platonic erotics (and as in Plato, seduction occurs through *logos*, here the book *The Anointment of the Catamite*), ascends to an epic version of *Death in Venice*, and degenerates into a Wildean horror of Narcissus tiring of his mirror. Shunsuké alternately plays Socrates, Aschenbach, and Lord Henry to Yuichi. Sexual identities, gender roles, names, ages, marriages, all are unstable signifiers. Mishima drops many familiar names (Wilde, Beardsley, Alcibiades, Hadrian) and recites from a vast storehouse of world literature. Students, amazed by Mishima's modernity, investigate his literary appropriations. I introduce the quintessential Japanese icon: the samurai. Adult samurai often established bonds with boys before their coming-of-age ceremony. This is also an excellent time to address a common charge against gay literature: misogyny. We contrast the reactions of Yuichi's wife and his mother to his (forced) coming out. Yasuko is praised by students for her understanding; maybe she even knew all along. What do we make of the ending? Is Yuichi just despicable? Does Mrs. Kaburagi play Diotima to Yuichi? Minoru, who desires Yuichi to be his hero, seems to give true love. We began with Plato. Shunsuké may very well offer the most devastating verdict on Platonic love: "Briefly, you know very well that there is no such thing as emotion that is unconnected with sexual attraction. . . . [T]he word 'love' [is] a synonym for animal desire" (228).

For the second part of the course, I assign Sappho's poems. Students probe her relationship with Aphrodite and Eros, the former being her patroness, the latter often her antagonist. A love triangle? Sappho can also be claimed as the first feminist, rewriting the Homeric account of the Trojan War: "Helen whose beauty far outshone / The rest of man's chose to desert / The best of men: Willingly sailed away to Troy" (*Love Songs* 83). Sappho's Helen chose love over family, just as Sappho says, "I cannot mind my loom" (133). We also look at Sappho's self-awareness, her lyrical "I," her subjectivity—commonplace to us but revolutionary in her time. Too, her poetry is remarkably free of modern stereotypes of lesbians (butch, unemotional, coarse), while at the same time her relationships rely more on equality and thus differ markedly from the hydraulic model in Plato. I bring in Catullus's poem 62, a problematic but typical heterosexualization of Sappho (Reynolds, *Sappho Companion* 76 [fragment 31]). Another good activity is to have students complete some of Sappho's fragments or, since we are using an illustrated edition, to add appropriate drawings. How often do they get to write love poetry in class? Student reports deepen our understanding of Sappho's poetry of love and loss.[8] We finish with Sappho in popular culture. I play famous songs, such as Diana Ross's "Where Did Our Love Go?" or Madonna's "Like a Virgin," which draw on Sapphic images, or I offer my own impressions of Sappho in contemporary culture, who has lent her name to a stiff cocktail served in Mykonos, to dirty bookstores worldwide, and to Greek tavernas (with the store sign "Sappho Ate Here").

We then look at all the other extant sources on lesbianism in antiquity (culled from Hubbard). Plato's Aristophanes acknowledges lesbian love, but—given the homoerotic atmosphere of the dinner party—he is not interested in it. The Romans, however, grew increasingly preoccupied with women loving women and came to dismiss lesbianism as "monstrous, lawless, licentious, unnatural, and shameful" (Brooten 29), an attitude that remained, as students are quick to point out, unchanged for

Christian writers until recently. In groups, students analyze Seneca the Elder's two *tribades* (from Greek *tribein*, "to rub"), who are caught in bed; Ovid's Iphis and Ianthe and their sex change; Seneca the Younger's bald lesbians, who wrestle and vomit; Phaedrus's mythological tale of misplaced genitals; Martial's Philaenis with her strap-on dildo and predilection for cunnilingus; Juvenal's virulently misogynistic sixth satire; Plutarch's praise of Spartan women who loved virgins and his simultaneous abhorrence of such love in his own time; Lucian's account of perverse lesbian marriages and penis substitutes; Pseudo-Lucian's notion of lesbianism as both unspeakable and, because it does not lead to procreation, undesirable. Students also provide artistic evidence (in Brooten). I summarize the main representations of classical lesbians, such as masculinization, hellenization, and anachronization (see also Hallett). Equipped with a good understanding of lesbian desire in classical antiquity, we proceed to the twentieth century.

A great attention getter for Radclyffe Hall's *The Well of Loneliness* is to circulate pictures of Hall with her close-cropped hair, tailored jackets, flamboyant shirts, shrill ties, and wide-brimmed hats. Do lesbians today still look like her? What did they look like in Martial or Juvenal? We then collect the stereotypes of Stephen Gordon as a lesbian. For background, I have students research the various sexologies (Havelock Ellis, Richard Krafft-Ebing, Edward Carpenter, Karl Heinrich Ulrichs, Sigmund Freud) available to Hall. In groups, students look for images of wounds and sin and for other biblical symbols; contrast Stephen's parents, Sir Philip and Lady Anna; compare Stephen's relationships with Angela Crossby and Mary Llewellyn; decode Jonathan Brockett's gayness; and gather the various spaces in the novel and how they encode sexual desire. The most fruitful class discussions develop around the ending ("How depressing," students usually exclaim) and the merits of the trial of *The Well*, which was found obscene (interestingly, in the UK but not in the US). It is quite enlightening to look at the transcripts and early reviews (in Doan and Prosser). I also bring in a little biography to underline a central paradox in Hall's life. Despite a lifetime commitment to Una Lady Troubridge, Hall depicts lesbians in *The Well* as essentially doomed, unable to sustain meaningful relationships. How come? Could we set the novel in our time? Have we overcome the strictures Hall faced?

Rita Mae Brown's *Rubyfruit Jungle* invites comparison with Petronius. Encolpius and Molly Bolt play the picaro, the outsider who does not fit in. Refreshingly, Molly feels no need to apologize for her lesbianism (or for anything), defying stereotypes and refusing to conform:

> So now I wear this label "Queer" emblazoned across my chest. Or I could always carve a scarlet "L" on my forehead. Why does everyone have to put you in a box and nail the lid on it? I don't know what I am—polymorphous and perverse. (107)

We compare and contrast Molly's life in New York City with Jim Willard's, Molly's lovers with Sappho's addressees, Molly's in-your-face approach with the coyness of Proust's Albertine, and Molly's happiness with Stephen Gordon's depression. Other issues we go over are the choice of title, sexism in academia, origins, the famous lesbians on whom Molly models herself, the penis as a commodity, and Molly as a modern-day Huckleberry Finn (Brown's lesbianization of the canon). We end with all the examples of romantic love in the novel, most of which are embodied by movie stars. Since Molly aspires to make films, we eventually discuss the role of Hollywood in gay and lesbian culture. Inevitably, we finish with the beauties and faults of *Brokeback Mountain*, but that is another story.

The last week is taken up by group presentations. I remember great work on the laissez-faire world of the 1970s in Andrew Holleran's *Dancer from the Dance*, race and sexual deviancy in Audre Lorde's *Zami: A New Spelling of My Name*, or (my favorite) athletics and homosexuality in Patricia Nell Warren's *The Front Runner*. I expect these presentations to be well rehearsed, polished in both content and delivery, and accompanied by handouts. For the final exam, I try to provide questions that pull together many of our works:

1. Several gay and lesbian authors struggled with the representation of sexuality in their texts. What models did they use? How did they appropriate or deviate from these models? What constraints did they have to consider?
2. Discuss the problems associated with change. What kinds of change confront the characters? Is change recognition? Does change equal progress?
3. All our texts stress sexual difference. How does this trait interplay with other differences, such as race, class, age, ethnicity, gender?
4. Gaydar. How do our authors convey same-sex desire both in the texts and to their readers?

5. Location, location, location. How do various sites encode and facilitate same-sex attraction?

Judging from student evaluations and peer observations, the course works well. Students enjoy the open-forum format, the readings' historical reach, queer theory supplements, and IT ancillaries. They also appreciate our truly global approach, which has taken them to the worlds of ancient Mesopotamia, Mediterranean Lesbos, Persian harems, post–World War II Japan, and Coffee Hollow, Pennsylvania.

Notes

1. I am not a big fan of anthologies, which rely too much on snippets. Still, I draw on the following compilations to supplement class readings: Castle; Hubbard; Faderman; Fone. Also, I encourage my students to visit the online *GLBTQ: An Encyclopedia of Gay, Lesbian, Bisexual, Transgender, and Queer Culture*, whose entries are arranged by subject and exhaustively cross-referenced.

2. For example, Dover; Foucault, *History . . . Introduction* and *History . . . Use*; Halperin; Halperin, Winkler, and Zeitlin; Williams; Winkler. For later periods, see Rocke; Ruggiero.

3. Instructors will find a world of gay and lesbian movies in Daniel and Jackson.

4. My lecture is based on Boswell; Burger and Kruger; Burgwinkle; Dinshaw.

5. For Shakespeare, I assign Hammond; Pequigney; Oscar Wilde's "The Portrait of Mr. W. H." For Marlowe, see Bray, *Homosexuality* and "Homosexuality"; Bredbeck; DiGangi; Summers, "Sex."

6. For a more detailed proposal on how to teach *Dorian Gray* as a "gay" text, see Endres.

7. The presentations are based on Corber; D'Emilio; Summers, *"City"*; the Kinsey Report (Kinsey, Pomeroy, and Martin) or now the movie *Kinsey*.

8. Their reports are based on DuBois; Reynolds, *Sappho Companion* and *Sappho History*; Snyder; Vanita; Winkler 162–87.

Works Cited

Ackerman, Susan. *When Heroes Love: The Ambiguity of Eros in the Stories of Gilgamesh and David.* New York: Columbia UP, 2005. Print.

The Angelic Conversation. Dir. Derek Jarman. Perf. Paul Reynolds, Phillip Williamson, Judi Dench, Dave Baby, Timothy Burke. British Film Inst., 1985. Film.

Bernstein, Leonard. *Serenade for Solo Violin, Strings, Harps, and Percussion.* Perf. Hilary Hahn. Cond. David Zinman. Rec. 8 June 1998, Joseph Meyerhoff Symphony Hall, Baltimore. Sony, 1998. CD.

Boccaccio, Giovanni. *The Decameron.* Trans. G. H. McWilliam. New York: Penguin, 1972. Print.

Boswell, John. *Christianity, Social Tolerance, and Homosexuality: Gay People in Western Europe from the Beginning of the Christian Era to the Fourteenth Century.* Chicago: U of Chicago P, 1980. Print.

Bray, Alan. "Homosexuality and the Signs of Male Friendship in Elizabethan England." *Queering the Renaissance.* Ed. Jonathan Goldberg. Durham: Duke UP, 1994. 40–61. Print.

———. *Homosexuality in Renaissance England.* New York: Columbia UP, 1995. Print.

Bredbeck, Gregory W. *Sodomy and Interpretation: Marlowe to Milton.* Ithaca: Cornell UP, 1991. Print.

Brooten, Bernadette J. *Love between Women: Early Christian Responses to Female Homoeroticism.* Chicago: U of Chicago P, 1996. Print.

Brown, Rita Mae. *Rubyfruit Jungle.* New York: Bantam, 1973. Print.

Burger, Glenn, and Steven F. Kruger, eds. *Queering the Middle Ages.* Minneapolis: U of Minnesota P, 2001. Print.

Burgwinkle, William E. *Sodomy, Masculinity, and Law in Medieval Literature: France and England, 1050–1230.* New York: Cambridge UP, 2004. Print.

Castle, Terry, ed. *The Literature of Lesbianism: A Historical Anthology from Ariosto to Stonewall.* New York: Columbia UP, 2003. Print.

Chaucer, Geoffrey. *The Canterbury Tales.* Trans. Nevill Coghill. New York: Penguin, 2003. Print.

Cohen, William A. *Sex Scandal: The Private Parts of Victorian Fiction.* Durham: Duke UP, 1996. Print.

Corber, Robert J. *Homosexuality in Cold War America: Resistance and the Crisis of Masculinity.* Durham: Duke UP, 1997. Print.

Daniel, Lisa, and Claire Jackson, eds. *The Bent Lens: A World Guide to Gay and Lesbian Film.* 2nd ed. Los Angeles: Alyson, 2003. Print.

D'Emilio, John. *Sexual Politics, Sexual Communities: The Making of a Homosexual Minority in the United States, 1940–1970.* Chicago: U of Chicago P, 1983. Print.

DiGangi, Mario. "Marlowe, Queer Studies, and Renaissance Homoeroticism." *Marlowe, History, and Sexuality: New Critical Essays on Christopher Marlowe.* Ed. Paul Whitfield White. New York: AMS, 1998. 195–212. Print.

Dinshaw, Carolyn. *Getting Medieval: Sexualities and Communities, Pre- and Postmodern.* Durham: Duke UP, 1999. Print.

Doan, Laura, and Jay Prosser, eds. *Palatable Poison: Critical Perspectives on* The Well of Loneliness. New York: Columbia UP, 2001. Print.

Dover, Kenneth. *Greek Homosexuality.* Cambridge: Harvard UP, 1989. Print.

DuBois, Page. *Sappho Is Burning.* Chicago: U of Chicago P, 1995. Print.

Edward II. Dir. Derek Jarman. Perf. Steven Waddington, Andrew Tiernan, Tilda Swinton, Nigel Terry. BBC and Columbia Tristar, 1991. Film.

Endres, Nikolai. "Teaching *The Picture of Dorian Gray* as a 'Gay' Text." *Approaches to Teaching the Writings of Oscar Wilde.* Ed. Philip E. Smith. New York: MLA, 2008. 62–74. Print.

Faderman, Lillian, ed. *Chloe plus Olivia: An Anthology of Lesbian Literature from the Seventeenth Century to the Present.* Harmondsworth: Penguin, 1994. Print.

Farinelli: Il castrato. Dir. Gérard Corbiau. Perf. Stefano Dionisi, Enrico Lo Verso, Elsa Zylberstein. Columbia Tristar, 1995. Film.

Fellini Satyricon. Dir. Federico Fellini. Perf. Martin Potter, Hiram Keller, Salvo Randone, Max Born. MGM, 1968. Film.

Fone, Byrne R. S., ed. *The Columbia Anthology of Gay Literature.* New York: Columbia UP, 1998. Print.

Foucault, Michel. *The History of Sexuality: An Introduction.* Trans. Robert Hurley. New York: Pantheon, 1978. Print.

———. *The History of Sexuality: The Use of Pleasure.* Vol. 2. Trans. Robert Hurley. New York: Vintage, 1990. Print.

Gide, André. *The Immoralist.* Trans. David Watson. New York: Penguin, 2001. Print.

GLBTQ: An Encyclopedia of Gay, Lesbian, Bisexual, Transgender, and Queer Culture. Ed. Claude J. Summers. Glbtq, 2002–07. Web. 30 Mar. 2008.

Hall, Radclyffe. *The Well of Loneliness.* New York: Anchor, 1990. Print.

Hallett, Judith P. "Female Homoeroticism and the Denial of Roman Reality in Latin Literature." *Yale Journal of Criticism* 3 (1989): 209–27. Print.

Halperin, David M. *"One Hundred Years of Homosexuality" and Other Essays on Greek Love.* New York: Routledge, 1990. Print.

Halperin, David M., John J. Winkler, and Froma I. Zeitlin, eds. *Before Sexuality: The Construction of Erotic Experience in the Ancient Greek World.* Princeton: Princeton UP, 1990. Print.

Hammond, Paul. *Figuring Sex between Men from Shakespeare to Rochester.* Oxford: Clarendon, 2002. Print.

Hoberman, Ruth. "Masquing the Phallus: Genital Ambiguity in Mary Renault's Historical Novels." *Twentieth Century Literature* 42 (1996): 277–93. Print.

Hubbard, Thomas K., ed. *Homosexuality in Greece and Rome: A Sourcebook of Basic Documents.* Berkeley: U of California P, 2003. Print.

Kinsey. Dir. Bill Condon. Perf. Liam Neeson, Laura Linney, Chris O'Donnell, Peter Sarsgaard, and Timothy Hutton. Twentieth Century Fox, 2004. Film.

Kinsey, Alfred C., Wardell B. Pomeroy, and Clyde E. Martin. *Sexual Behavior in the Human Male.* Philadelphia: Saunders, 1948. Print.

The Love Songs of Sappho. Trans. Paul Roche. New York: Signet, 1966. Print.

Mann, Thomas. Death in Venice*: A New Translation, Backgrounds and Contexts, Criticism.* Trans. Clayton Koelb. New York: Norton, 1994. Print.

Marlowe, Christopher. *Edward II.* Doctor Faustus *and Other Plays.* Ed. David Bevington and Eric Rasmussen. Oxford: Oxford UP, 1995. 323–402. Print.

Mishima, Yukio. *Forbidden Colors.* Trans. Alfred H. Marks. New York: Vintage, 1999. Print.

Musa, Mark, ed. *The Portable Dante.* New York: Penguin, 1995. Print.

O'Brien, Justin. "Albertine the Ambiguous: Notes on Proust's Transposition of Sexes." *PMLA* 64.5 (1949): 933–52. Print.

Pater, Walter. *The Renaissance: Studies in Art and Poetry.* Ed. Donald L. Hill. Berkeley: U of California P, 1980. Print.

Pequigney, Joseph. *Such Is My Love: A Study of Shakespeare's Sonnets.* Chicago: U of Chicago P, 1985. Print.

Petronius. *Satyricon*. Trans. Sarah Ruden. Indianapolis: Hackett, 2000. Print.

Plato. *Symposium*. Trans. Alexander Nehamas and Paul Woodruff. Indianapolis: Hackett, 1989. Print.

Proust, Marcel. *Sodom and Gomorrah*. Trans. John Sturrock. New York: Viking, 2004. Print.

Renault, Mary. *The Persian Boy*. New York: Vintage, 1988. Print.

Reynolds, Margaret, ed. *The Sappho Companion*. London: Chatto, 2000. Print.

———. *The Sappho History*. New York: Palgrave-Macmillan, 2003. Print.

Richlin, Amy. "Not before Homosexuality: The Materiality of the *Cinaedus* and the Roman Law against Love between Men." *Journal of the History of Sexuality* 3 (1993): 523–73. Print.

Rivers, J. E. *Proust and the Art of Love: The Aesthetics of Sexuality in the Life, Times, and Art of Marcel Proust*. New York: Columbia UP, 1980. Print.

Robinson, Christopher. *Scandal in the Ink: Male and Female Homosexuality in Twentieth-Century French Literature*. London: Cassell, 1995. Print.

Rocke, Michael. *Forbidden Friendships: Homosexuality and Male Culture in Renaissance Florence*. New York: Oxford UP, 1996. Print.

Ruggiero, Guido. *The Boundaries of Eros: Sex Crime and Sexuality in Renaissance Venice*. New York: Oxford UP, 1985. Print.

Saslow, James M. *Ganymede in the Renaissance: Homosexuality in Art and Society*. New Haven: Yale UP, 1986. Print.

———. *Pictures and Passions: A History of Homosexuality in the Visual Arts*. New York: Viking, 1999. Print.

Sedgwick, Eve Kosofsky. *Epistemology of the Closet*. Berkeley: U of California P, 1990. Print.

Skinner, Marilyn B. *Sexuality in Greek and Roman Culture*. Malden: Blackwell, 2005. Print.

Smith, Bruce R. *Homosexual Desire in Shakespeare's England: A Cultural Poetics*. Chicago: U of Chicago P, 1991. Print.

Snyder, Jane McIntosh. *Lesbian Desire in the Lyrics of Sappho*. New York: Columbia UP, 1997. Print.

Stephan, Ed. *The Greek World of Mary Renault*. Stephan, n.d. Web. 30 Mar. 2008.

Summers, Claude J. "*The City and the Pillar* as Gay Fiction." *Gore Vidal: Writer against the Grain*. Ed. Jay Parini. New York: Columbia UP, 1992. 56–75. Print.

———. "Sex, Politics, and Self-Realization in *Edward II*." *"A Poet and a Filthy Play-maker": New Essays on Christopher Marlowe*. Ed. Kenneth Friedenreich, Roma Gill, and Constance B. Kuriyama. New York: AMS, 1988. 221–40. Print.

Time Regained. Dir. Raoul Ruiz. Perf. Catherine Deneuve, Emmanuelle Béart, John Malkovich, Vincent Perez, Pascal Greggory. Artificial Eye, 1999. Film.

Troy. Dir. Wolfgang Peterson. Perf. Brad Pitt, Eric Bana, Orlando Bloom, Brian Cox, Peter O'Toole. Warner, 2004. Film.

Vanita, Ruth. *Sappho and the Virgin Mary: Same-Sex Love and the English Literary Imagination*. New York: Columbia UP, 1996. Print.

Vidal, Gore. The City and the Pillar *and Seven Early Stories*. New York: Random, 1995. Print.

———. *Palimpsest: A Memoir*. New York: Random, 1995. Print.

———. *United States: Essays, 1952–1992*. New York: Random, 1993. Print.

Wells, Stanley, ed. *Shakespeare's Sonnets and* A Lover's Complaint. Oxford: Oxford UP, 1987. Print.

Wilde, Oscar. *The Picture of Dorian Gray*. Ed. Donald L. Lawler. New York: Norton, 1988. Print.

Williams, Craig A. *Roman Homosexuality: Ideologies of Masculinity in Classical Antiquity*. New York: Oxford UP, 1999. Print.

Winkler, John J. *The Constraints of Desire: The Anthropology of Sex and Gender in Ancient Greece*. New York: Routledge, 1990. Print.

Woods, Gregory. *A History of Gay Literature: The Male Tradition*. New Haven: Yale UP, 1998. Print.

Zilboorg, Caroline. *The Masks of Mary Renault: A Literary Biography*. Columbia: U of Missouri P, 2001. Print.

Carol Fadda-Conrey

Middle Eastern Literature: An Introduction

The course Middle Eastern Literature is designed to offer graduate students a wide-ranging introduction to the field, extending from the pre-Islamic era to the present and including works in translation as well as texts written in English. The selection of texts by Arab and non-Arab authors writing in the Middle East and beyond is meant to situate Arab and Islamic literatures in a broader world context, with special emphasis placed on the multitude of cultures, religions, historical backgrounds, and ethnicities that fall under the Middle Eastern rubric. The thematic focus developed in this course offers a wide representation of prominent as well as emergent writers and texts. The course objective is to help students incorporate feminist, historical, transnational, and cross-cultural methodological tools in their textual analysis. With these tools, students can better negotiate many cultural perspectives both inside and outside the classroom and achieve a better understanding of aesthetics, culture, and history as presented through Middle Eastern literature.

The course syllabus is divided into five sections. Each section develops a theme that draws on a selection of writers and texts from different time periods, genres, and geographic locations. The first, entitled "Spirituality and Religion," features a mix of religious and nonreligious texts that represent some of the faiths originating in the region. With primary attention given to Islam, this section includes Qur'anic scripture and poetry dating from the Islamic period to the present, followed by Orhan Pamuk's novel *Snow*, which underscores the current religious debates and tensions, in Turkey and elsewhere, between Islamic fundamentalism and Western and secular values.

The second section, "Literature of War, Resistance, and Nationalism," introduces students to literary selections covering some key historical milestones and events that continue to define the contemporary Middle East, including the Palestinian-Israeli conflict and the Lebanese civil war. In addition to writers like Mahmoud Darwish, Fadwa Tuqan, and Etel Adnan, a group of new voices is featured to mark the continuation of the struggle amid war and occupation from one generation of Middle Eastern writers to another. Reacting to more recent events like the United States–led wars against Afghanistan and Iraq, writers like Suheir Hammad and Dima Hilal articulate their concerns from outside the geographic boundaries of the Arab and Middle Eastern world, thus widening the borders of national belonging to encompass Arab-American identities.

From religious and nationalist discussions, the third section of the syllabus moves on to topics of gender, love, and sexuality as handled in literature from the pre-Islamic period to the present. Although poetry, a staple genre of Middle Eastern literature, dominates this section, it is complemented by selections of fiction, drama, and an essay on the famous Egyptian singer Umm Kulthum. The four short poems by Wallada, along with Layla B'albakki's short story "A Space Ship of Tenderness to the Moon" (for which B'albakki was put on trial, on the charge of obscenity), emphasize the outspokenness of many of this region's writers when it comes to issues of love and sex. The portrayal of homosexual desire in the selected texts by Rabih Alameddine and Hanan al-Shaykh further breaks down the sexual taboos prevalent in many Middle Eastern cultures. Other taboo topics, such as incest, rape, and pedophilia, are handled by Ahdaf Soueif and Betty Shamieh. The section closes with Tahar Ben Jelloun's novel *The Sand Child*, in which a Moroccan father's longing for a son drives the father to raise his daughter as a boy.

The next section, "Feminism and Islam," develops issues raised in the previous texts. A comparative approach traces the historical development of feminism in Islam, highlighting works by early feminist thinkers like Warda al-Yaziji and Huda Shaarawi, followed by works by some of their intellectual descendants, such as Nawal El Saadawi and Leila Ahmed.

Other important feminists like Fatema Mernissi and Assia Djebar add a francophone element to the course readings. Ending this section with Marjane Satrapi's graphic novel *Persepolis*, another work translated from French, exposes students to the historical repercussions of the Iranian Revolution and the subsequent Iran-Iraq war, as depicted from the narrator's point of view. Recent contributions to Muslim feminist writing include pieces that discuss Afghani women under Taliban rule, written by Alison Donnell, by Binar Sharif, and by the Revolutionary Association of the Women of Afghanistan. These three texts are important additions, since they offer up-to-date discussions of women and Islam, even though Afghanistan falls outside the scope of the Middle Eastern region.

The last section, "Flexible Identities: Literature of Home and Exile," facilitates an international approach to the study of Middle Eastern literature by mainly focusing on an array of Arab American writers, including immigrant writers from the early twentieth century (Gibran Khalil Gibran and Ameen Rihani) as well as contemporary diasporic writers (Edward Said, Ella Shohat, and Pauline Kaldas). Their works provide insights into the lives and concerns of Arab Americans and are used to trace commonalities and differences between these writers and their Middle Eastern counterparts. Also in this section is the Palestinian writer Mourid Barghouti, who has spent most of his life in exile. Barghouti's *I Saw Ramallah*, a moving autobiographical narrative about the writer's return to his Palestinian home, complements Satrapi's return narrative to Iran in *Persepolis 2*, thus linking the different sections of the syllabus in ways that reinforce its thematic coherence.

Despite the converging global concerns and issues raised by these interconnections, there still exist strong regional traits, which are underscored and featured by each of these texts. The Middle Eastern rubric is helpful as an umbrella term but should not eclipse the differences (in dialect, religion, politics, etc.) that exist between one Middle Eastern country and another or even those traits (whether related to class, ethnicity, political affiliation, education, or religion) that differentiate various groups in the same country. In other words, even though the pieces selected for this syllabus collectively represent Middle Eastern literature as a whole, the intrinsic nuances that result from their national and regional roots cannot be ignored. Both Adnan's *Sitt Marie Rose* and Satrapi's *Persepolis: The Story of a Childhood* portray war experiences (the first in the Lebanese civil war [1975–90], the second in the Iran-Iraq war [1980–88]), but each portrays armed conflict from different national, historical, and cultural vantage points, thus underscoring the variations that exist among the national literatures of the region. This type of syllabus, then, emphasizes not only the importance of the regional roots of world literature but also the vast array of characteristics distinguishing these regional connections.

Course Syllabus

Spirituality and Religion

Week 1   Fatima Bint Muhammad (605–32) was daughter of Prophet Muhammad and his first wife, Khadija. Rabi'a al-Adawiyya (c. 714–801), born in Iraq, was one of the first Sufi poets. Al-Ghazali (1058–111), mystic, philosopher, and theologian, was born in Tus, Khorasan, a province of Persia. Hafiz (meaning one who has memorized the entire Qur'an by heart), a well-known Sufi poet and mystic, was born in Shiraz, Persia (c. 1320–89).

Monday   Introduction

Wednesday The Qur'an: sura 12, Joseph, in Kritzeck (37–45)

Fatima Bint Muhammad (early Islamic period), "Those Who Smell the Soil," "The Sky Turned Grey" (poetry), in Al-Udhari (64–67)

Friday   Rabi'a al-Adawiyya (Abbasid period), "I Put You in My Heart," "I Love You a Double Love" (poetry), in Al-Udhari (102–05)

Al-Ghazali (early Islamic Persia), "Confessions of a Troubled Believer" (essay), in Kritzeck (170–79)

Hafiz (early Islamic Persia), selections from Divan (poetry), in Kritzeck (267–73)

Week 2   Winner of the 1988 Nobel Prize for Literature, Naguib Mahfouz (1911–2006) is one of the most acclaimed contemporary Egyptian writers. Tayba Hassan is a protection officer for the United Nations High Commission for Refugees and the International Rescue Committee in Egypt. 'Abd al-Wahhab al-Bayati (1926–99), a pioneer of modern Arabic poetry, was born in Baghdad but lived outside Iraq for more than half his life. Mohja Kahf is a Syrian American poet, novelist, essayist, and short story writer. She is an associate professor of comparative literature at the University of Arkansas, Fayetteville, and a regular contributor to the "Sex and the Umma" column on the *Muslim WakeUp!* Web site.

Monday   Naguib Mahfouz (Egypt), "A Voice from the Other World" (short story), in Mahfouz (59–75)

Wednesday Tayba Hassan al Khalifa Sharif (Sudan), "Sacred Narratives Linking Iraqi Shiite Women" (essay), in Badran and Cooke (436–45)

'Abd al-Wahhab al-Bayati (Iraq), "The Birth of Aisha and Her Death," "Elegy for Aisha" (poetry), in Jayyusi (171–79)

Friday	Mohja Kahf (Syria and US), "Little Mosque Poems" (poetry), in Afzal-Khan (116–23), "The Muslim in the Mirror" (essay), in Abdul-Ghafur (130–38)
Week 3	The novelist Orhan Pamuk was born in Turkey in 1952. His work has been translated into more than thirty languages, and he is the recipient of major Turkish and international literary awards.
Monday	Orhan Pamuk (Turkey), *Snow* (novel)
Wednesday	Orhan Pamuk (Turkey), *Snow* (novel)
Friday	Orhan Pamuk (Turkey), *Snow* (novel)

Literature of War, Resistance, and Nationalism

Week 4	The Palestinian writer Fadwa Tuqan (1917–2003) was one of the leaders of the use of free verse in Arabic poetry. Yehuda Amichai (1924–2000) was born in Würzburg, Germany, to an Orthodox Jewish family. One of Israel's best-known poets, he was among the first to compose poems in colloquial Israeli Hebrew. Born in Palestine, the writer and journalist Mahmoud Darwish is widely recognized as one of the major voices of the Palestinian struggle. Ghassan Kanafani (1926–72) was a well-known novelist, short-story writer, and dramatist whose works are marked by the themes of displacement, exile, and national struggle. Dahlia Ravikovitch and Nessia Shafran were both born in Israel. The former is a celebrated poet, and the latter's memoir is entitled *Farewell Communism* (1981).
Monday	Fadwa Tuqan (Palestine), "Enough for Me," "Song of Becoming" (poetry), in Davis et al. (539–40)
	Yehuda Amichai (Israel), "Sort of an Apocalypse" "God Has Pity on Kindergarten Children" (poetry), in Davis et al. (541–42)
	Mahmoud Darwish (Palestine), "Diary of a Palestinian Wound," "Poems after Beirut" (poetry), in Jayyusi (200–02, 207–09)
Wednesday	Ghassan Kanafani (Palestine), "Men in the Sun" (short story), in Kanafani (21–74)
Friday	Dahlia Ravikovitch (Israel), "One Cannot Kill a Baby Twice" (poetry), in Cooke and Rustomji-Kerns (46–47)
	Nessia Shafran (Israel), "Long Live Jewish-Arab Friendship" (memoir), in Cooke and Rustomji-Kerns (105–16)
Week 5	Born in Algiers, Marie-Aimée Helie-Lucas is a sociologist and social anthropologist interested in feminist issues involving women and Islam. Adnan was born in Beirut in 1925 and has lived in the United States and France for long periods of time. An acclaimed writer and thinker, she works in fiction, poetry, drama, essays, and visual art.
Monday	Marie-Aimée Helie-Lucas (Algeria), "Women, Nationalism, and Religion in the Algerian Liberation Struggle" (essay), in Badran and Cooke (104–14)

Wednesday	Etel Adnan (Lebanon), *Sitt Marie Rose* (novel)
Friday	Etel Adnan (Lebanon), *Sitt Marie Rose* (novel)
Week 6	Born in Syria in 1930 and now living in Lebanon, Adonis (Ali Ahmad Said Asbar) is considered to be one of the most important modern Arab poets. Nazım Hikmet (1902–63) is a well-known figure in twentieth-century Turkish literature. His works are celebrated in the West, but he was condemned in his country for his Marxist thinking and imprisoned for seventeen years. Saadi Youssef, born in Basra in 1934, is one of the leading poets in the Arab world. Nada Elia was a war correspondent in Beirut during the 1980s and received her doctorate in comparative literature from Purdue University. Suheir Hammad, a Palestinian American poet and activist, was born in Jordan in 1973, then moved with her family to Brooklyn at the age of five. Nathalie Handal is a Palestinian American poet, playwright, and a cultural and literary activist who has lived in the United States, Europe, the Middle East, Latin America, and the Caribbean. Dima Hilal is a poet and writer, born in Beirut and raised in California, where she studied at the University of California, Berkeley.
Monday	Adonis (Syria and Lebanon), "I Am Confused, My Country," "In the Murderous Age," "Approach, You Wretched of the Earth" (poetry), in Adonis (15, 39, 69)
	Nazım Hikmet (Turkey), "Istanbul House of Detention," "Some Advice to Those Who Will Serve Time in Prison" (poetry), in Hikmet (80–83, 143–44)
Wednesday	Saadi Youssef (Iraq), "Days of June," "America, America" (poetry), in Youssef (107–09, 172–76)
	Nada Elia (Palestine and US), "A Woman's Place Is in the Struggle: A Personal Viewpoint on Feminism, Pacifism, and the Gulf War" (essay), in Kadi (114–19)
Friday	Suheir Hammad (Palestine and US), "First Writing Since" (poetry), in Afzal-Khan (90–94)
	Nathalie Handal (Palestine, Caribbean, US), "First Bombing" (poetry), in Afzal-Khan (94–96)
	Dima Hilal (Lebanon and US), "America" (poetry), in Darraj (104–06)

Gender, Love, and Sexuality

Week 7	ʿAntara, of the sixth century ʿAbs tribe, is believed to have been born to a slave of his father's, but then he rose to become the chief of his tribe. He is the hero of the celebrated *Romance of ʿAntar*. Aaʿisha bint Ahmad (d. 1010) was a poet and calligrapher living in Moorish Cordoba. The poet Wallada (c. 1001–80) was the daughter of the Umayyad Caliph Mustakfi of Cordoba. Qabbani (1923–98) was widely known around the Arab world for his

sensual and romantic poems. Ibtisam al-Mutawwakal was born and raised in Yemen, where she studied at Sana'a University.

Monday   'Antara Ibn Shaddad (pre-Islamic period), *The Mu'allaqa* (poetry), in Sells (45–56)

Wednesday   Aa'isha bint Ahmad al-Qurtubiyya (Muslim Andalusia), "I Am a Lioness" (poetry) in Al-Udhari (160)

Wallada bint al-Mustakfi (Muslim Andalusia), "If You Were Faithful," "Ibn Zaidun, in Spite," "Ibn Zaidun, Though," "Is There a Way" (poetry), in Al-Udhari (188, 190, 192, 194)

Friday   Nizar Qabbani (Syria), "Two African Breasts," "Language" (poetry), in Jayyusi (371–73, 375)

Ibtisam al-Mutawwakal (Yemen), "How to Become a Man," "The First Letters" (poetry), in Badran and Cooke (419–21)

Week 8   Born in Tehran to a middle-class family, Furugh Farrukhzad (1935–67) was a modern poet known for her courage and outspokenness. Layla B'albakki, born into a traditional Lebanese Shi'ite family, writes about controversial topics such as women's sexuality and the positions women occupy in the Arab world. Betty Shamieh is a Palestinian American playwright and actor whose plays have toured widely in the United States. Daisy Al-Amir was born in Baghdad in 1935. She has published seven volumes of short stories, a selection of which (*The Waiting List*) is available in translation. Economist, activist, and poet, Su'ad al-Mubarak al-Sabah has published numerous books on the Kuwaiti economy and three volumes of poetry.

Monday   Furugh Farrukhzad (Iran), "The Hidden Dream," "The Sin" (poetry), in Fernea and Bezirgan (295, 297)

Layla B'albakki (Lebanon), "A Space Ship of Tenderness to the Moon" (short story), in Fernea and Bezirgan (273–79)

Wednesday   Betty Shamieh (Palestine and US), *Chocolate in Heat: Growing Up Arab in America* (play), in Afzal-Khan (303–25)

Friday   Daisy Al-Amir (Iraq), "The Cat, the Maid, and the Wife" (short story), in Cohen-Mor (129–32)

Su'ad al-Mubarak al-Sabah (Kuwait), "Mad Woman," "You Alone" (poetry), in Handal (258)

Week 9   Trained to sing traditional Islamic songs with her father, Umm Kulthum (1904?–75) rose to stardom during the 1930s and 1940s to become the most famous singer in the Arab world. The Lebanese American fiction writer and painter Rabih Alameddine lives between the United States and Lebanon, and his works poignantly address the horrors of the Lebanese civil war. The fiction writer Ahdaf Soueif, educated in Cairo and England, writes in both English and Arabic. Her most recent work is *Mezzaterra* (2004). One of the most acclaimed contemporary

	Lebanese authors, Hanan al-Shaykh has garnered a lot of attention and praise for her novels and short stories alike.
Monday	Umm Kulthum (Egypt), "The Umm Kulthum Nobody Knows" (memoir), in Fernea and Bezirgan (135–65)
Wednesday	Rabih Alameddine (Lebanon and US), "Remembering Nasser" (short story), in Alameddine (177–93)
	Ahdaf Soueif (Egypt and England), "The Water-Heater" (short story), in Soueif (65–85)
Friday	Hanan al-Shaykh (Lebanon and England), "Suha" (excerpt from novel), in al-Shaykh (3–80)
Week 10	Tahar Ben Jelloun was born in Fez in 1944 and has lived in France since 1971. He is an internationally known novelist, playwright, poet, and essayist and has won numerous awards for his writing.
Monday	Tahar Ben Jelloun (Morocco), *The Sand Child* (novel)
Wednesday	Tahar Ben Jelloun (Morocco), *The Sand Child* (novel)
Friday	Tahar Ben Jelloun (Morocco), *The Sand Child* (novel)

Feminism and Islam

Week 11	Warda Al-Yaziji (1838–1924) was born in Lebanon and then moved to Egypt in 1899 after the death of her husband. She was skilled in the Arabic language and began writing poetry at the age of thirteen. May Ziyada (1886–1941), a leading intellectual, was born to a Palestinian father and a Lebanese mother. She emigrated to Cairo with her parents in 1908, where she lived for the rest of her life. Huda Shaarawi (1879–1947), born in Upper Egypt to a landowning family, was a leading feminist activist and writer of her time. Nawal El Saadawi, a trained medical doctor, is one of the most prominent contemporary Arab feminist writers and thinkers. Her works include essays that led to her imprisonment in 1981. Leila Ahmed teaches at Harvard Divinity School, where she is the first professor of women's studies and religion. Her works include *Women and Gender in Islam* (1993) and her memoir, *A Border Passage* (2000), about growing up in Egypt and emigrating to the United States.
Monday	Warda al-Yaziji (Lebanon), "Epistolary Poem to Warda al-Turk" (poetry), in Badran and Cooke (21–22)
	May Ziyada (Palestine), "Warda al-Yaziji" (essay), in Badran and Cooke (239–43)
	Huda Shaarawi (Egypt), "Pan-Arab Feminism" (lecture), "Farewell, Betrothal, and Wedding" (memoir), in Badran and Cooke (337–40, 42–48)
Wednesday	Nawal El Saadawi (Egypt), "Women and Islam," "Why Keep Asking Me about My Identity?" (essays), in Saadawi (73–92, 117–33)

Friday	Leila Ahmed (Egypt), "The Discourse of the Veil" (essay), in Ahmed (144–68)
Week 12	Assia Djebar was born in a small coastal town near Algiers in 1936. Her feminist voice is well known in North Africa and around the world. In her fiction, films, and essays, she tackles pertinent issues about women and Islam. Fatema Mernissi is a contemporary Moroccan feminist writer and thinker. Her memoir, *Dreams of Trespass* (1995), narrates her experience of being born in a harem in Fez. Alison Donnell is a senior lecturer in postcolonial literatures at Nottingham Trent University. Her work deals with women's writing and Caribbean literature. Bina Sharif, a Pakistani American, is an actress, playwright, poet, and director whose plays have been shown in the United States, Pakistan, and Europe. The Revolutionary Association of the Women of Afghanistan, established in Kabul in 1977, is a social and political organization of Afghani women fighting for freedom and women's rights. Marjane Satrapi has received great acclaim for her graphic novels. She grew up in Tehran and currently lives in Paris.
Monday	Assia Djebar (Algeria), "Forbidden Gaze, Severed Sound" (essay), in Djebar (133–51)
	Fatema Mernissi (Morocco), "The Mind as Erotic Weapon," "Scheherazade Goes West" (essay), in Mernissi (43–60, 61–78)
Wednesday	Alison Donnell (England), "Visibility, Violence, and Voice? Attitudes to Veiling Post-11 September" (essay), in Bailey and Tawadros (122–35)
	Bina Sharif (Pakistan and US), "An Afghan Woman" (one-woman play), in Afzal-Khan (246–53)
	Revolutionary Association of the Women of Afghanistan (RAWA), "Bin Laden Is Not Afghanistan" (essay), in Hawthorne and Winter (37–38)
Friday	Marjane Satrapi (Iran), *Persepolis: The Story of a Childhood* (graphic novel)
Week 13	
Monday	*Persepolis: The Story of a Childhood*
Wednesday	*Persepolis 2: The Story of a Return*
Friday	*Persepolis 2: The Story of a Return*`

Flexible Identities: Literature of Home and Exile

Week 14	Ameen Rihani (1876–1940) was born in Lebanon and emigrated to the United States at the age of twelve. He is one of the first Arab American writers to gain wide critical acclaim for his essays, poetry, short stories, and plays. Along with Gibran Khalil Gibran, he was one of the major figures of the New York Pen League, established in 1920. Gibran (1883–1931) is another major figure in early-twentieth-century Arab American literature. He was born in

a small village in the north of Lebanon and left for the United States at a young age. Writing alongside such greats as D. H. Lawrence, Sherwood Anderson, and Robert Frost, Gibran had a remarkable influence on Arabic literature, and his works became well known in the United States. Edward Said (1935–2003) is considered one of the most influential writers and thinkers of the contemporary period, his book *Orientalism* (1978) being a major work of postcolonial studies. Rabab Abdulhadi is a Palestinian American scholar who writes on transnational feminism, globalization, and postcolonialism. Naomi Shibab Nye is one of the best known Arab American poets. Her numerous works include poetry collections, children's books, and edited anthologies. The Arab American scholar, poet, and political activist Lisa Suheir Majaj has published extensively in the field of Arab American, Arab, and postcolonial literature.

Monday
Ameen Rihani (Lebanon and US), "I Dreamt I Was a Donkey Boy Again," excerpt from *A Chant of Mystics* (poetry), in Orfalea and Elmusa (5–6, 11–15)

Gibran Khalil Gibran (Lebanon and US), "Dead Are My People," excerpt from *Khalil the Heretic* (poetry), in Orfalea and Elmusa (31, 23–25)

Wednesday   Edward Said (Palestine and US), "Reflections on Exile" (essay), in Said (173–86)

Rabab Abdulhadi (Palestine and US), "Where Is Home? Fragmented Lives, Border Crossings, and the Politics of Exile" (essay), in Afzal-Khan (71–83)

Friday
Naomi Shihab Nye (Palestine and US) "Arabic," "Blood," "My Father and the Figtree" (poetry), in Davis et al. (1386–89)

Lisa Suheir Majaj (Jordan and US), "Boundaries: Arab/American" (essay), in Kadi (65–84)

Week 15
Born in 1944, Mourid Barghouti is an acclaimed Palestinian poet. He spent most of his life in exile, living in places like Budapest, Kuwait, and Egypt. He currently lives in Cairo.

Monday   Mourid Barghouti (Palestine), *I Saw Ramallah* (novel)

Wednesday   Mourid Barghouti (Palestine), *I Saw Ramallah* (novel)

Friday   Mourid Barghouti (Palestine), *I Saw Ramallah* (novel)

Week 16
For a description of Handal, see above, week 6. Evelyn Alsultany is a scholar working in the field of Arab American studies. With Rabab Abdulhadi and Nadine Naber, she edited the issue of the *MIT Electronic Journal of Middle East Studies* titled *Gender, Nation and Belonging, Arab and Arab-American Feminism.* Pauline Kaldas is an Egyptian American writer who is the editor, with Khaled Mattawa, of the first anthology of Arab American short stories, titled *Dinarzad's Children.* Ella Shohat is an Arab Jewish

writer and activist who is professor of cultural studies and women's studies at the City University of New York (CUNY).

Monday   Nathalie Handal (Palestine, Caribbean, US), "El almuerzo de Tia Habiba" (poetry), in Darraj (42–43), "Shades of a Bridge's Breath" (essay), in Anzaldúa and Keating (158–65)

Wednesday   Evelyn Alsultany (Iraq, Cuba, US), "Los Intersticios: Recasting Moving Selves" (essay), in Anzaldúa and Keating (106–11)

Pauline Kaldas (Egypt), "Home" (poetry), in Handal (146–47)

Friday   Ella Shohat (Iraq, Israel, US), "Coming to America: Reflections on Hair and Exile" (essay), in Amireh and Majaj (284–300)

Note

I would like to thank Mohja Kahf, Steven Salaita, and Ghia Osseiran for suggesting texts to include in this syllabus.

Works Cited

Abdul-Ghafur, Saleemah, ed. *Living Islam Out Loud: American Muslim Women Speak*. Boston: Beacon, 2005. Print.

Adnan, Etel. *Sitt Marie Rose*. Trans. Georgina Kleege. Sausalito: Post-Apollo, 1989. Print.

Adonis. *A Time between Ashes and Roses*. Trans. Shawkat M. Toorawa. Syracuse: Syrcause UP, 2004. Print.

Afzal-Khan, Fawzia, ed. *Shattering the Stereotypes: Muslim Women Speak Out*. Northampton: Olive Branch, 2005. Print.

Ahmed, Leila. *Women and Gender in Islam: Historical Roots of a Modern Debate*. New Haven: Yale UP, 1992. Print.

Alameddine, Rabih. *The Perv*. New York: Picador, 1999. Print.

Amireh, Amal, and Lisa Suhair Majaj, eds. *Going Global: The Transnational Reception of Third World Women Writers*. New York: Garland, 2000. Print.

Anzaldúa, Gloria E., and Analouise Keating, eds. *This Bridge We Call Home: Radical Visions for Transformation*. New York: Routledge, 2002. Print.

Badran, Margot, and Miriam Cooke, eds. *Opening the Gates: An Anthology of Arab Feminist Writing*. 2nd ed. Bloomington: Indiana UP, 2004. Print.

Bailey, David A., and Gilane Tawadros, eds. *Veil: Veiling, Representation, and Contemporary Art*. Cambridge: MIT P, 2003. Print.

Barghouti, Mourid. *I Saw Ramallah*. Trans. Ahdaf Soueif. New York: Anchor, 2003. Print.

Ben Jelloun, Tahar. *The Sand Child*. Trans. Alan Sheridan. Baltimore: Johns Hopkins UP, 2000. Print.

Cohen-Mor, Dalya, ed. *Arab Women Writers: An Anthology of Short Stories*. Albany: State U of New York P, 2005. Print.

Cooke, Miriam, and Roshni Rustomji-Kerns, eds. *Blood into Ink: South Asian and Middle Eastern Women Write War*. Boulder: Westview, 1994. Print.

Darraj, Susan Muaddi, ed. *Scheherazade's Legacy: Arab and Arab American Women on Writing.* Westport: Praeger, 2004. Print.

Davis, Paul, et al., eds. *The Bedford Anthology of World Literature: The Twentieth Century, 1900–the Present.* Boston: St. Martin's, 2003. Print.

Djebar, Assia. *Women of Algiers in Their Apartment.* Trans. Marjolijn de Jager. Charlottesville: UP of Virginia, 1992. Print.

Fernea, Elizabeth W., and Basima Qattan Bezirgan, eds. *Middle Eastern Muslim Women Speak.* Austin: U of Texas P, 1977. Print.

Handal, Nathalie, ed. *The Poetry of Arab Women: A Contemporary Anthology.* New York: Interlink, 2001. Print.

Hawthorne, Susan, and Bronwyn Winter, eds. *After Shock: September 11, 2001: Global Perspectives.* Vancouver: Raincoast, 2003. Print.

Hikmet, Nazım. *Poems of Nazım Hikmet.* Trans. Randy Blasing and Mutlu Konuk. Rev. ed. New York: Persea, 2002. Print.

Jayyusi, Salma Khadra, ed. *Modern Arabic Poetry: An Anthology.* New York: Columbia UP, 1987. Print.

Kadi, Joanna, ed. *Food for Our Grandmothers: Writings of Arab-American and Arab-Canadian Feminists.* Boston: South End, 1994. Print.

Kanafani, Ghassan. *"Men in the Sun" and Other Palestinian Stories.* Trans. Hilary Kilpatrick. Boulder: Rienner, 1999. Print.

Kritzeck, James. *Anthology of Islamic Literature.* New York: Meridian, 1975. Print.

Mahfouz, Naguib. *Voices from the Other World: Ancient Egyptian Tales.* Trans. Raymond Stock. Cairo: Amer. U in Cairo P, 2002. Print.

Mernissi, Fatema. *Scheherazade Goes West: Different Cultures, Different Harems.* New York: Washington Square, 2001. Print.

Orfalea, Gregory, and Sharif Elmusa, eds. *Grape Leaves: A Century of Arab-American Poetry.* New York: Interlink, 2000. Print.

Pamuk, Orhan. *Snow.* Trans. Maureen Freely. New York: Vintage, 2005. Print.

Saadawi, Nawal El. *The Nawal El Saadawi Reader.* London: Zed, 1997. Print.

Said, Edward, W. *"Reflections on Exile" and Other Essays.* Cambridge: Harvard UP, 2000. Print.

Satrapi, Marjane. *Persepolis: The Story of a Childhood.* New York: Pantheon, 2003. Print.

———. *Persepolis 2: The Story of a Return.* New York: Pantheon, 2004. Print.

Sells, Michael A., trans. *Desert Tracings: Six Classic Arabian Odes.* Middletown: Wesleyan UP, 1989. Print.

al-Shaykh, Hanan. *Women of Sand and Myrrh.* Trans. Catherine Cobham. New York: Doubleday, 1989. Print.

Soueif, Ahdaf. *Sandpiper.* London: Bloomsbury, 1996. Print.

Al-Udhari, Abdullah, ed. *Classical Poems by Arab Women.* London: Saqi, 1999. Print.

Youssef, Saadi. *Without an Alphabet, without a Face: Selected Poems of Saadi Youssef.* Trans. Khaled Mattawa. Saint Paul: Graywolf, 2003. Print.

Raymond-Jean Frontain

Cosmos versus Empire: Teaching the *Ramayana* in a Comparative Context

The philosopher Martha C. Nussbaum observes:

> People from diverse backgrounds sometimes have difficulty recognizing one another as fellow citizens in the community of reason. This is so, frequently, because actions and motives require, and do not always receive, a patient effort of interpretation. The task of world citizenship requires the would-be citizen to become a sensitive and emphatic interpreter. (63)

The University of Central Arkansas's two-semester sophomore-level world literature course proposes to instill in students a critical appreciation of cultural difference that will in turn make them more culturally self-aware. The complexity of this task is compounded by the fact that contemporary American popular culture increasingly privileges the visual over the verbal, leaving general education students indifferent to, if not actually resistant to, their own literary tradition, much less one that they find unsettlingly alien. The challenge, as I see it, is to reduce the number of texts covered in the general education survey even while, paradoxically, expanding the range of traditions. Under such circumstances, my primary aim becomes to teach students to think comparatively.

The most successful unit in my course World Literature I pairs the *Ramayana* of Valmiki with Vergil's *Aeneid*, two epic poems founded on the paradox of a hero whose glory depends in large part on an act of self-abnegation rather than, as occurs more traditionally in heroic narrative, one of self-assertion.[1] Whereas my students ultimately have little difficulty understanding Aeneas's sacrifice of personal desire for the good of an empire that will eventually glorify him as its founder, they are often confounded by Rama's commitment to honoring the word of his father, no matter what cost to the kingdom or himself, especially when the narrative makes clear that the situation is being manipulated for personal gain by Rama's stepmother, Kaikeyi. Thus, even as the actions of Rama and Aeneas prove remarkably similar, their motives are so radically different that, as Nussbaum insists, the *Ramayana* calls for a "patient effort of interpretation" that will allow students to recognize blue-skinned Rama as a "fellow citizen . . . in the community of reason."

Visualizing Cultural Assumptions

My students—perhaps because they are the products, variously, of *Sesame Street*, MTV, and Web iconography—seem increasingly more responsive to visual rather than verbal stimuli. Thus I begin my unit by helping them visualize cultural difference.

Both the *Aeneid* and the *Ramayana* are deeply grounded in religious values. Aeneas is praised for his piety and Rama is a man "dedicated to righteousness" (Valmiki 901). However, while ancient Rome and medieval Ayodhya were both polytheistic cultures, their temple styles were so dramatically dissimilar as to model for students two radically different concepts of the cosmos and of an individual's divinely ordained duty. The Roman Empire, observes the antiquarian Mortimer Wheeler, "was in large measure monolithic" (14), and the Roman temple, like other public structures erected during the reign of Augustus, functioned as a sign of that empire's greatness (20).[2] The Roman temple is elegant in design, its columns perfectly symmetrical, bespeaking a belief in the primacy of reason and modeling a social harmony obtained through the disciplining of unruly personal impulses. Although Roman religion was polytheistic, the will of Jupiter ultimately overrode that of all the other gods, establishing an absolute in relation to which everything in society was hierarchically organized.

A North Indian Hindu temple, conversely, is baroquely tiered, the curved shape of its tower "enhanc[ing] the effect of a mountain peak" (Elgood 94) and bespeaking the temple's cosmic function. The darkened central space of the interior is conducive to a "regeneration or rebirth" of the devotee, who visits the temple in order to engage "the potential divinity" that is present in every person (93). The rich carvings on the exterior of a Hindu temple are in keeping with a religion whose Upanishads claim has one, three, 303, or 3,003 gods (Davis 3). Such a system, I attempt to impress on students, admits more ambivalent conflict into the religion's thought—as when Rama and Kausalya debate whether her dharma ("duty") as Rama's mother preempts her dharma as Dasaratha's wife.

Any generalization about a culture as vast as either the Roman or the Hindu risks betraying, not describing, that culture. But by contrasting these respective temple architectures, students are able to distinguish between, on the one hand, a culture in which religion is a means of inculcating imperial self-consciousness and encouraging the pursuit of an earthly absolute and, on the other, a culture in which religion is cosmic, primarily transformative, and uneasily admits absolutes in the earthly sphere. Some ultimate significance is obtainable in Vergil's culture (indeed, Vergil was writing in the very golden age of Augustus that the actions in his text were fashioned to prophesy), whereas belief in cycles of reincarnation prepares a Hindu reader to accept the relativity of individual actions and the postponement of an absolute, making for a very different way of telling a story.[3] Helpful analyses of the *Ramayana* as a richly complex and continuously evolving tradition are available in Stuart Blackburn and in the essays collected in the anthologies edited by Mandakranta Bose and by Paula Richman (*Many Ramayanas* and *Questioning Ramayanas*).

This divergence in temple representations of the cosmos is replicated in iconographic representations of the heroes, Aeneas and Rama. In Vergil's epic, Aeneas is presented as modeling the virtues that allow empire to thrive: he is grave, pious, patient, long-suffering, and dignified. Not surprisingly, in Roman art he is invariably presented as the epitome of Roman *virtus* or manly excellence. The moral perfection of Aeneas is rendered in the classical symmetry of his nude or seminude form, his maturity suggested by his thick but well-kempt beard and by the gravity of his bearing. (Compare the Roman relief *Aeneas Sacrificing* with Bernini's imitation of a classical group, *Aeneas, Anchises and Ascanius Fleeing Troy*

[Liversidge, figs. 1b and 8].) In Roman culture, gods and demigods are made in the likeness of humans; they differ in being more powerful, physically perfect, and immortal. Apart from some uneasiness with the gods' indulgence in very human passions, American students generally have little difficulty accepting Roman anthropomorphism.

But students are invariably taken aback to look at such seemingly unrealistic, yet nonetheless equally idealized, images of Rama having blue skin and Hindu deities possessing multiple heads or arms. (A wealth of such images is to be found in Dekejia; Kam; Prime.) Such images suggest a divine world that is totally other, nonhuman, and requiring a more "patient effort of interpretation" than the *Aeneid*. I work at length to explain the Hindu concept of dharma and to distinguish Rama's sense of righteousness from Aeneas's. Juxtaposing Aeneas's inner debate over leaving Dido with Rama's instantaneous acquiescence to the will of his father, Dasaratha, for example, stimulates student discussion of the extent to which each culture values individuality and interiority. The Roman world idealizes Aeneas but locates his individuality in his struggle to put his will in accord with the will of Jupiter. Rama's spiritual superiority is proved by the erasure of what Anglo-European readers would call his individuality and by his being visually distinguished from others by his blue skin. Rama is the perfection to which all people may aspire and eventually reach in the course of their soul's evolution across the cycles of existence.

Dido, Sita, and the Social Role of Women

The hero's relation to a woman is essential to each of these two epics, yet Dido and Sita play very different roles in their respective narratives. Aeneas's and Rama's love relations can be used to focus class discussion on the role of women in a homosocial society in general and, more specifically, on how Roman and Hindu culture variously understand the nature of female passion.

In Roman culture, a man who succumbs to his passions or devotes himself to satisfying the demands of his body is considered soft and lacking in *virtus* or manly excellence. By the same scheme, a woman is respected insofar as she is "a *univira*, a matron of high moral character who is faithful to [her] husband" (Engar 184). Thus, by lingering in Carthage with Dido, Aeneas risks rendering himself effeminate, just as by forgetting the memory of her dead husband, Sychaeus, and succumbing to her passion for Aeneas, Dido loses honor in her people's eyes. In homosocial heroic narrative, women are often associated with the distraction of unruly passion and men with acts of self-mastery.

Like Dido, Sita finds her reputation compromised after she is abducted by Ravana and kept secluded by him in his remote island kingdom. Her behavior, however, has consequences beyond the history of her kingdom. In his "rage" to possess Sita sexually, Ravana admonishes her not to "worry about scriptural definitions of righteousness" (915), and "surely, dharma has come to an end, as Ravana is carrying Sita away," observers lament (914). Consequently, on her return to Rama, her integrity must be tested by fire for the rule of dharma to be restored. Thus, like Dido, Sita eventually finds herself atop a burning pyre, but in her case the purifying flames testify to the strictness of her conduct. She is heroic in her perseverance in her dharma as Rama's wife; she keeps the world on its course instead of, like Dido, throwing it off its track.

An analysis of the differences between Sita's and Dido's behavior challenges students to consider how they judge equality in a love partnership. My students rarely question Dido's right to pursue amorous gratification and are generally frustrated by a system of values that sees her lapse redeemed only by suicide. But as much as students deplore the practice of suttee by which a widow voluntarily or involuntarily joins her husband's body on his funeral pyre—a custom that Sita's test by fire invariably draws into our discussion—they agree that Sita is far more the equal of Rama in their story than Dido is of Aeneas in theirs.

Cosmos versus Empire

The Aeneid is an epic of empire, telling of how "hard and huge / A task it was to found the Roman people" (1.48–49). The *Ramayana* is an epic of the role of dharma in sustaining the harmony and order of the universe. The consequence of this essential difference in orientation is manifested in the poems' attitudes toward nature.

In the *Aeneid*, nature is the raw stuff of passion that must be controlled to ensure the advance of empire. The destructive fury of passion, for example, is figured by the storm that an enraged Juno raises to shipwreck Aeneas on the shore of Carthage in the opening movement of the poem, just as Dido's passion for Aeneas is represented by the storm that drives her and Aeneas to seek shelter in a cave where they consummate their relationship in a ceremony that parodies the Roman marriage rite. Later, lovesick Dido is compared to a wounded deer that thrashes about the forest in an attempt to dislodge the fatal arrow embedded in its side. Just as the Judeo-Christian Bible commands humankind, "Be fruitful and multiply, and replenish the earth, and subdue it: and have dominion over the fish of the sea, and over the fowl of the air, and over every living thing that moveth upon the earth" (Gen. 1.28 [King James Vers.]), Roman culture assumes that nature, like passion, is something to be dominated and subdued.

Nature in the *Ramayana* is far more beneficent, an indicator of the harmony in which all creatures will live if they all perform their dharma. "Pious and noble souls are found even amongst subhuman creatures," the narrator says of Jataya the Vulture, who dies in the service of Rama (921). Consequently, far from being a hindrance to human accomplishment, other species work in tandem with human beings toward a universal good. When the demon king Ravana disrupts the cosmic order by abducting Sita, the trees, mountains, and rivers eagerly aid Rama in his search for her (920); the deer and other forest animals turn southward to point out the direction in which Ravana has fled (912). A universal mourning settles on the land, the waterfalls causing the mountains to look as though they were "shedding tears" of sorrow over Ravana's violation of dharma (914). Students are particularly engaged by the character of Hanuman, the leader of the monkey forces whose heroic (and oftentimes mischievous) exploits lead to the discovery of Sita and defeat of Ravana. In Hanuman's heart is inscribed the image of Rama and Sita, making Hanuman not a wild brute to be subdued by a civilized superior but the poem's greatest witness, after Rama, to the workings of dharma.

Religious Authority

What is the religious authority of each epic? Rhetorically, Vergil's request for divine inspiration at the opening of the *Aeneid* must have been granted: had it not been, there would presumably have been no poem. By Vergil's day, however, such invocations were conventional and could not have had the same effect on the reader of a written text as they presumably had on the audience at a bard's oral performance of, say, a Homeric epic. Significantly, at no time in its history has the *Aeneid* been treated as a sacred text. Rather, by presenting a hero who models the piety, gravity, and virile dignity on which the Roman Empire was built, the poem was constructed to make a religious institution out of empire, in much the same way as some Americans speak with religious fervor of democracy and the flag.

Valmiki's *Ramayana*, like the *Mahabharata*, is included with the sutras and puranas among the *smirti*—that is, religious texts that are composed by human beings but based on revealed truth. The epic thus forms an important part of the Hindu scriptures, and Valmiki is often referred to as Bragwan Valmiki, meaning "Lord Valmiki," as a god is called "lord." A blessing prefaced to Valmiki's epic promises, "The deeds of Rama are purifying, cleansing, meritorious, and equal to the Vedas, / Whoever recites them is freed of all evils." Recitation of the story is "life-giving" (Alles 130–31). No European epic tradition promises the moral perfection of a reader through a text; not even the Judeo-Christian Bible promises complete spiritual transformation through the act of reading. The closest analogue to this claim of which I am aware is the Muslim belief that even an illiterate person can find holiness by memorizing and reciting as little as one verse of the Qur'an. Anglo-European readers classify as secular literature an epic of heroic deeds like the *Ramayana*. One of the reasons that its tradition continues to thrive in South Asian communities, however, is that the poem is associated with the sacred rather than the secular. Contrasting the *Ramayana* with the *Aeneid* in this regard asks students to evaluate what they consider holy, why Judeo-Christian culture assigns absolute value to only one text, and what the cultural consequences are of this distinction between sacred and secular texts.

One immediate consequence of asking students to read the *Ramayana* in conjunction with the *Aeneid* is that it makes Vergil's work seem more familiar and accessible. Aeneas may lose his wife, Creutia, and be forced to renounce Dido, but ultimately he secures Lavinia (who is as "hot" as but less temperamental than Dido, at least one student in every class is certain to comment). However simplistic such a reading of the *Aeneid* may be, it is in keeping with the epic as a paean to empire in which the individual's defeat of personal *furor* is necessary for the community to prosper. And however unlikely contemporary students are to put communal good before the fulfilment of their personal desires or ambitions, the American notion of manifest destiny has been ingrained in their thinking, and they have little difficulty conceptualizing the sacrifices required of individuals by empire.

Conversely, even at the end of this unit some students continue to struggle to understand the motivation of Rama. In the several years that I have been teaching this text, I have yet to have a male student agree that, without a moment's hesitation, he would leave the fast track to material success by dropping out of college, donning a pair of jockey shorts made of tree bark, and moving to a mosquito-infested swamp for fourteen years, all in order to honor a vague promise made by his father years before. Most students conclude that if, for instance, their father were so foolish as to lose the family fortune gambling, then it would be his responsibility to repay his debt, not theirs; their lives should not be adversely affected by a parent's foolish action. It is difficult to engage American undergraduates, raised on the Emersonian notion of self-reliance and rugged individualism, in a discussion of the network of duties and responsibilities that sustains the Hindu cosmos's harmony. I try to frame discussion of dharma in terms of students' own behaviors. For example, one person's coming late to class could affect the concentration of the entire group; one person's playing loud music while driving at night could disrupt the sleep of an entire neighborhood. On a larger scale, one nation's appropriating a lion's share of the world's natural resources could impoverish hundreds of millions of people in other parts of the globe. Students identify easily enough with Aeneas, whose story, crudely put, says that the gods assure an eventual payoff for any suffering that one undergoes on their behalf. But how can an American undergraduate identify with the notion of doing the right thing in order to preserve a seemingly nebulous order in the world? Rather than ask whether one person's decision to recycle can halt global warming, I ask students for their own examples of how one person's selfishness may disrupt the harmony of a community and possibly of the world.

It is the very strangeness of the *Ramayana* that allows it to stimulate debate over individual responsibility and social duty in my general education classroom. With "a patient effort of interpretation," the blue-skinned god may remain alien but is a "fellow citizen . . . in the community of reason" nonetheless.

Notes

1. Included with the *Ramayana* and the *Aeneid* in the syllabus for World Literature I are Homer's *Iliad*, *The Tale of the Heike*, *The Epic of Son-Jara*, and Dante's *Inferno*. As time and the changing contents of the *Norton Anthology* allow, I have on occasion included or substituted *The Song of Roland*, *Beowulf*, and John Milton's *Paradise Lost*.

2. Images of both the interior and the exterior of the Maison Carrée at Nîmes, the most complete remaining example of Augustan Age temple architecture, are readily available on the Web, and can be used to intimate to students the extent to which, as Wheeler notes, the Romans believed in a coherent cosmos, expressed politically by an empire (13).

3. *The Norton Anthology* (Lawall and Mack) contains only selections from each poem, so the instructor must fill in important gaps in the story. In lecture, I emphasize that although Aeneas will make the transition from mortal to god outside the *Aeneid*, in the poem he is the incarnation, however imperfect, of public virtue. (I am indebted to James J. Clauss's superb analysis of the complex manner in which Aeneas modeled moral heroism to Augustan Rome.) Conversely, Rama's full identity is revealed in the *Ramayana*; he is not godlike but a god, because of his ability to control his passion. This difference is highlighted by the nature of what is at stake, respectively, in Aeneas's battle with Turnus and Rama's with Ravana. When Aeneas sees that Turnus is wearing the belt taken from Pallas, he gives himself over to the passionate *furor* that compromises him as a hero, whereas Rama's victory over Ravana depicts the victory of the enlightened mind over maya (illusion or self-delusion), making for a metaphysical battle, not a geopolitical one. Thus, although the epics are similar in that both climax in the battle between the hero and a principal antagonist, the enormous difference in thematic values suggests very different reasons culturally for each epic's telling. I ask students to discus the possibility that because the *Aeneid* frames a culture that understands itself to be historically the ne plus ultra, its language began a slow death when Roman supremacy was eventually undermined and Vergil's poem became a relic of what had been. Conversely, although the culture that produced Valmiki's *Ramayana* has long since disappeared, the story of Rama continues to play a pivotal role in South Asian life. As time allows, I summarize for students the cultural-religious warfare that occurred in the 1990s surrounding the Ayodhya mosque that had been built over what some Hindus believed to be the birthplace of Rama, the appropriation by the Hindutva movement of the year-long televised dramatization of the *Ramayana* (episodes of which are available on video for use in the classroom), and the continued vitality of the story and its characters in such popular forms of culture as puppet plays and village festivals. By asking students to contrast the fates of the two epic traditions, the instructor is able to address the larger question of what makes for a living versus a dead cultural tradition.

Works Cited

Alles, Gregory D. *The* Iliad, *the* Ramayana, *and the Work of Religion: Failed Persuasion and Religious Mystification.* University Park: Pennsylvania State UP, 1994. Print.

Anderson, William S., and Lorina N. Quartarone, eds. *Approaches to Teaching Vergil's* Aeneid. New York: MLA, 2002. Print.

Blackburn, Stuart. *Inside the Drama House: Rama Stories and Shadow Puppets in South India.* Berkeley: U of California P, 1996. Print.

Bose, Mandakranta, ed. *The* Ramayana *Revisited.* New York: Oxford UP, 2004. Print.

Clauss, James J. "Vergil's Aeneas: The Best of the Romans." Anderson and Quartarone 87–98.

Davis, Richard H. "A Brief History of Religions in India." *Religions of India in Practice*. Ed. Donald S. Lopez, Jr. Princeton: Princeton UP, 1995. 3–52. Print.

Dekejia, Vidya, ed. *The Legend of Rama: Artistic Visions*. Bombay: Marg, 1994. Print.

Elgood, Heather. *Hinduism and the Religious Arts*. London: Cassell, 1999. Print.

Engar, Ann. "Tragedy and Vergil's *Aeneid*." Anderson and Quartarone 182–89.

Kam, Garrett. Ramayana *in the Arts of Asia*. Singapore: Select, 2000. Print.

Lawall, Sarah, and Maynard Mack, eds. *The Norton Anthology of World Literature: Volume A: Beginnings to A.D. 100*. 2nd ed. New York: Norton, 2002. Print.

Liversidge, M. J. H. "Virgil in Art." *The Cambridge Companion to Virgil*. Ed. Charles Martindale. Cambridge: Cambridge UP, 1997. 91–103. Print.

Nussbaum, Martha C. *Cultivating Humanity: A Classical Defense of Reform in Liberal Education*. Cambridge: Harvard UP, 1997. Print.

Prime, Ranchor. Ramayana: *A Journey*. New York: Welcome Rain, 1997. Print.

Richman, Paula, ed. *Many Ramayanas: The Diversity of a Narrative Tradition in South Asia*. Berkeley: U of California P, 1991. Print.

———, ed. *Questioning Ramayanas: A South Asian Tradition*. Berkeley: U of California P, 2001. Print.

Valmiki. *The Ramayana*. Trans. Swami Venkatesananda. Lawall and Mack 890–953.

Vergil. *The Aeneid*. Trans. Robert Fitzgerald. Lawall and Mack 1052–134.

Wheeler, Mortimer. *Roman Art and Architecture*. New York: Thames, 1985. Print.

Elizabeth Horan

Off to Join the Online Circus: The Comic Heroic Journey of World Literature

Institutional Contexts

This article describes the first semester of a two-semester world literature course that I've offered in avatars from primarily face-to-face to primarily electronic meetings and assignments. Arizona State has supported hybrid and online courses to address problems of limited classroom space and parking associated with the state's exploding population growth. In the English Department, World Literature has been an anomaly, the only lower-division course among a handful of upper-division literature courses with global, postnationalist foci and, in my version, the only literature course that encourages students to write creatively. For these and other reasons, enrollments in World Literature have been and continue to be robust, attracting the maximum number of forty students from the freshman through senior levels. While World Literature fills no specified requirements for majors in English or other languages and literatures, students can use the course to satisfy general, university-wide requirements in global awareness and in historical breadth.

Developing and teaching online and hybrid forms of World Literature has led me to emphasize the circulation of texts in global contexts and in multiple retellings. Working with the theme of travel literature moves comparative literature past the structuralism that cans and condenses journeys, whether epic, heroic, or comic, into a bland, generalized Joseph Campbell soup of plots and archetypes. The enrollment includes sophomores to seniors, full-time and part-time students, nineteen-year-olds alongside older, working students, and the occasional retiree. All benefit from practicing comparative literature's habitual modes of close reading, global perspective, and growing attention to cultural specifics. At the onset, students say that they're drawn by the reading list, the convenience of completing some or all of their work online, and the absence of prerequisites. In their final evaluations, they indicate that they are most satisfied with the two class projects, in which they imaginatively recast the course's texts in contemporary versions.

Texts and Topics

I take the global and area studies approach that Gayatri Spivak cites as a possible new incarnation of the comparatism in which I was trained. While my choice of texts conforms to the catalog's traditionalist description of "classical, medieval, and Renaissance periods, with lectures and discussions on the historical and cultural background," I interpret the world aspect as broadly global, present and circulating across many cultures. This contemporary formulation leads me to classical, canonical texts that begin in disparate traditions that involve or relate episodes of transculturation. The texts circulate through once separate, now contiguous and overlapping locations on the globe. As low expense, portability, and availability recent, colloquial translations are high among my criteria for text selection, I've jettisoned anthologies in favor of having students purchase four key texts, and that reading is supplemented with extensive online work. Working with and around the theme of travel leads the students to grapple with the tension between local and global concerns. Working with satire and comedy keeps us entertained even as we subvert the notion of travel as progress or forward movement by reading our texts chronologically backward.

The course is divided into four modules, with about five weeks each devoted to *Quixote* and the *Odyssey*, our two longest books, and about three weeks each to *Monkey* and the *Popol Vuh*, our shorter ones. The semester begins with the most recent and most recognizably realistic text, part 1 of *Don Quixote* (1605). I've often presented Hayden White's analysis of narrative modes (adapted, in turn, from Burke's rhetorical theories) as a bridge from our work with *Quixote* to the similarly episodic tale of *Monkey*, Arthur Waley's translation and abridgement of the *Hsi-yu Chi*, better known as *Journey to the West* (c. 1555). This fabulous yet historically based comic novel attributed to Wu Ch'eng-en is widely regarded as "one of the four or five lasting monuments of traditional Chinese fiction" (*Journey* x). After reading *Quixote* and *Monkey* as travel narratives, we step back and consider the uses of Mary Louise Pratt's insights into travel narrative, both for the texts we've read and to anticipate aspects of our next text, the *Popol Vuh*, a Quiché Maya creation story or collection of stories beginning in pre-Columbian oral traditions. Initially made available as a single Quiché-Spanish bilingual manuscript, this work has an ongoing redaction history that involves past and present, local and global contexts. From survival of the Conquest, we turn to the *Odyssey*, concluding our sampling of travel literature with the hero's extended peregrinations and difficult homecoming.

As we begin each work, we watch films and engage in close readings of its opening chapters, and in those readings we approach narrative development through attention to original cultural contexts. The first writing assignment for each module involves collaborative online work: students search out, evaluate, and post examples of contemporary retellings, especially those that involve transculturation. In posting this information on our online discussion board, students respond to prompts about how the text changes with each telling and about what remains the same. We also use the discussion board to post drafts in which we proceed, step by step, to construct parodic or serious rewritings, contemporary versions of selected scenes from our core texts. We are constantly moving, then, from films to online searching, posting to the board and reading hard-copy texts all the while. In each module we play with collaborative, experimental writing forms, drawing from the texts to produce macaronic verse, renga, and cento, appropriating and developing materials from the three most conventionally canonical of our texts, *Quixote*, *Monkey*, and the *Odyssey*. Students can choose to embed this work into their two individual class projects—for example, as found manuscripts, satiric poetry, or take-offs on heroic epithets.

Reading in reverse chronological order foregrounds the thematic importance of time in the narratives, all of which, including the *Popol Vuh*, open with frustrated beginnings and have frustrated closures. All involve round-trip travel to and from the land of the dead. *Quixote* and *Monkey* unfold in more or less recognizable temporal frameworks, while the *Popol Vuh* brings us into another time, one that begins with creation and ends with "the death of the first people to come from the sea" (175). Concluding rather than beginning with the *Odyssey* lets us focus on the problems surrounding the ending of this story.

Most students have at least superficially encountered *Don Quixote* before enrolling in the course. Some will have seen a production of *Man of La Mancha*. But not even wonderful film versions such as the Russian *Don Quixote* (Kozyntsev) offer what a literature class can: immersion in the experience of reading, beginning with Cervantes's hailing us in the prologue, "desocupado lector"—that is, idle, leisurely reader, not making money, not earnestly learning, not improving anyone's soul (1: 19). Although we make side trips into slapstick, we concentrate on what's self-consciously literary in Cervantes's novel, from the prologue to the circumstances of the hero's madness, from the multiple narrators to the competitive jealousy that motivates the village priest and spurs on both Sancho's Quixotification and Quixote's humiliating forced return.

With *Don Quixote* we take on the recurring question of reading for entertainment as opposed to moral instruction, a theme that hovers at the edge of the travel narrative and pilgrimage stories generally. Exposing students to the controversies about reading that pervade and surround these texts leads students to identify and distinguish, for example, between purely slapstick versus pointedly satirical episodes in *Quixote* and *Monkey*. They benefit from knowing about disagreements in the critical tradition—for example, how English recourse to a funnybook tradition (Close 1) has sought to displace a range of romantic approaches to *Quixote*, from Ortega y Gasset to Américo Castro, who observes that "we heard picaresque laughter cackling as Olympus is brought down low" (29). They learn, too, how a metaliterary Cervantes may be giving way to one who stresses place and failure of empire, whether looking toward the occidental Indies or from captivity in Algiers (Wilson 1, 8; Garcés). In *Monkey*, Waley's short preface (Wu Ch'eng-en, *Monkey*) contrasts with Anthony C. Yu's approach (Wu Ch'eng-en, *Journey*). The students initially follow Waley in regarding the story as primarily comic with moralistic aspects, but the slightest attention to the religious background leads to the allegorical aspects that Yu's fine work elucidates, while the political aspects provide insight into China's relations with neighboring non-Chinese peoples. The culturally ubiquitous monkey king character, who appears in Japanese manga and anime, Chinese opera, kung fu movies, United States novels, and even the massive, multiplayer online role-playing game *Westward Journey* becomes the students' key to discovering this text's enormous and constantly shifting range of influence (see *Monkey*).

We begin the *Popol Vuh* by watching Patricia Amlin's superb film version. We read Dennis Tedlock's excellent introduction, then his translation, *Popol Vuh: The Mayan Book of the Dawn of Life*. This approach differs somewhat from our work with *Quixote* and *Monkey* in that we begin with immersion in visual representation and attention to the text's transmission modes and move more gradually into reading the text. Because Tedlock and Amlin reproduce the Mayan glyphs, they encourage our thinking beyond print modes, while Tedlock's introduction, coupled with work from Pratt that I summarize for the students, helps us think about travel in relation to colonialism and the rise of anthropology. To further develop an understanding of contexts for the *Popol Vuh*, the class has sampled the travel narratives of J. L. Stephens, Miguel Angel Asturias's legends, and Rigoberta Menchú's autobiography (Menchú and Burgos-Debray) along with documentary films on the modern-day Quiché Maya. This localized world approach moves comparatism past the more isolated 1990s multiculturalism described in Charles Bernheimer and toward both David Damrosch's and Emily Apter's twenty-first-century stress on the recovery, circulation, and global transmission of texts.

By the time we are reading the *Odyssey* in the final weeks of the course, students anticipate the rhythm of our work and need little prompting. They know that our preliminary work will relate select episodes to controversies about the texts and their transmission and that our online collaborative search assignments and watching film clips will examine contemporary adaptations. We watch John Barnes's visually arresting 1965, black-and-white BBC *Odyssey*, a sixty-minute narrative in three parts, narrated by Gilbert Highet, which we contrast with the last twenty minutes of Andrei Konchalovsky's Canadian, 1997, made-for-TV movie. There, a buff, almost Jason-like Odysseus manages to reunite with Penelope sans the effort of bed riddle, final battle, or dea ex machina on Ithaca's craggy heights. Concluding the course with *Odyssey* lets us draw on the unique combinations that each meeting of this class has developed in the course of speculating on the nature of travel narratives, the representation of foreigners, the nostalgia for or rejection of staying at home.

Students generally need some convincing that they'll benefit from reading lengthy texts peppered with terms from foreign languages. To deflect their reliance on Web-posted or CliffsNotes summaries, I give them my own rather unconventional summary rewritings. To develop some awareness of the original languages, we play with the meanings of the characters' personal names. Working with names also forestalls the students' discussion-dampening anxiety about seemingly unpronounceable non-English names. I relay the excellent advice that I recall, given by William Strunk, Jr.: "If you don't know how to pronounce a word, say it loud!" (qtd. in E. White xvi). We play a lot with translations, faux and otherwise: would Cervantes's Quesada or Quejada be Cheesy or Choosy, should the giant Caraculiambro be Buttface or Butthead? Waley's translation represents such play by detailing the Stone Monkey's several name changes, from first-among-equals Monkey King; to the disciple Aware of Vacuity; to the bureaucratic honorific Pi-ma-wen—that is, "Stables-hand"; to the hubristic Great Sage, Equal to Heaven. (For all these translations from the Chinese I thank my colleague Tim Wong.) We note how the names in the *Popol Vuh* combine terms for numbers and animals that appear in the Mayan glyphs that both Tedlock and Amlin reproduce. We look at the Greek love of puns via the wily Odysseus, whose name, according to my colleague Diane Rayor, means "trouble" or "man of wrath." Odysseus takes on the sheepish disguise of Nobody but can't resist triumphantly revealing himself as son of Laertes (the thief), followed by his full address, practically down to the zip code.

Overview, Individual Assignments

In the first substantial individual project, due at midterm time, students imagine how selected scenes from Cervantes's novel would appear in a contemporary setting. We begin with the question of what kind of reading would provoke a contemporary Don Quixote. This departs from the text's basic premise of someone whose judgment has been twisted by "la razón de su sinrazón" ("the sane madness") of overindulgence in books (37; 20). The students who most easily imagine someone who, reading "x," goes mad and decides to take seriously the conventions of a literary genre, to enact them, are those students who've been reading-addicted themselves. They are, we are, as my teacher Joseph Silverman used to say, like the village priest, readers who are "prone to Don Quixote's ontological sin," inclined to mistake fantasy for reality.

Students' creative projects have invoked a reader driven mad by immersion in diet books, glamour magazines, various strains of science fiction and fantasy, superhero comics, and the "left behind" series of Christian novels premised on imminent apocalypse. When students propose to have an imagined hero enact a favorite television show, I stress the project as involving not one book but a whole genre that even the illiterate Sancho learns to recognize and parrot and turn to his advantage, via Don Quixote. While I accept that even television could mimic literature, I insist that their best versions will aim for the same wealth of elements as Cervantes's narrative, with its multiple narrators, new identities, appropriately chosen horses or wheels, invented sweethearts, episodes of slapstick and pastoral, and serious questions of freedom and honor.

The second project, due at the semester's end but developed in drafts over the online bulletin board, has students imagine and rewrite in the present selected scenes from either *Monkey* or the *Odyssey*. The best versions include naming and equipping their heroes, interactions with a worthy adversary, significant divine interventions, an underworld journey, alternative homecomings—scenarios, whether serious or not, that we find throughout all our travel narratives.

Course Goals

By semester's end, students demonstrate a range of skills in identification and synthesis, stated in the current parlance of "learning outcomes." They can identify specific historical and cultural circumstances of the texts, relating them to subsequent events and to the present. They can identify modes of narrative and representation relating to the course theme of the comic, heroic journey. They've broadened their global awareness through reading and discussing verbal and visual texts from different cultures, times, and places, with attention to colonialism, transculturation, representation of selves and others.

I use the creative and electronic aspects of the class to pursue an unwritten goal of keeping students in the class and on track to graduate—both major institutional concerns at Arizona State. Regularly posting to the course Web site and being accessible to students by quickly, cheerfully answering their e-mail messages, I provide the feedback that students want. My course Web site hit statistics indicate that regular, predictable, positive feedback leads students to log on more frequently, to respond more substantively to other students online, and to spend more time exploring the site. I hope that the creativity and camaraderie of the online writing assignments and class projects encourages students to regard university-level humanities courses as interesting, experimental places. I hope that the thematic of the course allows an introduction to comparatism's literary and cultural underpinnings through the work of Hayden White and Pratt, work that can guide students as they spin out their own retellings.

Working with a limited number of texts instead of an anthology lets us engage the cultural specifics of the postcolonialist and classicist backward glance, whether it is Golden Age Spain's musing on the chivalric age or Ming China's looking back on the T'ang Dynasty. Working with oral texts that have survived from Homeric Greece and the pre-Columbian Mayas to the present day, with so much of their original contexts still stunningly evident, testifies to the power of storytelling, transformed in global circulation. That students can even now add to, transform, and be transformed by these old texts is, for me, the best possible argument for the value and pleasure of idle reading.

Online Resources

Cervantes Saavedra, Miguel de. *The Adventures of the Ingenious Gentleman Don Quixote de la Mancha*. Trans. John Ormsby. *Project Gutenberg*. Web. 2 Apr. 2008.

Homer. *Odyssey*. Trans. Samuel Butler. *Internet Classics Archive*. MIT. 1994–2000. Web. 2 Apr. 2008.

Hsi-Yu Chi / Journey to the West. *China the Beautiful*. 1995–2006. Web. 2 Apr. 2008.

———. *World Literature Classics*. Xah Lee Web. Web. 8 Apr. 2008.

The Popol Vuh: The Sacred Book of the Mayas: The Book of the Community. Trans. Delia Goetz, Sylvanus G. Morley, and Adrián Recinos. 1950. Rainbow Mystery School. Web. 16 June 2008.

Popol Wuj. Newberry Lib. Ohio State U. Web. 16 June 2008. In K'iche', Spanish, and English.

Works Cited

Amlin, Patricia, dir. *Popol Vuh: Creation Myth of the Maya*. Berkeley Media LLC, 1988. DVD.

Apter, Emily. *The Translation Zone: A New Comparative Literature*. Princeton: Princeton UP, 2006. Print.

Asturias, Miguel Angel. *The Mirror of Lida Sal: Tales Based on Mayan Myths and Guatemalan Legends.* Trans. Gilbert Alter-Gilbert. Pittsburgh: Latin Amer. Lit. Rev., 1997. Print.

Barnes, John, dir. *The Odyssey.* Encyclopaedia Britannica Films, 1965. Film.

Bernheimer, Charles, ed. *Comparative Literature in an Age of Multiculturalism.* Baltimore: Johns Hopkins UP, 1995. Print.

Burke, Kenneth. *A Rhetoric of Motives.* Berkeley: U of California P, 1969. Print.

Castro, Américo. *El pensamiento de Cervantes.* Rev. ed. Ed. Castro and Julio Rodríguez-Puértolas. Barcelona: Moguer, 1980. Print.

Cervantes y Saavedra, Miguel de. *Don Quixote.* Trans. Edith Grossman. New York: Ecco, 2003. Print.

———. *El ingenioso Hidalgo Don Quixote de la Mancha.* Ed. Martín de Riquer. 2 vols. Barcelona: Juventud, 1971. Print.

Close, Anthony. *The Romantic Approach to* Don Quixote. Cambridge: Cambridge UP, 1977. Print.

Damrosch, David. *What Is World Literature?* Princeton: Princeton UP, 2003. Print.

Garcés, María Antonia. *Cervantes in Algiers: A Captive's Tale.* Nashville: Vanderbilt UP, 2003. Print.

Homer. *Odyssey.* Trans. Stanley Lombardo. Indianapolis: Hackett, 2000. Print.

Konchalovsky, Andrei, dir. *The Odyssey.* Amer. Zoetrope, 1997. Film.

Kozyntsev, Grigori. *Don Kichot.* Lenfilm, 1957. Film.

Menchú, Rigoberta, and Elisabeth Burgos-Debray. *I, Rigoberta Menchú.* Trans. Ann Wright. London: Verso, 1987. Print.

Monkey. BBC, 1978–79. Television. Trans. of *Saiyuki.*

Popol Vuh: The Mayan Book of the Dawn of Life. Ed. and trans. Dennis Tedlock. New York: Simon, 1996. Print.

Pratt, Mary Louise. *Imperial Eyes: Travel Writing and Transculturation.* New York: Routledge, 1992. Print.

Spivak, Gayatri. *Death of a Discipline.* New York: Columbia UP, 2003. Print.

Stephens, J. L. *Incidents of Travel in Central America, Chiapas and Yucatan.* 2 vols. New York: Dover, 1969. Print.

White, E. B. Introduction. *The Elements of Style.* By William Strunk, Jr., and White. 3rd ed. New York: Macmillan, 1979. xi–xvii. Print.

White, Hayden. *Metahistory: The Historical Imagination in Nineteenth-Century Europe.* Baltimore: Johns Hopkins UP, 1973. Print.

Wilson, Diana de Armas. *Cervantes, the Novel, and the New World.* Oxford: Oxford UP, 2000. Print.

Wu Ch'eng-en. *Journey to the West.* Trans. Anthony C. Yu. 4 vols. Chicago: U of Chicago P, 1984. Print.

———. *Monkey: Folk Novel of China (Journey to the West).* Trans. Arthur Waley. New York: Grove, 1994. Print.

Ellen Peel

Imagining the Constructed Body: From Statues to Cyborgs

Did I request thee, Maker, from my clay
To mould me Man, did I solicit thee
From darkness to promote me?
—John Milton, Paradise Lost, 10.743–45[1]

Why?

Complete coverage has never been a very attainable pedagogical goal, especially in a single world literature course, and the goal is receding even farther as our concepts of world, literature, and course expand—or perhaps explode. Nevertheless, when teaching world literature, I still aim for a degree of breadth. At the same time I also seek some focus as a way to avoid dilettantism and to make the material more comprehensible. Imagining the Constructed Body succeeds as a study of world literature because it balances breadth of place, time, and genre with focus on a single theme. As I explain below, a constructed body can be thought of metaphorically as the translation of an ordinary body and so affords an apt theme for a world literature course, which itself is of necessity taught largely in translation. The readings include fiction, drama, poetry, and memoir and are supplemented by a few films, for the subject invites visual treatment. The course has attracted, in addition to literature majors, students from cinema, creative writing, and women's studies. After studying brief introductory texts that serve as touchstones, we read the rest, which are grouped roughly by type of bodily construction.

Along with readings from Western Europe and North America, we draw on literature from El Salvador, Argentina, Poland, and what is now the Czech Republic.[2] The study of these texts, coming from different places and different times, entails a certain responsibility for the instructor to know about a variety of cultures. That is one reason I have chosen largely Western materials, which at least share some ancestry of Judeo-Christian or Cartesian attitudes toward the body, if only to rebel against them. Needless to say, despite this shared ancestry, each of the cultures is unique, as we observe, for example, in Christa Wolf's "Self-Experiment": the translators' introduction situates the story in the German Democratic Republic, showing the text to be a critique not just of patriarchy but also of the GDR's particular scientific Marxism.

How have various cultures imagined constructed bodies in world literature? Many examples come to mind: the man who adores a feminine automaton in E. T. A. Hoffmann's "The Sand-Man" (and in Jacques Offenbach's opera *Tales of Hoffmann*), Mary Shelley's creature—victimized and victimizing—in *Frankenstein*, the mermaid who becomes human in Hans Christian Andersen's "The Little Mermaid," and the man who turns anorexia into performance art in Franz Kafka's "A Hunger Artist." In this upper-division undergraduate course—the most enjoyable I've ever taught—we trace the constructed body through world literature from classical times (Pygmalion's statue in Ovid's myth) to our times (stories of cyborgs).[3]

Bodies have always been attention grabbers, perhaps never more so than at the current moment. While it may seem that a talking statue and a lovesick mermaid have little to do with ordinary life, students find the course's subject matter highly relevant to what's going on around them, from pop culture sensations on television such as *Extreme Makeover* to scientific breakthroughs in stem cell research. And, as technology advances, some techniques for constructing bodies, such as cloning, move from fiction to fact. Class members are constantly bringing in newspaper clippings and Web site references that tie in with course themes. Meanwhile, in the fictional realm, creators of literature and film are increasingly employing fantasy and science fiction, the genres that most often depict the constructed body. Among popular novels in recent decades, for instance, we seem to be undergoing a bit of a golem renaissance (as in Marge Piercy's *He, She, and It* [1991] and Michael Chabon's *The Amazing Adventures of Kavalier and Clay* [2000]). Scholars are devoting increasing attention to those genres, as in the *PMLA* special issue on science fiction ("Special Topic"). Talking about the growing stature of fantasy and science fiction offers a chance for the class to contemplate canonicity.

The body is also salient in the theoretical realm, where, for example, a century of psychoanalytic theory has foregrounded bodily desire. The last few decades have introduced still more topics concerning the body in general, largely through the influence of Michel Foucault and of scholars who read through the lenses of race, sex, gender, sexuality, and disability. In addition, scholars such as Judith Butler have asked how bodies are constructed, especially through performance. The forest of theory can overwhelm undergraduates, but because our class focuses on the particular group of subjects concerning the constructed body in literature, students have a path to follow through the forest.[4]

What?

The constructed body gives rise to a number of questions. By posing the same ones more than once—in relation to different texts—our class is able to get a more nuanced sense of the answers, as if a photograph were gradually showing more detail while being developed. I present some of the questions here, most often using *Frankenstein* and Ovid's "Pygmalion" as examples, since my readers are likely to be most familiar with them and since Shelley's novel is commonly considered to have inaugurated the genre of science fiction. I also refer frequently to *R. U. R. (Rossum's Universal Robots)* (1920), a play by the Czech writer Karel Čapek. Although less well known than *Frankenstein* and "Pygmalion," *R. U. R.* is a paradigmatic constructed-body text and the source of the word *robot* (from the Czech for "work"). As Čapek's human characters manufacture robots more and more like people, the robots rebel more and more, ultimately killing all but one human being.

As I define it, "constructing a body" can refer either to mentally conceptualizing a body or to physically building one by artificial means. If the body is being physically built, construction can mean either changing it or creating it from scratch.[5] What is the nature of some of these constructed bodies? If, like Pygmalion's ivory statue or the Grecian urn in John Keats's poem, a constructed body is not flesh, does that lack of flesh make it undying or unliving? Patched together from parts of dead bodies in a grotesque parody of Christ's resurrection, even Frankenstein's creature could be considered both undying and unliving. It may at first seem desirable to be undying and disturbing to be unliving, but might the reverse be true? In the face of such challenges to death and life, what can time mean? And how else does a constructed body relate to time? In *Blade Runner*, having memories at first seems to prove one is human, yet it turns out that they too can be just another constructed element in a replicant.

How indeed can one tell a human body from a constructed one? By the ability to feel physical pain? the experience of emotions? the presence of a soul? Some characters in *Blade Runer* cannot themselves tell that they have been constructed. Similarly, in Jorge Luis Borges's "The Circular Ruins," one man creates another by dreaming, unaware until afterward that he himself was created the same way.

A surprisingly revealing question concerns the choice of pronouns used during class discussions—and in this essay—to refer to constructed bodies: at what point during the construction process does an "it" become a "she" or a "he"? If most characters perceive a body as an "it" or a "he" but the protagonist mentally constructs that body as a "she," what word should we use? And how does translation complicate all this? Such pronoun problems grow especially acute when they infect the self-image of a constructed body it-/her-/himself. In "The Mask," by Stanislaw Lem, the narrator first comes to awareness while being mechanically assembled, then suddenly finds herself a woman at a royal ball, then eviscerates herself, releasing the self at her core: a silvery, beetle-like killing machine. This narrator usually refers to the self as "I" but occasionally, disconcertingly switches to a third-person form—sometimes "she," sometimes "it."

To take another tack, can a human self merge with computers, more tangible tools, or medical implants such as pacemakers or simple dental fillings? In Anne McCaffrey's "The Ship Who Sang," does Helva become one with the space ship whose brain she becomes? In fact, might fundamental oppositions be deconstructed: not only between self and other (as in the immediately preceding examples or a clone) but also between subject and object (as in an anorexic who shrinks her own body or the scientist in Wolf's "Self-Experiment" who turns herself into a man) or between human and machine (as in an android)? Does the coming to life of Pygmalion's statue deconstruct the opposition between the representation of a body and the body itself? Although the thought of deconstruction intimidates some students, the constructed body affords a concrete way to introduce it: after students have learned to observe oppositions that break down, I let them know that the practice in which they have been engaging is a deconstructive one.

Questions of power also emerge. Who actually controls the construction of a body, the person who requests it or the person who carries it out? In plastic surgery, is it the patient or the doctor? In Andersen's "The Little Mermaid," is it the mermaid or the sea witch? And where does the desire for such a body come from in the first place? If the desire comes from forces beyond the individual who expresses it, how do institutions and other historical and societal forces shape the desire and the resulting power relations? Again one thinks of plastic surgery, as well as of makeovers and Nathaniel Hawthorne's "The Birthmark," in which a husband convinces his wife to let him remove her birthmark. In *R. U. R.*, some who manufacture robots do so less because of individual choice than because of the avalanche of consumer demand. In like fashion, Lem devotes much of "The Mask" to issues of power. His woman / killing machine knows the king has fated her/it to assassinate his rival, but she/it cannot figure out whether her/its rebellious moments are authentic or are themselves part of the king's plan. Such texts sometimes prompt class members to debate the possibility of choice, with the accompanying paradoxes of false consciousness and of free will and determinism.

More generally, we ask who has greater power, the creator or the creation. It might seem that of course the creator is in charge, but to some extent statues, portraits, androids, cyborgs, and even ordinary children escape the control of their makers. Frankenstein's creature and the *R. U. R.* robots are exemplars for such a rebellion, but even Pygmalion's bride talks back to him in modern rewritings such as the Salvadoran poet Claribel Alegría's "Galatea before the Mirror":

> I am only the mirror
> in which you preen yourself
> and for that very reason
> I despise you.   (85)

Shelley's novel and some golem tales raise the further problem of the creator who tries to escape his creation, the father who betrays his son.

Indeed creator and created body are in some ways like parent and child, and the process of creation resembles that of reproduction. This analogy leads us to a number of inquiries, such as why these narratives portray so few female creators, so few "mothers." The topic of reproduction can also bring students to ponder whether constructed bodies can produce another generation; since most are not fully or not at all human, they certainly cannot reproduce themselves in the same way in which they were made (by human beings). Some created beings wish in vain for offspring. Just before the humans are exterminated in *R. U. R.*, for instance, one woman destroys the manuscript that explains how to make robots, and in the last act the created beings, who last only twenty years, lament that they cannot figure out how to replace themselves. The play ends, however, with a female and a male robot who have developed the capacity to love and perhaps to reproduce.

Such topics lead to the aesthetic realm, where a key theme is self-referentiality: How is creating a human body akin to creating the body of a text? Since people have long noted that producing art resembles producing human beings in the traditional way, by reproduction, the course asks whether the production of art can also resemble nontraditional production—and enhancement—of human beings. Shelley makes the analogy explicit, and unsettling, when she uses the term "my hideous progeny" for the book she has written about Frankenstein and his hideous progeny (25). I bring up another aesthetic concern, the recurrent theme of perfection: Can it be found only in nature or, on the contrary, only in artifice? Pygmalion's whole reason for sculpting an artificial woman is the imperfection he sees in the women created by nature, but—in a cascade of ironies—he is not totally satisfied until Venus artificially turns his artificial woman into a natural one.

Power and aesthetics swirl together with ethics in the problem of evaluation. As the *R. U. R.* factory managers themselves ask in a heated debate, When is it admirable to construct a body, and when is it heinous? One can also ask, When is the result beautiful, and when is it hideous? I have been taken aback to find how unthinkingly I favor some constructed bodies and dismiss others. Asking students to examine my assumptions and their own can lead to thought-provoking debates.

Finally, the constructed body invites the question of whether it is real. My course title includes the word "imagining" because we deal primarily with the constructed body as represented in various fictional, artistic forms, not as it exists in life.[6] Imaginary constructed bodies do, however, engage in a complex dialectic with real ones, and so in order to understand the former, we need some sense of the latter, such as the constructions resulting from assisted reproductive technology or bodybuilding. Yet there seems to be little time, in class or outside it, for students to acquire much factual information on such phenomena.

One way I deal with this difficulty is by making such topics an option for the oral presentations. Students have talked on organ transplants, veiling, corsets, Chinese eunuchs, voodoo curses directed at another's body, sex-change operations, and of course Barbie. Once I also invited a guest lecturer who spoke about her experience wearing TENS, a "transcutaneous neurostimulator." While it lessens her chronic pain, her description of its many disadvantages dashed our fantasies that a cyborg utopia might lie in the near future. In addition, I have addressed this matter of real-world phenomena by going into some detail on one of them, suggesting that each of the others would reward an equally deep exploration. I chose eating disorders, because I know the most about them, they afflict so many college-age women, and I can assign a wrenchingly beautiful memoir about eating disorders—*Wasted*, by Marya Hornbacher. This topic is valuable, but its roots in reality mean I must be prepared to hear and respond to some painful accounts of how students themselves have contended with such disorders.

Not being trained as a scientist or psychologist, I wonder about the quality of the information the class receives on this and other factual matters, and I am still working on ways to address this concern. In fact, I see this lack of reliable information as part of a broader, underacknowledged problem: as scholars reach out to fields beyond their training, especially as the humanities reach out to the social and natural sciences, it becomes harder and harder to teach and write responsibly. This issue can itself provide fuel for class discussions.

The course could be modified to underline other themes. Although I do not emphasize how notions of the constructed body have evolved through time, the syllabus could be adapted to do so. Another option would be to add non-Western film and literature, such as Yasunari Kawabata's "One Arm," a surreal Japanese tale in which a young woman lends one of her arms to a man for the night. Non-Western sources might offer provocative alternatives to the genre of science fiction and the theme of Promethean overreaching, which characterize a number of the materials I currently use, as exemplified in *Frankenstein*. Furthermore, cross-currents between East and West could be studied through materials such as *The*

Pillow Book, a French, British, and Dutch film about people in Japan and China who write on each other's bodies. Or the class could trace the Indian myth about a woman who places her husband's head on his friend's body, and the friend's head on the husband's body: this story influenced the German novelist Thomas Mann, who in turn influenced the Indian playwright Girish Karnad (see Mahadevan).

Whence?

Tying together threads from a number of cultures, the study of world literature creates an opportunity for students to struggle with and savor cultural diversity, not only the relations that exist among the texts but also the relations between the texts and us as readers—the texts and readers by definition usually from different cultures. We inquire into these diverse cultures by asking both how they think about the body and how they think about the construction of both bodies and art.

Many of the texts themselves thematize cultural diversity. Most texts about constructed bodies can be read as allegories about the other, especially about the racial other. *Blade Runner*, for instance, is a film about passing, and the replicants' rebellion can be read as a slave revolt. More specifically, some of the plots hinge on perceptions or misperceptions of cultural difference. In both Honoré de Balzac's "Sarrasine" (1830) and David Henry Hwang's *M. Butterfly* (1986), a Frenchman goes to another country and falls in love with someone onstage whose body he mentally constructs as female, not knowing that in the other culture female roles are played by men. In "Sarrasine," a French sculptor is attracted to a castrato in eighteenth-century Italy, and in *M. Butterfly*, a twentieth-century French diplomat is attracted to an actor in the Chinese opera. Both texts ask discomfiting questions about how we construct the foreign, the exotic, the other in general.

I also encourage students to think about the specific nationalities and historical periods involved. For instance, *M. Butterfly* weaves an extremely intricate web involving France, China, Japan, Vietnam, and the United States, to mention only its major nationalities. Written by a Chinese American after the Vietnam War, the play comments not only on French attitudes toward China but also on French attitudes toward what used to be Indochina, and on United States attitudes toward Vietnam and toward Asia more broadly. Later in the course, I ask the class to compare "Sarrasine" and *M. Butterfly* with Germaine de Staël's comedy

The Mannequin (1811), in which a pompous man is attracted to a half-concealed mannequin, set up to mock him by his reluctant fiancée and the man she actually loves. Unlike the two texts studied earlier, Staël's does not rely on a difference in stage customs and so need not be set in a culture other than her own (France), yet she too chose to make the self-centered man a Frenchman visiting another place (Germany). Students may well wonder why all three men deluded by their own projections have been represented as French, and so I present some background on the history of French chauvinism as well as on its critics in France and elsewhere.

Since cultural diversity is often manifested by linguistic diversity, I raise the question of translation. Especially at the undergraduate level, world literature courses need to be taught in translation. Some students in this course come from outside comparative literature and may know only English. While all our comparative literature majors must know at least one language in addition to English, even they—and their professor— can hardly be expected to read literature in nine different languages. At the beginning of the course I make sure that we contemplate the problems and pleasures of translation, in a session that is often an eye-opener for students who have taken the process for granted. The discussion can be lightened by amusing examples of mistranslations, and students who know more than one language can often provide engaging tales of their own pursuit of the mot juste in another tongue. I stress that, although a computer might be able to convert simple technical prose, literary translation still requires the human touch. I explain the process in terms of trade-offs: few translations, for instance, can simultaneously preserve a poem's exact rhyme scheme along with its literal meaning, and so no perfect translation is possible, though we can distinguish better from worse. Moreover, for elements like tone and metaphor, literary translation always requires human judgment to make interpretations.

From presenting translation in the narrow sense, I move to presenting it in several broad senses, which I mention only briefly here, although they sometimes require a fair amount of classroom time. To begin with, any sign can be thought of as a translation of what it represents, so that the word *tree* is, roughly speaking, a translation of the tree it refers to. More significant, any artistic object or text, especially a realistic one, can be seen as a translation of what it represents: Balzac's *Père Goriot* translates nineteenth-century Paris. I urge students to try this approach in pondering the fantasy and science fiction we read. It is relatively easy to compare *Père Goriot* with the original from which Balzac was translating, for historical accounts of Paris abound. It is impossible, however, to find a historical account of a golem, much less to find a golem itself, against which to compare a fictional account. In the same vein, I sometimes get a laugh when I tell students about an argument I had concerning what dragons "really" look like: I asserted they had potbellies, while my friend, influenced by Chinese images, claimed they were snakelike.

Most important, the notion of translation can be extended to constructed bodies, for in life or literature to construct a body is, in a metaphorical sense, to translate—a metaphor that runs throughout the course. We can consider a robot, for example, as a rendering of an ordinary body. Reminding students that most literary translations are inevitably interpretations, I ask how constructed bodies interpret ordinary ones. For instance, if we interpret emotion as a physical response, then a robot that drips tears when damaged is arguably translating sadness. If, however, we interpret emotion as an inner state, the damaged robot needs to translate sadness more internally, perhaps as a particular electronic state, though that too seems hardly adequate. A more complex and comic example of interpretation involving emotion occurs in "Helen O'Loy," by Lester Del Rey. Two men who are trying to build a robot housemaid decide that the robot must feel emotion in order to perform the tasks properly. They interpret human housecleaning and translate it into robotic form—with unexpected results, as you might expect.

I ask students to play around with the metaphor of construction as translation: What might familiar terms like "faithful" and "unfaithful" translation mean in this context? Some robots on automobile assembly lines translate human appearance unfaithfully, looking at best like arms that have been detached and flayed, but these contraptions weld quite skillfully: appearance has been traded off for function. Finally we interrogate the notions of faithful and unfaithful themselves, asking whether we should necessarily prefer fidelity. The more like humans the *R. U. R.* robots become, the more domineering and murderous they become. Conversely, one might assume that an unfaithful rendering always causes the original to "lose in translation." But, as writers such as David Damrosch have argued, sometimes a text "gains in translation" (288). Frankenstein makes his creature in some ways better than normal—bigger and stronger. And it has almost become a cliché to make literary characters with constructed bodies ironically more humane than the average human being: Isaac Asimov's Rules of Robotics, for example, are meant to ensure that his robots cannot hurt people. In fact, gaining in translation turns out to be a major motivation for constructing bodies.

How?

Classroom activities consist of lecture and discussion, plus individual presentations and a workshop in which class members split into groups to get feedback on their ideas for the final paper or project. In addition to questions mentioned above, suggested paper topics include the representation of feminine or female power; the importance of clothing; the presentation of lies, silences, and other deviations from conventional communication; the presentation of boundaries; the role of literal or metaphorical rebirth; and the importance of the particular material from which a body is constructed. Students write three short papers or write two and do a final project. They are also evaluated on brief exercises, an oral presentation, writing mechanics, and effort.

An unusual feature is the option just mentioned of substituting a creative project for the last of the three papers. Students may choose almost any medium (as long as they don't emulate Frankenstein's assemblage of dead body parts) and must write a brief commentary on why they carried out the project as they did and how it relates to concepts in the course. I encourage but do not require them to present these projects to the rest of the class. Many welcome the creative opportunity, and this assignment has produced some surprising, exciting, and funny results, sometimes involving cultures or media not on the syllabus. One student translated part of *Kojiki*, the oldest Japanese text, in which a goddess's body humorously and tragically becomes a hill; another student created a temporary construction of her own body as performance art: she spent twenty-four hours tied to a male friend by a six-foot rope, then analyzed her experiences. Other examples have been short stories, sculpture, computer animation, and a retelling of the Pygmalion story in Ming Dynasty style (complete with a fan as an all-purpose prop), in which Pygmalion's mother comes to size up Galatea. Presentations of final projects stretch people's minds and create a feeling of community and closure.

Which?

Literature studied in recent semesters has largely been drawn from among the texts already mentioned in this essay, plus those listed below, which are novels or stories unless marked otherwise. For texts that are not well known, I have added brief explanations of how they involve the constructed body. The annotations are of necessity reductive—almost comically so—but I hope that above I have conveyed the richness of constructed body materials.

Margaret Atwood. "This story was told to me by another traveller, just passing through." Canadian prose poem, 1974. Boys have sex with a female figure they have made of mud.

———. *The Edible Woman*. Canadian, 1969. A woman undergoes an eating disorder, ultimately constructing and consuming a cake in the shape of her own body.

Avram Davidson. "The Golem." United States, 1955. A bickering retired couple comically deflates the pretensions of a threatening golem. I supply a glossary of Yiddish vocabulary (Peel and Peel).

Rebecca McClanahan Devet. "He Says He Doesn't Want to Change Her." United States poem, 1987. A man denies that he wants to resculpt a woman.

H[ilda] D[oolittle]. "Pygmalion." United States poem, 1917. Pygmalion reflects on the statues he has made of gods, wondering who created whom.

Nathaniel Hawthorne. "Rappaccini's Daughter." United States, 1844.

Larissa Lai. "Rachel." Canadian, 2004. Based on *Blade Runner,* from the point of view of a character coming to realize she is a replicant.

Ursula K. Le Guin. "Nine Lives." United States, 1969. Nine of a group of ten clones die, leaving the survivor devastated.

Artur Lundkvist. "The Statue." Swedish poem, 1974. A man's wife turns to stone because he could not love her enough.

Vonda McIntyre. "Aztecs." United States, 1977. In order to become a space pilot, a woman has her heart replaced by a mechanical one.

William Shakespeare. *The Winter's Tale*. English play, 1611.

Bram Stoker. *Dracula*. Irish, 1897.

David Wisniewski. *Golem*. United States, 1996. Children's book with cut-paper illustrations. It retells the traditional story of the golem, created out of mud by a rabbi to save the Jews of Prague in 1580.

As for film, *Blade Runner* and *Robo-Cop* are studied in detail. Other films, from which clips are studied, are usually drawn from among the following. Other possibilities abound.

Aria. 1987. Different directors, from various countries, were in charge of each of ten segments, each set to a different aria. In "Nessun dorma," the process of bedecking a woman with jewels turns out to be a vision she has while being operated on after a car accident. In "Armide," men work out in a gym, oblivious to women who caress and threaten them.

Edward Scissorhands. United States, 1990. A scientist dies before completing the young man he is creating. Left with scissors for hands, the young man finds lust, love, and ostracism in suburbia.

The Pillow Book. French, British, Dutch, 1996.

Some Like It Hot. United States, 1959.

Notes

1. These lines from John Milton's epic appear as the epigraph to Mary Shelley's *Frankenstein.*

2. While the syllabus contains more items from the United States than I would ordinarily assign in a world literature course, their predominance stems from the predominance until recently of the United States in the history of science fiction—a history that itself can be explored in the classroom.

3. I have also taught the course at the graduate level but am describing the undergraduate version, as probably more broadly useful to world literature faculty members. Some of my later examples of student projects come from the graduate version.

4. When I teach the course at the graduate level, I emphasize theory more. I assign readings by or lecture in greater depth on theorists such as Donna Haraway, Judith Butler, and Lennard Davis, and I list theoretical texts among the options for oral presentations.

5. I realize that these distinctions have gone out of fashion, but they are necessary for understanding the texts in the course. For instance, the distinction between mental and physical construction is needed to read Balzac's "Sarrasine." If everything is just mentally constructed, then it is as valid for the protagonist to believe La Zambinella is female as it is for everyone else to believe the singer is a castrato, and the story has no point. Similarly, the distinction—or at least a spectrum—between natural (or traditional or conventional) and artificial is needed for a robot story to make sense. Of course not every student shares my position, and the controversies surrounding constructivism make for lively class debates.

6. Although some find that distinction meaningless, I still consider it crucial (if at times difficult to determine). For instance, it matters that, while a number of science fiction texts depict human clones, we do not yet know of any real ones. If any are announced, that will be a key date in human history.

Works Cited

Alegría, Claribel. "Galatea before the Mirror." *Fugues.* Trans. D. J. Flakoll. Willimantic: Curbstone, 1993. 84–85. Print.

Andersen, Hans Christian. "The Little Mermaid." 1837. *Tales and Stories.* Trans. Patricia L. Conroy and Sven H. Rossel. Seattle: U of Washington P, 1980. 34–58. Print.

Aria. Dir. Robert Altman et al. 1987. Miramax, 1988. Film.

Asimov, Isaac. *I, Robot.* Garden City: Doubleday, 1950. Print.

Atwood, Margaret. *The Edible Woman.* 1969. New York: Popular Lib., 1976. Print.

———. "This story was told to me by another traveller, just passing through." *You Are Happy.* New York: Harper, 1974. 61. Print.

Balzac, Honoré de. "Sarrasine." 1830. *S/Z: An Essay.* By Roland Barthes. Trans. Richard Miller. New York: Hill, 1974. 221–54. Print.

Blade Runner. Dir. Ridley Scott. Warner Bros., 1982. Film.

Borges, Jorge Luis. "The Circular Ruins." 1956. Trans. James E. Irby. *Labyrinths: Selected Stories and Other Writings.* Ed. Donald A. Yates and Irby. New York: New Directions, 1964. 45–50. Print.

Čapek, Karel. *R. U. R. (Rossum's Universal Robots).* Trans. P. Selver. 1920. *R. U. R. [and] The Insect Play.* By the Brothers Čapek. London: Oxford UP, 1961. 1–104. Print.

Chabon, Michael. *The Amazing Adventures of Kavalier and Clay.* New York: Picador, 2000. Print.

Damrosch, David. *What Is World Literature?* Princeton: Princeton UP, 2003. Print.

Davidson, Avram. "The Golem." 1955. *The Fantasy Hall of Fame.* Ed. Robert Silverberg and Martin H. Greenberg. New York: Arbor, 1983. 318–24. Print.

Del Ray, Lester. "Helen O'Loy." 1938. *Science Fiction Hall of Fame.* Ed. Robert Silverberg. Garden City: Doubleday, 1970. 42–51. Print.

Devet, Rebecca McClanahan. "He Says He Doesn't Want to Change Her." *Mother Tongue.* Orlando: U of Central Florida P, 1987. 54. Print.

D[oolittle], H[ilda]. "Pygmalion." 1917. *Collected Poems of H. D.* New York: Liveright, 1929. 70–73. Print.

Edward Scissorhands. Dir. Tim Burton. Twentieth-Century Fox, 1990. Film.

Hawthorne, Nathaniel. "The Birthmark." 1843. *Hawthorne: Selected Tales and Sketches.* 3rd ed. New York: Holt, Rinehart, 1970. 264–81. Print.

———. "Rappaccini's Daughter: From the Writings of Aubépine." *Mosses from an Old Manse.* Ed. William Charvat, Roy Harvey Pearce, and Claude M. Simpson. Columbus: Ohio State UP, 1974. 91–128. Print. Vol. 10 of *The Centenary Edition of the Works of Nathaniel Hawthorne.*

Hoffmann, E. T. A. "The Sand-Man." 1816–17. Trans. J. T. Bealby. *The Best Tales of Hoffmann.* Ed. E. F. Bleiler. New York: Dover, 1967. 183–214. Print.

Hornbacher, Marya. *Wasted: A Memoir of Anorexia and Bulimia.* 1998. New York: Harper, 1999. Print.

Hwang, David Henry. *M. Butterfly.* 1986. New York: Plume, 1989. Print.

Kafka, Franz. "A Hunger Artist." 1924. *"The Metamorphosis," "In the Penal Colony," and Other Stories.* Trans. Willa Muir and Edwin Muir. New York: Schocken, 1995. 243–56. Print.

Kawabata, Yasunari. "One Arm." *"House of the Sleeping Beauties" and Other Stories.* Trans. Edward G. Seidensticker. Tokyo: Kodansha Intl., 1969. 102–24. Print.

Keats, John. "Ode on a Grecian Urn." 1820. *The Norton Anthology of English Literature.* Vol. 2. Ed. M. H. Abrams et al. New York: Norton, 1968. 530–32. Print.

Lai, Larissa. "Rachel." *So Long Been Dreaming: Postcolonial Science Fiction and Fantasy.* Ed. Nalo Hopkinson and Uppinder Mehan. Vancouver: Arsenal Pulp, 2004. 53–60. Print.

Le Guin, Ursula K. "Nine Lives." 1969. *The Wind's Twelve Quarters.* New York: Bantam, 1976. 119–47. Print.

Lem, Stanislaw. "The Mask." 1976. *Mortal Engines.* Trans. Michael Kandel. New York: Seabury, 1977. 181–239. Print.

Lundkvist, Artur. "The Statue." 1974. Trans. Diana Wormuth. *Scandinavian Review* 4 (1980): 22. Print.

Mahadevan, Anand. "Switching Heads and Cultures: Transformation of an Indian Myth by Thomas Mann and Girish Karnad." *Comparative Literature* 54 (2002): 23–41. Print.

McCaffrey, Anne. "The Ship Who Sang." 1961. *Women of Wonder: Science Fiction Stories by Women about Women.* Ed. Pamela Sargent. New York: Vintage-Random, 1975. 82–107. Print.

McIntyre, Vonda N. "Aztecs." 1977. *"Fireflood" and Other Stories.* New York: Timescape-Pocket, 1981. 183–237. Print.

Ovid. "Pygmalion." *Bulfinch's Mythology: The Age of Fable.* Comp. Thomas Bulfinch. 1855. Garden City: Doubleday, 1968. 65–66. Print.

Peel, Ellen, and Evelyn Peel. "Yiddish Vocabulary in [Davidson's] 'The Golem.'" TS.

Piercy, Marge. *He, She, and It.* 1991. New York: Fawcett Crest–Ballantine, 1993. Print.

The Pillow Book. Dir. Peter Greenaway. 1996. Columbia Tristar Home Entertainment, 1998. DVD.

Robo-Cop. Dir. Paul Verhoeven. Orion, 1987. Film.

Shakespeare, William. *The Winter's Tale.* 1611. Ed. Baldwin Maxwell. Baltimore: Penguin, 1956. Print.

Shelley, Mary. *Frankenstein.* 1818, 1831. Ed. Johanna M. Smith. 2nd ed. Boston: Bedford–St. Martin's, 2000. Print.

Some Like It Hot. Dir. Billy Wilder. United Artists, 1959. Film.

"Special Topic: Science Fiction and Literary Studies: The Next Millennium." *PMLA* 119.3 (2004): 429–546. Print.

Staël, Germaine de. "The Mannequin." *An Extraordinary Woman: Selected Writings of Germaine de Staël.* Trans. and ed. Vivian Folkenflik. New York: Columbia UP, 1987. 325–47, 396–97. Print.

Stoker, Bram. *Dracula.* 1897. New York: Signet, 1992. Print.

Wisniewski, David. "A Note." *Golem.* New York: Clarion-Houghton, 1996. N. pag. Print.

Wolf, Christa. "Self-Experiment: Appendix to a Report." 1973. Trans. Jeanette Clausen. *New German Critique* 13 (1978): 109–31. Print.

C. A. Prettiman

"Literature That Changed the World": Designing a World Literature Course

In this essay I briefly explore some general conceptual and pedagogical issues inherent in world literature course construction for nonmajors. I built a two-semester, electronic-format survey course for a small college that did not have such a course. At the beginning of this undertaking, I supposed that acquiring the appropriate computer skills and the technical ability to create a completely online course environment would be my biggest challenge. Instead, I found that selecting, single-handedly, a year-long dream list of great non-English-language literature was a task both fascinating and daunting. I found myself questioning, weighing, and relearning many tenets crucial to the comparatist. These questions may seem tired, simplistic, or self-evident to some, but I felt myself in terra incognita. As both an undergraduate and a graduate student in comparative literature, I was never once counseled on how to build a comprehensive world literature course worth offering at an institution of higher learning.

How to proceed? One might build on the basis of pure intellectual substance, or worry about balance, or make salability to the undergraduate market—invidious though that prospect is to many—the main criterion. I phrase these issues collegially, informally, but they are serious, and the most theoretically sophisticated of us must grapple with them when confronting the task of course development or revision and when explaining our vision to curriculum and instruction committees. Unfortunately, I have just enough space here to pull many troubles out of Pandora's box but not to catch them and cram them back in. So the following pretends to be nothing grander than my questions and my saga as I made decisions in designing a course called Literature That Changed the World, parts 1 and 2.

The very terms we begin with are fraught with problems, and we have no tidier ones to substitute them, even in the new millennium. As Claudio Guillén might say, we are what we are and what we have been. The term *world literature* itself is at once both admirably catholic and ridiculously tautological: does there exist any work of literature that is not written in the world? Even more fundamentally, we must decide where we personally—or as a department—delineate the outer limits of literature. Could a case be made for including *On the Origin of Species*, Sun Tsu's *Art of War*, *Summa Theologiae*, the Upanishads, or Einstein's *Relativity* as texts? What about Andreas Capellanus, Freud, the Qur'an? Then there is the old polemic concerning the term *world literature* as opposed to *comparative literature*. Is world literature, as some have said, the widest extension of comparative literature, (but) strictly a dimension? Do we really mean *Weltliteratur*? In practical terms, world literature often ends as simply comparative literature in translation (as it was in my undergraduate courses), but there may be theoretical and procedural differences too, depending on the instructor and the program in question. (The course I designed was certainly ab ovo a comparative course, if by comparison we mean the dialectic between similarity and difference.)

Next, there is the issue of whether to represent American and British literatures in a world literature survey course, and if so, in what proportion. We may decide to exclude them because they are already known, because they are covered in other courses, or because we are uneasy about usurping the territory of our English department colleagues. Or perhaps we underrepresent them for contrastive reasons. Or perhaps the enterprise drives one to adopt the solution of W. J. T. Mitchell and write an article on why comparisons are odious. Ideally, of course, one could teach a course that need not attempt to be a smorgasbord. It goes without saying that here I am confining myself to the conception of an undergraduate world lit survey course, not a topics course, a genre course, or a course with some mandated geographic limitations. I look at syllabi for East/

West courses, and wish I had even that luxury, of being able to eliminate North and South at least. (I wistfully wish I could teach a course entitled World Literature between the Tropic of Cancer and the Tropic of Capricorn. No reason this focus would be any more arbitrary than many other geografico-literary gerrymanderings we use as organizational devices.)

The concept of a world literature survey becomes almost hopelessly complex. The analogy I used with my husband (who is mercifully concentrated in one national discipline) is that one might as well try to conduct a fifteen-week cooking class on world cuisines. Italian food alone could not be done justice in such a time span. To that, add Chinese food, French, Middle Eastern, Eastern European, Japanese, Mexican, German— everything that defines the gastronomy of a culture, from sushi to schnitzel, from cordon bleu to chop suey. Add to that gargantuan task the fact that your students may have tasted little other than hamburgers in the course of their lives.

This culinary analogy may not be a felicitous one, but it is essentially accurate, as I'm sure most of us can attest to. We may find ourselves with two weeks of the semester to cover . . . Russia. Three class periods for Germany. We want to cover something, anything in Chinese literature? That may mean jettisoning France. Inconceivable. Well, maybe we can cut all of French literature down to *two* selections, so we have time to squeeze in one Chinese author . . . After a while, we begin to feel like Rowan Atkinson as Mr. Bean, packing his shoebox-sized suitcase to go on holiday: chopping off pant legs, squeezing toothpaste out into the sink to make a smaller tube, even considering cutting off his teddy bear's head so it will fit (*Mr. Bean*). And the constraints of the length of college semesters make it impossible for us simply to take a bigger suitcase.

So, survey course design is the task laid before us. How do we choose texts for inclusion? What are the criteria? We could choose texts, as I attempted to do, on the basis of their degree of influence rather than on the more nebulous basis of excellence. But influence on whom? Perhaps on us in the West, and on our literary forms. Or on other writers, or nations, or the educated population. How widespread should the influence be, and how enduring, to make the cut? And then what? Do we succumb to the quest for the recognizable name: Dante, Vergil, and Goethe as opposed to Maimonides, Akhmatova, and Lao-tzu? Are we covertly or overtly teaching great books? Perhaps we are teaching great thinkers instead, or cultural literacy, or (if we are honest) stuff we like. Or (if we are even more honest) stuff we can find scholarly reference material on.

We stare the old conundrum in the eyeballs, that of the canonical versus the multicultural. If we take time genuinely to teach Africa, India, Latin America, the Far East, we find ourselves skimming Germany, Italy, Spain, Russia. Do we give Homer short shrift to squeeze in Machado de Assis? (I might trade that catalog of Greek ships for *Quincas Borba*, at that.) Part of the coverage issue hinges on number of class hours, but as well on the amount of student reading per term that makes us blink: 1,500 pages, 3,000 pages, and 5,000 pages per term yields dramatically different amounts of coverage—and of course dramatically different levels of student digestion and retention, not to mention simple compliance. I once had a colleague who assigned a different full-length novel for each class period, and was both bewildered and incensed when his honors-level students regularly failed to complete the reading on time—or at all. There looms the specter of the sublimest failure one can make in decisions of coverage: one puts together a course so beautifully comprehensive that a full-time student would have to be crazy to take it.

Another question is what to do about translations. We could go with revered and venerable translators, with their *thee*s and *thou*s. Or we could take a chance on a colloquial new rendering (which may be the only rendering, in some literatures). Or, as I did with some Leopoldo Lugones poetry, we can translate the damn things ourselves for the students. It becomes easier—a little easier—to make decisions if we articulate our personal pedagogical and philosophical objectives, if only for ourselves, in words of one syllable. I do not include Dante on my syllabus just because I want to use him as a vehicle to teach Italian culture. But one might put Yukio Mishima on the syllabus to get at Japanese culture and ideas of honor.

Even if we keep to the literary, we might model Tzvetan Todorov's dictum that the object of study is not the work but the potentialities of literary discourse that have made it possible. Do I teach Solzhenitsyn or Kundera not only for their own excellence but also to convey something about Soviet repression? If I am teaching at a large, multicultural university, perhaps not. If I am standing before a roomful of overwhelmingly Caucasian middle-class Judeo-Christian women from rural eastern Pennsylvania, whose families are of western European descent, many of whom might have difficulty indicating Japan on a map . . . well, then what do I do? Do I always keep clear the distinction among great works, great authors, and great cultures? Can I responsibly teach the first two without the third? How important is "balance" to us personally, and of what sort?

Chronological balance, gender balance, continent balance, linguistic balance, cultural balance?

Many of us possibly have a difficult time imagining the need to conceive something as basic as a lower-level world lit survey course. Such things have probably been in place since time immemorial at most institutions. But we may have to update or refurbish such a survey course to meet the needs of changing times and constituencies, and all of us have had to emerge from the relative shelter of our specialty fields to teach such a course for the first time.

To what extent do you worry about making the course feasible for a grader other than yourself? If it generates large enrollments and you must use a grader, how outré can you get? (As a senior colleague once growled in my hearing, "If no one has bothered to write a Twayne on it, I don't want to teach it.") Is this attitude hopelessly uninformed or provincial? It can be grimly realistic at institutions like my own, where our modest library's budget often does not cover many purchases straying from canonical-minded volumes, and even our most senior scholars teach four-four loads. I am not for a moment insinuating that we should not be teaching literature that is genuinely world—whether or not one's students have ever heard of someone named something like Tawfiq al-Hakim. I am saying that we as professors still face, and will always face, issues of inclusion versus exclusion in survey course design, and there are still no easy solutions.

Another troubling path is that of representative sampling. If we do not have time to teach a dozen great novels, we could consider whether a dozen great excerpts will do. If the *Reader's Digest* approach to literature appalls, what about genre trade-offs? If we do not have time for a Tolstoy novel, we could resort to a Tolstoy short story. We could eliminate an epic from the syllabus to make way for a flock of sonnets. We could try a Cervantes *entremés* instead of a full-length play, or a *novela ejemplar* instead of *Don Quijote*. I confess that I excerpted mercilessly in my course, but it seems to have worked after a fashion. The chemistry major who went off to peruse the entire *Divine Comedy* after we studied a few cantos from *Inferno* is my prize success. She thought the excerpts were the best thing she ever read and wanted to find out for herself if Dante ever got Beatrice in the end.

When we have chosen our all-star lineup of authors, we must decide how to present them. We could resort to period, genre, or theme approaches, or the still oddly seductive parade of isms of our own undergraduate days (realism, naturalism, Romanticism, neoclassicism . . .), or geo-graphic groupings. In designing my course, I tried a few different categorizations—thus I cheerfully admit to a lack of structural consis-tency on my first time out. (But I'll call my approach eclectic.) I think that for me and my class of honors students, the thematic units worked best. With so drastically selective a course, I abandoned much of my pretense of coverage. So I did units like "Love in the Ancient World," with readings from Ovid, Catullus, Sappho, Rumi—even *The Arabian Nights*, translated by the Iraqi American scholar Husain Haddawy, al-though I was sad to jettison the Sir Richard Burton edition so many of us remember.

I introduced the issue of translation, theoretical and practical, in my lecture and assignments on Omar Khayyám and Fitzgerald. Other the-matic units I tackled were Eastern Thought, The Soviet Experience, and Postcolonialism. I tried generic units too. The Birth of the Novel, for in-stance, took us from Petronius's *Satyricon* to *The Tale of Genji* to the *Quijote*. Into this mélange I mixed units on the Renaissance, the Enlight-enment, the medieval masters—yes, I tried a bit of everything. My crite-rion for selection of authors was influence. Confucius's *Analects* influ-enced millions of people. So did *The City of God*. Ovid and Catullus changed the way we write of love, so I included them too.

But the ultimate question for me is what the student carries away from the course. Objectives will vary according to college resources and course offerings. At small, liberal-arts institutions in which resources in-creasingly go to sciences, business, and technology programs, there may be no comp lit department, or indeed even a separate English department anymore. Victims of the moneymakers and the bottom line, some of us may languish in a departmental bouillabaisse called Humanities or lan-guish still further under a four-four or worse teaching load. A world lit survey course is a different beast when you are one of several full-time, tenure-track professors in comparative literature at your university and not, as I am, one of only two gurus for your institution of all non-En-glish-language literature in existence.

But back to the tale of what my students carried away from my ex-periment. Most of them were bright science majors, the kind you often can't get out of the lab with a crowbar, who with innocence bestow on you the troubling compliment, "I really hated literature until I came to this class." Teaching Lacan to this population seems superfluous. I tell them little of theory as such. I mostly try to teach them the practical aspects of how to read literature intelligently, how to evaluate widely divergent critical interpretations of a text, how to write about complex abstractions. How to make connections between a twelfth-century Japanese woman's life and their own. How to write a research paper on a historical or literary topic. How to reflect on the constants in great literature and in our lives: finding and keeping love, surviving loss, struggling through parenthood and childhood, making honorable choices, reacting to societal pressures and political institutions, preparing for death. How to read about and listen to strange worldviews; how to contemplate alien creeds, celebrations, resolutions.

In my class, we did not whitewash over differences. I remember the young woman who tried anxiously to convince the class that Sappho couldn't have been writing about sexual passion for another woman; surely Sappho was just talking about friendship. This student was not comfortable with my answers. But we survived; so, I hope, did the spirit of Sappho. I am not sure that I taught correctly. When I looked through Dante's *Purgatorio* recently, my eye fell on these words: "E Virgilio rispuose: 'Voi credete / forse che siamo esperti d'esto loco; / ma noi siam peregrin come voi siete'" (2.61–63; "And Virgil answered: 'You may be convinced that we are quite familiar with this shore; but we are strangers here, just as you are'"). Some might say that I involve my students too little in current polemicizing and too much in a positivistic search for old-fashioned themes. Perhaps we are still grappling with the problems Robert Clements observed when he wrote, some years ago now:

> We are still lacking the concepts and tools which will permit us truly to study literature at the global level. These concepts and tools will gradually materialize. While waiting and searching for them, we must beware of ever again confusing "world literature" with the literature of our inherited culture. (xxx)

Nevertheless, I have no regrets about my experiment (which has become a regular offering of our honors program). Apparently neither did the students: after the first half of this year-long course, the second half, in the spring semester, was dramatically overenrolled. The conclusion that I made somebody want to read books and think and talk about them makes me hopeful that world literature, however we blunder into it and through it, can find a place in and revitalize the undergraduate academic experience.

Works Cited

Clements, Robert J. *Comparative Literature as Academic Discipline: A Statement of Principles, Praxis, Standards.* New York: MLA, 1978. Print.

Dante Alighieri. *Purgatorio 2. The Comedy.* Trans. Allen Mandelbaum. *Digital Dante.* Inst. for Learning Technologies, Columbia U, Nov. 1997. Web. 22 July 2008.

Guillén, Claudio. *The Challenge of Comparative Literature.* Trans. Cola Franzen. Cambridge: Harvard UP, 1993. Print.

Mitchell, W. J. T. "Why Comparisons Are Odious." *World Literature Today* 70.2 (1996): 321–24. Print.

Mr. Bean Packing. Metacafe Video Entertainment, 24 July 2007. Web. 3 Apr. 2008.

Todorov, Tzvetan. "The Notion of Literature." *New Literary History* 38.1 (2007): 1–12. Print.

Eric Sterling

Teaching World Masterpieces through Religious Themes in Literature

In my course Survey of World Literature I at Auburn University, Montgomery, which covers literature from *Gilgamesh* through John Milton's *Paradise Lost* and employs the first volume of the *Norton Anthology of World Masterpieces*, I focus on the dichotomy between polytheistic and monotheistic works. The exploration of this demarcation is very productive pedagogically, because the plots, characterizations, and themes of most of the literary works in the anthology pertain, to some extent, to religion and faith in a supernatural being or beings. The belief in a deity markedly affects the characters' behavior, an author's attitudes toward political and social hegemony, and an author's treatment of women in a particular society. Moreover, students discern that although polytheistic and monotheistic texts share similar themes, such as the subordination of human beings to the gods or God, crucial distinctions exist between portrayals of protagonists and deities in these two types of works.

Although this class is a general survey of world literature, not a course in spiritual literature, I have found that the exploration of the significance of religion in the literary works of the ancient, medieval, and early modern eras allows students to attain a thorough and sophisticated understanding of world literary masterpieces in these periods. (In this essay, I focus solely on texts of ancient literature.) Furthermore, the study of the transformation of Western literature from polytheistic to monotheistic texts provides students with a profound insight into the evolution of world literature and Western culture.

Religion is a helpful theme in the course because of the large number of devout Christians at Auburn University, Montgomery. Montgomery is located in the heart of the Bible Belt. In 2003, Alabama Supreme Court Chief Justice Roy Moore installed a huge stone replica of the Ten Commandments in the state courthouse, about six miles from campus, and embarked on a highly publicized campaign to maintain it there. Many die-hard supporters from all over the United States came and held daily vigils outside the courthouse, begging the state and federal courts to save the commandments. In October 2005, Moore announced that he was running for governor of Alabama, counting primarily on the large support of evangelical Christians. Montgomery is called the cradle of the Confederacy, because it was the first capital of the Confederacy and contains the Confederate White House, where Jefferson Davis stayed during the Civil War. Montgomery, however, is also known as the birthplace of the civil rights movement, for it is the city where Rosa Parks refused to move to the back of the bus, inciting the bus boycott, and where Martin Luther King, Jr., preached at his church on Dexter Avenue. The famous Selma-to-Montgomery march, in which policemen attacked African American marchers, ended in Montgomery. Montgomery is also near Tuscaloosa, where former Governor George Wallace stood by the door of the school building, attempting to prevent African American students from attending the University of Alabama, and near Birmingham, where in 1963 the infamous Sixteenth Street Baptist Church bombing occurred.

Auburn University, Montgomery, has five thousand students and is the only branch campus of Auburn University. Auburn University, Montgomery, was lauded in *US News and World Report* for having a diverse student body, consisting of approximately thirty percent African American students ("America's Best Colleges"). There is also a large nontraditional student base, with many students in their thirties, forties, fifties, and even sixties. Because of a lenient admissions policy, faculty members find themselves with a diverse mix of students. Highly motivated and well-read students sit next to others who barely graduated from high school and who are not well prepared for college. With this mix and the city's history in mind, the class begins with the exploration of the works and how they relate to other works, both polytheistic and monotheistic.

The first work is Sophocles's *Oedipus the King*, which is relatively manageable for students to read and discuss (more manageable than the Homeric epics). We continue with Euripides's *Medea* and the anonymous *Gilgamesh*, discussing the power of the gods and their influence on human beings. These three work well together in the classroom. All address the theme of the gods' roles in the lives and actions of mortals. The characters can achieve their goals only with the support and approval of the gods. But students discern differences in the role of the gods in *Oedipus the King*, *Medea*, and *Gilgamesh*. They are intrigued by the didactic function of the gods in *Oedipus* and the lack of this function in the play by Euripides; this contrast always leads to fruitful discussion. Students believe that *Gilgamesh* is also didactic, in that the protagonist often thrives or is punished depending on how he treats the gods. For example, he loses his close friend, Enkidu, shortly after insulting the goddess Ishtar. The themes of pride and destiny permeate all three works, and students enjoy discussing them, particularly how they relate to each protagonist's quest.

My students and I discuss the characters' attitudes toward the gods and ponder whether human beings such as Oedipus have free will or whether fate and predestination determine human destiny. Students need to know what people in the days of Sophocles, Euripides, and the anonymous author of *Gilgamesh* believed about the gods and about their relationship with human beings. My students realize that *Oedipus the King* is more than simply a play about a tragic fall of a hero caused by hubris. Some students assert that during the course of the drama, Oedipus sees tragedy not only in his marriage to his mother and murder of his father but also in his place in the universe and subservience to the gods.

After the class has thoroughly explored the relationship between the gods and human beings in these three works, we turn our attention to selections from three monotheistic literary works: the Old Testament, the New Testament, and the Qur'an. Although the students have previously read the story of creation from the Book of Genesis, this time they read it in the light of other works, such as the creation of Gilgamesh and Enkidu. That the great flood in *Gilgamesh* appears in the Old Testament as well leads to lively discussion. One question that arises is whether *Gilgamesh* influenced the Old Testament treatment of the flood. This discussion can be emotional, considering that the university is firmly nestled in the Bible Belt. In most semesters, none of my students is familiar with the Qur'an, so I am pleased that they get to read selections from it. We read sura 1 (The Exordium), sura 5 (Table), and sura 12 (Joseph). Sura 5 provides students with an Arabic view of Jews and Christians, and we compare sura 12 with the story of Joseph from the Old Testament. Some students express surprise that Joseph and other figures from the Old Testament are discussed in the Qur'an; before the course began, they thought that the Qur'an contained only Muslim figures such as Muhammad. One important distinction occurs in the story of Joseph and his master's wife in Egypt: the Qur'an provides an interpretation quite different from that of the Old Testament. We discuss the significance of these markedly different interpretations of the Joseph story.

When I tell about Ancient Greek stagecraft and how Oedipus's drama might have been staged, students sometimes form visual images in their minds of the characters. I also show a video of the play, although I stress that what students see is not necessarily Sophocles's play as the dramatist saw it but rather an interpretation of it. Robert McMahon says:

> Real-life interactions have an advantage over reading a play because we can hear the tones in a person's speech. We respond not only to what others say but to how they say it, and the *how* often means more to us than the *what*. As every director knows, the same play can be performed in many different ways. (125)

Students enjoy the Sir Tyrone Guthrie version of *Oedipus Rex* (1957), in which Guthrie's actors don masks as the actors did in the days of Sophocles. The production provides my students with a sense of how the play might have been staged in approximately 430 BC. Students should also see the play, because drama is meant to be staged and seen, not merely read. Instructors can do performance teaching and ask theater majors—or other students—in the class how they, as a director, would do the blocking in the play. I also like to begin with *Oedipus the King*, because I find it constructive pedagogically to pair it with Euripides's *Medea* and because I like to save *Gilgamesh* for later so that I can juxtapose it with parallel sections from the Old Testament. Establishing helpful thematic connections among texts is more important than proceeding in chronological order.

I break the students into six groups of five and provide each group with the specific task of discussing thoroughly one question concerning *Oedipus the King*. I do not request or even desire students to agree with one another. They should not withhold their opinions in order to conform, and sometimes disagreement in a group results in a discussion more complex and substantial than when the group reaches a consensus. The students address their group's question and subsequently share highlights of their deliberations with the rest of the class. After each group reports details from the discussion, I ask the rest of the class to respond to the group's conclusions. I repeat this procedure for all six groups. Beginning this activity early in the course allows students to become comfortable with one another, and those who participate in class discussion early in the semester tend to continue to provide their opinions to the class throughout the semester. Furthermore, this activity proves advantageous to shy students, who often are well prepared for class and have excellent answers in their heads but are reluctant to share their opinions in front of large groups of people.

Students enjoy reading and discussing *Medea*. They are intrigued by the intensity of the protagonist's emotions and her sense of honor. Ironically, students admire her pride, even though they criticize Oedipus for exhibiting the same sin. Some identify with her and defend her vigorously in class—at least until she murders her own children. Some focus on Medea as a victim of discrimination and as a minority in the culture. This perspective is not surprising, given that the course is taught in a city that played an important role in the civil rights movement. Students claim that Medea has virtually no rights and is a victim of discrimination as a nonnative and a woman. She helped Jason enormously, but in Thebes he kept his rights and will ascend socially by marrying Kreon's daughter, while Medea has lost her rights and power. I suggest that Medea's willingness to take matters into her own hands, the absence of divine intervention or even a divine presence, and the lack of divine or poetic justice—in contrast to *Oedipus*—indicate why the drama of Sophocles was more readily accepted and praised than that of Euripides in their time.

Gilgamesh, like *Oedipus*, contains the strong presence of and intervention by the gods. Many students claim that this work contains a much greater presence of the gods than do the plays by Sophocles and Euripides. A few students disagree, however, arguing that there is as much supernatural control in *Oedipus* as in *Gilgamesh*; the only difference is that the gods in Sophocles's play act before the drama begins and the protagonist's fate is already sealed. Although many students see Gilgamesh's defeat of Humbaba as a sign of the hero's power, I point out that perhaps the victory actually shows his weakness, because he relies so much on the help of the gods. Similarly, when Gilgamesh spurns the romantic advances of Ishtar, the reader perceives how vulnerable he is, for the goddess demands revenge, which leads ultimately to the death of Enkidu. Without divine favor, Gilgamesh is actually helpless.

Gilgamesh serves as an effective transition to the monotheistic works. Students readily make connections between this epic and the Old and New Testaments and the Qur'an. *Gilgamesh* and the Old Testament begin with the story of Creation, and both texts depict verbal interaction between deities and human beings. Shamash accepts Gilgamesh's plea and chastises Enkidu for cursing the harlot. Gilgamesh engages in a verbal altercation with Ishtar. Similarly, Adam speaks with God, and God confronts Adam and Eve in the Garden of Eden after they eat from the fruit of the Tree of Knowledge of Good and Evil. Students notice that God does not speak directly to Joseph but instead communicates with him through dreams. Astute classmates observe that much of the communication and warnings in the beginning of *Gilgamesh* also derive from dreams. Students wonder if this indirect communication results from living in a postlapsarian world, that the fall from God's grace results in his reluctance to speak directly with human beings.

When students are asked how God differs from the gods, some say that God is paternal; it is as a parent that he punishes Adam and Eve for disobeying. I wonder aloud why God puts the tree in the garden if he does not want them to eat from it. Is he setting them up to fall, just as the gods set up Oedipus?

One controversial connection that I make is between the flood scenes in *Gilgamesh* and Genesis. Students notice immediately the correlation between the stories of Utnapishtim and Noah. Initially, some suggest that the anonymous author of *Gilgamesh* borrowed (or plagiarized) his or her story from the Old Testament account of Noah and the flood. Observant students point out that the story of Utnapishtim could not have been taken from the Bible, having been created centuries before the Old Testament was written; if any borrowing took place, the biblical story borrowed from *Gilgamesh*. This idea is upsetting to some of my students, particularly those who are deeply religious. Some suggest that the similarity is only a coincidence or that the dating of *Gilgamesh* could be wrong—that the work was actually written after the Old Testament account. This passage from *Gilgamesh* can lead to tense moments in class, particularly if a student suggests that the striking similarity between the two texts indicates that those who wrote the Bible were inspired not by

God but by other writings. Students do mention that the contrast between the two accounts suggests that God is a just deity, because he creates the flood to destroy evil, while the gods in *Gilgamesh* simply want to
sleep better. Other students make a connection between the two texts
because of the similar use of the word "babel" to describe confusion and
bad behavior (Genesis 11; *Gilgamesh* 41). I like to wait until the class has
discussed both *Gilgamesh* and the Old Testament before making connections between the two texts, but often students cannot wait and, knowing the Old Testament so well, start comparing and contrasting while we
are discussing *Gilgamesh*.

When the class reads about the birth of Jesus in Luke 2 of the New
Testament, students are immediately struck by the element of social class.
They discern that Joseph and Mary are common citizens, far from wealthy,
as are the country shepherds whom the angel of the Lord tells of tidings
of joy. It is not until we reach the New Testament that students recognize
that the heroes of the polytheistic texts are wealthy and powerful and that
the protagonists of the Old and New Testament are commoners, at least
socioeconomically. I explain that in classical, polytheistic literature, tragedy derives from a great fall and a great loss by a man with great power
and wealth—in other words, someone who has much to lose. Commoners were not considered tragic heroes, because people of their social class
were not respected or valued. Commoners in tragedies merely serve as
messengers who bring information to the royalty but are not perceived by
those in power to have much worth in themselves. But in the Bible, nobil-
ity derives from spirit, virtue, and God's plan, not from material wealth.
Students acquire a better understanding of Judeo-Christian values when
they contrast these values with the ethos present in the polytheistic
works.

The hardest text that I teach in the class is the Qur'an, hardest because some students are resistant to studying the work, even though they
have never read it before. This resistance has increased markedly since
9/11. Recently a few of my students asked to be excused from the reading
for spiritual reasons, but I denied their request, believing that it is important for them to read a work of another spiritual literature, one that pos-
sesses another perspective. Also, they should not dismiss a text before
reading and understanding it. Before we discuss the Qur'an, I encourage
students to read the text with an open mind, and to those students who
do not want to read the work because of 9/11 I stress that a huge distinction exists between peaceful, law-abiding Muslims and the hijackers.

392 Religious Themes in Literature

Practically all my students already know this, but I speak to the few who do not wish to read the text in protest.

Students are surprised to learn that Joseph and other figures of the Bible appear in the Qur'an, but they are disappointed that he seems to be stripped of his heritage as a Jew. Some are quite offended by statements in sura 5 that Jews and Christians have broken their covenants to God and thus no longer have his love. I point out that although these statements seem prejudicial, Muslims today are insulted by prejudiced comments by Americans about their faith and ethnicity. Current examples can make students realize that the literature of centuries ago still holds relevance today, that issues from *Oedipus, Medea, Gilgamesh*, the Old and New Testaments, and the Qur'an can affect students' lives today.

Although this unit on religious literature covers only the first six works on the syllabus, clearly the unit could be expanded to fill the entire semester, by incorporating other works: Sophocles's *Antigone*; Homer's *Iliad* and *Odyssey*; and literary pieces that contain the presence of one God, such as *Beowulf* (a work that has pagan elements but was transcribed and most probably revised with a monotheistic perspective by a Christian), Dante's *Divine Comedy*, the anonymous *Sir Gawain and the Green Knight, Everyman*, and Milton's *Paradise Lost*. I have enjoyed success when extending the syllabus to incorporate some of these works. As one can see by reading the table of contents of world literature anthologies by Norton (Lawall, Mack, et al.) or Longman (Damrosch et al.), most works of the era contain spiritual themes. Thus, instead of serving as one unit, the theme of religious literature can inspire students for a whole semester.

Works Cited

"America's Best Colleges, 2008." *US News and World Report*. Web. 22 July 2008.

Damrosch, David, et al., eds. *The Longman Anthology of World Literature*. 3 vols. New York: Longman, 2004. Print.

Gilgamesh. Lawall, Mack, et al. 1: 16–47.

Guthrie, Tyrone, dir. *Oedipus Rex*. 1957. Image Entertainment, 2002. DVD.

Lawall, Sarah, Maynard Mack, et al., eds. *The Norton Anthology of World Masterpieces*. 7th ed. 2 vols. New York: Norton, 1999. Print.

McMahon, Robert. *Thinking about Literature*. Portsmouth: Heinemann, 2002. Print.

Kathryn A. Walterscheid

Ancient and Contemporary Texts: Teaching an Introductory Course in Non-Western Literatures

The Pierre Laclede Honors College of the University of Missouri, Saint Louis, requires all freshmen to take Non-Western Traditions, which deals with a variety of ethnic literatures spanning the globe. Depending on the particular semester, my sections might require works from Asia, Africa, Australia, the Americas, and the Middle East. The course focuses on cultural traditions and the fact that such traditions rarely die; they reappear instead in a different form. Thus, we investigate a global tradition through sources from a culture—perhaps myths, religious texts, poetry, fiction, or autobiography. Then we read recent literature from the same culture to see how that tradition is still enduring, being contested, or has been transformed in some way.

Our very first discussion has to be about what the "non-Western" of the course title might mean. It is difficult to explain or to find a more appropriate label. Clearly we are not speaking geographically (and even then, what is west depends on where on the globe you stand). Are we choosing by technology? No, because lots of the places we will study have advanced technology. Students know that United States culture and European culture have been strongly influenced by Ancient Greece and Rome. But using that influence as a test does not really help, since many countries that are not usually represented in Western anthologies have been greatly influenced by Ancient Greece and Rome, Egypt to name only one. *Non-Western* is not a very appealing term, because is it defining by a negative, which implies that the positive side is more important. We finally decide, because we can spend only so much time on this topic, that our course is about cultures that do not have marked Anglo-European roots.

For this course, I choose texts written by the peoples from the regions we address, which means that almost everything must be read in translation. This fact leads naturally to a discussion of how meaning can differ depending on the translation. I give a few short excerpts of other translations for comparison with the one we are using. For example, there is an alternative translation of the *Mahabharata*'s story of Savitri in the John Yohannan anthology, and students are asked to compare and contrast the two versions.[1]

To prepare the students for the literature, we discuss myth (as in "a universal truth," not as in "a lie"). Our discussion is focused by essays by Mircea Eliade and by Joseph Campbell on myth, religion, and art from the anthology *Transformations of Myth through Time* (Eisenberg et al.). This discussion usually opens the students up for the rest of the class. Some are enthralled; others feel that at least they know what they will be in for this semester.

We move to Native American topics. The students are required to read several essays about myth and Native American culture in the Diane Eisenberg anthology; they are also given a handout describing the Spider woman story of the Navajo. It is only after several days discussing these texts that we begin Leslie Marmon Silko's novel *Ceremony*. Presaging the novel with the articles has made the novel much easier to teach and much more appreciated by students. In previous courses in which I did not assign the articles, not only did students feel disoriented by Silko's novel but also many disliked it because of its unusual style. After reading articles like those on myth and religion, most students can accept the mythic poetry that seems to float through Tayo's head. After reading Barre Toelken's "How Many Sheep Will It Hold?" and Sam D. Gill's "The Shadow of a Vision Yonder," they are willing to try to view the world from another perspective. In fact, by now they feel like experts, and it is they, not I, who explain the cyclical structure of the novel and the importance of the interspersed poetry (although they always need help with the poem apparently told by Emo). Through Silko's interweaving of twentieth-century attitudes with Laguna Pueblo songs, prayers, and stories, the students are given a concrete example of how old traditions can be reused, and they are shown that traditions can still have immediate importance.

For Africa, we start with D. T. Niane's retelling of *Sundiata*. This work leads to discussion of, among other themes in the story, the nature and function of the griot or West African bard. It segues beautifully into *Keita: The Heritage of the Griot*, a film from Burkina Faso set in the twentieth century. The story follows a traditional-style griot who journeys to the city to tell a young boy about his name and heritage. Because the youngster is a descendant of the Keita princes of Mali, the griot begins telling the story of the Malian epic hero Sundiata. As the film moves among the boy's life at home and school, his time with the griot, and the flashbacks to the story of Sundiata, the griot theme is continued by showing a modern, mercenary griot and also the griot of Sundiata's father. Once again we have plenty of examples to discuss the change in traditions. At the end of the film, when the griot has left because of conflicts with the schoolmaster, the boy himself tries to tell the griot's story. The film inspires discussion of the nature of education, women's roles, and of course the griot. The griot tradition continues, despite changes in culture, because there are still griots who feel it is their mission to continue to tell the story of their people, although those same griots might expand their media, telling the tales not just orally but perhaps also through film. The griot in the film is a real-life griot, and his son, the director of *Keita*, is also a griot; their family has traditionally been the griots for the Keita family.

We continue this unit with several short stories by African writers from the anthology *Other Voices, Other Vistas* (Solomon). In choosing texts for this unit (actually for the whole course), I tried to find texts from the same region that I could pair together (like *Sundiata* and *Keita*). I also tried to expose the students to a variety of cultures in the unit grouping, if that was possible. In an introductory course like this, students need constant reminders that, for example, Africa is a huge continent with many different peoples. Thus the stories come from authors from around Africa: Nigeria, Kenya, Botswana, South Africa, and Zimbabwe.

When we discuss the Middle East, we start with some works from ancient Persia and Arabia: excerpts from the *Shahnamah* and a tale from the *Thousand and One Arabian Nights* (both found in Yohannan's *Treasury of Asian Literature*). These texts are chosen for being very different from the images that the United States media shows about the Middle East. The texts show strong women, humor, epic heroism, and real tragedy. We then read the anthology's selections from the Qur'an. That discussion begins with a disclaimer: perhaps the Qur'an should not be read in a course on non-Western literature, because theologians consider Islam to be in the Western tradition. Most of my students are stunned by this revelation. We decide to read it anyway, because how can we understand Middle Eastern texts written after 621 CE if we did not? The selections from the Qur'an facilitate discussion of Islam's relation to Judaism and Christianity, alcohol's place in Middle Eastern culture, visions of paradise, the status of women, and the nature of God (which we can relate nicely to *Ceremony*). Then we read Hanan al-Shaykh's *Women of Sand and Myrrh*. The novel is set in an unnamed desert country, similar to Saudi Arabia, in which women must be veiled and not do anything in public (like work or drive cars). This is a wonderful text, because it presents the Arab world from four different female points of view. It allows us to follow themes that we addressed with the traditional texts, such as the status of women, and it adds new concerns, such as the question of whether a people has a right to self-determination (and change from inside) rather than enforced change from an outside power.

For India, we read William Buck's translation-abridgement of the epic the *Mahabharata*, coupled with selections from the *Bhagavad Gita* (the *Gita* is a part of the *Mahabharata* that Buck removed). The students benefit from a lot of ancillary support here. For example, even though there is a list of main characters in the back of the text, I distribute another, shorter list for students to use as they start reading. Because the beginning of the epic has so many characters, students are confused about who the protagonists are, so I discuss the shorter list the class period before they start reading the *Mahabharata*. Combined with the *Gita*, this text opens lots of elements for discussion: caste, duty, Hindu gods, the nature of God. Students often do not know what India looks like, so photographs, drawings, and film clips are useful. There is a film of parts of the *Mahabharata* directed by Peter Brook; however, my students have always preferred to discuss the reading rather than see many film clips. (Students who do view the film usually notice that the griot in *Keita* plays Bhishma in this film.) Visual aids are particularly helpful when reading the descriptions of Krishna in the *Gita*; in his divine image, he has many eyes, faces, hands, and so on. Showing images of a multi-headed or multiarmed Hindu god both illustrates the text and offers an opportunity to discuss Hindu iconography.

After the length of the *Mahabharata*, students are happy to read some modern short stories in the *Other Voices, Other Vistas* anthology. "Dhowli" brings up the subject of caste and the status of women. "The Wog" is a sad treatment of the problem of colonial culture in India. "A Horse and Two Goats" is a humorous treatment of miscommunication between a villager and an American tourist.

For China, which is often our last unit, we start with the philosophical and religious giants: selections from the *Analects* of Confucius, from the *Tao Te Ching*, and from the *Dhammapada* (although the historical Buddha was born in Indian territory, his teachings affected Chinese thought so much that I put him in this unit). We discuss these traditions independently and as a mixture, since much of Chinese culture has been influenced by the interaction among them. Themes would include duty, filial piety, correct relationships, the nature of life, Chinese medicine, the teachings of the Buddha.

Chinese communism is the focus of our next reading, *Red Azalea*, by Anchee Min. The novel begins during China's Cultural Revolution and follows the main character, Anchee, from childhood through her emigration to the United States. Students invariably love this book. It is an easy read, and it is from a younger person's point of view. *Red Azalea* also opens good topics for discussion: Why did the government reassign a university professor to work in a shoe factory? Why would a student betray a teacher who had been nice to her? Why would committed Communist Party members become disillusioned? How would you survive working at Red Fire Farm? We also make sure to notice the traditional themes and values, many of which were overturned during the Cultural Revolution: family and ancestors were no longer revered; the family group was routinely broken up, since there had to be one farmer-peasant from each family; females were considered equal and expected to do equal jobs.

In addition to the regular class reading and discussion, each student gives a presentation on a preapproved topic about one of the cultures, to provide more background for understanding the texts. The report is scheduled for presentation during one of the class periods in which we are discussing that particular culture. Other assignments include a paper discussing a student's site visit (to a non-Western site such as a Buddhist temple or Cahokia Mounds, a local world-heritage Native American site) and a movie review of a non-Western film. In the review, students evaluate how well the movie reflects the culture it depicts.

The two-step approach of reading both ancient and contemporary texts reduces the disappointments teachers encounter when teaching multiethnic literature. Class discussion can be challenging for both teachers and students when engaging a book and a culture remote from undergraduate life. Students are uncomfortable because they do not know relevant background material (especially if they have skipped the headnote or other textual helps). Teachers are frustrated because there is not time to teach everything—history, culture, and literature—in a three-hour multiethnic college class. But when students have read and discussed a traditional text, such as the *Bhagavad Gita*, they feel more comfortable with modern short stories set in India. They learn that just because the *Bhagavad Gita* originates before the common era, it has not lost its relevance. And after students read and discuss the traditional African epic *Sundiata*, they can better understand *Keita*. The multiethnic approach also allows students to see that the relevance of such texts crosses cultures as well as time.

Note

1. The Buck translation of the *Mahabharata* is abridged, not literal, and in a couple of places not accurate, but it has the right tone and, most important, excites the students into wanting to read more. The most accurate translations run to eight or more volumes, which would be too long for an introductory course (there is an unabridged late-nineteenth-century version by Kisari Mohan Ganguli available online at www.sacred-texts.com/hin/maha/index.htm). The chief problem with Buck is that he excludes the *Bhagavad Gita* section, but the Yohannan text offers excerpts. Teachers can also supplement with the complete text, other excerpts, or a summary. Chakravarthi V. Narasimhan offers a translation of selected verses and includes a summary of the *Bhagavad Gita*. R. K. Narayan's 1972 version is beautiful but too condensed. Another consideration when choosing texts is cost (if cost is a major factor, there are translations of most ancient texts available online). Although the translations of the scriptural texts in the Yohannan anthology are somewhat stilted because they are old, the diction adds a sort of reverence that is appropriate when discussing religious ideas, especially when one wants the students to give unfamiliar religions the same kind of respect that they offer their own traditions. However, the Analects of Confucius do suffer from the difficulties of an old translation. If money were no barrier, I would choose Thomas Cleary's *Essential Confucius* for this introductory course. His translations are more accessible, and he provides useful notes. His organizing principle is also more effective than simply restating the analects in their original order. On the other hand, the Yohannan choices for the *Shahnamah*, the tale from the *Thousand and One Arabian*

Nights, and for the *Tao Te Ching* work fine for students in an introductory course. The *Tao Te Ching* is sufficiently complex that supplementing with other translations (available online at several sites, including www.chinapage.com/gnl.html) helps them understand the meaning better.

Works Cited

Buck, William, ed. and trans. *Mahabharata*. New York: Meridian-Penguin, 1993. Print.

Cleary, Thomas, ed. and trans. *The Essential Confucius: The Heart of Confucius' Teaching in Authentic* I Ching *Order*. San Francisco: Harper, 1993. Print.

Eisenberg, Diane U., et al., eds. *Transformations of Myth through Time*. New York: Harcourt, 1990. Print.

Keita: The Heritage of the Griot. Dir. Dani Kouyaté. California Newsreel, 1995. Film.

Min, Anchee. *Red Azalea*. New York: Berkeley, 1995. Print.

Niane, D. T., ed. and trans. *Sundiata*. Essex: Longman, 1965. Print.

Shaykh, Hanan al-. *Women of Sand and Myrrh*. New York: Anchor-Doubleday, 1992. Print.

Silko, Leslie Marmon. *Ceremony*. New York: Penguin, 1977. Print.

Solomon, Barbara H., ed. *Other Voices, Other Vistas: Short Stories from Africa, China, India, Japan, and Latin America*. New York: Mentor-Penguin, 1992. Print.

Yohannan, John D., ed. *Treasury of Asian Literature*. New York: Mentor-Penguin, 1956. Print.

Part V

Resources

Valerie Henitiuk

Print Resources

Theory of World Literature

Carroll, Michael Thomas, ed. *No Small World: Visions and Revisions of World Literature.* Urbana: NCTE, 1996.
  Fifteen essays discussing theory and practice in teaching world literature courses, with an emphasis on expanding genres and texts beyond the traditional Western canon.

Casanova, Pascale. *La république mondiale des lettres.* Paris: Seuil, 1999. English trans.: *The World Republic of Letters.* Trans. M. B. DeBevoise. Cambridge: Harvard UP, 2004.
  Discusses literary power relations on a global scale, where languages and genres compete for dominance, in an attempt to understand the production, circulation, and valuing of literature.

Damrosch, David. *What Is World Literature?* Princeton: Princeton UP, 2003.
  Analyzes the scope and purposes of world literature conceived in broad terms, from the more commonly taught traditions to hieroglyphics and Nahuatl.

Damrosch, David, Natalie Melas, and Mbongiseni Buthelezi, eds. *The World and the Text: A Comparative Literature Sourcebook.* Princeton: Princeton UP, 2009.
  Thirty influential essays on the theory and practice of comparative literature, from the nineteenth century to the present. Many of the essays include discussion of world literature.

Lawall, Sarah, ed. *Reading World Literature: Theory, History, Practice.* Austin: U of Texas P, 1994.
  A dozen essays address issues such as teaching the unfamiliar, the canon, language, and literacy. Includes an extensive introduction by Lawall on the history and theory of world literature.

Miner, Earl. *Comparative Poetics: An Intercultural Essay on Theories of Literature.* Princeton: Princeton UP, 1990.
  A provocative and readable attempt to define a true intercultural poetics. Miner examines how various cultures define the nature of poetics, in terms of whether drama, lyric, or narrative is their most esteemed genre.

Moretti, Franco. *Graphs, Maps, and Trees: Abstract Models for a Literary History.* London: Verso, 2005.
  Makes the case for a less random and unsystematic study of literature, as Moretti redefines aesthetic form. Develops the notion of "distant reading" into an elaborate literary historiography, where the canon is absorbed into the larger literary system.

Pizer, John. *The Idea of World Literature*. Baton Rouge: Louisiana State UP, 2006.
A history of Goethe's concept of *Weltliteratur* in German intellectual history and in American pedagogical practice.

Posnett, Hutcheson McCauley. *Comparative Literature*. 1885. New York: Johnson Rpt., 1970.
This book, by one of the pioneers of transnational literary study, has a global focus and contains an important chapter on the relativity of literature.

Prendergast, Christopher, ed. *Debating World Literature*. London: Verso, 2004.
Includes Moretti's influential essay "Conjectures on World Literature" as well as important pieces by fourteen other leading scholars.

Schulz, Hans-Joachim, and Phillip H. Rhein, eds. *Comparative Literature: The Early Years*. Chapel Hill: U of North Carolina P, 1973.
This sourcebook contains "Some Passages Pertaining to the Concept of World Literature" by Goethe as well as seminal pieces by Chasles, Brunetière, Posnett, Croce, and others arguing for the study of literature beyond boundaries of nation and language.

Spivak, Gayatri Chakravorty. *Death of a Discipline*. New York: Columbia UP, 2003.
A provocative and challenging book. Spivak argues that comparative literary studies should adopt the area studies model and insists on the primacy of linguistic competence if we are to avoid merely colonizing the literature of the other.

Wellek, René, and Warren, Austin. *Theory of Literature*. New York: Harcourt, 1942.
An important early study attempting to see beyond national literatures to the literary phenomenon itself. Sections include important definitions in the field as well as various aspects of the extrinsic and intrinsic study of literature.

Anthologies, Literature Series, and Other References

General Literature

Arkin, Marian, and Barbara Shollar, eds. *Longman Anthology of World Literature by Women, 1875–1975*. New York: Longman, 1989.
Prose and poetry by an international selection of almost three hundred women writers, with biographical notes and bibliographies of their literary traditions.

Caws, Mary Ann, and Christopher Prendergast, eds. *The HarperCollins World Reader.* New York: Harper, 1994.

A truly global presentation in 2,800 pages, with selections from some 475 authors.

Damrosch, David, et al., eds. *The Longman Anthology of World Literature.* 6 vols. New York: Pearson Educ., 2004. 2nd ed. 2009.

A wide range of poetry, prose, and drama, with many works provided in their entirety. An innovative feature is that texts are placed not only in their cultural contexts but also in juxtapositions that encourage comparative readings across eras, regions, and genres.

Davis, Paul, et al., eds. *The Bedford Anthology of World Literature.* 6 vols. Bedford–St. Martin's, 2003.

Thematic groupings of literature from all over the world; social and historical contexts; comparative time lines, maps, and many images.

Lawall, Sarah, et al., eds. *The Norton Anthology of World Literature.* 6 vols. New York: Norton, 2003.

An updated version of an authoritative classic. Aims to provide comprehensive and diverse coverage. Contains an expanded collection of prose fiction, lyric poetry, and women's writing.

Poetry

McClatchy, J. D., ed. *The Vintage Book of Contemporary World Poetry.* New York: Vintage, 1996.

A broad sampling of poetry being written in our day around the world. The editors have excluded poets from major English-speaking countries (e.g., Britain, the United States, Canada) in order to bring less readily accessible voices to the fore.

Paine, Jeffrey, ed. *The Poetry of Our World: An International Anthology of Contemporary Poetry.* New York: Harper, 2001.

Poetry produced since 1950 in the English-speaking world, Latin America, Europe, Asia, and Africa. Has introductions to each section as well as a brief biography for each poet represented.

Major Area Anthologies and Series

Barnstone, Willis, and Tony Barnstone, eds. *Literatures of Asia, Africa, and Latin America.* Upper Saddle River: Prentice, 1999.

A representative sampling for lesser studied literatures from antiquity to the present day, with extensive introductions and bibliographies. Includes pre- and post-Columbian literature and orature from Native American languages. The selections are ordered chronologically, in sections structured to reveal cultural influence.

Carter, Steven D., trans. *Traditional Japanese Poetry: An Anthology*. Stanford: Stanford UP, 1991.
An extensive selection from ancient to modern times, with the originals provided in *hiragana* syllabics beneath each translation.

Frangieh, Bassam K. *Anthology of Arabic Literature, Culture, and Thought from Pre-Islamic Times to the Present*. New Haven: Yale UP, 2005.
This book is evenly divided between classical and modern Arabic writers, with brief selections demonstrating the breadth of styles. The accompanying CD offers readings of poetry.

Heinemann. African Writers Series.
Represents the work of sixty-five writers (ranging from Chinua Achebe to Steve Biko to Leila Aboulela). Novels, short stories, poetry, and drama from over twenty countries in Africa. The Heinemann Web site (www.heinemann.co.uk/secondary/series/index.aspx?n=541&s=671& skey=2013&d=s) allows you to select books based on country of origin, theme or genre, or title and also provides a biography for each author.

Irwin, Robert. *Night and Horses and the Desert: An Anthology of Classical Arabic Literature*. New York: Anchor, 2002.
Arabic literature written in countries as diverse as Afghanistan and Spain, from the fifth through the sixteenth century. Famous works such as the *Thousand and One Nights* are set against lesser known pieces. Irwin provides erudite commentary to bring the selections to life.

Keene, Donald. *Anthology of Japanese Literature from the Earliest Era to the Mid-Nineteenth Century*. New York: Grove, 1955.
This anthology of prose, poetry, and drama remains authoritative and widely used in classrooms.

MLA. Approaches to Teaching World Literature.
A large and growing series of volumes that contain essays devoted to the teaching of major works of world literature, chiefly European and North American but now also including non-Western works. The MLA also has titles relevant to world literature courses in other of their series: Options for Teaching; Texts and Translations; Teaching Languages, Literatures, and Cultures; and World Literatures Reimagined.

Owen, Stephen. *An Anthology of Chinese Literature, Beginnings to 1911*. New York: Norton, 1997.
Traditional Chinese poetry, stories, excerpts from novels and plays, and philosophy, all arranged chronologically. Period introductions establish a political and social framework in which to read the selections.

Rimer, J. Thomas, and Van C. Gessel, eds. *The Columbia Anthology of Modern Japanese Literature: Volume 1: From Restoration to Occupation, 1868–1945*. New York: Columbia UP, 2005.
A comprehensive sampling of modern prose and poetry, with many new translations of classic works as well as of lesser-known writers. Arranged chronologically and by genre.

Shirane, Haruo, ed. *Early Modern Japanese Literature: An Anthology, 1600–1900*. New York: Columbia UP, 2004.
The first comprehensive anthology for a time of extraordinary transition in an important world literature. Covers genres ranging from philosophy to poetry to the prototypes of today's popular manga, with many newly translated works.

Simpson, William Kelly. *The Literature of Ancient Egypt: An Anthology of Stories, Instructions, Stelae, Autobiographies, and Poetry*. 3rd ed. New Haven: Yale UP, 2003.
Includes monument inscriptions, songs and hymns, and tales from the ancient and middle kingdoms through to the late period.

Encyclopedias and Other Reference Works

Boardman, John, et al., eds. *The Oxford History of the Classical World*. Oxford: Oxford UP, 1986.
Provides a comprehensive overview of the Greco-Roman world. Each of the three main sections (Greece, Greece and Rome, and Rome) contains chapters on politics and society, history, literature, philosophy, and the arts. Maps, chronological charts, and illustrations are included, as are bibliographies and an index.

Dimock, Edward C. *Literatures of India: An Introduction*. Chicago: U of Chicago P, 1978.
A seminal work by one of the foremost scholars in Indian studies.

Josephy, Alvin M., ed. *America in 1492: The World of the Indian Peoples before the Arrival of Columbus*. New York: Knopf, 1993.
Enlightening essays on religion, art, language, and systems of knowledge seek to move beyond myths and stereotypes of the pre-Columbian civilizations. Contains an annotated bibliography.

Miller, Barbara Stoler, ed. *Masterworks of Asian Literature in Comparative Perspective: A Guide for Teaching*. Armonk: ME Sharpe, 1994.
A collection of essays identifying texts, themes, and comparative concepts for Indian, Chinese, and Japanese literature, both lyric and narrative. Includes topics for discussion and reference lists. Of particular interest are the entries on the imaginative universe of each literary tradition.

Monture-Angus, Patricia, and Renée Hulan, eds. *Native North America: Critical and Cultural Perspectives*. Toronto: ECW, 1999.
A collection of essays that deal provocatively with issues of racism, colonialism, and assimilation in the various indigenous cultures of North America.

Serafin, Steven R., ed. *Encyclopedia of World Literature in the Twentieth Century*. 4 vols. Detroit: St. James, 1999.
Entries cover many aspects of world literature in the twentieth century. Includes bibliographies.

Translation Studies

Álvarez, Román, and Carmen-África Vidal, eds. *Translation, Power, Subversion*. Clevedon: Multilingual Matters, 1996.
Essays concerned with the political implications of any act of linguistic and cultural transfer.

Apter, Emily. *The Translation Zone: A New Comparative Literature*. Princeton: Princeton UP, 2005.
Argues for translation studies as the basis for a twenty-first-century comparative literature, which must take stock of the political implications of translation technologies and recognize the complexity of language politics.

Baker, Mona, ed. *Routledge Encyclopedia of Translation Studies*. London: Routledge, 2004.
Comprehensive and informative entries on terms and topics central to the study of translation. An essential reference work.

Bassnett, Susan, and Harish Trivedi, eds. *Post-colonial Translation: Theory and Practice*. London: Routledge, 1999.
Essays dealing with the intersection of postcolonial theory and translation studies. Contributors are from Britain, the United States, Brazil, India, and Canada.

Bassnett-McGuire, Susan. *Translation Studies*. London: Methuen, 1980.
This early book still provides an excellent and highly readable overview of the history of translation theory, the field's central issues, and specific problems of literary translation.

Bermann, Sandra, and Michael Wood, eds. *Nation, Language, and the Ethics of Translation*. Princeton: Princeton UP, 2005.
This collection of essays deals with a dozen languages and myriad topics. Translation is conceived of as broadly as possible, to incorporate any remaking of a text. An important volume for anyone interested in the globalization of culture.

Dingwaney, Anuradha, and Carol Maier, eds. *Between Languages and Cultures: Translation and Cross-Cultural Texts*. Pittsburgh: U of Pittsburgh P, 1995.

These essays examine translation as a cultural practice that, when approached critically, encourages interrogation of our relation to the world.

Lefevere, André. *Translation, Rewriting and the Manipulation of Literary Fame*. London: Routledge, 1992.

A major contribution to translation theory by one of its central figures.

Simon, Sherry. *Gender in Translation: Cultural Identity and the Politics of Transmission*. London: Routledge, 1996.

The first comprehensive study of feminist issues in translation theory and practice.

Tymoczko, Maria, and Edwin Gentzler, eds. *Translation and Power*. Amherst: U of Massachusetts P, 2002.

A collection of essays dealing insightfully with translation as the production and reception of texts in real social and political contexts.

Venuti, Lawrence. *The Scandals of Translation: Toward an Ethics of Difference*. London: Routledge, 1998.

In this book on the stigmatization of translation as a form of writing, Venuti argues that critical awareness of translation can encourage the questioning of dominant cultural values.

———, ed. *The Translation Studies Reader*. 2nd ed. New York: Routledge, 2004.

Seminal essays on every conceivable aspect of translation, arranged by decade, along with foundational statements by Saint Jerome, Goethe, and others. Includes Benjamin's "The Task of the Translator."

Cross-Cultural Reception and Influence

Aldridge, A. Owen. *The Reemergence of World Literature: A Study of Asia and the West*. London: Assoc. UP, 1986.

An influential argument for expanding the world literature canon and for recognizing the value of translation as a legitimate tool.

Caracciolo, Peter L., ed. *The Arabian Nights in English Literature: Studies in the Reception of* The Thousand and One Nights *into British Culture*. Basingstoke: Macmillan, 1988.

Fine essays analyzing the influence that this major world text has had in the West.

De Gruchy, John Walter. *Orienting Arthur Waley: Japonism, Orientalism, and the Creation of Japanese Literature in English*. Honolulu: U of Hawai'i P, 2003.

Useful for anyone interested in the intersection of Japanese and English literature or postcolonial studies. De Gruchy analyzes the impact Waley's renditions of East Asian literature have had on how Japanese literature was and is read.

Griffiths, Eric, and Matthew Reynolds, eds. *Dante in English*. London: Penguin, 2005.

An anthology of passages in English translation as well as of English poetry (from Chaucer to Seamus Heaney) influenced by Dante. Contains a lengthy introduction.

Hockx, Michel, and Ivo Smits, eds. *Reading East Asian Writing: The Limits of Literary Theory*. London: Routledge, 2003.

A stimulating contribution to the debate concerning the application of Western critical theory to non-Western literature. The essays, mostly dealing with Chinese literature, examine the question from both practical and theoretical approaches.

Ishihara, Tsuyoshi. *Mark Twain in Japan: The Cultural Reception of an American Icon*. Columbia: U of Missouri P, 2005.

Discusses the translation and adaptation of this quintessentially American author into Japanese. The emphasis is on Twain's localization, with a view to challenging overly simplistic conceptions of cultural imperialism.

Miller, J. Scott. *Adaptations of Western Literature in Meiji Japan*. New York: Palgrave, 2001.

This readable analysis highlights the confrontation of broadly divergent cultures and problematizes our assumptions respecting the limits and objectives of cross-cultural or literary transfer.

Moore, Cornelia N., and Raymond A. Moody, eds. *Comparative Literature East and West: Traditions and Trends: Selected Conference Papers*. Honolulu: Coll. of Lang., Linguistics, and Lit., U of Hawai'i; East-West Center, 1989.

These proceedings contain papers on such authors as Brecht and the Samoan Albert Wendt as well as on the concept of world literature in general.

Stevenson, Barbara, and Cynthia Ho, eds. *Crossing the Bridge: Comparative Essays on Medieval European and Heian Japanese Women Writers*. New York: Palgrave, 2000.

This interesting collection encourages readers to note striking similarities among women writers who lived and worked in very different places and cultures.

Yokota-Murakami, Takayuki. *Don Juan East/West: On the Problematics of Comparative Literature.* Albany: State U of New York P, 1998.
This book argues against the assumption that certain themes, patterns, and concepts can be considered universal. Yokota-Murakami demonstrates how even concepts such as love and lust are historically and culturally defined.

Zhang Longxi. *Allegoresis: Reading Canonical Literature East and West.* Ithaca: Cornell UP, 2005.
Examines the possibility of cross-cultural understanding through a study of allegorical readings in Confucius and the Bible.

Zhang Yingjin, ed. *China in a Polycentric World: Essays in Chinese Comparative Literature.* Stanford: Stanford UP, 1998.
This book moves beyond literary parallels and influence to a critical rereading of Chinese texts. Its essays cover topics such as the impact of literary theory on sinological research, canon formation, gender and sexuality, and the challenges inherent to East-West comparative literature.

Ziolkowski, Theodore. *Ovid and the Moderns.* Ithaca: Cornell UP, 2005.
Taking a comparatist rather than classicist approach, this book explores the reasons for this Latin poet's continued popularity. Covers Ovid's reception from 1912 to 2002.

Web Resources

Association Web Sites

American Comparative Literature Association: www.acla.org

Association of Departments and Programs of Comparative Literature: www.adpcl.org

International Comparative Literature Association: http://www.byu.edu/~icla/. Has links to various national associations worldwide.

Literary Anthology Companion Web Sites

The Bedford Anthology of World Literature: http://bcs.bedfordstmartins.com/worldlit/default.asp?uid=0&rau=0
Has interactive quizzes, culture and context overviews, a discussion of world literature in the twenty-first century, and various links.

The Longman Anthology of World Literature: http://wps.ablongman.com/long_damrosch_wl_1

Has research links, audio table of contents and glossary, and a section evaluating different translations of key poems. Also offers a syllabus manager tool.

The Norton Anthology of World Literature: www.wwnorton.com/nawol/
Has review materials, audio glossary, discovery modules, interactive time lines, maps, Web-based resources, and instructor resources.

Online Journals

CLCWeb: Comparative Literature and Culture: A WWW Journal: http://clcwebjournal.lib.purdue.edu/
Offers scholarship in comparative cultural studies, defined as a contextual approach to global culture in all its forms.

Comparative Literature Studies: www.cl-studies.psu.org/
Research in literary history, the history of ideas, critical theory, studies between authors, and literary relations in and beyond the Western tradition.

Words without Borders: The Online Magazine for International Literature: www.wordswithoutborders.org/
Seeks to promote international understanding through the translation and circulation of contemporary writing from around the world.

World Literature Today: www.ou.edu/worldlit/
Offers original poetry and fiction, interviews, essays, and coverage of news and conferences.

General Portal Web Sites

Humanistic Texts: www.humanistictexts.org/
Introductions to and excerpts from a wide selection of cultures and specific authors are represented on this site devoted to promoting world peace.

Literary Resources on the Net: http://andromeda.rutgers.edu/~jlynch/Lit/
See especially "Other National Literatures" for a fine array of links.

Perseus: www.perseus.tufts.edu/hopper/
Extensive database on ancient Greek civilization.

Voice of the Shuttle: http://vos.ucsb.edu/
This online guide to humanities research includes both primary and secondary resources. See especially the "Literatures other than English" section, which contains a vast number of links.

Selected Literatures and Authors

The major survey anthologies suggest various Web sites of interest. The list below, while not pretending to be exhaustive, should also prove useful for researching certain world literatures as well as specific authors and their works.

Africa South of the Sahara, African Literature and Writers on the Internet: http://library.stanford.edu/africa/lit.html
An extensive list of links to literatures, authors, reviews, publications, and so on.

Arabic Literature: www.al-bab.com/arab/literature/lit.htm
Designed as an introduction to Arabic culture in general, this site provides information on both classical and modern works and authors, with useful links.

Bashô: http://darkwing.uoregon.edu/~kohl/basho/
A fine source for the *Narrow Road to the North* (*Oku no Hosomichi*), offering the text in English (four translations to choose from) and Japanese, with links explaining allusions and providing images. Also has information on Matsuo Bashô's life and a separate time line.

Cervantes: http://quixote.mse.jhu.edu/
Offers two online tours for *Don Quixote*, in both English and Spanish. The first walks you through a thirty-five-station exhibit on the novel, with images. The second is text-based, providing information on Cervantes, the novel, the translations, Hogarth's engravings, and so on.

Chinese literature: www.yellowbridge.com/literature/
A survey of classic and contemporary Chinese literature available in English, some texts presented with the original and a translation side by side. A who's who of Chinese American authors is also provided, with links to additional resources.

Dante Online: www.danteonline.it/english/home_ita.asp
Information on the life and works of Dante, with many links. One interesting feature is a creative interview with Dante himself.

Dostoevsky: www.fyodordostoevsky.com/
Contains a biography, images, links to e-texts and essays, and so on.

Expanding East Asian Studies: www.exeas.org
This site offers teaching materials and resources, syllabi, and links. It is designed to help instructors incorporate East Asia into their teaching, by suggesting a range of thematic, transnational, and interdisciplinary contexts.

Ghalib, A Desertful of Roses: www.columbia.edu/itc/mealac/pritchett/00ghalib/

An attractive and engaging site devoted to this Urdu poet's *ghazal*s.
Contains many images and useful links, as well as indices of names and
terms.

Goethe: www.aspirennies.com/private/SiteBody/Romance/Poetry/Goethe/
jwvgoethe.shtml
This site offers a biography, discussions of various relevant themes, a
reading list, and links to Goethe's poetry (in English translation). Among
the many wonderful German-language sites is www.goethe-bytes.de/,
which has audio files of readings from Goethe, as well as other useful
resources.

Homer Homepage: www.gpc.edu/~shale/humanities/literature/world_
literature/homer.html
Filled with extensive links, this site offers a variety of essays and commentary, an audio file, maps, and images related to the *Iliad* and the
Odyssey.

Indian literature: http://dmoz.org/Arts/Literature/World_Literature/
Indian/
Compiled by the Open Directory Project, this site deals with the literatures of India, providing links to a dozen major authors, as well as
themed links.

Literatures of the Middle East: www.columbia.edu/cu/lweb/indiv/mideast/
cuvlm/literatures.html
Informative links for Arabic, Armenian, Hebrew, Kurdish, Maltese,
Persian, and Turkish literature and literary history.

Marie de France: www.people.vcu.edu/~cmarecha/#Treasure
This site offers a wealth of resources on Marie de France. Many links to
texts and translations and to other sites discussing the author's life and
work. Links also provided for a range of online syllabi and articles.

The Modern Word: www.themodernword.com/authors.html
This excellent site provides access to very useful pages for over two dozen
twentieth-century writers, from Abe Kôbô to Jeanette Winterson.
Another forty or so authors are also represented, albeit only by (extensive)
links to other sites, while awaiting fuller treatment here. The pages
devoted to Beckett, Borges, Eco, Joyce, Kafka, García Márquez, and
Pyncheon are especially fine.

Molière: www.site-moliere.com/intro.htm
A bilingual (English-French) site that offers biographical information, a
searchable concordance, and a variety of other resources. The plays are
also provided in full, but in the original French only.

Murasaki Shikibu: www.meijigakuin.ac.jp/~watson/genji/genji.html

Provides many useful links to both English and Japanese sites containing text, images, and commentary on *The Tale of Genji*.

Native American Literature: www.ipl.org/div/natam/
Part of the Internet Public Library, this site provides extensive information on Native North American authors and their works, with links to online resources such as interviews, texts, and tribal Web sites. Primarily concerned with contemporary authors—Paula Gunn Allen, Louise Erdrich, and many others—although some historical authors are also listed.

Négritude: www.unc.edu/depts/europe/francophone/negritude/eng/index .htm
This fine compact site offers a general overview; texts by major figures such as Césaire and Senghor, along with discussion questions; audio and video clips of interviews; and numerous links. Some of the material is bilingual (English-French).

Nobel Prize in Literature: http://nobelprize.org/nobel_prizes/literature/
This Nobel Foundation site provides resources such as biographies, bibliographies, interviews, and a handful of links for all literature prize winners since 1901 (including Elfriede Jelinek, Naguib Mahfouz, and Derek Walcott).

Postcolonial Literature: www.postcolonialweb.org/
Maintained by Brown University, this site provides information and links for a wide range of authors and works from Africa, Australia, Canada, the Caribbean, New Zealand, Singapore, South Asia, and the United Kingdom.

Proust: www.tempsperdu.com/
Although dedicated to Marcel Proust's great novel (with chronology, character lists, etc.), this site offers a variety of other resources as well, including reviews of books on the author's life and work. Links to many additional sites, including one with the text of a relevant Monty Python sketch.

Shakespeare: http://shakespeare.palomar.edu/
Well-organized links to a plethora of other sites and resources. Provides access to lesson plans, critical essays, information on the authorship controversy, films, and even directs the reader to a copy of the Klingon *Hamlet*.

South Asian Women's NETwork: www.sawnet.org/books/authors.php
Lists a vast number of women writers from across South Asia, each with a brief biography, bibliography, and often links to reviews, interviews, essays, and more.

Tolstoy: www.online-literature.com/tolstoy/
  Part of the Literature Network, a searchable online resource for a great
  number of authors. Includes a biography, e-texts, forums, quizzes, and
  additional links.
Woolf: http://orlando.jp.org/VWW/
  The most extensive listing of links for Virginia Woolf, including discussion groups and e-texts.

Notes on Contributors

Emily Apter is professor of French and comparative literature at New York University. Her books include *Continental Drift: From National Characters to Virtual Subjects* (1999) and *The Translation Zone: A New Comparative Literature* (2006). She is editor of the series "Translation/Transnation" for Princeton University Press.

Carolyn Ayers is associate professor of English at Saint Mary's University of Minnesota. A Slavicist by training, she has published articles on the nineteenth-century Russian tale. She teaches world literature and literary theory.

Thomas Beebee is professor of comparative literature and German at Pennsylvania State University. His most recent book is *Millennial Literatures of the Americas* (2008). He is editor-in-chief of *Comparative Literature Studies*.

Monika Brown is professor of English at the University of North Carolina, Pembroke. A contributor to the MLA teaching volumes on *Madame Bovary* and *The Turn of the Screw*, she has taught world literature for twenty years at a regional university recognized for student diversity.

Vilashini Cooppan is associate professor of literature at the University of California, Santa Cruz. Her articles on comparative literature and world literature have appeared in *Symploke, Comparative Literature,* and *Gramma*. Her book *Worlds Within: National Narratives and Global Connections in Postcolonial Writing* will appear in 2009.

David Damrosch, professor of English and comparative literature at Columbia University, is the author of *We Scholars: Changing the Culture of the University* (1995), *What Is World Literature?* (2003), *The Buried Book: The Loss and Rediscovery of the Great Epic of Gilgamesh* (2007), and *How to Read World Literature* (2008). He is general editor of *The Longman Anthology of World Literature* (2004).

Wai Chee Dimock is William Lampson Professor of English and American Studies at Yale University. Her books include *Through Other Continents: American Literature across Deep Time* (2007). She is coeditor, with Lawrence Buell, of *Shades of the Planet: American Literature as World Literature* (2007).

Margaret Doody is John and Barbara Glynn Family Professor of Literature at the University of Notre Dame. Her critical works include *The Daring Muse: Augustan Poetry Reconsidered* (1985) and *The True Story of the Novel* (1996). Her most recent book is *Tropic of Venice* (2006). Her works of fiction are *The Alchemists* (1980) and a series of mystery stories set in ancient Athens, beginning with *Aristotle Detective* (1978).

Caroline D. Eckhardt is head of the Department of Comparative Literature, Pennsylvania State University, and president of the Association of Departments and Programs of Comparative Literature. A medievalist, she has published on Chaucer, chronicles, and professional topics.

Nikolai Endres, associate professor of world literature at Western Kentucky University, is the author of articles on Greek and Roman homosexuality, Oscar Wilde, André Gide, Mary Renault, and Gore Vidal.

Carol Fadda-Conrey is assistant professor of English at Syracuse University. Her essays on Middle Eastern and Arab American literature have appeared in *Studies in the Humanities, MELUS, The Greenwood Encyclopedia of Multiethnic American Literature*, and *Al-Raida*, as well as in the edited collections *Arabs in America: Interdisciplinary Essays on the Arab Diaspora* (2006) and *Arab Women's Lives Retold: Exploring Identity through Writing* (2007).

John Burt Foster, Jr., is university professor of English and cultural studies at George Mason University. He is the author of several books and articles in comparative literature, including *Nabokov's Art of Memory and Literary Modernism* (1993), and he coedited *Thresholds of Western Culture: Identity, Postcoloniality, Transnationalism* (2003).

Raymond-Jean Frontain, director of the Humanities and World Cultures Institute at the University of Central Arkansas, has edited or coedited five collections of essays on biblically inspired literary traditions. The most recent is *Reclaiming the Sacred: The Bible in Gay and Lesbian Culture* (rev. ed. 2003).

Jeanne Gillespie is associate professor of Spanish and women's studies and associate dean of the College of Arts and Letters at the University of Southern Mississippi. She is the coeditor, with Jennifer Eich and Lucia Guzzi Harrison, of *Women's Voices and the Politics of Spanish Empire: From Convent Cell to Imperial Court* (forthcoming).

Gary Harrison, professor of English and presidential teaching fellow at the University of New Mexico, is coeditor of *The Bedford Anthology of World Literature* (2004).

Valerie Henitiuk is lecturer and associate director of the British Centre for Literary Translation at the University of East Anglia. Her monograph *Embodied Boundaries* (2007) explored images of liminality in women's writing in English, French, and Japanese. She is currently completing a manuscript on modern translations of a classical Japanese text.

Margaret R. Higonnet, professor of English at the University of Connecticut, Storrs, is the editor of *Borderwork: Feminist Engagements with*

Comparative Literature (1994) and *Lines of Fire: Women Writers of World War I* (1999).

Elizabeth Horan, professor of English and comparative literature at Arizona State University, is the author of a book on Gabriela Mistral and editor of editions of Mistral and of Carmen Lyra.

Oscar Kenshur is professor emeritus of comparative literature and chair emeritus of the Comparative Literature Department at Indiana University. He has published books and articles on seventeenth- and eighteenth-century literature and thought and on the status of facts and theories in the sciences and humanities. He is currently working on the theory of taste.

Kathleen L. Komar, professor of comparative literature at the University of California, Los Angeles, is the author of books on modernist narrative and on Rilke and most recently of *Reclaiming Klytemnestra: Revenge or Reconciliation* (2003).

Sarah Lawall, professor emerita of comparative literature at the University of Massachusetts, Amherst, was editor of the modern period and then general editor of the Western and the full-world versions of the *Norton Anthology of World Literature.* She is author of *Critics of Consciousness* (1968) and of translations and studies of Greek literature, modern French poetry, literary criticism, and the theory and teaching of world literature. She edited *Reading World Literature* (1994).

Carol J. Luther is professor of English at Pellissippi State Technical Community College, Knoxville, where she teaches world literature and other freshman and sophomore English courses.

Joseph A. Massad is associate professor in the Department of Middle East and Asian Languages and Cultures at Columbia University, where he teaches modern Arab politics and intellectual history. He is the author of books on nationalism in the Middle East. His most recent book is *Desiring Arabs* (2007), which won the 2008 Lionel Trilling Book Award.

Collin Meissner is assistant professor in the Department of American Studies and associate director of the PhD in Literature Program at the University of Notre Dame. He is the author of *Henry James and the Language of Experience* (1999).

Anuradha Dingwaney Needham, Donald R. Longman Professor of English at Oberlin, is the author of *Using the Master's Tools: Resistance and the Literature of the African and South-Asian Diasporas* (2000).

Jane O. Newman, professor of comparative literature at the University of California, Irvine, is the author of studies of baroque German drama and lyric poetry. She is at work on a study of Walter Benjamin.

Michael Palencia-Roth, Trowbridge Scholar in Literary Studies and professor of comparative literature at the University of Illinois, has written or edited books on García Márquez, Mann, Joyce, the Conquest period in Latin America, the Holocaust, comparative literature as a discipline, and comparative civilizational analysis.

Ellen Peel is professor of English and comparative and world literature at San Francisco State University. She is the author of *Politics, Persuasion, and Pragmatism: A Rhetoric of Feminist Utopian Fiction* (2002).

C. A. Prettiman is associate professor of international languages at Cedar Crest College, Pennsylvania, where she teaches Spanish, French, and Italian languages, Spanish and Latin American literature and history, and world literature. She has written on Golden Age Spanish literature and Anglo-Hispanic literary relations in the seventeenth century.

Elvira Pulitano teaches in the Ethnic Studies Department at California Polytechnic State University. She is the author of *Toward a Native American Critical Theory* (2003).

Marjorie E. Rhine is associate professor in the Department of Languages and Literatures and director of the University Honors Program at the University of Wisconsin, Whitewater. Her publications include articles on Kafka, Kundera, Mishima, and Rushdie.

Eric Sterling, professor of English at Auburn University, Montgomery, is the author of *The Movement towards Subversion: The English History Play from Skelton to Shakespeare* (1996) and editor of *Life in the Ghettos during the Holocaust* (2005) and *Arthur Miller's Death of a Salesman: Dialogue* (2008).

Lawrence Venuti, professor of English at Temple University, is author of *The Translator's Invisibility* (2nd ed., 2008) and *The Scandals of Translation* (1998) and is editor of *The Translation Studies Reader* (2nd ed., 2004). His recent translations include Massimo Carlotto's crime novel *The Goodbye Kiss* (2006).

Kathryn A. Walterscheid is director of undergraduate research for the College of Arts and Sciences at the University of Missouri, Saint Louis. Her publications include a book on D. H. Lawrence and articles on the *Mahabharata* and on works by Ngũgĩ wa Thiong'o, Leslie Marmon Silko, Zora Neale Hurston, and Umberto Eco.

Zhang Longxi, chair professor of comparative literature and translation at the City University of Hong Kong, is the author of *The Tao and the Logos: Literary Hermeneutics, East and West* (1992), *Mighty Opposites: From Dichotomies to Differences in the Comparative Study of China* (1998), *Allegoresis: Reading Canonical Literature East and West* (2005), and *Unexpected Affinities: Reading across Cultures* (2007).

Index

Modern Language Association of America
Options for Teaching

Teaching World Literature. Ed. David Damrosch. 2009.

Teaching North American Environmental Literature. Ed. Laird Christensen, Mark C. Long, and Fred Waage. 2008.

Teaching Life Writing Texts. Ed. Miriam Fuchs and Craig Howes. 2007.

Teaching Nineteenth-Century American Poetry. Ed. Paula Bernat Bennett, Karen L. Kilcup, and Philipp Schweighauser. 2007.

Teaching Representations of the Spanish Civil War. Ed. Noël Valis. 2006.

Teaching the Representation of the Holocaust. Ed. Marianne Hirsch and Irene Kacandes. 2004.

Teaching Tudor and Stuart Women Writers. Ed. Susanne Woods and Margaret P. Hannay. 2000.

Teaching Literature and Medicine. Ed. Anne Hunsaker Hawkins and Marilyn Chandler McEntyre. 1999.

Teaching the Literatures of Early America. Ed. Carla Mulford. 1999.

Teaching Shakespeare through Performance. Ed. Milla C. Riggio. 1999.

Teaching Oral Traditions. Ed. John Miles Foley. 1998.

Teaching Contemporary Theory to Undergraduates. Ed. Dianne F. Sadoff and William E. Cain. 1994.

Teaching Children's Literature: Issues, Pedagogy, Resources. Ed. Glenn Edward Sadler. 1992.

Teaching Literature and Other Arts. Ed. Jean-Pierre Barricelli, Joseph Gibaldi, and Estella Lauter. 1990.

New Methods in College Writing Programs: Theories in Practice. Ed. Paul Connolly and Teresa Vilardi. 1986.

School-College Collaborative Programs in English. Ed. Ron Fortune. 1986.

Teaching Environmental Literature: Materials, Methods, Resources. Ed. Frederick O. Waage. 1985.

Part-Time Academic Employment in the Humanities: A Sourcebook for Just Policy. Ed. Elizabeth M. Wallace. 1984.

Film Study in the Undergraduate Curriculum. Ed. Barry K. Grant. 1983.

The Teaching Apprentice Program in Language and Literature. Ed. Joseph Gibaldi and James V. Mirollo. 1981.

Options for Undergraduate Foreign Language Programs: Four-Year and Two-Year Colleges. Ed. Renate A. Schulz. 1979.

Options for the Teaching of English: Freshman Composition. Ed. Jasper P. Neel. 1978.

Options for the Teaching of English: The Undergraduate Curriculum. Ed. Elizabeth Wooten Cowan. 1975.